Wordsworth's Poetry, 1815–1845

Wordsworth's Poetry, 1815–1845

Tim Fulford

PENN

UNIVERSITY OF PENNSYLVANIA PRESS

PHILADELPHIA

A volume in the Haney Foundation Series, established in 1961
with the generous support of Dr. John Louis Haney.

Published by
University of Pennsylvania Press
Philadelphia, Pennsylvania 19104-4112
www.upenn.edu/pennpress

Printed in the United States of America
on acid-free paper

10 9 8 7 6 5 4 3 2 1

A Cataloging-in-Publication record is available from the Library of Congress

ISBN 978-0-8122-5081-7

Contents

PART IV. LATE GENRES

Abbreviations

1807	William Wordsworth, *Poems, in Two Volumes* (London: Longman, 1807)
1815	*Poems by William Wordsworth: Including Lyrical Ballads, and the Miscellaneous Pieces of the Author. With Additional Poems, a New Preface, and a Supplementary Essay*, 2 vols. (London: Longman, 1815)
1827	*The Poetical Works of William Wordsworth*, 5 vols. (London: Longman, 1827)
1845	*The Poems of William Wordsworth, D.C.L* (London: Moxon, 1845)
BL	S. T. Coleridge, *Biographia Literaria*, ed. James Engell and W. Jackson Bate, 2 vols. (Princeton, NJ: Princeton UP, 1983)
BLJ	*Byron's Letters and Journals*, ed. Leslie A. Marchand, 12 vols. (London: Murray, 1977–82)
BPW	Byron, *The Complete Poetical Works*, ed. Jerome J. McGann and Barry Weller, 7 vols. (Oxford: Oxford UP, 1991–93)
CN	*Collected Notebooks of Samuel Taylor Coleridge*, ed. Kathleen Coburn, 5 vols. (Princeton, NJ: Princeton UP, 1957–2002)
CPW	S. T. Coleridge, *Poetical Works*, ed. J. C. C. Mays, 6 vols. (Princeton, NJ: Princeton UP, 2001)

Duddon	Wordsworth, *The River Duddon, a Series of Sonnets: Vaudracour and Julia: and Other Poems. To which is annexed, a topographical description of the country of the Lakes, in the North of England* (London: Longman, 1820)
Excursion	Wordsworth, *The Excursion*, ed. Sally Bushell, James A. Butler and Michael C. Jaye (Ithaca, NY: Cornell UP, 2007)
EY	*The Letters of William and Dorothy Wordsworth: The Early Years, 1787–1805*, ed. Ernest De Selincourt, rev. Chester L. Shaver (Oxford: Oxford UP, 1967)
Last Poems	Wordsworth, *Last Poems, 1821–1850*, ed. Jared Curtis (Ithaca, NY: Cornell UP, 1999)
LB	Wordsworth, *Lyrical Ballads and Other Poems, 1797–1800*, ed. James Butler and Karen Green (Ithaca, NY: Cornell UP, 1992)
LY	*The Letters of William and Dorothy Wordsworth: The Later Years*, ed. E. de Selincourt, rev. Alan G. Hill, 4 vols. (Oxford: Oxford UP, 1978–88)
MY	*The Letters of William and Dorothy Wordsworth: The Middle Years, 1806–20*, ed. E. de Selincourt, rev. Mary Moorman and Alan G. Hill, 2 vols. (Oxford: Oxford UP, 1969–70)
Prose Works	*The Prose Works of William Wordsworth*, ed. W. J. B. Owen and Jane Worthington Smyser, 3 vols. (Oxford: Oxford UP, 1974)
Shorter Poems	Wordsworth, *Shorter Poems, 1807–1820*, ed. Carl H. Ketcham (Ithaca, NY: Cornell UP, 1989)
Sonnets	Wordsworth, *Sonnet Series and Itinerary Poems, 1820–1845*, ed. Geoffrey Jackson (Ithaca, NY: Cornell UP, 2004)
TT	S. T. Coleridge, *Table Talk*, ed. Carl Woodring, 2 vols. (Princeton, NJ: Princeton UP, 1990)
YR	Wordsworth, *Yarrow Revisited, and Other Poems* (London: Moxon, 1835)

Introduction

For the best part of a century, the poems that Wordsworth wrote over the last thirty years of his career have been neglected. This was not in the case in his lifetime or in the post-1850 Victorian era, when works such as the *River Duddon* collection of 1820 and the *Yarrow Revisited* volume of 1835 attracted good reviews and healthy sales. Wordsworth was valued then not principally for the blank-verse "Greater Romantic Lyrics" he wrote between 1798 and 1810, but for odes, sonnets, inscriptions, and "memorials" (a name he gave to poems that aimed in an impersonal voice to bear witness to history as embodied in monuments, ruins, and relics). Indeed, before 1820 the nature meditations and rustic lyrical ballads that led Keats to refer to Wordsworth's "egotistical sublime" were commonly viewed as ridiculous exercises in self-worship—the poems of an eccentric who absurdly overvalued the observations of his "mean," "puerile," and "namby pamby" mind.[1] It was the tougher, more stoical, more traditional Wordsworth of *The Excursion*, the Duddon sonnets, and the Evening Voluntaries whom the nineteenth century appreciated.[2]

By the 1960s and '70s, the picture had been reversed. Generations of professional literary critics had held up the earlier work as the apogee of lyric poetry; Wordsworth had become the high priest of what, in a largely post-religious age, was taken to be Romanticism's chief contribution to literature and culture—its ability to transcend both the mundane, industrialized world and the commodified self which that world produced by discovering, via nature, the freedom of the individual imagination (or at least by exhibiting the heroism of the quest).[3] *The Prelude* became a new bible because it sanctified self-exploration as a mode of self-healing and self-elevation: poet and reader arrived at a deep, psychologized self able to face its isolation and eventual extinction at the hands of time because they could, in poetry, renew the lost past.[4] Thus, for example, Geoffrey Hartman argued of *The Prelude* that Wordsworth's resistance of "tradition in favor of imagination" produced the poetic "progress" that gave birth to "contemporary poetry." The imagination as expressed in *The Prelude* was revolutionary and foundational: it "dominates modern poetry."[5] The Cornell Wordsworth—that great editorial enterprise of twentieth-century academe—was the ultimate expression of this critical consensus. It devoted tome after tome to poems of the so-called Great Decade, producing no less than three editions of *The Prelude*, but then grouped the works written between 1820 and 1845 into a volume entitled *Last Poems*, as if the verse of Wordsworth's early fifties and late seventies was all of a piece—the final sputterings of a career at its end.

As Wordsworth's oeuvre was divided and the status of the earlier work rose, that of the later work fell. In 1923 H. W. Garrod, reflecting Matthew Arnold's preference for the earlier poems,[6] called the last forty years of Wordsworth's life "the most dismal anti-climax of which the history of literature holds record."[7] By 1935 Willard L. Sperry could already assume that there was a critical consensus as to a decline: the task was merely to explain its causes.[8] It fell to Thomas McFarland to reduce the consensus to its most basic expression. In a polemic so crude as to be counterproductive, he wrote of Wordsworth's "forty-year death-in-poetic life"—a "melancholy" period of desiccated poetry—but the evidence he amassed to support this judgment consisted of just two poems.[9] Hartman's verdict was more considered but just as damning: "Almost all [the] poetry written after 1806 fail[s] to show . . . progress" (toward modernity); Wordsworth "not only fails to condense his thought into a clear structure or dialectic but begins to use poetry purely as a defensive reaction to strange sympathies and apocalyptic stirrings."[10] The later poetry represented a "falling-off" because it did not prioritize lonely struggles toward imaginative self-discovery or attempt to find an intense lyric form to represent such moments. Hartman mourned as an uncourageous decline Wordsworth's turn away from post-religious prophecy, justifying his judgment, however, by discussing only three of the hundreds of later poems. Harold Bloom, wanting Wordsworth to have been the progenitor of a "Visionary Company" of poets culminating in John Ashbery, took a similar course: "Wordsworth's dreadful poetic dotage . . . went on drearily from 1807 to 1850 . . . the longest dying of a major poetic genius in history."[11] *The Excursion* (1814) became, in the wake of such views, the last poem worth considering in detail—though even it was chiefly summoned to evidence Wordsworth's decline since the 1805 *Prelude*.

In the 1980s, the critical consensus about Wordsworthian imagination as the epitome of Romanticism and the inauguration of modernity was challenged. Marxist scholars cast a cold eye on the assumption that "nature" and "imagination" were transcendent and universal values; they argued that they were instead signs of Wordsworth's displacement of history and politics.[12] Critics who devoted themselves to detailing how Wordsworth's verse made him a "prophet of imagination" were said to be uncritically complicit with the poet's ideological maneuver to cut himself free of historical demands he could not or would not meet.[13] Nature poetry and prophetic vision would no longer be constitutive of Romanticism: Wordsworth's indifference to newly popular genres such as the historical novel, women's poetry, and the magazine essay made his verse again seem to many, as it had to reviewers before 1820, self-secluding and marginal.

The New Historicist critique of Wordsworth, and of Wordsworth criticism, had two effects. It provoked a reaction from critics who argued that it misunderstood the poet's key relationships to nature and imagination: the best of these critics set about providing nuanced re-readings of the verse.[14] It also stimulated an effort to explore its engagement with historical discourses: new perspectives were offered on Wordsworth's uptake of feminism, natural history, colonialism, geology, cartography, and several other contexts.[15] Curiously, in view of this paradigm-shift in critical procedure, and the massive expansion of scholarly knowledge that it precipitated, the poetry discussed remained little changed, save that *The Excursion* (1814) and *The White Doe of Rylstone* (1807–15) came in for renewed scrutiny.[16] Scores of books and articles consider Wordsworth's relationship to history in one form or another; few consider the large body of writing, much of it historical, written after the works published in 1814. In this respect, many contemporary critics have perpetuated the bias of the mid-twentieth-century criticism they sought to supersede: they have inherited their teachers' neglect of the later poems. Jerome J. McGann, for instance, declared the later work to be poetry "we are spared from having to remember."[17] No longer even read, the post-1810 (or even post-1807) work became an omission passed down the critical generations in graduate school.

There were exceptions to the general neglect. One of the first to look again at the post-1814 poetry was, somewhat surprisingly in view of his earlier opinions, Geoffrey Hartman. In "Blessing the Torrent: On Wordsworth's Later Style" (1978), he discussed an 1824 sonnet, and in "Words, Wish, Worth: Wordsworth" (1979), he examined the 1816 poem "A little onward lend thy guiding hand."[18] These seminal essays renewed Hartman's emphasis on a Wordsworth engaged in a struggle to derive a vatic voice from a natural world encountered as sounds and traces. But Hartman now showed that the terms of the struggle were not repeated, in diminished form, but altered by the anxieties attendant upon age—the responsibilities of fatherhood, fear of incapacity, the weight of earlier work to be lived up to. Wordsworth's profound explorations of the poet's task and searching meditations on the sources of power were no longer confined to the Great Decade: he had an afterlife that was not dismissible as decline.

Hartman's phenomenological Wordsworth was joined a decade later by William H. Galperin's deconstructive poet. In *Revision and Authority in Wordsworth: The Interpretation of a Career*, Galperin made persuasive arguments for seeing the later poems as neither an anticlimax nor a betrayal of the earlier but as a reworking that restaged their central tension in self-deconstructive terms: "They make clear what is already detectable in the earlier poetry; namely, the arbitrariness of authority in general. Wordsworth does not 'become' an orthodox Christian in his later phrase. Instead, his orthodoxy cancels the authority it supersedes so as to cancel *all* authority, including, of course, the authority of orthodoxy itself."[19] This insight informs my reading not just of Wordsworth's explicitly religious poetry—his *Ecclesiastical Sketches* (1822), for instance—but also of poems in which authority is represented through historical institutions and their edifices or through literary form itself—although I prefer destabilization to cancellation as the apposite concept. Wordsworth is not Sterne or a postmodernist avant la lettre: his later poetry dramatizes the conflict between a recurrent concern to situate the self (writer and reader) in a larger whole within which it can find meaning (a historical institution or poetic tradition) and a restless need to reshape that whole or to preserve difference from it. But Galperin is perceptive: Wordsworth's expressions of conformity deform that which they conform to, and put conformity itself in question, but leave no place outside history for individual freedom. That is why they were of interest to young Victorian intellectuals[20] and why they should interest us in today's world of jihad and selfies.

Peter J. Manning has investigated the later work as a "complexly situated rhetoric" in which the restless self-troubling of the early 1800s is still present in altered form.[21] Manning illuminates the poetry in a variety of contexts: in "Cleansing the Images," he explores Wordsworth's use of Latin and his responses to German Romanticism in the 1820s and 1830s; in

"Wordsworth in *The Keepsake*, 1829," he investigates the poet's uneasy involvement in the popular periodical press, initiating print-culture approaches that replace the stereotype of the isolated, unworldly bard with an account of an author prepared to take advantage of the latest trends in the publishing business. The work of Lee Erickson on the marketing strategies that Wordsworth adopted in tandem with his publisher Edward Moxon is also instructive in this regard.[22] Further articles have explored Wordsworth's travel poems—in Scotland and Italy—in their relationship, both critical and admiring, to the historical romanticization of these places by Walter Scott.[23] At home in the Lake District too, Wordsworth's politics of place, Manning shows, involved anxious negotiations of divided political loyalties related to patronage relationships. He reveals that there was no simple shift from Jacobinical youth to conservative, Tory-supporting age but, instead, a tension between the expression of loyalty to authority (both to the political interests of aristocratic landowners and to traditional literary form) and its displacement.[24] A comparable argument is made by James K. Chandler, who analyzed the Burkean influences in both early and late work.[25] I attempt something similar here in Chapter 2.

For Peter Larkin, the complex rhetoric of the later poems—the turbulent selving that it crystallizes—comes into focus when viewed in relation to the earlier ones. He examines a series of poems that are clearly belated with regard to the self-questioning nature verse of the earlier career.[26] Rather than examine these late meditations in order to demonstrate the superiority of the pre-*Excursion* poetry of imagination, Larkin considers them as intricate comings-to-terms with being the poet who once intimated immortality but who now no longer wishes to do so. These late poems are not rejections of past work; they are not attempted recollections or repetitions of it, either, but recessions from it. Larkin's pondering of the poetics of lateness informs my discussions of the "evening" poems Wordsworth wrote from the 1820s on.

Wordsworth's politics in the Waterloo period have been discussed by Philip Connell, who notes "his imaginative identification of Britain's imperial and domestic civilizing missions" in *The Excursion*.[27] Philip Shaw has traced the need to define this mission after the defeat of France to the lack of an "other" against whom England could be defined.[28] Richard Gravil has explored the rhetoric of the "Thanksgiving Ode" in terms of its Biblical resonances,[29] while Jeffrey N. Cox has pioneered the study of its reception in a contentious and politicized literary sphere, in which it was one of many new discourses competing for attention in the reviews, journals, and magazines.[30] Reconstructing reactions to Wordsworth by Keats and Leigh Hunt and by him to them, Cox has reminded us that Wordsworth was not, after 1814, simply a past body of writing by which a budding poet might be inspired and/or intimidated, but a living writer and as such a potential ally or rival.[31] The poetry of the younger generation was written and read in this context, as was Wordsworth's own new work. The line of influence was not necessarily one way; nor was there, as literary history tended to assume, a "natural" progression from first to second generation. The later Wordsworth becomes a key figure in a redrawn Romanticism that reveals not the decline of the once-revolutionary 1790s poets into reaction, to be superseded by a new crop of radical young poets, but a continuing contest for authority in a divided public sphere.[32]

Stephen Gill's work on Wordsworth's late poems has been instructive in two ways.[33] Gill reveals how revision and reorganization became Wordsworth's creative modus operandi—a moving forward to new work not by harking back to but by continual self-parturition from the old; as a corollary of this, he also shows that Wordsworth became an astute, market-oriented writer who actively shaped his publications for success and was prepared to travel to do so. Gill's later Wordsworth was no solitary recluse but an experienced man of the world who recorded his engagement with places at home and abroad at least in part because tourist poetry was popular.[34] As Peter Simonsen shows, to appeal to posterity he paid considerable attention to the formatting of these publications—typography, layout, design—even thematizing the printed appearance of the poetry within poems, as if to make them ekphrases of themselves.[35] By the end of his career, Wordsworth had moved beyond the hostility to the public that had led him to be self-defensive up to 1815:[36] his anti-commercialism had proved to have considerable commercial appeal, at least within a specialist sector of the public. He was an early example of the niche marketing today beloved of indie bands, sold on the basis of their resistance to the mainstream.

To these critics can be added several who have elucidated particular poems of the later period: Theresa Kelley explored the move to an aesthetics of beauty and containment and discussed later poems invoking waters;[37] Robin Jarvis demonstrated how the terms of Wordsworth's negotiation with Milton were altered in the tour poems he composed at Vallombrosa; Philip Shaw revealed a productive tension between paternal authority and

Ovidian classicism in a late poem addressed to Wordsworth's daughter.[38] These essays took up the mantle of Hartman in delineating a poet engaged in finding new terms for his old struggle to claim a prophetic voice. So too Richard Gravil and James Garrett, who examined the gradual identification of that voice with the nation of which, increasingly, the later Wordsworth claimed to be the bard.[39] My own *Late Poetry of the Lake Poets* explores a similar tussle over sources of the authority that accrues to poetic form—history, prehistory, the Biblical god, pagan divinities.

Simon Jarvis and Eric C. Walker discussed the elaboration of a flexible poetic language for pondering late-life experiences in the poetry of 1819–20—Jarvis from a phenomenological standpoint, Walker from a historicist position that juxtaposes Wordsworth with Jane Austen as writers responding to the impact of war on gender relations.[40] Judith Page extended the consideration of gender in *Wordsworth and the Cultivation of Women*, offering a nuanced portrait of a poet less egotistically assertive in his later years and therefore able, within limits, to imagine women other than as helpmeets and nature-spirits.[41] Noah Heringman discussed the "Kirkstone" ode as an encounter with stone that proved too other to be invoked, precipitating a turn from the sublime.[42] Christopher R. Miller studied the Evening Voluntaries as responses to an eighteenth-century tradition of crepuscular poetry.[43] My work has benefited from all these accounts, which exemplify ways of reading the different language of a later poet whom they show to be surprisingly various. Together they suggest that the tide of critical neglect has begun to turn.

*   *   *

My intention in *Wordsworth's Poetry, 1815–1845* is not to reverse the biases that Galperin, Manning, Cox, Gill, Larkin, Gravil, Shaw, and others have begun to correct. This book does not advance the claims of "Humanity" over the 1805 *Prelude* or of the ode "On the Power of Sound" over the Immortality Ode. Nor does it provide a comprehensive survey: thirty years' worth of writing cannot be explored in one book, and the varied writings of such an extended period do not produce a single consistent "achievement." I aim, rather, to explore what seem to me the pieces that are most illuminating about the later work and/or that make the strongest claims on our attention; to allow us to read them again, alongside the earlier work and in their own right—and to place in literary history a different Wordsworth—a wholler Wordsworth, not predicated on youth but continuing to write beyond most of the Byron generation that many critics thought to have superseded him.

It is as a history poet that the later Wordsworth most frequently speaks to the preoccupations of critical readers today, and much of the verse I explore responds to historical issues and events and to the issue of historicity itself.[44] The response is often but not always explicit or made at the level of content. Frequently, historical pressures are refracted at the levels of form, style, genre, and prosody; form, style, genre, and prosody also shape historical interventions. My concern is to analyze this two-way process of refraction from both ends: I aim to track the logic of the verse so that historical quiddities and ideological battles appear not as externalities but within, as the animating forces of the poems.[45] In the first three chapters I explore historical contexts beyond the literary, as they bear upon the poetry's voice, form, diction, and meter; in the next five I investigate the literary as a historical actor in its own right: forms, genres, and styles, each of which possessed a history and/or currency of its own and did not just reflect but brought into being Wordsworth's views on political and religious history.

Wordsworth's Poetry, 1815–1845 is organized chronologically, within sections that focus on particular genres and themes. In Part I, "Producing a Poet for the Public," I examine Wordsworth's self-fashioning in his 1815 collection of poems. Chapter 1 investigates manuscript revision to show how an old poem was reworked for publication: I take my cue here from studies of Romantic poetry as a matter of multiple versions rather than originary inspiration and from accounts that place Wordsworth as an agent in the print culture of his times rather than as a lonely wanderer on the fells.[46] In Chapter 2 I take a Marxist approach to the local and national politics of landscape writing, developing the work of Raymond Williams, John Barrell, Stephen Daniels, and David Simpson, to clarify the poetic effects of anxieties about labor produced by Wordsworth's acceptance of patronage.[47]

Part II, "Spots of Space: Materializing Memory," considers the poetry of 1814–29, focusing on the effects of particular historical engagements in generating a highly varied formality through which "history" is not evaded, denied, or even displaced into hymns to nature or the individual imagination, but commemorated in what Wordsworth called "memorials." The later Wordsworth increasingly wrote poems on tour, focusing, in the spaces he traversed, on specific sites in which the past was evident—monuments and ruins.[48] Recollecting the history that made these sites significant to him and to others, he articulated them as places through which the past was recollected: they became, in his memorialization, spots that stood out from surrounding space as they focused times past. What they memorialized was not just the formative incidents of Wordsworth's mental education, as in *The Prelude*, but a public history—events through which, once revived by the poet, a local and national community could find itself. He now sought out spots in space, further afield, when once, having returned to home turf in 1800, familiar spots returned a personal past to him willy-nilly.

In Chapter 3 I suggest that Wordsworth's tours of Scotland were crucial in his development as a history poet: he adapted, from the examples of Scott, Hogg, and Burns, terms for thinking about the material remains of nationalist and independence struggles, about conflicts between loyalty and rebellion, and about the legacy of historical dispossession and trauma. Here I intervene in recent critical debates about the romanticization of the political and literary cultures of Scotland, as a nation colonized by England.[49]

In Chapter 4 I benefit from recent studies of book history and manuscript culture in reading Wordsworthian memory in the context of the material practice of writing and transcription in the Wordsworth household.[50] I look at a single poem that Wordsworth revised in response to the new perspective on historical time and on extinction produced by a geological discovery, but what I reveal about its formal alteration (and its thematization of its own altered form) has implications for understanding the oeuvre as a whole. Wordsworthian recollection did not precede the acts of writing words down on paper and then storing, retrieving and altering them (often repeatedly), producing more manuscripts. Memory materialized on paper, as transcribed and curated and reassembled by the scriptorial assistants—Dorothy, Mary, Dora, and Sarah Hutchinson. It was not spontaneous, or given, but constructed in the act of inscribing and rescribing. The published poems were neither "overflows" nor organic, but assemblages of fragments: to have a "spot of time," Wordsworth had to write a spot of time and have his family store it for rewriting and patching into the pieces of paper that were joined (or grown) into the "poem on the growth of my own mind."

In Part III, "The Politics of Diction," I examine the language of poems of 1819 and 1835 with the purpose of altering the received picture of the later Wordsworth as having defaulted to an authoritarian and declarative style—preachy generalities. I show that he was able to rework his earlier style—the sensual Ovidian diction of 1814 and the plain language of *Lyrical Ballads*—in competition with his younger imitators. In this process what occurred was not merely restatement but also renovation, with the older influenced by and taking on aspects of his followers' versions of his work. Not only was Wordsworth revitalized by his rivalry, he was also put into dialogue with a younger generation. He was not, that is, a Lake dinosaur ignoring or opposing new developments but, like the later Yeats and Hardy, an elder poet producing new work alongside that of his juniors.[51] What was at work here was an anxiety of influence felt by the older, influencing poet as much as by the younger, influenced one, and in the process Wordsworth's own characteristic poetic voice was altered. He became more like his admirers than he cared to admit. Seeing Wordsworth in this way allows us to breach traditional accounts of influence and to reimagine Romantic periodicity so it no longer is divided into pre-and post-1814 epochs and into first and second generations who are, for the most part, studied separately. Within this section, Chapter 5 construes Wordsworth through the lens of scholarship into debates about sex and gender provoked by the poetry of Byron and the mores of the governing aristocracy.[52] Chapter 6 puts Wordsworth in contact with laboring-class poetry that he precipitated, "recovering" a poet neglected by critics in the process. Here I expand the Romantic canon in the wake of Marxist literary historians, including John Goodridge, Ian Haywood, and Anne K. Janowitz.[53]

"Late Genres" (Part IV) examines how form shapes Wordsworth's presentation of the passage of time—history both public and private. Chapter 7 approaches Wordsworth's sonnets through a Historical Poetics methodology, exploring how the history of the form is not only developed by Wordsworth but is itself materialized in his practice in relation to the social issues of his time.[54] The observation of the historical form of the sonnet leans Wordsworth toward, and even shapes, his representation of the church as a historical materialization of the past in the present. Chapter 8 also examines formal innovation, reading Wordsworth's "evening" poems in the wake of critics who have considered late style, including Peter Larkin, Edward Said, and J. H. Prynne.[55] The experience of living beyond a past practice of formal experimentation is itself a pressure refracted in the formal developments of Wordsworth's late poetry. The late career is overdetermined by the past: how to write without repeating or to write anew without the new being judged in relation to the old—especially when the past work, and its formal innovation, is already public and thus a matter of literary history beyond the author's revisionary control? The Evening Voluntaries, a new hybrid form, are stunning late-life responses to these questions, revealing a poet able to put his superb technical control to the service of the most subtle and delicate articulations of time passing (articulations that restructure time as poetic meter and movement even while accepting its ultimate escape from the poet's hold).

What escapes, as I show in the coda, "Elegiac Musing and Generic Mixing," was confronted in a series of poems that hybridized the traditional genre of elegy with genres such as the epistle, the inscription, and the nature poem. This generic hybridization,[56] I suggest, is the refraction of tensions arising from the understood complexity of the poetic task: for Wordsworth to be an elegist meant the serving of contrasting purposes—the expression of personal grief and the doing of commemorative duty toward friends who were also public figures. Not just public figures, but renowned *writers*, so that the issue of what kind of elegy they received was shaped by that elegy's relationship with their own work. Form and style became issues in themselves, because they were received in relation to the recent literary past—to the dead writer's form and style; because also, they could not help resonate, for Wordsworth and his readers, with his own earlier writing. As a young man, already long an orphan, he had written about older men marked by loss in the figures of Matthew, Michael, the Old Cumberland Beggar, and the Discharged Soldier. As an old man himself, finding himself deprived of friends and loved ones, he was not only late in life but anticipated in this lateness by his own earlier evocations of it. How was he to find poetic words appropriate for his need to mourn, remember, and commemorate without their seeming already superseded, or at least shaped, by the prequel written when he had not yet experienced the aged perspective he now was forced to take by the death of his own generation and the younger generation too?[57] He found those words by crossing the genres in which he had previously imagined death and loss—chiefly the pastoral lyrical ballad—with that traditionally associated with mourning—the elegy—so as to benefit from the formal conventions by which, historically, the elegy conferred gravity upon mourner and mourned while still preserving the freedom to write in a personally resonant way that did not simply recapitulate the grief-stricken paralysis of Michael or the burnt-out silence of the old beggar. By this means, although he published no poems called elegies, he put elegiac form self-reflexively into question even as he commemorated the lives of the illustrious dead.

In sum, *Wordsworth's Poetry, 1815–1845* explores the work of a varied and surprising, rather than desiccated and reactionary, older poet. It presents him probing the experiences and perspectives of later life so as to discover fragile poise in the evocation of transience and diminution, as a poet formally and stylistically adapting the past—his own past verse and others'—to sketch ways of writing beyond the ways of recollecting the past that had been so central to his earlier art. A poet able to acknowledge the debt of his writing to women—to the counsel, rather than, as in 1798, to the naive naturalness of Dorothy. A poet modifying his writing in light of his younger followers' work. A love poet of companionate tenderness rather than passionate lament. An angry poet—bitter at capitalist exploitation of others and at a world in which vanity is rewarded while worth goes mad or dies. First and foremost, a history poet more probing and more clear-sighted than any of his time in his understanding of the responsibilities and temptations of all who try to find forms in which to put the past onto the page.[58] It is this restless and transformative Wordsworth I explore in these pages—a poet who is sometimes consolatory, and sometimes testy, but who always demands of himself and his readers that they think hard and differently from the ways to which they have become accustomed.

PART I

Producing a Poet for the Public

HERE I EXAMINE THE WAYS in which Wordsworth fashioned himself as a poet in his first collected works—the *Poems* of 1815. Chapter 1 shows how, in this edition, he defined himself for the first time in public as a "poet of imagination" to give himself finally, aged forty-five, the authority that readers and critics had refused him. Thus, "imagination" was no transcendent term neutrally applicable to the poems of the Great Decade, but an 1815 category that Wordsworth adopted for the self-interested purpose of escaping his reputation as a poet concerned with trivial matters unworthy of poetry. It had not featured strongly in the collections he published in 1800, 1802, and 1807; it did not play an important role in the volumes he issued in 1820 and after. In 1815, however, it was central to his effort to fashion himself as a different kind of poet, and to this end it involved the revision of old poems to fit a new agenda. I examine the textual history of one of these poems, "Yew Trees"—first drafted in 1804 but first published only in 1815—revealing how Wordsworth revised so as to occlude its relationship to contemporary contexts and to fellow poets. The result was a more impersonal and mysterious text, a text apparently independent of current political debates, of others' verse and even of its author's own subjectivity—a text revered by no less a critic than Hartman as the height of mythic power.[1] Produced as such, it was the successful outcome of a rebranding strategy that came with a cost.

A striking feature of the post-1814 Wordsworth is his changed rural politics, as epitomized by the dedication of *The Excursion* and the 1815 *Poems* to great landowners. Distancing himself from Jacobinical solidarity with the rural poor, the poet began in 1803 to accept the patronage of gentlemen and aristocrats. By 1815 a new poetic style, no longer close-up and personal but marked by distance and by overlooking (in both senses of that word), accompanied this changed social position. Focusing on Wordsworth's relationship with Sir George Beaumont, Chapter 2 traces the development of this later style to the politics of landscape in which the poet became uneasily involved at the landowner's country estate in Coleorton. Investigating the material context of labor relations between Beaumont and his employees, I show that Wordsworth's increasing use of the traditional genre of the inscription was an attempt to contain, by adoption of a formal and distant voice, the conflicting sympathies and viewpoints produced when an independent poetic laborer found himself working for a patron. Containment was not repression:[2] the remarkable achievement of the inscriptions that Wordsworth published in 1815 was to use his own ambiguous position as an independent yet patronized poet to dramatize, if not resolve, the tensions between landowner, land agent, and laborer that the capitalization and industrialization of the country were bringing to a crisis. These were the issues that occupied Jane Austen in the early years of the nineteenth century. Wordsworth's new embrace of an impersonal voice, distant viewpoint, and traditional genre can be compared with her novels—also apparently affiliated to the tastes and views of the landowning classes yet revealing their limitations by registering the tensions that they ignored.[3]

Chapter 1

Learning to Be a Poet of Imagination

Wordsworth and the Ghost of Cowper

Packaging for Posterity

In 1815 the bookseller Longman, Hurst, Rees, Orme, and Brown issued two volumes that were more significant for what they showed about their author's view of his career than they were for their sale. *Poems by William Wordsworth, Including Lyrical Ballads, and Miscellaneous Pieces of the Author. With Additional Poems, a New Preface and a Supplementary Essay* was the first collected edition and, as such, a publication designed to establish its author as a mature poet whose canon was substantial enough to be gathered as a whole.[1] It was a public bid for authority—a bid that seemed speculative to many, since the poet of *Lyrical Ballads* and *Poems, in Two Volumes* was more belittled than admired. The massive *Excursion* of the previous year had been brutally dismissed by Francis Jeffrey, the leading reviewer of the day, for its perverse egotism, while the *White Doe of Rylstone*, issued alongside the collected poems in an expensive format to demonstrate its importance, was termed "the very worst poem we ever saw imprinted in a quarto volume."[2] Wordsworth, in short, had neither the reputation nor the popularity to make the publication of his collected edition an uncontroversial sign of an established cultural significance: the volumes, carefully arranged for effect and prefaced with advice about how they should be read, embodied their author's anxious aspirations rather than acknowledged achievements.

Collected editions are a mark of lateness to the extent that, on the one hand, they require retrospection and reordering and, on the other, they look to futurity—to one's posthumous reputation.[3] Wordsworth surveyed his old poems and sorted them into aesthetic categories of his own devising, aiming to fulfill the promise he had made when, prefacing *The Excursion*, he had written that his "minor pieces, which have been long before the public, when they shall be properly arranged, will be found by the attentive reader to have such connection with the main work as may give them claim to be likened to the little cells, oratories, and sepulchral recesses" of a Gothic church, parts of which were not yet complete (*Excursion*, p. 38). Now, making that proper arrangement, he went further toward finishing the Gothic edifice of his oeuvre, pitching his collection as far beyond the moment of its issue as was one of the great monumental abbeys that survived—built and maintained over centuries—from England's earliest recorded history.[4]

Arranging poems into categories was a business as timebound as it aimed to be timeless.[5] It was part of a makeover designed to redeem Wordsworth's damaged reputation in a contemporary print culture of which he had learned to be suspicious. He had been criticized for his Jacobinical ballads, and still more for the 1800 Preface that argued that his model was the speech of rustic villagers—"the best part of language" (LB, p. 744). He had been ridiculed for the confessional poems that philosophized about his feelings for everyday objects: in the eyes of critics and parodists, such poems as "I wandered lonely as a Cloud" revealed him as a perverse oddball who invested trivial things with far greater emotional significance than they merited and who then assumed that his feelings must be important to others.[6] Resenting this response and suffering its consequences (poor sales left him unable to support his family), Wordsworth knew he could not escape the power of reviews and magazines: the literary world, in the wake of Scott and Byron, was now a marketplace subject to fashion—an "age of personality"[7] in which mass sales could be achieved if reviews were favorable and if an author presented a public image that fascinated consumers.[8] The new poem groupings were a modest attempt to transform his public image by demonstrating his seriousness and his centrality—none more so than the one entitled "Poems of the Imagination." This category sounded the collection's keynote, for it was justified in a preface in which Wordsworth set out his claim to be a poet of the highest class—not a "namby pamby" eccentric but a worthy successor to Spenser and Milton. It was here that Wordsworth first publicly staked his reputation on being a poet of imagination; it was also here that imagination was first announced, in print, as the central feature of the Romantic aesthetic.

"Imagination" had not featured strongly in the Prefaces to *Lyrical Ballads*;[9] the concept did not appear in the 1807 *Poems, in Two Volumes*. Although Coleridge had used the concept, he had not yet published his extensive discussion of it in *Biographia Literaria*. In the 1815 *Poems*, Wordsworth used it to depict his writing as philosophical and scientific: poetry of imagination "denot[ed] operations of the mind . . . and processes of creation or of composition, governed by certain fixed laws." Imagination provided its own validation: it fulfilled the old philosophical injunction "know thyself," for it was "conscious of an indestructible dominion;—the Soul may fall away from it, not being able to sustain its grandeur; but, if once felt and acknowledged, by no act of any other faculty of the mind can it be relaxed, impaired, or diminished" (1815, I, pp. xx–xxi; xxxv). The poet of imagination, therefore, was sublime, and his work was the highest expression of the mind's ability to exert itself upon the world and upon itself. Wordsworth was unexpectedly revealing about his motives in making the claim: if, he declared, he was "justified by recollection of the insults which the ignorant, the incapable, and the presumptuous, have heaped upon these and my other writings, I may be permitted to anticipate the judgment of posterity upon myself, I shall declare (censurable, I grant, if the notoriety of the fact above stated does not justify me) that I have given in these unfavourable times evidence of exertions of this faculty upon its worthiest objects, the external universe, the moral and religious sentiments of Man, his natural affections, and his acquired passions" (1815, I, p. xxxi). Here Wordsworth's self-congratulation emerges directly from his resentment of criticism: it is a self-defensive formation that indicates the depth of his need for acknowledgement and reveals the self-interested nature of his arguments.[10]

Despite the polemical context of its first expression, "imagination" was endorsed by professional literary critics in the twentieth century as a disinterested, generally valid, characterization of Wordsworth's poetry—and often of all poetry. Some made it the criterion for deciding whether particular poems were of the highest class; others explored how it operated in Wordsworth's account of his own mental development. Consequently, *The Prelude* became the defining work, although never published by Wordsworth because he considered it incomplete without the epic to which it was a preface. Critics defined and redefined imagination in relation to German philosophy,[11] to psychoanalysis,[12] to deconstruction,[13] and to phenomenology:[14] it was the means by which Wordsworth voiced the freedom of his mind from nature, his oedipal relation to his dead father and his surrogates,[15] his dependence on figuration, and his being in a universe of death.[16] But few of the critics who elevated the concept as the subject of investigation considered that Wordsworth was neither publicly a poet of imagination nor necessarily thought of himself as a poet of imagination until 1815—years after many of the poems they discuss had been drafted and/or published. The contemporary purpose of the concept as a means of rebranding an unpopular poet was (at least before the work of McGann[17]) ignored.

In this chapter I examine imagination as a situated, self-interested repackaging of an unpopular poet by investigating the textual history and prehistory of a poem first published in the 1815 collection. "Yew Trees," first drafted in 1804, was not born a "poem of imagination" but had imagination thrust upon it. It was a key part of Wordsworth's 1815 effort to be a poet of imagination, and it was reworked in order to play this role. It was made more gnomic and less personal by a poet who was trying to live down a reputation for garrulous subjectivity. Its imaginative qualities were accentuated by acts of revision that altered it so as to efface its relationship to another poet's text, to which it was indebted and with which it was in conversation. With that effacement, the poem's relationship to a tradition of political symbolism was also all but removed. In desubjectivizing his poem, Wordsworth increased what Geoffrey Hartman called its "mythic" power[18] by highlighting a trope that late twentieth-century critics singled out as a hallmark of imaginative lyric verse—prosopopoeia, calling the dead into imagined life by giving them a face or voice. This highlighting, however, came at the cost of mystifying the poem's relation to Wordsworth's poetic forebears as well as his readers and quietening its political resonance. Imagination stood alone, summoning the absent into textual voice, only because of acts of concealment made by doctoring an old text so it served a new agenda. In this process, I shall show, the poem was made to turn its back on the text that, when Wordsworth encountered it in 1804, had galvanized him, offering him a way out of a poetic quandary caused by his political disenchantment and social isolation. "Yew Trees" had begun as a response to "Yardley Oak": William Cowper's posthumously published poem was responsible for a significant turn in Wordsworth's poetic language and in his conception of the poet's responsibility to history.

The Context for "Yew Trees": 1804 and Earlier

When "Yew Trees" first germinated, Wordsworth was still, to the few who had read him, the Jacobin balladeer of *Lyrical Ballads*. He was not yet a byword for childish egotism, nor did he predicate his writing on his "imagination." He faced different problems, and sought other solutions, because the social sources and private audience on which his work depended were in a state of collapse. A tour of Scotland in the autumn of 1803 had revealed as much: he, Dorothy, and Coleridge had traveled together in an effort to renew the fertile companionship they had enjoyed in 1797–98. But Coleridge had left the party after days of tension, caused, in part, by his frustration that Wordsworth was content to write short poems about tiny objects instead of working on his great philosophical epic. To produce slight verses attributing great significance to encounters with daisies, celandines, and the like was to continue in the vein that had led to public criticism; it was to neglect his true vocation and to give his enemies further opportunities to attack him.[19] There were political tensions too: the rustic diction of *Lyrical Ballads* had been received as poetic Jacobinism, but Wordsworth now became disconcerted by the kind of Jacobinical speech he heard in rural Scotland. Napoleon's revolutionary armies were amassed on the French coast, and the Highland clansmen welcomed the planned invasion: one of them, Dorothy recorded, "speaking of the French, uttered the basest and most cowardly sentiments" (Coleridge called him a "Jacobin traitor of a boatman").[20] Wordsworth found himself disgusted by the rural speech on which he had modeled his radical poetry; recoiling from their professions of enthusiasm for a French revolutionary liberty he had come to distrust, he could not henceforth be a poet of the common people. But neither could he simply dissociate himself from them. Though shocked that the clansmen would refuse to fight the French, the Wordsworths understood their reasons:

> In talking of the French and the present times, their language was what most people would call Jacobinical. They spoke much of the oppressions endured by the Highlanders further up, of the absolute impossibility of their living in any comfort, and of the cruelty of laying so many restraints on emigration. Then they spoke with animation of the attachment of the clans to their lairds: "The laird of this place, Glengyle, where we live, could have commanded so many men who would have followed him to the death; and now there are none left."[21]

Sympathetic toward the plight of the speech community on which he had based his revolutionary poetry while simultaneously appalled by its politics,

Wordsworth was in danger of being stymied. Retreat was ineffective: after the Preface to *Lyrical Ballads* and Jeffrey's *Edinburgh* review, even poems about flowers were Jacobinical if written in simple, rustic form and style. Reaction was impossible: resenting the "oppressions" suffered by ordinary people, he could not simply take up the language of the lairds who, having exploited and impoverished them, now urged them to fight.

Over the next year, Wordsworth cast around for ways out of his impasse. He joined the Volunteers—the local militia—performing weapons drill alongside Grasmere shepherds, farmers, and gentlemen in readiness to defend his beloved vale against the French.[22] This action spoke more loudly and simply than his words could of a patriotic loyalty and a local solidarity, but it scarcely satisfied his needs as a poet.[23] Those needs had, in recent years, been met, in part, by conversation and collaboration with Coleridge, but Coleridge, his health having collapsed, decided in early 1804 to leave the Lakes for warmer climes. Wordsworth would be without his friend and mentor; he suspected that Coleridge might never return, and anticipating his loss, he began recomposing the prelude to the philosophical poem that Coleridge had always wanted him to write—the "poem to Coleridge."

While the prospect of Coleridge's absence prompted Wordsworth to the autobiographical verse that made his friend an intimate sharer of his upbringing, it did not stimulate him to a public poetry capable of resolving the dilemmas caused by political developments. The political sonnets of Milton offered one model of such poetry.[24] Writing sonnets in their vein, Wordsworth produced public verse that demonstrated patriotism—the onetime admirer of the French revolution called the English to arms against French invasion—only to register his critical reservations about the moral and political state of present-day England.

Wordsworth's most potent poetic influence in 1804 was, however, not the sonnet but an in-between genre: not quite an ode, not quite an epitaph, not quite an inscription—a nameless form that mixed private with public, personal with political. "Yew Trees" was his response to this genre—not a "poem of imagination" but a guide to a particular, named place that mixed social and political commentary with natural history and with observations on history. Also present, at least implicitly, was consideration of the poet's role in articulating that history (the history of place, of public affairs, and of literature). The genre in question was epitomized by a poem published posthumously in William Hayley's *The Life and Posthumous Writings of William Cowper* and read by Wordsworth in autumn 1804.

Hayley's *Life* presented Cowper as a poet who in his last years had written, without publishing, poems about age, loss, decay, and death. Its culmination was a poetic fragment, probably from a longer unfinished work, that was presented as a separate, integral, if incomplete, poem. Although Cowper wrote it in 1792,[25] Hayley placed it last, after a number of later poems. The effect of this placing was to present it as the final text, retrieved from the grave, of a mad and suicidal poet: a literary testament to a life fragmented by the anticipation of death. Hayley gave the poem a title—"Yardley Oak"—and prefaced it with paratextual material signaling its importance: a letter from a friend welcoming its retrieval from the waste paper of Cowper's uncompleted projects, and natural history notes describing the actual tree that features in the poem. Readers are assured of the poem's accuracy: Cowper, we are told, visited the tree; it can be measured; it grows on the Earl of Northampton's estate; it is a local landmark and a byword for longevity. "Yardley Oak" is thus established as the poem's proper title because of its reliable affiliation to a real, local tree. The named tree and poem bespeak lateness and decay: the tree is broken by age; the poem is an unresolved fragment, yet they open upon the deep past, looking back to the birth of modern England and beyond. They are presented as growths from a current English landscape, typical in that it is owned by a great aristocrat. The poem, so introduced, is about the poet's contemplation of the national as well as the local, the past as well as what is present to his eyes—and this recommended it to Wordsworth as a model for his own new writing. Moreover, for a poet disenchanted with both the Jacobin common people and their masters and expecting an invasion by Napoleonic France, it was also a fragment that reflected the broken nature of history—its resistance to the redeeming unity that a Christian might wish to intimate in his own life and in nature. The tree is neither teleological nor cyclical; it has grown and decayed so long and so slowly that neither renewal nor extinction seem possible: it embodies death-in-life.

From its beginning, "Yardley Oak" adopts the trope of apostrophe as a means toward making the tree bear witness to the history that has passed since it first began to grow. Cowper asserts his own poetic voice by addressing the oak: like a mirror it represents his own being, revealing his own age, vulnerability, and decrepitude in its decayed trunk.

Survivor sole, and hardly such, of all
That once liv'd here thy brethren, at my birth,

Since which I number three-score winters past,
A shatter'd vet'ran, hollow-trunk'd perhaps,
As now, and with excoriate forks deform,
Relic[t] of Ages . . .

(lines 1–6)[26]

Apostrophe is associated with prosopopoeia and has been viewed as the poet of imagination's hallmark procedure. According to Jonathan Culler and Paul de Man, lyric poetry depends on apostrophic invocation of the other that simultaneously calls it and the poet into words: "invocation is a figure of vocation."[27] "Yardley Oak," a poem wholly consisting of invocation, is, on this model, a seminal modern lyric, a poem of imagination avant la lettre. It is a prototype of Wordsworth's Greater Romantic Lyrics, a blueprint for the kind of poem that makes its author a "prophet of nature" (*Prelude* (1805), XIII, 442).

In Cowper, though, apostrophic invocation is not so straightforwardly empowering as Culler suggests: Cowper talks to the tree only to discover its reluctance to be made-over into language. Apostrophe involves the alienation of the imaginative power: it gives the poet voice so as to articulate the insignificance of his present speech in the face of the tree's silent embodiment of the past. Cowper finds his invocations refused; no dryad answers him from the trunk. Instead, the tree keeps its own counsel, its silence stretching the credibility of the apostrophe trope to its limit. It will neither easily become the death he resurrects nor simply be a living form sponsoring his lively song, and for this reason it repeatedly both provokes and frustrates his efforts to speak—to establish his poetic vocation. Here apostrophe brings nature and poet into words, but as a way of blurring, without transcending, the distinction between self and other. It leads to displacement rather than, as Culler suggests, the "self-authorization" of a poet of imagination who re-creates the world transformed by his mind.[28]

Yardley oak is disabled by age ("Thine arms have left thee. Winds have rent them off," line 125) but still it survives. And it evokes as well as defies death, seemingly rooted in the fall with which the lapse of time began and death entered the world. For this reason it is both macabre and curiously protective. Its shade suggests the grove, both ghastly and sheltering, in which Adam hid after sinning and bringing death into the world: "into gloom / Of thickest shades, like Adam after taste / Of fruit proscrib'd, as to a refuge, fled" (lines 14–16). The tree is a memento mori yet also a helpmeet of sinful man, frightened by his mortality. Thus it allows Cowper to articulate both the inevitability of his own decline into the grave and the persistence of the life-force even in such reduced circumstances. It helps him to come to terms with the mutability of nature, within which the individual organism dies, and by so doing lets him avoid the self-pity and vanity that accompany the confessional mode. In this respect, apostrophe is a trope by which there is some (cold) comfort to be had: it lets the poet lose the burden of a sole self even as it brings the self to words; it lets him face both ways, inside and out, and to the lost past and the unknown future.

That the tree blurs the life/death opposition is its most significant feature. In invoking it, and thus envisaging the possibility of its reply, Cowper articulates this blurring in a blurring of the oppositions of subject and object, speech and silence. What goes on here is not the prosopopeia that de Man sees as the master trope of autobiography—and especially the summoning of self to words that characterizes the imaginative poetry of Wordsworth. For de Man, apostrophe bases the representation of the living self on a personification of the past, the absent, the deceased—figures of Death.[29] And so it zombifies (or, in de Man's term, defaces) the apostrophist's account of himself.[30] He is haunted by the death he makes live, and by the absence he makes present. Cowper's apostrophized oak, however, is neither an absent, deceased past that the poet's words make live anew, nor does it regain a face or voice when the poet invokes it. It stays silent, both present and alive yet also apparently "fixed and dead" (to use Coleridge's term for the unimagined object world; BL, I, p. 304).

Cowper both apostrophizes and charts the failure of his apostrophizing as the tree resists his call and undermines the gesture that would establish his imaginative power. He returns, again and again, from discursive time (in which poet and past-in-tree coexist) to empirical time (in which loss and absence is not repaired). "O, couldst thou speak," Cowper writes, calling the tree to disclose its knowledge of the history that it fully embodies: "By thee I might correct, erroneous oft, / The clock of history, facts and events / Timing more punctual, unrecorded facts / Recov'ring, and misstated setting right" (lines 45–48). This is a fantasy of a poetic discourse that would overcome referential temporality because it is founded on a tree that is a surviving witness of the past, incorporating absence within presence. Sitting above the fray, it would survey all, losing nothing, understanding everything. Yet it remains a fantasy, because Cowper finds his invocation refused; he is turned back on himself, forced to call his invocation—his poem—(with a disturbing allusion to Macbeth's mad urgency to make nature reveal itself) "desperate . . . till trees shall speak again" (line 49). As a result, the poet's sanity in trying to summon prophetic words from a nature that is already both past and present, dead and alive, familiar and strange, becomes the implicit issue that the poem dramatizes. Sobered, he falls back on the admission that his words are only his own. They are not imaginative modifications of the oak's inner nature: "since . . . / . . . no spirit dwells in thee, nor voice / May be expected from thee . . . / . . . I will perform myself the oracle, and will discourse / In my own ear such matter as I may" (lines 138–43). But a self-performed oracle, unsupported by the absent spirit that oracles summon to presence, turns out to be no sort of oracle at all. Cowper's apostrophe leaves him hearing his own voice echoing in the silence, reminding him of man's loneliness in a world that does not, in the end, acknowledge him, however strongly he wants to recoup the past.

Unsure of redemption—at least for himself—Cowper has no alternative but to bear the weight of what the tree shows him: an inextricable co-presence of past and present, death and life, object and subject, that is not convertible to a playing off of one against the other in a timeless, lossless time of poetic discourse. Thus the poem ends by placing the tree and fallen man, crippled and vulnerably mortal, in opposition to prelapsarian Adam. Adam, Cowper shows,

> survey'd
> All creatures, . . .
>   . . . assign'd
> To each his name significant, and fill'd
> With love and wisdom, render'd back to heav'n
> In praise harmonious the first air he drew.
> He was excus'd the penalties of dull
> Minority. No tutor charg'd his hand
> With the thought-tracing quill, or task'd his mind
> With problems; history, not wanted yet,
> Lean'd on her elbow, watching Time, whose course
> Eventful, should supply her with a theme[.]

(lines 133–44)

Here Eden is a place of exactitude, a paradise of language in which words not only fit things precisely but are a gift given to God in return for the gift of breath. It is a paradise too fragile to be sustained, watched by "history" and "Time"—and by Cowper, who seems to image himself as a writer-in-the-making as he identifies "the thought-tracing quill" as one of the penalties by which the fallen world is characterized. Is "task'd" even a punning allusion to his own *The Task* and the mental pain its writing cost? The lines contrast the timeless spiritual reciprocity of Edenic speech—a temporality of discourse in Culler's terms[31]—with writing (including poetic writing), showing the latter to be a penalty rather than a gift, an expression of, rather than escape from, historical bondage.

After representing learning to write as one of the penalties of the fallen world, the poem fades into uncompleted silence. Cowper's own text, like the oak to which it compares him, lacks a resolving conclusion. It, like the tree and everything else in the post-Edenic world, is shown to be a form in which time is not regained nor overcome, but not lost either. It is preserved, enshrined, as decay—a form therefore that is necessarily incomplete, broken, fragmentary. Outside Eden, language, like the oak, is disabled by the consequences of the first fall: Sin, Death, and Time. But the millennium is not at hand: the poet can make no prophecy that renews the Edenic by substituting the temporality of poetical discourse—tropological time—for historical time. The sad fate of the writer is to be in-between and compromised: he will preserve loss over and again as he tries to word his way beyond it, and thus re-create the inevitability of its consequences for his own—and all—writing. He is always too late yet never late enough.

Hayley's paratext framed the poem uncontroversially as part of a tradition of landscape writing that took the measure of England and Englishness, country and character, by observing local places. This, however, was to occlude the fact that, in 1792, when Cowper wrote the poem, the ideological use of the oak to symbolize Englishness had become a hotly contested issue. His immediate spur was his reading of Burke's defense of the constitution in *Reflections on the Revolution in France* (1790), a text that both employs the oak as an icon of Englishness and argues for the vital importance of such icons in ensuring a stable polity. Long a brilliant rhetorician, Burke understood the power of rhetoric, over time, to familiarize people to a political system. Symbols, he saw, made power seem attractive and, if used for long enough, customary and even natural. The British constitution was a case in point: the people were loyal to it because they were accustomed to the terms in which it was shaped. Burke quite deliberately practiced what he preached, using the old patriotic symbols to make the domination of power by the landed classes appear traditional, attractive, natural, and native. Thus he gave Britain's form of government a face, personifying—or at least animating—it in the form of an oak tree of ancient growth: it "moves on through the varied tenour of perpetual decay, fall, renovation, and progression" in "the method of nature."[32] Oaks, too, symbolized the British constitution not just because they were native, organic, and slow to change, but also because they grew on the landed estates, ownership of which entitled a gentleman to represent his country. They symbolized the landowner's monopoly of power in the unreformed parliament: if one owned no land, one was unlikely to be able to vote, let alone become an MP.

Exposing the ideological nature of traditional symbols was a dangerous game. It gave readers a look behind the curtain—admitting that the iconography of Englishness was a political trick perpetuated by the classes who possessed power. And the extremity of Burke's use of the iconography also dramatized its class bias: when he wrote of a "swinish multitude" grazing on acorns below the "shade" of the aristocratic constitution, a people brought up to sing of themselves as "hearts of oak" now heard themselves likened to pigs.[33] In the polarized politics of the postrevolutionary era, the ideological function of the oak symbol was revealed: radicals turned Burke's image against him, criticizing the ruling classes for exploiting rather than protecting the ordinary people.

Cowper had long understood the association of the oak with the political power of the gentry and aristocracy. In *The Task* (1785), he lamented gentlemen's indifference both to the symbolism on which their power depended and to the duties which that power entailed upon them.[34] "Yardley Oak" develops this critique in the middle of a propaganda war in which the role of propaganda and ideology had itself become an issue. It is, in this context, a self-conscious examination of the decline of the personification of the constitution, and of the national character, in the symbol of the oak—an investigation of the collapse of an ideological use of nature. Hollow, aged yet "still erect," Yardley Oak stands for the destruction of an icon by the people it had been called upon to benefit—the landed classes:

> So stands a kingdom, whose foundations yet
> Fail not, in virtue and in wisdom laid,
> Though all the superstructure, by the tooth
> Pulveriz'd of venality, a shell . . .

(lines 120–23)

Cowper's tree indicates the failure of a once-powerful prosopopeiac use of the oak. Neglectful of their paternalist duties to shelter their dependants under the oak of their power, the landowners precipitate the revolution that threatens to remove them, as had happened to the aristocracy in France. Visibly decayed, his poetic oak suggests the inevitable decline of a national character too old for reform—the slow death-in-life of the ruling landowning classes and the symbols that were used to make their rule seem traditional and natural. Cowper's is an organicism of diminution, the bleak obverse of Burke's organicism of growth—the nature poetry of a poet whose scruples about the appropriation of nature into powerful words, whether by poets or politicians, prevent him from apostrophizing his way into a position of power.[35]

By 1804 the ideological struggle against Jacobins who admired revolutionary France had taken a new turn. It was harder than ever before to sustain a language of patriotism that was not either stigmatized, or subsumed, by the language of anti-French, anti-reform Toryism. Napoleon's armies were camped on the French coast, preparing for an invasion of Britain, and in the resultant alarm, criticism of war policy became more unpatriotic than ever, while radicals who had shown sympathy for revolutionary France risked seeming traitorous. "Yardley Oak" was published during an outpouring of crude propaganda that aimed to rally Britons to a defense of their soil and their government. Broadsides such as "Old England for Ever!" depicted ideological conformity to church and state as patriotic duty—an anti-war Briton is a disloyal, and, so the oak symbol suggests, an unnatural one:

I

Let BRITONS attend, and unite in the cause,
To save their Religion, THEIR KING, and their Law,
Against an Usurper, whose treacherous blow
Has laid throughout Europe all Potentates low!
Hearts of Oak

II

'Tis his wish and intention this land to invade,
To ruin our Commerce, and Credit degrade—
Our Birthright he threatens at once to enslave—
But BRITONS have e'er been courageous and brave!
Hearts of Oak

. . . .

IV

In a moment of danger let's rally around
TRUE LIBERTY's STANDARD ON OLD ENGLISH GROUND!
Should Neptune take charge of the Consul at sea,
BRITONS may boast, they STILL LIVE—and ARE FREE!
                                    Hearts of Oak.[36]

In this flood of bellicose revivals of the oak symbol, Cowper's probing meditation on a broken, self-divided tree seemed an isolated case: its pained
scruples about apostrophizing and personifying nature to gain vocational
and ideological authority were utterly absent from the reactionary and
aggressive discourse that dominated the public sphere.[37]

It was its pained scruples, and not its putative status as a poem of imagination, that made "Yardley Oak" so powerful a text for a Wordsworth not
yet categorizing his writing as "poetry of the imagination." Disillusioned by
Jacobinism, loving his country, afraid of invasion, yet opposed to the political reaction that had caused his friends to be tried for treason—or imprisoned without trial—he found "Yardley Oak" a godsend. It offered an
example of how description of a local landscape could let a poet ponder his
relationship with history—let him question what, during the long years of
political deeds witnessed by an ancient tree, had been done in England's
name. It showed that an Englishman's expression of love for England need
not be a knee-jerk endorsement of war but could, instead, be a counting of
costs—the costs of war and of other forms of contest for power. It offered
him a model wherewith to make his isolated position a vantage point of
disenchanted hindsight—a late view that refused enthusiasm about the ideology and politics of the present because they seemed, from a long historical
perspective, trivial and short-lived. That historical perspective showed a
continuity of development and diminution so slow that it seemed almost
static; one couldn't see it happening, save by witnessing its effects on the
aged and the ancient. Taking that perspective, Wordsworth built on Cowper's style: he echoed his symbolism and his very words; he formally continued a past poetry rather than begin anew, as he had in 1798. He self-
consciously wrote after the late-career belatedness of a posthumous poetry
that was itself written after Milton's late style. In this respect, he too became
a belated poet.

Wordsworth began drafting a tree poem of his own in late 1804 within
a few months of receiving Hayley's edition, completing it for publication

only in 1814.[38] When first drafted, "Ewtrees," as it was called, developed in a new direction a kind of poetry Wordsworth had already begun to try out in poems that monumentalized the local so as to bear witness to the effects of age and isolation. It was, however, newly impersonal in its focalization of a place shown to be ineluctably shaped by slow change through deep time—a place too late for departures and revolutions, too real to be merely a subjective impression. Enabled by Cowper's verse, it was a way forward for a writer alienated from both the Jacobinical speech of the common rural people and the anti-Jacobin language of contemporary patriotism—a writer, too, newly without Coleridge. In these daunting and isolating circumstances, Cowper's poem allowed Wordsworth to retrieve his poetic vocation without turning from historical pressures to a dehistoricized and unpoliticized nature. A seminal achievement, it began a vein of nature "memorials" that he would continue for the rest of his writing life. Detached in viewpoint, these are related to, but distinct from, the inscription and the epitaph (they commemorate particular places but do not affect to be written on stone, and they are much longer). Instead, they adopt the narrative address of a tourist guidebook or a natural history; they imitate impersonal prose rather than subjective speech or oracular song—print rather than apostrophe.

"Ewtrees," as drafted in 1804, is like "Yardley Oak" as prefaced by Hayley in that it treats readers as visitors to significant local sights—named, landmark trees—the yews of Lorton and Borrowdale:

There is a Yew-tree pride of Lorton Vale,
Which to this day stands single, in the midst
Of its own darkness, as it stood of yore:
Not loth to furnish weapons for the bands
Of Umfraville or Percy ere they marched
Oer Scotland's heaths; or those that crossd the sea
And drew their sounding boughs at Azincour,
Perhaps at earlier Crecy, & Poictiers.
Of vast circumference & gloom profound
This solitary Tree a living thing
Produced too slowly ever—to decay;
Of Form & aspect too magnificent
To be destroyed—yet worthier [?still] of note
Nor those fraternal four of Borrowdale,

Joined in one solemn & capacious grove;
Huge Trunks and each particular Trunk a growth
Of intertwisted fibres serpentine
Up-coiling, and inveterately convolved
Nor uninformed with phantasy and looks
That threaten the profane—a pillared shade,
Upon whose grassless floor of red-brown hue,
By sheddings from the pining umbrage tinged
Perennially, beneath whose sable roof
Of Boughs, as if for festal purpose decked
With unrejoicing Berries, ghostly Shapes
May meet at noontide;—Fear and trembling Hope
Silence and Foresight, Death the Skeleton
And Time the Shadow; there to celebrate,
As in a natural Temple scattered oer
With altars undisturbed of mossy stone
United worship or in mute repose
To lie and listen to the mountain flood
Murmuring from Glaramara's inmost caves
Pass not the place unvisited—Ye will say
That Mona's Druid Oaks composed a Fane
Less awful than this grove:—as Earth so long
On its unwearied bosom has sustaind
The undecaying Pile, as Frost & Droughth,
The Fires of heaven have spared it and the Storms,
So in its hallowed uses may it stand
Forever spared by man!—[39]

Wordsworth guides readers' view, directing them to "note" the trees as indices of history. The Lorton yew stands apart in the present but embodies a remote past of violence in which the tree has provided wood for the bows of English archers fighting the Scots and the French. Wordsworth's references to Agincourt are significant in a period of war with Napoleonic France renewed in 1803 after a year's tense peace. But there is no more jingoism here than there was in "Yardley Oak." He notes but does not celebrate the yew's association with war; he does not suggest that strength—and success—in battle is a native and rooted English characteristic. And if Agincourt was widely seen, after Shakespeare, as a miraculous vindication of English courage and honor in battle, then Robert de Umfraville was a border raider, known for burning and pillaging Scottish towns. The yews are used in wars both noble and petty but remain what they are: they do not glamorize the English character, the Burkean constitution, or the land-owning classes. On the contrary, the Lorton yew is the epitome of solitari-ness, "not loth" but not keen either to be used as a resource for men's wars, hardly to be recruited for propaganda. Wordsworth views it as an embodiment of nature's enduring independence of the human need to make it into a resource or a validation—save that, in viewing it so, he turns it into a stronghold for the cultural position he wishes his poetry to occupy. Beholden to no party, standing single, unmoving and unmoved, it config-ures an isolated disengagement on which Wordsworth, lacking Coleridge and disgusted by the revolutionary Jacobinism to which he had once been committed but equally disgusted by propagandistic appropriations of nature, wishes to stand. The recurrence of "stands single" in *The Prelude* makes this context even clearer: in Book X, Wordsworth says of Coleridge "To me the grief confined / That thou art gone / From this last spot of earth where Freedom now / Stands single in her only sanctuary" (*Prelude* (1805), X, 981–83). In "Ewtrees" the personal is omitted: the single tree is neverthe-less an outgrowth and focus of local, rather than national, "pride."

Disengagement means disembodiment: "Ewtrees" does not sound like "Yardley Oak." The third-person observation leaves the narrator out of the scene; the poem does not apostrophize but resembles the silent and imper-sonal narration of a guidebook or a natural history.[40] Wordsworth objecti-fies the narrative voice of "Yardley Oak" and avoids the autobiographical context that Hayley's *Life* had given it and that he was concurrently explor-ing in his own *Prelude*. "Ewtrees" is not, like its model, about the poet's effort to call nature into language and make it speak to and in his imagina-tion. Wordsworth claims no vatic mission. He neither invokes the muse nor attempts Culler's visionary substitution of referential time, with its constant lapse, by discursive time. History is not transcended by the nature/poet relationship as forged in the verse. "Ewtrees," composed as *The Prelude* was being composed but unlike that long poem put to the press, is the public positive to its private negative: it is an example of a chastened poetry that works within self-imposed limits, avoiding imaginative flight because it eschews the lure of mistaking verbal facility for special insight into the world's purpose, achieving weight because it distinguishes itself from dis-courses that treat nature as a resource to make political arguments. That is,

the narratorial stance of standing witness to history (history being embodied in objects surviving from the past), allows poetry's proper concerns to
be distinguished from those of politics. Poetry takes a view so long that it
is disenchanted and disinterested. It is a specific and located view, rooted
in experience, but also static and uninvolved.

But that is not the whole story. Although "Ewtrees" avoids apostrophizing the yews, it finds another way to affirm poetry's ability to reanimate
the past, the lost, the dead. Verbal borrowings from "Yardley Oak" renew
Cowper's voice, itself retrieved from death by Hayley's posthumous edition.
Wordsworth gains authority from this double revival; indeed, his poetic
vocation is restored by his ability to replay Cowper's scrupulous words of
witness in words that are both his own and Cowper's. If this leaves Wordsworth's language a discourse of both a living and a dead poet, it also ensures
that the past speaks in the poem's form and diction even if not in the
scenario it presents. The trees—nature—will not reply to the poet's call,
will not be spoken for, but the invocations of past poets can be renewed.
Borrowing is the gesture that empowers Wordsworth and enables him to
venture a historicist poetry: it is a form of prosopopoeia that is not the
granting of voice to a natural object apostrophized by the poet but the
finding of voice by bringing the words of a dead poet to life on one's own
page. In the process, as Hartman argues, his language is left haunted—his
own and not his own.[41] His empowerment by and discomfort with the
resultant uncanniness of his medium is revealed by the concluding passage
of the 1804 draft ("Pass not the place unvisited . . . / Forever spared by
man!"). The poet there appears in his poem—at least in the imperative
address to the reader, who is put in the place of a passerby. This gesture
diminishes the impersonality of the narratorial voice and relates the poem
to "Yardley Oak" and, beyond Cowper, to the classical tradition of inscription, wherein the poet brings to life the voice of a tombstone calling visitors
to pay attention (the very origin of the trope of prosopopoeia). Wordsworth
is empowered by others' words and ideas and lets the debt be seen ("Mona's
Druid Oaks" come both from Cowper and the long antiquarian tradition
that placed the druids' stronghold on Mona—variously identified as the
Isle of Anglesey or the Isle of Man). Thus his address functions not simply
to indicate the poet's imaginative ability to call others into words, but also
to reference the poet's indebtedness to poetic history, recent and remote.

The diction, too, is close to Cowper's: "sustain'd," "undecaying,"
"spared," and "stand" all appear in "Yardley Oak," as does the idea that the

trees, having survived storms, deserve to escape the axe. Wordsworth's trees are, however, less damaged by the years than Cowper's, though they too are characterized by a rate of change so slow that they mock the concerns of the moment; they are "living" yet almost inanimate "things"—the closest part of the organic world to the world of the fixed and the permanent. They partake, therefore, of both life and death, as if embodiments of the haunted language in which Wordsworth finds himself revoicing Cowper's posthumous poem:

> —and each particular trunk a growth
> Of intertwisted fibres serpentine
> Up-coiling, and inveterately convolved,—
> Nor uninformed with Fantasy, and looks
> That threaten the profane;—a pillared shade,
> Upon whose grassless floor of red-brown hue,
> By sheddings from the pining umbrage tinged
> Perennially—
>
> ("Yew Trees," lines 16–23)

Again, Wordsworth's description is sonically and semantically close to "Yardley Oak's" "gloom / Of thickest shades," and its "knott'd fangs / . . . crook'd into a thousand fancies" ("Yardley Oak," lines 116–18). Both poets allude to Milton's serpentine Satan as the agedness of the tree leads them to think on time, death, and the origins of both—the fall of man. Whereas the thickest shades of Yardley oak offer the shameful Adam shelter from the knowledge of sin brought about by taking what was not his, those of the Borrowdale yews provide a natural altar around which congregate the ghosts introduced to the world by the fall:

> Fear and trembling Hope,
> Silence and Foresight, Death the Skeleton
> And Time the Shadow; there to celebrate,
> As in a natural temple scattered o'er
> With altars undisturbed of mossy stone,
> United worship
>
> ("Yew Trees," lines 26–31)

The personified ghosts make Wordsworth's yews uncanny and startling, but they are not the poem's last word. Rather than dominate its narration, they are historicized—said to resemble Mona's druid groves—and they are prefaced by an address that recruits the reader as a conservationist of a real grove: they should be allowed "to stand / Forever spared by Man!" (line 29).[42] By this entreaty Wordsworth invokes Cowper again, placing his verse in the line of the appeals in "Yardley Oak," *The Task*, and (most famously) "The Poplar Field" to spare real, named, visitable trees from being felled for profit. His words stand rooted in literary history and a material world of social and economic praxis.

Thus in 1804 Cowper's poem helped Wordsworth move beyond the optimism and simplicity of his revolutionary lyrical ballads to a kind of poetry that looked from the present deep into the past; saw nature as the product of a violent history—the accumulation of deeds and misdeeds done over centuries; and resisted its appropriation for ideological purposes by means of apostrophe, personification, and symbolism. The manuscript "Yew Trees" is a view taken from late in the day—a work of hindsight, a poetic Tree of Knowledge—written after and in reflection on prior English poetry / poetry of Englishness. Pessimistic, it expresses no hopes for revolutionary change and portrays the human struggles that lead to war from so great a temporal distance that they seem trivial. A work of postrevolutionary disenchantment, it takes a poetic stance of proud separation: here to be English is to be, like Cowper, a witness to a deep past that is still manifest as local resistance to contemporary nationalist and classist propaganda. It is not to be a celebrant of potential, nor to be a prophet of change, but an observer for whom sight means hindsight, a recorder of an ineluctable process of aging that puts innovation out of the question. And it is at the same time to be marked off from the crowd. These trees stand by themselves and belong to no one. They suggest that their poet does likewise—vital for a Wordsworth who felt hostile both to reactionary nationalism and to the revolution he had once admired.

Reconstructing the Text: "Yew Trees" for 1815

According to Geoffrey Hartman, "Yew Trees"[43] has the "mythic" power of a great poem because of its use of two devices: "that *imaginative transference* which is at root of opposite yet related devices essential to poetry: impersonation (personification, animistic metaphor), on the one hand, and impersonal constructions eliding narrator or human intermediary on the other."[44] What Hartman does not say, in this celebration of poetry as mythic, mysterious imagination, is that "Yew Trees" was made to seem so in order to serve the new, self-defensive agenda of Wordsworth's first collected poems. In 1814, as Wordsworth gathered poems for the collection that he hoped would redeem his notoriety as a Jacobin balladeer and a perverse egotist, he revised the manuscript "Ewtrees." He subjected it to a process designed to make it an example of the new authority-seeking category that, in the preface to the edition, he defined as the highest form of poetry—Poems of the Imagination. The process involved presenting himself as an independent, original poet capable of masterfully transforming the world by the light of his own mind. It led him to remove traces of dependence on other poets, if those traces raised the specter of seeming to be obsessed with morbidly exploring the effects of trivial encounters on his overdelicate feelings. Publishing a poem clearly based on Cowper anxiously picking over the emotional turbulence caused by a tree's refusal to speak to him would only play into reviewers' hands. Being seen to associate with the mad poet presented by Hayley was now too much of a risk.

Revising the poem was a matter of excising evidence of indebtedness to and dialogue with Cowper. The passage beginning "Pass not the place unnoticed" and ending "Forever spared by man!" was deleted, as if Wordsworth wished to banish the part of his poem that most directly addressed the reader and most strongly marked the haunting of his language by Cowper's. The cut removed evidence that he had taken another poet's words as his own—a sin of originality; it asserted independence, and it strengthened the narrator's impersonality. The effect of this pruning was to remove the poem's immersion in a literary and social context and to focus attention more starkly on the ghostly personifications the narrator "sees" under the yews. Cut free of the words that once introduced them, these now, as Hartman shows,[45] loom before the reader in uncanny objectivity, apparently without the mediation of an authorial apostrophe to call them into presence. Prosopopoeia without apostrophe—the sudden materialization of spirit in forms that at least could, if they do not actually, speak—becomes the poem's salient feature. It is a technique of hyperrealism—a place concentrated upon so fiercely and with so little acknowledgement of the artist or his medium that it delivers more of itself to the viewer than is the case when it is not stilled and held up for scrutiny by art.[46] Unframed by a narratorial call that echoes Cowper's response to Yardley oak, the ghostly figures now seem to arise from the remotest past, taking phantom shape before the disembodied eyes of the third-person narrator. As personifications, Fear and its brother Hope, Foresight, and "Death the Skeleton" (a figure drawn straight from Milton where he is the offspring of Satan and Sin) all enter the world once Adam's sin makes time begin. They embody in the here and now the spiritual powers that lie at the origin of fallen nature—and these powers are grim and deadly. To de Man they are figures of the poem's figuration—of its imaginative transformation of the object world (a process of tropological personification that all poetry must employ[47]). They become tokens of the impersonality of the poetic imagination, summoning into words, beyond the poet's own insight, the unspeakable condition that language exists to defer knowledge of—Death.[48] Lorton and Borrowdale, 1804 and 1814, are merely local instantiations of the universal concerns that it is the poem's role to declare. "Yew Trees" becomes, as Hartman emphasizes, vatic, mythic.[49]

Examining the poem's textual history and publication context suggests that another, more specific encounter is represented by the personifications that come to dominate the 1815 text. The ghostly figures are the remnants of Wordsworth's unease at finding his language indebted to the dead Cowper's subjectivization of Milton's and Virgil's encounters with time and death. In effect, they locate the echoes Wordsworth had excised from his poem; they are the ghostly residue of the verbal and thematic borrowing of Cowper's poetic articulation of personal fears and anxieties that Wordsworth had mostly deleted so as to strengthen his presentation of himself as a strong, independent poet. They represent the obverse of prosopopoeia as formulated by de Man, for they are relics of the achievement of voice by displacing a past voice rather than by bringing one back to life. Personification here desubjectivizes a speaking presence (Cowper's anxious poetic speech haunting Wordsworth's) rather than conferring subjectivity, through speech, on the dead and gone. By doing so, it allows that anxious poetic speech to be contemplated with detachment, rather than recur uncannily within and as the poet's very words. We the readers, as tourist viewers, are to note from a safe distance the spookiness of history's continued presence, rather than to learn how the poet is spooked by that presence—by his revival of a past poetry of anxiety in his own present poetry.

Wordsworth's crystallization of the Cowperian anxieties that were held in solution in his poetic medium was a canny move toward presenting himself as an original, imaginative poet able, as an observer if not as a prophet, to act directly on the object world. Fear, Hope, Foresight, and "Death the Skeleton" generalized what Cowper, in Hayley's biography, portrayed as a personal anxiety; they also avoided autobiographical self-exposure in an ideological realm in which, in 1804 and 1814, not to be loyal—in the reactionary Church and King terms by which loyalism was defined—was to be a traitor. Wordsworth's anomalous and uncomfortable position as a man tainted, in the public eye, by a revolutionary sympathy he no longer felt would not be exposed if his discourse was dispassionate, his own feelings and views left inexplicit. As a poet posing as a putative guidebook writer viewing the ghosts of the past in the present, he was able to bear witness without having to explore feelings, express conflicted loyalties, or reveal indebtedness to oversensitive predecessors like Cowper.

Only at the very end of the poem did Wordsworth hint that, having borne witness, the observer might himself be imbued with special access to inner nature. The poem's final lines do not directly introduce the poet into the poem but do gesture toward such an introduction: they imagine a figure empowered by his presence at the yew bower to follow nature to its mysterious source: "in mute repose / To lie, and listen to the mountain flood / Murmuring from Glaramara's inmost caves" (lines 31–33). This is a displaced and tentative picture of inspiration: if the reposing witness is a figure of the poet, his imaginative power is a matter of quiet communion rather than orphic song.

The 1815 poem needed to seem restrained and depersonalized. To live down his reputation for undisciplined sensibility and excessive egotism, Wordsworth had both to claim imaginative power and show that power to be a reliable way of interpreting the world. To become authoritative he must appear experienced, disinterested, objective. The revised text sought to appear so by associating imagination with witness rather than spontaneous overflows of feeling or conversation with fellow sensitives, achieving this at the cost of removing dialogue with Cowper and with the discourses invoked by that dialogue. Personification made the ghosts of temporality stand out starkly, staging the present as in thrall to the past. Imagination saw how things become and stay as they are; it did not envisage them different in the future; it represented a sobering conservatism.

The 1815 "Yew Trees" reveals the Romantic imagination as far less personal, rapturous, and orphic than the texts that twentieth-century critics treated as poems of imagination but that were not written or first published as such by Wordsworth—the subjective, confessional "Tintern Abbey" and the Immortality Ode. It shows that when first put before the public, imagination was not what it has since been assumed to have been. In 1815 "imagination" was the name for a poetry carved away from its former immersion in the social and political issues, and in the personal relationships, that arose out of its dialogic embrace of literary history.

Imagination was not a notably successful strategy at the time. The early nineteenth-century public preferred the less "imaginative" Wordsworth: the Wordsworth, for example, of the 1820 Duddon collection—his first volume to garner critical success and good sales. The Duddon poems addressed moral issues intelligibly in a style and form that revealed, rather than elided, their relationship to poetic tradition—and it would be poems of the Duddon kind that would dominate Wordsworth's output post-1815. Imagination, in fact, was a strategy for a period in his career—not its be-all and end-all but a defensive poetic chiefly proposed between 1815 and 1817 in response to Coleridge, who also distanced himself from it after that time. In some respects Wordsworth's later poems would renew the potential of the larger, 1804, "Yew Trees." Written after visits to landmarks, monuments, and ruins, they would again bear witness to a present as ineluctably conditioned by its past—but without obscuring his subjectivity, and foregrounding rather than excising his relationship to other poets' work and to the historical issues which that relationship raised. There are profound and complex examples from as late as 1819, 1827, and 1835, as I shall show in later chapters. Each of them has the same hallmark: description of an ancient place of local significance, often invoking a previous poet of that place. In 1827 Wordsworth coined the term "memorial" for them. He would also term them, as he had before declaring himself a poet of imagination, inscriptions.

Chapter 2

The Politics of Landscape and the Poetics of Patronage

Collecting Coleorton

In "Yew Trees" Wordsworth pioneered a voice of belated historical witness, a detached and impersonal voice that would become one of the principal features of his later work. In this chapter I trace the development of this voice in other poems published in 1815, arguing that two interrelated influences were crucial: on the one hand, the failure of Wordsworth's publications in the book market and the consequent alienation from the literary public; on the other, the gradual acceptance of patronage from the landed gentry and a resultant anxiety about poetic independence. The two influences coalesced in a recurrent ambivalence about the meaning and value of labor—both his own poetic labor and the rural labor of the workers who produced the landscape owned by the gentry. Detachment and impersonality, in turn, were embraced as modes of coping with ambivalence. They were registers of reserve, indices of a need to maintain a distance from which to overlook the field (in both senses of these words[1]) without either asserting or yielding independence. From a distance, Wordsworth avoided both commitment to and definition against the rural politics and landscape aesthetics of the patrons for whom he increasingly wrote. Meanwhile, this very acceptance of patronage distanced him from the cultural politics he had formerly espoused: his ideal subjects were no longer independent shepherds and farmers; his ideal readers were no longer the reading public. And distance was geographic too: whereas in *Lyrical Ballads*, *The Prelude*, and *Home at Grasmere* he homed in on the Lake District, repossessing his childhood ground, from 1806 his new affiliations took him to Leicestershire, Lowther, and the landscape parks of earls and baronets. The poetry he wrote from those places was self-consciously at a remove.

With distance came poems that did not pursue his earlier poetic goals and methods. In these, Wordsworth put aside his earlier need to seize past places and times by, for, and as the self and instead held them up for scrutiny as scenes imagined from afar and already mediated by art—in pictures, texts, sculpture, and gardens. These poems were modes of remediation, not seizing directly on the world (either the present or the remembered past) but on the world as represented—and thus modeled, arrested, aestheticized.[2] They were self-reflexive (contemplating art reminded both Wordsworth the writer and his readers of his own art); they were also of reduced fervor because they were formally predicated on the inability to capture the world directly. The world's difference was already acknowledged, so that what Wordsworth imagined, poetically, was not the thing in itself but the thing imagined from a distance in response to a secondhand token. Poetry of this kind offered him a way of accepting the loss of the hour of splendor in the grass, while taking strength in the ability of art to stimulate, in a form that is diminished but reliable (insofar as it is controlled and repeatable), a partial and distant image of that hour. It also gave him a way of sharing the burden of imagination: he was not the solitary egotist but one of many who represented experience—part of a chain of mediation.

Remediating the mediations of others made much of the later Wordsworth a more traditional poet: after 1806 he did not just respond to pictures, poems, and parks but used the vocabularies and forms that painters, poets, and gardeners had used. As in youth, the poet of rustic speech now made allusions to Latin poetry and Greek myth; he wrote epistles and inscriptions—classical forms. In these works, he aimed at the authority that stems from formal control rather than at a spontaneous overflow of subjective feeling. Impersonality, restraint, terseness: a concentration of means rather than an effusion of selfhood became, much but not all of the time, his aesthetic. It was in the inscription that this development primarily came about, because it was in that classical genre that he was required to cope with the fact that his nature poetry was now written to praise his patrons and their parks—to be set up, indeed, on stone in those parks, as a monumental mediation of and guide to gardens that were already mediations designed to illustrate their owners' benevolent and proper ownership of the wider landscape.[3] A poetry that overlooked the ground from a distance and omitted the poet's subjectivity was traditional to the inscription genre; this tradition assisted Wordsworth in coping with the ambivalence produced by his new subordinate position and his residual radical sympathies. By 1815, inscriptions featuring his new, distanced, voice formed a whole section of his collected poems; if they collectively demonstrated his closer alignment with landowning patrons and with the classical and neoclassical verse associated with such patrons, they also contained an implicit declaration of independence.[4] Omitting Jacobinical politics and eschewing rustic genres, Wordsworth instead exploited the possibilities afforded by the layout of his lapidary verses in the public context of a print collection. He arranged his inscriptions so that a dialogic relationship was produced: old and new poems cast reflections upon each other across the pages of the book, putting the relations between poet and patron, laborer and landowner, nature and garden, stone and paper, text and context into question. Distance and impersonality, in other words, did not mean the end of Wordsworth's challenge to conventional assumptions: that challenge was now mounted less explicitly, occurring by the manipulation of formal traditions and print layout.

What's in a Dedication?

Wordsworth's changed politics of landscape were signaled at the very beginning of the 1815 *Poems*. Before the polemical preface was a dedication, in which Wordsworth expressed his thanks to "Sir George Howland Beaumont, Bart." for "the permission given me to dedicate these volumes to you" (I, p. iii). This deferential note must have disconcerted Wordsworth's radical friends of the 1790s: the Jacobin poet who vindicated the lives and language of the rural poor had not prefaced *Lyrical Ballads* by indicating his gratitude to a titled gentleman.[5] To do so was to revert to the literary politics of the eighteenth century, when volumes of poetry typically featured paratexts praising wealthy landowners who, in return for praise, had supported the publication and the poet, sometimes financially, sometimes by lending the imprimatur of their names. Wordsworth had caused consternation among radicals in 1814 when he had dedicated *The Excursion* to the Westmoreland landowner and Tory magnate Lord Lonsdale as "A token (may it prove a monument!) / Of high respect and gratitude sincere" ("To the Right Honourable, William, Earl of Lonsdale, K. G. &c &c," lines 7–8; *Excursion*, p. 37). Now he chose again to advertise his dependence on a titled patron in a flattering dedication (Beaumont was Lonsdale's friend). And although he omitted the panegyric, he nevertheless included in the edition a series of poetic inscriptions in praise of Beaumont's landed estate.

The dedication also linked Wordsworth's volumes not just to Beaumont the man, but to the estate he, and his ancestors before him, owned: "several of the best pieces," Wordsworth declared, "were composed under the shade of your own Groves, upon the classic ground of Coleorton, where I was animated by the recollection of those illustrious Poets of your name and family, who were born in that neighbourhood, and we may be assured, did not wander with indifference by the dashing stream of Grace-Dieu, and among the rocks that diversify the Forest of Charnwood" (1815, I, p. iv). This was a surprising statement: Wordsworth was known to readers as a Lake poet, not as a bard of Leicestershire. Coleorton, moreover, was not Stratford upon Avon: so far was it from being "classic ground" that few had ever heard of it, of Grace Dieu, or of Charnwood. Fewer still would recognize the "illustrious poets" of Beaumont's lineage who were here claimed as the genii loci. And some might be bemused to find Wordsworth, who attacked "poetic diction" and tinkling couplets, quoting Augustan verse. The phrase "classic ground" derives from Joseph Addison's "Letter from Italy," in which it expresses the excitement of visiting places made famous by the great Latin poets:

> For wheresoe'er I turn my ravished eyes,
> Gay gilded scenes and shining prospects rise
> Poetic fields encompass me around,
> And still I seem to tread on classic ground.
>
> (lines 9–12)[6]

This is about as far removed, in style and sentiment, from Michael's sheep-fold and the leech gatherer's pond as it is possible to get.

What was Wordsworth up to? Why package in this way the collected poems with which he wished to make his mark on the present and on posterity? The allusion to Addison provides a clue: it appeals to a readership well-enough educated to identify the allusion and share the excitement about classical poets—a readership of gentlemen and women rather than radical democrats or Lakeland shepherds. And the reference to Grace Dieu provides further evidence of a changed literary politics. Like Bolton Abbey, in which Wordsworth set The White Doe of Rylstone, Grace Dieu was a monastic foundation dissolved in the time of Henry VIII. It had been bought by John Beaumont in 1539 and was the country seat of the Beaumont family until 1684. In 1815 it still survived in the Leicestershire landscape; its nuns had long been banished but the Gothic church remained, though ruined—a relic of a tradition of spiritual reflection inhering in a specific rural place. It was a monument, in Wordsworth's eyes, that had inspired the poets John and Francis Beaumont with whom he now aligned himself: religious spirituality, lingering in an ancient ruin, was renewed as poetic spirituality. Succeeding to these poets and invoking the old priory, his collected poems, were, in function as in form and arrangement, like an ancient church, a monument in which a historical tradition of spiritual reflection was invested. Classic ground, in this sense, was Gothic ground.

Invoking ruined abbeys and Gothic churches, Wordsworth placed his *Poems* in the context of the eighteenth-century practice of antiquarian study of historical remains. Pursued by gentleman amateurs, mostly on a regional basis, this practice involved the collection of documents and relics; it bore fruit in a series of county histories, of which John Nichols's *The History and Antiquities of the County of Leicester* (1795–1811) was one of the most comprehensive. Grace Dieu is there pictured and its associations with the Beaumont poets, when turned into a residence after 1539, are discussed.[7] It also features in the 1807 volume of the illustrated series *The Beauties of England and Wales, or, Delineations, Topographical, Historical and Descriptive of Each County.*[8] Antiquarian history, obsessive about the architecture, heraldry, and lineage of the local gentry, was the epitome of conservatism: by courting comparison with it, Wordsworth's dedication distances the *Poems* from his reputation as a Jacobin who overturned aesthetic canons and social hierarchies.

Overall, the dedications of the 1815 *Poems* and the 1814 *Excursion* show Wordsworth, as if he had never been a radical opponent of the established order, affiliating himself with the landed gentry who were its main supporters and chief beneficiaries. The 1815 *Poems* thus constituted a retrospective repackaging that consolidated the new self-positioning declared in 1814: Wordsworth now fashioned himself as a traditional and respectable poet and downplayed the radicalism of his past work.

Coleorton Style

Downplaying and repositioning was heralded in the dedications but executed in the poetry by alterations of style and structure. *The Excursion* and the 1815 *Poems* both contained writing that bore the traces of Wordsworth's Jacobinical politics of the 1790s; this writing was variously revised to lessen

its radicalism and subsumed within new frameworks that contained its leveling sympathies. In *The Excursion*, a series of emblematic character
sketches raised, only to allay, the politics of landscape in the new era of
industrial capitalism. In *Poems 1815*, economic and political tensions in
rural society were evoked in thematic sections in which new poems were
carefully placed alongside older pieces, thus suggesting a continuity of pre-
occupation, rather than a sudden break with a radical past. In what follows,
I investigate one of the *Excursion* character sketches and one of the 1815
sections—that entitled "Inscriptions" and featuring poems about Beaumont's estates at Coleorton. My aim is to assess what was lost and what
gained by Wordsworth's careful presentation of his move from independent
radical to patronized poet. How, I ask, did the affiliation to Lonsdale and
to Beaumont change Wordsworth's politics—and, more specifically, how
did Wordsworth's tendency to incorporate aspects of his radical past change
the form and style of the verse in which those politics were expressed? It is
often argued that Wordsworth simply became a hypocritical servant of the
landed classes who cooperated in the mystification of their economic
exploitation of others' labor as stewardship and paternalism. The dedication reference to Grace Dieu could be seen as a case in point: Wordsworth
used the old priory to portray Beaumont's landholding as the preservation
of ground on which spirituality and poetry could flourish, yet it had not
actually belonged to his family for over a century—it had been sold in 1684.
That Wordsworth overlooked this fact might seem symptomatic of a certain
self-interested self-blinding in his later evocations of landscape. To the
younger poets who lamented his acceptance of patronage, this later work
was too often vitiated by the cant, flannel, and fudge that were attendant
upon a former Jacobin glamorizing Tory landowners. There were sins of
omission in reverting to the eighteenth-century Georgic mode of treating
landowners' estates as expressions of their traditional paternal care for the
country—the main unmentioned matter being money. Property, as the sale
of Grace Dieu showed, was at bottom a matter of wealth rather than paternalism. Wealth bought power: it allowed landowners to purchase seats in
parliament; it helped them buy the praise of poets and painters. In consequence, both government and the arts were corrupted. Wordsworth had
sold out and, worse, could not admit that he had done so: he was the "lost
leader" criticized in Browning's poem of that name.

If Browning lamented, Byron parodied. Cleverly, he attacked Wordsworth as a compromised placeman in the very genre in which Wordsworth

had expressed his gratitude to his patrons. The "Dedication" to *Don Juan* was mockingly addressed to the Lake poets, and its satiric strategy was to undermine their claims to poetic greatness by insisting they had sold their independence to reactionary grandees: their words were those of hirelings; Wordsworth was a "shabby fellow" rather than an independent gentleman ("Dedication," stanza vi, BPW, V). Byron, though frequently in debt, accepted patronage from nobody. In the polarized public sphere of the early nineteenth century, patronage was no longer compatible with honor; in his view the poet should trust to the public or possess an independent income of his own. It was impossible to revert to the eighteenth-century practice of writing about the beauty of landed estates without revealing that one had, at best, silenced one's opposition to, or at worst, explicitly voiced one's support of, their owners' political influence. In accepting a sinecure arranged through Lonsdale's influence, Wordsworth had become a servant of a reactionary and corrupt oligarchy.

The poems Wordsworth wrote about Lonsdale's and Beaumont's estates are not directly Tory or simply reactionary; they are conflicted, rather than strident, about the politics of landowners. They are more uncertain than Browning's and Byron's verdicts allow. They do suggest that there was an aversion of attention, a self-limiting avoidance of issues that should have mattered to a political reformer. Studying them in their immediate histori- cal context lets us see what Wordsworth turned a blind eye to and allows us to assess the moral costs to his art. Yet it also shows us something else less stark—a residual skepticism about the landowning, patronizing classes, and the kind of landscape poetry that glamorizes them: authorial unease and attempts to banish it are both manifest in the Coleorton inscriptions. The unease appears in phrases and allusions that sit uncomfortably with the poetry's overall endorsement of the landowners and their taste as embodied in their estate. The attempts to banish the unease are evident in the development of the voice Wordsworth had pioneered in "Yew Trees"—a distanced, depersonalized, detached voice now, however, also characterized by a generalized and neoclassical diction. This voice was increasingly prevalent in the poetry Wordsworth wrote after accepting patrons: it features strongly in *The Excursion*, the work he dedicated to Lord Lonsdale. It is, perhaps, the most common voice of his later poetry. But it was in the Beaumont poems that it was first combined with classical and neoclassical form: Wordsworth revived, in a move that inaugurated a salient feature of his later work, the epistle and the inscription as a means of dealing with the anxieties that stemmed from the effort to align his views with those of his titled patrons. William Hazlitt, Wordsworth's most perceptive critic at the time, noted as much, writing that the later poems were "classical and courtly," "a departure from, a dereliction of, his first principles" that "seem to have been composed not in a cottage at Grasmere, but among the half-inspired groves and stately recollections of Cole-Orton."[9]

Classical form mattered because, as Hazlitt's comment suggests, Coleorton was a style as well as a location—a classical revival. Like James Thomson at Hagley, an eighteenth-century park he visited with Beaumont in 1810, Wordsworth depicted the landed estate in the impersonal terms of the inscription intended for a stone, seat, or tablet. This was a specialized form of Georgic writing, a way of poetically representing the landowner's paternal care for his land on his land that derived from Greek and Roman roadside tombs.[10] Eighteenth-century Georgic, however, owed as much to contemporary contexts as it did to Virgil. It was normally an idealization that effaced the economic relations of laborer, farmer, and landowner and instead imagined agricultural productivity—wealth—as a benefit conferred by nature on the master.[11] The idea of "patrimonial Grounds" (to use the phrase Wordsworth chose for one of the inscriptions at Coleorton[12]) was vital: if the power conveyed by landownership was to seem natural rather than a matter of expropriation of land and exploitation of labor, then the origin of ownership must be lost in the mists of the past. Inherited from a line of ancestors, property and wealth seemed to be the landed gentleman's by tradition and by right. The poet was then able to depict his patron as a native of the soil and to portray the results of primogeniture (a social and legal arrangement for the preservation of property in one line) as natural succession. Born and raised like his forefathers in the place he owned, he and his family were easily pictured as organic: like the trees on their estate, they seemed a *natural* as well as stable presence. As Burke had argued, the aura of naturalness and of stability was then usable to justify their monopolization of political, legal, and cultural authority, so long as it was accompanied by evidence of their care for the health of their land and the well-being of their laborers. The landscape poet sustained this aura by depicting the landowner in terms provided by revered classical models: thus Virgil's poems about husbandry and cultivation were adapted to portray gentlemen as paternalist agriculturalists rather than as rentiers whose main concern was to maximize the profits produced by the labor of tenant-farmers and laborers. They were to seem disinterested guardians rather than self-interested exploiters of the country. Some Georgics, however, involved more of a stretch than others: to write Georgics on Thomas Coke and Joseph Banks, landowners who were deeply concerned with improving agriculture and whose holdings were ancient, was one thing—they fitted the mold; to create the Georgic illusion for a nouveau riche purchaser with little historical connection to the locale was another; another still was to produce it for a man whose wealth came not from the traditional practices of tending crops and husbanding of animals celebrated by Virgil, but from activities that despoiled, rather than cultivated, the land. Industrialization was a problem for the Georgic at the turn of the eighteenth century: it was difficult to incorporate mills, manufactories, and mines in a genre that naturalized its own idealizations of a class in terms of broad acres, fertile fields, and pastoral plenty. For the landscape gardener Humphry Repton, the art of designing the estate so it visually represented its owner's paternal care and native rootedness was compromised when he found himself employed by a nouveau mill owner who wanted a quick-fix pastoralization of his park while a few miles away his mill hands labored in the smoky factory or languished in the workhouse.[13]

Georgic Ground?

Sir George's Beaumont's grounds at Coleorton were not as patrimonial as Wordsworth suggested. They had only passed to Beaumont's father, from whom Beaumont inherited them, in 1738, when the local branch of the family, his cousins, died without issue. They were then left without a resident lord; Beaumont, who had inherited them while still a boy, was so little a son of Coleorton soil that he lived 120 miles away in Essex. An absentee landlord, he took about £2,000 a year in rent from the property,[14] and he made his first visit to the estate in 1791, when he was thirty-eight. What he found there was not a model for the Georgic: the hall was in a tumbledown state, part inhabited by the steward; the woods had been stripped and sold for timber; the fields were pocked with brickmakers' diggings; and the "park [was] quite gone; the trees having given place to coal-mines."[15] Coleorton had little in the way of waving crops, fleecy sheep, or fat cattle; it was not fertile but polluted, not agricultural but industrial: "the land," noted one visitor, "is as black as if the coal were above the ground."[16]

Beaumont was not directly in charge of the "dirty coal mines" that polluted his land.[17] Like many a rentier aristocrat, he leased out mining rights to a bidder. The Joseph Boultbees, father and son, ran the Beaumont pits, agreeing a price and a maximum annual tonnage with Beaumont's lawyer.[18] Matters were complicated because the Boultbees were, as well as the lessees of the mine, also Beaumont's stewards. For a miserly salary of £20 a year, they managed the estate in the owner's absence—a long-term arrangement that made them responsible, on their master's behalf, for preserving its stocks of timber, water, and soil; for maintaining buildings; and for keeping tenants to the terms of their leases. Boultbee, the father, was one of these tenants himself: it was he who from 1757 leased, and lived in, the decaying hall, an arrangement that suited Beaumont as an absentee landlord. Boultbee senior was thus the authority in residence over the mines and the house; as the steward he was the person charged with supervising his own activities as tenant. If this was a conflict of interests, it was one that, for over thirty years, enriched both Boultbee and Beaumont, who effectively conceded the hands-on running of the estate so long as it yielded sufficient rental income. Boultbee ensured that it did so by developing the pits: he overhauled Beaumont's Paddock Colliery, paying for a Newcomen pumping engine himself and sinking new shafts when Beaumont proved reluctant to invest. In 1764 he advised Beaumont to buy some neighboring land at the "Rotten Row" pit to prevent coal deposits beneath it being worked in competition with his mines. When Beaumont did not, Boultbee raised capital, bought the land himself, and sunk his own pit. Thus he was now running adjacent collieries in Beaumont's interest and his own; indeed, he connected his own pit with the Paddock mine underground, arguing that Beaumont's "deep coal" could "never be got to . . . advantage" without the new mine.[19] Geological necessity, if such it was, proved profitable: Boultbee was soon enriching himself by selling more than the 10,000 loads a year agreed in his lease; meanwhile, the issue of what was his coal, derived from Rotten Row, and what was Beaumont's, from Paddock, was utterly blurred.

It was Boultbee's spectacular new wealth that aroused Beaumont's interest in Coleorton. In the mid-1770s Boultbee was able to loan £20,000 to Lord Wentworth—a sum equivalent to about £1,400,000 at 2018 values. Beaumont began to feel that more of this wealth should be his as the landowner; nevertheless, as a connoisseur of art making the Grand Tour, Beaumont had little desire to manage his property closely as only a resident lord could. Thus in 1784 the Boultbees' mining lease was renewed, but only after negotiations designed to make the contract yield more for Beaumont. The Boultbees were then left to continue their enterprises, which included a new pit at Coleorton Field, to which they removed the Newcomen engine they had earlier installed in Paddock Mine. By 1789 they ran the largest and most successful mining concern in the area and had won, it seemed, Beaumont's approval of the highly unorthodox business relationship between them and his estate. When Boultbee senior died, Boultbee junior duly inherited the position of Beaumont's steward.

When Beaumont finally visited in 1791, he must, as an aesthete, have been shocked at the pitted, treeless landscape and the poor, grimy inhabitants. His villagers were not the idealized shepherds who featured in the pastoral landscapes he painted in imitation of the pictures by Claude and Rubens that he collected; they lived in "meagre looking" homemade shacks.[20] Most depended in the summer months, when pit work was slack, on half-acre plots of land they had taken from the common to raise pigs and grow vegetables. Many of the miners were children; for as little as 8 pence, boys as young as eleven worked for twelve hours a day in the pits, pulling wagons laden with seven hundredweight of coal along tunnels no more than four feet high.[21] Their labor, and their deformed and stunted bodies, resulted from a system that was a far cry from the Georgic ethic of paternalism that legitimized the landed gentleman's profit from his tenants' labor. Beaumont presided over a chain of monetarized relationships: he leased mining rights to the Boultbees, and they in turn, as was typical, subcontracted the getting of the coals to "butties"—men who agreed with them a price for a load and then organized their own work teams. By this means, both owner and lessee avoided responsibility for working practices, pay rates, and miners' welfare. They themselves did not force children down the pits, but the subcontracting, piece-rate system meant that the cheapest labor available was used, while keeping the Boultbees' and Beaumont's costs down.

It was to keep costs down, not to investigate the welfare of child miners, that Beaumont visited his estate. By 1791, Coleorton coal was being outcompeted at market by coal from Derbyshire and Staffordshire. Like many local owners, Beaumont, facing losses, had invested in a canal scheme designed to lower transport costs. The canal was behind schedule; Beaumont came to investigate. In the event, it proved impossible to overcome its problems, and as the 1790s progressed, Coleorton collieries began to close. The consequences for the villagers were severe: unemployment and poverty. Lady Beaumont offered some charitable relief, but protests became common. In 1793 the magistrates suppressed a riot by calling in a detachment of troops from Nottingham; three miners were imprisoned. In 1795, after another protest, James Edwards was sentenced to seven years' transportation for breaking a colliery pumping engine (Beaumont spent £50 on bringing the prosecution[22]). The Boultbees and Beaumont had sufficient capital to keep a mine working, but the Coleorton area faced closures and unemployment into the 1810s. By that time, Luddite protests were sweeping the area as colliers joined textile workers in campaigning against the mechanization that was driving down the price of their labor. In 1812 the zealous Rector of Loughborough informed the Home Office that, acting as local magistrate, he had committed for trial a father and son of Coleorton who had broken the knitting frame they rented. That year, the Beaumonts avoided visiting Coleorton for fear of the Luddites.

It was against this background of shrinking profits and local protest that Beaumont, still an absentee owner, embarked upon a retrenchment of his Coleorton concerns. His first motive was economic. In 1799, with wealth harder to come by, he went to court against the Boultbees, claiming that they had profited excessively from their lease and sold, for personal benefit, coal, minerals, and timber that they should, as stewards, have managed for the benefit of the estate. The Boultbees defended the case by arguing that their costs in repairing and extending the mines counterbalanced the profits made from exceeding agreed production levels. They cited their purchase of the pumping engine; they argued that Beaumont's mine could not have been worked had they not, as they had advised Beaumont to do, bought Rotten Row and opened a pit there. At issue, in essence, was whether they should be bound strictly by the terms of the lease between them and Beaumont or whether, as stewards, they acted fairly in benefiting personally from Beaumont's properties (while also benefiting Beaumont) in return for the ingenuity and expense they invested in them and their own mines. The judges were asked to resolve a dispute that had arisen because the eighteenth-century landowner's means of managing his estate was not, in the face of his perpetual absence, adequate to supervise the development of a new kind of machinery-driven and thus capital-intensive business. The Boultbees were part of a new class of entrepreneurial industrialists who had built the businesses on the spot; Beaumont was a rentier landlord who did not contribute his own labor and skill and (in the Boultbees' opinion) left the business deprived of the investment in equipment and infrastructure that it needed to prosper. In 1800 the court, judging as it must from the terms of the written lease, found in Beaumont's favor, awarding him

£20,000 in compensation for the Boultbees' excessive production of coal from his land. Boultbee junior appealed, and in 1802 the compensation was reduced to £15,000, and one of the collieries was accepted as part payment. The matter returned to court in 1805, when Lord Eldon not only refused Boultbee's claim for costs and for increased wages as steward but also refused Beaumont's application to have interest added to underpayments made before 1798. Bemused, Eldon remarked that Beaumont's long complicity in the arrangement counted against him: "One of the circumstances, upon which I think I ought not to give interest prior to the filing of the bill, is that long before the bill filed, all parties knew very well what was the excess of the getting."[23]

Beaumont's legal victory enriched him just as the Coleorton mines endured a depression.[24] It was then, in a scene of closed pits and reduced prospects, that he decided to restore the hall and park that he had once been content to leave Boultbee to exploit. In 1801 he commissioned George Dance to design a new house; the foundation stone was laid in August 1804. In 1803 he borrowed Uvedale Price's landscape gardener to lay out the grounds as the apparent center of a paternalist estate. The profits of the old industrialization financed this makeover, but evidence of the industrialization—meager cottages, slag heaps, pit heads, quarries, rusting engines—was kept out of sight, as if Coleorton was a long-established agricultural estate.

Beaumont and Wordsworth

The effect of Beaumont on Wordsworth's language of nature—his articulation of a politics of landscape—was immediate. It was manifested first in letters that circle around questions of patronage and property. In 1803 Beaumont, having been introduced to *Lyrical Ballads* by Coleridge, whose neighbor he became while summering in the Lakes, bought some land at Applethwaite, under Skiddaw, and presented it to Wordsworth. Beaumont, exhilarated by Coleridge's enthusiasm, hoped that Wordsworth would build there, and so be able to live close to his friend and collaborator. It was a generous but impractical gift and, coming to Wordsworth from a stranger, one that put him in an awkward position. Embarrassed, Wordsworth waited eight weeks to send Beaumont his thanks; his letter of 14 October began with pages of tortuous excuses and awkward apologies before explaining that he lacked the capital to build a house and that it was likely that Coleridge would go abroad to recover his health. He then asked if he could be viewed merely as "steward of the land with liberty to lay out the rent[25] in plant[ing] or . . . other improvement" and if he might then be allowed to return it to Beaumont so that it might be presented to another worthy person (EY, p. 408).

Given what had happened to Beaumont's steward at Coleorton, Wordsworth's request to be the land's steward, rather than owner, seems strange. It seems stranger still when his personal history is remembered. In 1803 he had only just received payment of a claim arising from his father's employment as Lord Lonsdale's steward in the 1780s. When John Wordsworth died, in 1783, his executors calculated he was owed £4,625 for legal work he had done for Lonsdale's estate and for his own monies disbursed on Lonsdale's behalf as his agent.[26] Lonsdale refused to accept the claim, and so the executors went to law. The case was a mirror image of *Beaumont v. Boultbee*: Lonsdale's lawyers argued that Wordsworth had exceeded his authority and also benefited personally from his stewardship: much of the disputed money had been spent by Wordsworth in his own interest, so Lonsdale was not liable for it. As at Coleorton, the case concerned the degree of independence given by an often-absent landlord to his professional man of business. To fellow professionals such as the lawyer Richard Wordsworth, the steward of a great landowner could not act without—and in practice was not expected to act without—using his independent judgment and own resources in his master's interest. He was employed to micromanage the estate precisely because the landowner did not himself want to do so. Lonsdale now impugned his steward's sincerity for the dishonorable reason that, after years of lucrative service, he wanted to maximize his profit at his employee's expense (Lonsdale was locally known as an avoider of debts to tradesmen; as an aristocrat he regarded only debts to gentlemen as debts of honor). From Lonsdale's point of view, Wordsworth appeared as Boultbee did to Beaumont: as an employee who had been favored with a fine house and who had enjoyed credit locally by virtue of being known as Lonsdale's agent. The attempt to transfer debts incurred in his own interest to his employer was an imposition by a canny man of business who was not a gentleman.

The verdicts were different: Beaumont won; Lonsdale lost. But there were further parallels: as wealthy landowners, Beaumont and Lonsdale could afford the best lawyers; they could also cope with the law's delay, whereas the Wordsworths, even more than the Boultbees, could not. Lonsdale's lawyers used delay as a strategy; by 1794 the case had still not been resolved, but the Wordsworths were facing £1,073 in legal costs. Even after the court found against Lonsdale, payment was not forthcoming; the lord was so wealthy and powerful he could effectively ignore the law. By 1802 it was clear that legal action had failed; the Wordsworths had been deprived of their patrimony.

Lonsdale had not just deprived the Wordsworth children of their monetary inheritance, he had left them without a home; he had also led them to be dispersed and raised with different relatives. Wordsworth was radicalized by this injustice and left distrustful of aristocrats' power. So after Lonsdale died in May 1802, he was suspicious as well as eager when the new lord announced in the local newspaper his intention to pay all outstanding debts. Determined to take advantage while this initial act of generosity lasted, Wordsworth decided to present a claim merely for the sum owed and not request interest or legal costs. This brought him into conflict with his brother Richard, who had worked on the claim in the 1790s and now found his advice to press for costs and interest disregarded. William, who wished to make a settlement with Annette Vallon and to marry, was reluctant to wait to prepare such a claim and rudely told Richard he would act by himself if a claim was presented without consulting him. When Richard counseled patience, he condescendingly replied that "such exhortations are the common language of hackney men of business" (3 July 1802; EY, pp. 372–73). William had his way: the claim was entered quickly, without additions for costs and interest. It was important to be independent of landlords' capricious power.

Given this history, Wordsworth's sensitivity when the Beaumonts made him a gift of Applethwaite was understandable. If he knew of the Boultbee case—and he may have done so via Coleridge although he had himself met the Beaumonts only briefly—he must have seen parallels between the Boultbees' position and his father's and been all too aware of Beaumont's ability, like Lonsdale, to use his resources to manipulate the law against his stewards. Wordsworth's reasons in October 1803 for being reluctant to accept Beaumont's gift are then not far to seek: he was wary of aristocrats' power; he did not want to be Beaumont's client. But why, in this case, did he suggest he would rather be the land's steward and maintain and improve it till Beaumont was ready to present it to someone else? Was this not to put himself in a more vulnerable, more dependent position than he would be as its owner? In fact, the suggestion indicated Wordsworth's changing perspective: if he was suspicious of dependence on the landowning classes he also, paradoxically, discovered that he wanted to be appreciated by them. The new Lord Lonsdale was finally making good the dead lord's injustice; now Beaumont, Lonsdale's friend, offered a gift in tribute to *Lyrical Ballads*—as if, having read "Michael," he wanted to endow its writer with the landed independence that the poem's hero tragically lacked. Thus, as a sign of the readerly appreciation that Wordsworth rarely received, the gift was highly appropriate. Perhaps, despite Boultbee, Beaumont was a new kind of patron/landowner who acted generously rather than in his own interest. Wordsworth was unsure and ambivalent, but even as he expressed his reluctance to accept the land, he sent Beaumont unpublished poems, as if making return for the gift. An exchange of verse for land, of aesthetic value for property value, might allow each to give the other something he had at his disposal but the other did not. It might seem a fair exchange between equals, especially since the verse that Wordsworth sent Beaumont did not flatter him and, in fact, was not concerned with him at all; it was not a client-poet's praise of the benefactor he hoped would continue funding him. On this basis, becoming steward at Applethwaite in return for his poetry attracted Wordsworth because it allowed him to replay his father's role but with the proper acknowledgement from a fair landowner that his father never received and that was refused the children after their father's death. In other words, portraying his acceptance of the Applethwaite tribute to his poems as stewardship was a means by which Wordsworth gained compensation for his father's treatment. The land he would steward signified the recognition his father's labor never received. By holding it for Beaumont, and by sending Beaumont more works of his hands (poems), he would rehabilitate his father through his own actions, replacing an exploitative relationship in which a steward had been treated merely as an employee with one in which value was aesthetic rather than financial. Perhaps, with Beaumont, the relationship of amateur patron and professional poet,[27] landowner and versemaker, could remain above the "common language of hackney men of business" to which Lonsdale's treatment of their father had reduced the Wordsworths.

Such was Wordsworth's hope, intertwined with his fear of the subjugating effects of landowners' wealth and authority. Both are evident in the correspondence that deepened his relationship with Beaumont over the next eight years and in the poetry featured in that correspondence. In March 1805, after much of the money Wordsworth had won from Lonsdale seemed to have been lost when his brother John's ship was wrecked,

Beaumont made him a substantial gift. In thanking him, Wordsworth justified the acceptance of "pecuniary assistance even from those who are not
. . . personal Friends" with a self-serving argument, implying that his very
inability to repay the gift was a sign that he was above the demeaning
mentality of business: "It is no part of my creed that money may not be
received . . . without a return equivalent in the way of a bargain." He then
declared that even though he had now discovered that his investment in
John's ship would be recouped, he would still keep Beaumont's donation,
on the grounds that "my bodily strength is not equal to much literary
drudgery; besides I am strangely unfit for exertion as far as it is mere labor
in the way of job and for money" (EY, pp. 554–55). Bodily weakness and
the lack of a business mentality were both tokens of social status; here
Wordsworth's excuse reveals his aspiration to identify his poetry as a gentleman's avocation rather than a laborer's work or a businessman's money-
making scheme. Ignoring the origin of Beaumont's money in the hard
bodies of miners and field hands and in the sharp minds of stewards and
lawyers, Wordsworth was keen to let it transform his own life, as it had
Beaumont's, into one of leisure rather than labor. He was implicitly distancing himself from his former solidarity with, on the one hand, shepherds
and farmers like his neighbors, and, on the other, attorneys and sea captains
like his uncle and brother.

Subsequent letters steered a difficult course between the language of
equals—one gentleman talking to another—and that of an indebted infe-
rior anxious to find terms to rebrand an economic relationship as an artistic
one: to convert money value into aesthetic value.[28] Wordsworth repeatedly
returned to the importance of making an aesthetic display that, if it did not
reveal the origin of the landowner's wealth in others' labor, did symbolize
his social duty to the dependants who worked for him. As the new house
and park took shape at Coleorton, Wordsworth told Beaumont that it was
necessary to show that great houses belong "to the country, which will of
course lead us back to the simplicity of nature"; "it is a substitution of little
things for great when we would put a whole country into a nobleman's
livery." Here his leveling politics are still present, though heavily modulated
by an idealization of the Georgic estate, assuaging real differences in rank
and wealth—the landowner, he says, should show "a true relish of simplicity": "let him do his utmost to be surrounded by tenants living comfortably" among "flourishing fields and happy-looking houses." Wordsworth
declares himself glad that the Beaumonts do not think of removing the

villagers from proximity to the hall. To "strip the neighbourhood" of people leaves "the poverty of solitude," though he admits, perhaps in reference to Coleorton's uncouth miners—who, not being employees or direct tenants of the squire, were not deferential—that whether to remove the village depends on "with what kind of inhabitants, from the nature of the employments in that district, the village is likely to be stocked" (17 and 24 October 1805; EY, pp. 622–29). Here, Wordsworth's gaze is aligned with the landowner's: he sees the villagers, en masse, from a distance, as a potential problem, rather than speaking from among them as individuals, as he had done in "Goody Blake and Harry Gill" and "The Last of the Flock." Although meaning to guide Beaumont toward a traditional, protective paternalism rather than to a disregard of the rural poor that bespoke class division and condescension, he is nevertheless co-opted by the landowner's authoritative point of view.

It was in late 1806 that the Wordsworths, their relationship deepened by Beaumont's kindness after John Wordsworth's death, first went to Coleorton, availing themselves of the generous offer of a farmhouse to live in rent free for the winter. In the event, they stayed until June 1807, as Beaumont's guests and, to a degree, dependants, although Beaumont himself was away in Essex and London. What they found there was neither a traditional estate nor a completed landscape garden. The new hall was incomplete, the garden still full of rubble. Much of the area was a postindustrial wasteland. It all presented a stark contrast between labor and leisure, poor and rich, engineer and rentier, capitalist improver and gentleman aesthete—linked in one pitted place by the commodity of coal. Coleorton was new and raw, a landscape that presented class divisions and provoked divided loyalties, an utter contrast to Grasmere's "vale so beautiful."[29] Nights brought the glow of fires at the pit furnaces, rather than starlight. Sundays revealed the poverty and distress of the inhabitants: at church, Wordsworth noted that the girls were "clean, but not *tidy*; they were in this respect a striking contrast to our congregation at Grasmere" (10 November 1806; MY, I, p. 94).

The Wordsworths dealt with the situation by concentrating on the parts of Coleorton where mining, and miners, could be overlooked. Dorothy reported a visit to an elderly couple who lived in a cottage screened by woods; she was impressed by their pride in the holly trees that they had themselves planted years before. Veteran locals, they represented the kind of sturdy, dignified villagers that the Wordsworths sought out and revered in Grasmere—Leicestershire as Greenhead Ghyll. Wordsworth, meanwhile, busied himself with a winter garden in an old quarry adjacent to the new house. He embraced the role of designer, writing to Beaumont concerning the aesthetics of plantings, waterfalls, and grottos as one connoisseur of landscape to another but also showing himself to his patron as his reliable man on the spot.[30] In effect, he volunteered to take the "office," as he termed his role, normally performed by a land agent. He supervised and instructed the groundsman Beaumont had employed to create the garden—somewhat, Dorothy detected, to the groundsman's annoyance. He checked on the gardeners twice a day to ensure his and Beaumont's wishes were carried out exactly—as if he were the kind of loyal steward his father had been and the Boultbees had failed to be. The aim was to create a bower, enclosed by evergreens, in which the harsh winds of winter would not be felt and the grim evidence of industry would not be seen. "Shelter, and seclusion" would be "essential to the *feeling* of the place": "no image of chillness, decay or desolation" must penetrate it (MY, I, p. 112). Wordsworth conceived the garden in the image of poets' idealizations of meditative retreats—he quoted Thomson's yearning to enter a "secret Cell / And in . . . deep recesses dwell / . . . / Where Meditation has her fill" (MY, I, p. 113) and cited Chaucer's bower in "The Flower and the Leaf" (MY, I, p. 117). Lines from Burns, Coleridge, and James Grahame also illustrated the plan: the winter garden would allude to poetic bowers both old and new, both real and imagined. Two derelict cottages would be covered in ivy and become picturesque ruins. Mounds and ridges of "rubbish" would become rustic banks. Plants and poems would cloak, as a bower that seemed a natural sanctuary for contemplation, the disused quarry left by the Boultbees' industrial works.

At the center of the garden, a nook within a nook, recessed within the bank that had once been the quarry wall, was a niche meant to resemble the stone stall of a monk or nun in a Gothic abbey. This seat was inspired by outings in November and December 1806 to the ruined priory Grace Dieu, which, after the dissolution of the monasteries, Beaumont's ancestor had turned into his country house. The poets John and Francis Beaumont had lived there in Shakespeare's time. The niche was meant to recreate at Coleorton one of the features of a building that associated the Beaumonts with an ancient spiritual tradition rather than with industrial wealth. A retreat for a poet to compose in, it would link the writer who used it with a religious and poetic past, transferring that past from the ruins of Grace

Dieu to the new Beaumont seat. Wordsworth, Dorothy, and Mary began the act of carving it out of the soft sandstone with their own hands. When, in 1814, Wordsworth compared his minor poems to the "cells, oratories, and sepulchral recesses" of a Gothic church, he may have been modeling his poetry on this act, imagining his poetry in the terms that, at Coleorton, let him associate his labors with the traditional, the spiritual, and the contemplative as embodied in the grounds of an old landowning family. What was not perceived, either in the winter garden or in *The Excursion*, was that the token voluntary labor involved in carving the niche ironically mirrored the lifelong, involuntary labor of the quarrymen and miners who hacked profit out of the earth all around it.

While at Coleorton, Wordsworth was reminded of his inability to provide, from the sales of his literary labors, the Lakeland nook he desired for his family. Dove Cottage, a rented property, was now too small, and he had been unable to afford to buy a small estate in Patterdale without the assistance of Lord Lonsdale—unsolicited assistance that, like Beaumont's gift of Applethwaite, made him uneasy but that he nevertheless accepted. In April 1807 he found it necessary to draw on his brother to find the £200 required to complete the purchase; by late May he was writing to Lady Beaumont making an accurate (if self-fulfilling) prophecy: his poetry would be harshly reviewed and rarely purchased. Justifying his own alienation from the market, he avowed himself both unwilling and unable to write to please the "worldlings" who composed the book-buying public: "it is an awful truth," he declared, "that there neither is, nor can be, any genuine enjoyment of Poetry among nineteen out of twenty of those persons who live, or wish to live, in the broad light of the world" (MY, I, pp. 145–46). Flattering Lady Beaumont, he implied that her appreciation of his newly published *Poems, in Two Volumes* would demonstrate her superiority to a public that was obsessed with trivialities and whose taste was vitiated. In these circumstances, gifts from wealthy supporters among the gentry were, even if uncomfortable reminders of his lack of independence, also signs of the recognition he deserved and would one day receive from posterity. Wordsworth was finding a means of persuading himself that his inability to make a living by literary work vindicated that work: patronage was a proper substitute for a popularity he sacrificed by aiming "to teach the young and the gracious of every age" rather than pandering to the "vanity" of this one (MY, I, p. 146).[31]

Wordsworth's prediction proved still more accurate than he expected. Reviewers damned *Poems, in Two Volumes*; sales were dismal. Whereas *Lyrical Ballads* had become a modest success, selling almost 2,000 copies across three editions, the new collection sold a mere 770 copies in eight years.[32] It became clear Wordsworth could not earn enough to support his family; he grew still more defensive about his writing and more suspicious of the public. His ideal audience was now a small coterie—his family, Coleridge, Southey, and Lamb (whose approval was not always unequivocal)—and the Beaumonts (whose approval was). The Beaumonts thus became vital: their gifts were tokens of a reader response that Wordsworth desperately needed as well as essential means of financial support. Thus, in February 1808 Wordsworth welcomed Beaumont's present of an illustration for "Peter Bell" but worried that the sale of the poem would be insufficient to "carry the Expense of the Engraving" (MY, I, p. 194). However gratifying as an aesthetic response, the picture must remain a private sign of value because of the public's failure to buy his verse. Aesthetics and economics remained related in ways that Wordsworth, embarrassed, could not avoid. He was simply too poor to relate to Beaumont solely as one gentleman artist to another; awkward matters of money and labor dogged a correspondence he would have liked to keep on the level of disinterested aesthetic judgment of paintings and poems.[33]

Sonnets, Epistles, and Inscriptions: Coleortonizing Cumbria in 1811

Although Coleorton Hall was finished by 1808, the Beaumonts mostly lived in Essex and London. They were in Leicestershire in August 1811, however, when Wordsworth renewed a correspondence he had left in Dorothy's hands during the previous year. Away from home on the Cumbrian coast and anxious about his children's health, Wordsworth found himself outside his usual routines and resources. This situation jolted him to write both letters and poems in which he departed more than ever before from the genres and style in which he had been accustomed to write. In fact, his sojourn turned out to be pivotal. Feeling isolated and reaching out to Beaumont, he turned to the kinds of poetry he associated with Coleorton—traditional, neoclassical kinds that would henceforth feature heavily in his work. This new poetry germinated in a few short weeks in August 1811 that put him at such a distance from his home and his books that he was forced to reconceive his relationship to them, in effect developing a new voice that exploited, rather than tried to overcome, his remoteness from the places and times he had formerly struggled so hard to identify himself with. It was a poetry that often depended on the prior mediation of its subjects: Wordsworth wrote of place in response to others' pictures, poems, urns, and gardens, acknowledging a dependence on models that, by reducing the world to manageable scale and ordered form, stimulated memory without presenting all the tension and evanescence of the immediate, saturated spatiotemporal experience.

It was the landed estate that prompted him to write to Beaumont. Hearing that Beaumont's new steward at Coleorton was imposing new methods, Wordsworth hoped "that Mr Taylor's new laws and regulations are at least *peaceably* submitted to." He then turned to his recent experience of local landscape parks. Traveling past Muncaster castle, he had found that "the noble Proprietor has contrived to shut himself up so with Plantations and chained gates and locks, that whatever prospects he may command from his stately Prison, or rather Fortification, can only be guessed at by the passing Traveller." On the outside, rather than an invited guest, Wordsworth resented the exclusion and quoted Thomson's verse as an ironic counterpoint that also implied that such landscape gardens were unpropitious ground for poets: "You cannot rob me of free Nature's grace; / You cannot shut the windows of the sky." "The business," Wordsworth observed sardonically, "was done more thoroughly; for the sky was nearly shut out altogether." Likewise, Beaumont's friend Uvedale Price kept too much of his Foxley estate "exclusively to himself." Used to "a power to exercise . . . controul," the great landowner was tempted to make "his power . . . his law," banishing what displeased him from his view, "impoverishing and *monotonising* Landscapes." Receiving these comments, Beaumont must have felt reminded that the landowner's estate, for a client poet to flourish there, should represent his paternal protection of, rather than separation from, his tenants—although Wordsworth nowhere explicitly mentioned them. He did mention Coleorton, however, letting Beaumont know that his painting of the neighborhood hung over the chimney breast in the Wordsworths' new Grasmere house and that this, unlike the Muncaster estate, inspired poetry: "A few days after I had enjoyed the pleasure of seeing in different moods of mind your Coleorton Landscape from my fireside, it *suggested* to me the following sonnet." As before, Wordsworth thus characterized his relationship with Beaumont as one of aesthetic exchange rather than money or labor. He also suggested a politics of landscape poetry: Beaumont, he implied, did make room, when Price did not, for variety and humanity in his park. "The images of the smoke and the Travellers are taken from your Picture," Wordsworth said of his sonnet; the poet was inspired by the social inclusiveness of the picture (28 August 1811; MY, I, pp. 503–8). What he did not say, but was nevertheless fundamental, is that it was easier to see the smoke and travelers of Coleorton as aesthetically inspiring objects when they were viewed, from Cumbria, through the idealizing frame of a painting in Beaumont's distanced and generalized neoclassical manner. When seen in close-up on the spot, they reminded the viewer of the furnace fires that polluted the air and of the ragged coal miners. Deriving his sonnet from the picture, Wordsworth distanced, if he did not altogether efface, the industry and labor that underlaid Beaumont's patronage and that enabled the artistic exchange he would have liked to treat as purely aesthetic.

Praised be the Art whose subtle power could stay
Yon cloud, and fix it in that glorious shape;
Nor would permit the thin smoke to escape,
Nor those bright sunbeams to forsake the day;
Which stopped that Band of Travellers on their way,
Ere they were lost within the shady wood;
And shewed the Bark upon the glassy flood
For ever anchored in her sheltering Bay.
Soul-soothing Art! whom Morning, Noon-tide, Even,
Do serve with all their changeful pageantry!
Thou, with ambition modest yet sublime,
Here, for the sight of mortal man, hast given
To one brief moment caught from fleeting time
The appropriate calm of blest eternity.

(1815, II, p. 160)

The sonnet is not only a description but also the formal equivalent of Beaumont's distanced and generalized landscape painting. Influenced by Claude and by Reynolds, Beaumont aimed to achieve permanence by substituting a semblance of objectivity stemming from detachment for the revelation of subjectivity deriving from particularity. From his distanced viewpoint, the transitory, when framed at a remove, acquires the permanence required of art. Wordsworth achieves a similar Reynoldsian effect by eschewing the first person:[34] no narrator declares his viewpoint within the scenario presented by the poem. Lacking a speaker, the sonnet appears as a document to be read rather than an overflow of spontaneous conversation. This depersonalization extends to the addressee also: Wordsworth engages neither Beaumont nor the reader directly but only the idealized, abstract "Art," even eliding the optative verb "let" at the outset, so as to leave "praised be" detached from a putative speaker or writer exhorting his audience. Detachment and, consequent upon it, stasis are also effects of the rhyme scheme: the final sestet leaves behind the regular chimes of the octet for an *abcacb* pattern, where *a* and *b* are feminine half rhymes. This intricacy creates a delayed aural resolution, a slow and imperfect set of sonic echoes—stately progress to a reserved closure rather than unexpected harmony won from discord (as in the final couplet of a Shakespearean sonnet). Art, it seems, is "soul-soothing" because it creates a simulacrum of the world in which the subjective experience of time fleeting away is translated into a pattern of formal relationships by which change is slowed and arrested. This is not the conceit of so many Renaissance sonnets in which verse triumphs over time because it will be read in future ages; rather, it is an endorsement and enactment of artistic form as monumentality. For Wordsworth, it is a departure, in form and content, from his earlier work—developing the changed style he had begun to explore in "Yew Trees" and in the earlier response to a Beaumont painting "Elegiac Stanzas Suggested by a Picture of Peele Castle in a Storm."[35] If a root cause of this appreciation—and practice—of art that allowed him to counteract time's depredations was his brother's shipwreck and death (invoked here by "showed the Bark upon the glassy flood / For ever anchored in her sheltering Bay"), nevertheless Beaumont's representation of an unchanging landscape, both in his paintings and on the ground in Leicestershire, was the immediate spur. Wordsworth now seeks an "appropriate calm"—as if composing his art to appear dignified in public after grief—and the depth of this need is measured not only by his generalized diction, passive voice, and stately cadences but also by his reluctance to ask what is lost by a poetry that overlooks humanity from a distance. The contrast with the "Ode on a Grecian Urn" is instructive: whereas Keats questions what is given up by an art that freezes passionate human activity into the stasis of formal perfection—a "Cold Pastoral"—Wordsworth does not; his poem sees no sacrifice in art's (and its own) stilling of the excitements and vulnerabilities of the living; it is enough that it offers shelter and prevents loss.

The sonnet constitutes an art of overlooking: detachment militates against curiosity and prevents sympathy. What the travelers are doing and who they are is not a matter of interest: the variety and energy of people's activities are absent. And this is true not just of the idealized Leicestershire but also of Grasmere—now viewed from a distance via Beaumont's painting of the still more distant Coleorton. Far from the Lakes on the Cumbrian coast, Wordsworth writes to import the pictured Coleorton to the remembered Grasmere, bringing a detached view home to a Lakeland where he had once seen travelers up close in social and political terms—the discharged soldier, the Cumberland beggar, the leech gatherer. The sonnet thus begins a revision of Wordsworth's old poetic ground as well as a turn to pastures new: it heralds a later reworking of the sociopolitical stance and of the formal and stylistic preferences both of *Lyrical Ballads* and of *The Prelude*. In its context in the letter, it demonstrates that the cause of this revision was the changed perspective brought by a distance that placed Wordsworth beyond his familiar norms—and the consequent wish to show that he valued the patronage and friendship that Beaumont offered from a distance and the detached art to which Beaumont was committed. Yet the same letter also suggests Wordsworth's residual Jacobinism, a certain class resentment at the lord's domination of the locale revived by the pain of being excluded. The sonnet evinces his desire to exempt Coleorton and his own relationship with it from what he sees and feels about other gentlemen's country parks. But it also implies that the exemption can only survive what he sees on the spot at Foxley and Muncaster when Coleorton is seen in the idealizing mind's eye, responding to Beaumont's idealized paintings of it. Under the surface, Beaumont's difference from the other landowners whom Wordsworth criticizes is that he finds, in his art, a more effective way of disguising inequalities of labor and of wealth than they do on the ground.

Back in Grasmere in the autumn, Wordsworth produced more poetry in neoclassical forms for Beaumont, sending it in letters that once more circled uneasily around the issues of aesthetic values and market values, of labor, patronage, and stewardship. The poetry took the form of a series of inscriptions intended to be set up on stone in the Coleorton grounds—an idea that patron and poet had conceived in 1810 when they visited Lord Lyttelton's estate at Hagley and William Shenstone's at the Leasowes. Both of these landscape parks featured carefully situated plinths, tablets, and urns bearing inscriptions, in Latin and English, that related the view to scenes immortalized by poets and painters of the past. Wordsworth set out to do the same for Coleorton. On 11 November, for instance, he sent lines intended to be inscribed on a plinth carrying an urn in memory of Beaumont's mentor Reynolds. The urn was to be placed at the end of an avenue of lime trees at Coleorton. He also sent an inscription for a stone to be sited near a cedar he and Sir George had planted in 1807—this poem imagined present-day Coleorton as seventeenth-century Grace Dieu:

> Not mindless of that distant age renowned
> When Inspiration hovered o'er this ground,
> The haunt of Him who sang how spear and shield
> In civil conflict met on Bosworth Field;
> And of that famous Youth, full soon removed
> From earth, perhaps by Shakespear's self approved,
> Fletcher's Associate, Jonson's Friend beloved.
>   (lines 17–23; MY, I, pp. 513–15; 1815, II, pp. 284–85)

John and Francis Beaumont, invoked by the anonymous words chiseled into stone, made Coleorton seem to issue from its very rocks a script identifying itself as poetic, rather than industrial, ground. In the letter, Wordsworth further aligned himself with them as the new, local Beaumont poet by declaring he wished to see John's poems republished. He also sent an inscription for the poet's seat that he, Dorothy, and Mary had hollowed out of the stony bank of the winter garden in 1807. His intention, clearly, was to stamp his own words—albeit anonymously—on Beaumont's new park, using the ancient genre of the classical inscription to suggest that it was a place of deeply entrenched, ancient poetic tradition—"classic ground" because it was overwritten by the verse of ancestors and friends.

Five days later, Wordsworth sent Beaumont another letter in which he discussed painting, patronage, and the proper language for inscriptions. A crucial document in the evolution of his later poetry, the letter sets out Wordsworth's developing conception of the poet as a faithful steward of a landowning patron, a servant who dedicates his art to the monumentalizing of his patron's estate. Inscriptions are central to this conception because, rather than sell the poet's subjectivity on the book-buying market, they offer a disembodied, anonymous, uncommercial voice, the poet's identity remaining undeclared on the stone that "publishes" them to the viewer. Thus, discussing the inscription for Reynolds's urn, which, to Beaumont's surprise, he had composed in Beaumont's voice, Wordsworth declared, "I have always thought that in an epitaph or memorial of any kind a Father or Husband etc., might be introduced speaking, without any absolute deception being intended: that is, the Reader is understood to be at Liberty to say to himself; these Verses, or this Latin, may be the composition of some unknown Person" (16 November 1811; MY, I, p. 516). Effectively, Wordsworth was dedicating his voice, his art, to Beaumont, to effect the makeover, as both aesthetic and ancestral, of Beaumont's "patrimonial grounds"—a phrase Wordsworth avowed himself keen to preserve in the inscription, despite the problems of grammar it caused in context.

The discussion of inscriptional form followed an apparently unrelated paragraph in which Wordsworth commiserated with Beaumont over the conduct of his latest steward: "I am very sorry for Mr Taylor's misconduct both on account of his own numerous Family, and of his two Brothers who are most respectable Men, and cannot but be much hurt, if the particulars should ever come to their ears. For yourself the *extreme* impropriety of his behaviour must have rid you of all concern for him. I do sincerely wish that you may be more fortunate in your future connections of this kind; but it should seem that honest and judicious Agents are very rare." Like Boultbee, and like Boultbee's successor Bailey, Taylor had been entrusted with running the estate and the mine; like them he had now been dismissed—a bad steward, in Beaumont's and Wordsworth's eyes. Wordsworth's solicitude in the letter to meet Beaumont's wishes over the Coleorton inscriptions thus implies, in this context, that he is a better servant (though not salaried by his patron) than the agent who was paid to manage the estate. To make the affair still more pertinent to Wordsworth, Taylor had come to Beaumont from Cumbria on Lord Lonsdale's recommendation—thus another Lonsdale land agent was being summarily treated by his employer as Wordsworth's father had been. Beaumont, indeed, paid Taylor off to avoid the expense of again going to court. The affair could not but have echoed that of Boultbee and, before him, Wordsworth senior.[36] And though Wordsworth nowhere acknowledges the connection in the letter, he does state that he is about to ask Lonsdale "to serve me effectually"—that is, to arrange a job for him. He is anxious not to reveal any disapproval over landowners' treatment of their employees, because he has to admit that beneath his gift of inscriptions is an economic need that makes him more like Taylor than he would like to be. He needs a job from Lonsdale because "a considerable portion of my time *must* in some way or other be devoted to money-making"—and his poetry makes no money. So he must beg Lonsdale to use his political influence to procure him an office. This is the embarrassing economic truth beneath the relationship that Wordsworth wants to believe is a disinterested artistic one in which he confers aesthetic value on Beaumont's estate—as if it were not a place of industry and profit and he were not financially rewarded like Taylor, who had been employed by Lonsdale and then offered by Beaumont 10% of the annual colliery profits (on average £1,000 annually).

After discussing the latest drafts of his inscriptions, Wordsworth ends the letter by asking about Beaumont's other artistic protégés, the painters Wilkie and Arnald. Here, between the lines, his motive is to show Beaumont that his verbal rendition of Coleorton is superior to their pictorial representations. The painter, he says, needs to read books, for it is not "possible to *excel in landscape* painting without a strong tincture of the Poetic Spirit." As evidence of this spirit, Wordsworth then gives some new lines he has written to form a new beginning to one of his Lake District poems of 1800: "After I had written the Inscription for Coleorton, I looked at those in the Lyrical Ballads, and was tempted to alter the one for the Hermitage on St Herbert's Island in the following manner. I send it as the subject is elevated and serious, and therefore does not ill accord with those for Coleorton." A sincere report of the revisionary effect of being turned back to classical forms by Beaumont's commission of inscriptions for his garden, this remark was also an astute way of demonstrating his superiority to the other artists in his patron's stable. Not only was Wordsworth taking his inscriptional task seriously, like a good steward, he was also Coleortonizing the lyrical ballads that Beaumont admired, showing his patron how close to home he had brought the Leicestershire perspective that idealized Coleorton by association with the religious and poetic spirituality of Grace Dieu. The new lines that followed describe the ruined hermitage on a Derwentwater island that had once been occupied by St Herbert; they also refer to Herbert's friend Cuthbert—another retired monk, who was responsible for the production of many religious texts at the scriptorium of Lindisfarne:[37]

This Island, guarded from profane approach
By mountains high and Waters widely spread,

Is that Seclusion which St. Herbert chose;
After long exercise in social cares
And offices humane, intent to adore
The Deity, with undistracted mind,
And meditate on everlasting things.
Hither he came in life's austere decline:
And, Stranger! this blank heap of stones and earth
(Long be its mossy covering undisturbed!)
Is reverenced as a Vestige of the Abode
In which, through many seasons, from the world
Removed, and from the affections of the world,
He dwelt in Solitude.—But he had left
A Fellow-laborer, whom the good Man loved
As his own soul. And when within his Cell
Alone he knelt before the Crucifix, . . .

(MY, I, p. 518)

Preceding the *Lyrical Ballads* text, this revision turns it away from the heap of stones (line 9) and toward the hermit's meditation—materiality now becomes valuable insofar as it is a "vestige" of spirituality. Labor, in these lines, is associated with monks' contemplation rather than mason's craft or shepherds' handiwork. The lines contrast sharply with that other lyrical ballad of 1800, "Michael," in which the stones of a sheepfold betoken the shepherd's labor of wall building, a labor that has a non-monetary economic value (it protects the sheep from which Michael lives), is a skilled work of body and mind (dry stone walling is a difficult craft), and represents paternal inheritance (patrimony not as a money legacy but as a building made by father for son and as a skill passed down by hands-on teaching). In 1800 the sheepfold is a symbol of a local, traditional laboring society that dwells rather than sells, and the poem "Michael" is aligned with it, and the poet with its builder. The sheepfold's abandonment represents the vulnerability of this society—and poetry modeled on this society—to a money economy that spreads from the city. The poem laments the land's labor's lost and is uneasy about its own attempt to recoup that labor as the poetic work of a poet who, for all his locality and rejection of capitalism, has his books marketed in London.[38] In 1811, by contrast, the broken heap of stones is symbolically repaired by the hermit's labor of contemplation and the monk's labor of writing texts: the poet's labor is aligned with this work, not with that of the local shepherd builder. There is an abstraction of the bodily work of writing and building that reflects Wordsworth's increasing revulsion by the prospect of writing poetry for a market that does not buy his books. He idealizes the hermit and the monk not because he shares their Catholic beliefs but because they offer him a new model for himself as a poet: they are effectively secluded from the money economy by an institution that values thought and writing in doctrinal, rather than economic, terms—the monastery and church. Sending this fantasy to Beaumont, along with his inscription for a poet's seat that resembles a monks' stall, Wordsworth subtly asked Beaumont to give him shelter from the market, as did the prioress of Grace Dieu her nuns and as did Cuthbert protecting Herbert. The fruits of this protection would be verse dedicated to Beaumont, as if this were a paper version of the Gothic fantasy built into many eighteenth-century landscape parks, wherein a patronized poet was installed in a newly built hut and made to play at being a hermit to impress visitors.[39] Wordsworth would, of course, have been appalled at being asked to play the role that Stephen Duck had lived out: the patron/hermit fantasy was to remain an idealization that allowed him and Beaumont to imagine their relationship as one of paternal and institutional protection of spirituality.

The idealization did not bear close examination: if Coleorton, and now Derwentwater, were supposed to renew the Beaumont sanctuary of Grace Dieu, it was essential to overlook the fact that Beaumont's ancestors had in the 1530s helped arrange Grace Dieu's dissolution as a priory and, having done so, had profited by acquiring it as their residence, after winning a dispute over the spoils with another local nobleman. The Beaumonts' lands, if one looked back, were revealed as having been acquired through opportunism and expropriation, just as, if one saw beyond the screening trees in the new park, they disclosed slag heaps and child laborers. But Wordsworth did not look back or beyond: his poems, at least in their letter context, elide bodily labor, whether of miners, shepherds, or writers, and occlude the landed estate's implication in the capitalist economy. In form and function they are a kind of money laundering, enabling Beaumont to recycle his colliery wealth to a poet who makes clean depictions of his land. Profits become benefactions, a process that maintains Beaumont's credentials as a gentleman of taste because it shows him to be capable of disinterested acts of artistic appreciation. For Wordsworth, too, the inscriptions, tokens of his gratitude for Beaumont's appreciation and his gifts, are purer products of labor than poems written to be popular in an acquisitive society.[40] Beaumont cleanses him from the dirty work of writing for money; his poetic labors are no longer priced by the item at market value; instead he receives honorariums recognizing his work on the land, as if he were replacing his father's legal paperwork for Lonsdale's estate with poetic paperwork on Beaumont's.

Excursion *Sketches*

In the letter he wrote in February 1812 seeking Lonsdale's patronage, Wordsworth confessed that he had "erroneously calculated upon the degree in which [his] writings were likely to suit the taste of the times" (MY, II, p. 3). He offered himself as a poet prepared to contract debts of obligation to Lonsdale rather than monetary debts resulting from an unpopular style. Debts to Lonsdale, Wordsworth knew, meant upholding Lonsdale's political views—essentially supporting the system that had emerged from the rural economy of the eighteenth century in which local elections, and thus the national parliament, were dominated by the influence of great landowners. Those who now resisted this domination included capitalist entrepreneurs like Boultbee and Taylor and impoverished laborers like the Luddites. It is the former that Wordsworth addresses in one of the sketches he included in *The Excursion*. In Book VII he portrays a "peasant," a Cumbrian like Taylor, who has altered his social status by developing a traditional rural craft to meet the needs of the new industrial economy that was transforming landowners' estates into resource-fields for mills and manufactories. Here Wordsworth explores the meaning of the Coleorton disputes, articulating the social tensions produced by the new scale of economic activity and revealing the strain they placed on traditional rural paternalism and on its accompanying poetic form—the Georgic.[41]

> He was a Peasant of the lowest class:
> Grey locks profusely round his temples hung
> In clustering curls, like ivy, which the bite
> Of Winter cannot thin; the fresh air lodged
> Within his cheek, as light within a cloud;
> And he returned our greeting with a smile . . .
> . . . .
> . . . The Pastor answered, "You have read him well.

Year after year is added to his store
With *silent* increase: summers, winters—past,
Past or to come; yea boldly might I say,
Ten summers and ten winters of a space
That lies beyond life's ordinary bounds,
Upon his sprightly vigor, cannot fix
The obligation of an anxious mind,
A pride in having, or a fear to lose;
Possessed like outskirts of some large Domain,
By any one more thought of than by him
Who holds the land in fee, its careless Lord!

(*Excursion*, VII, 567–92)

Here the peasant and the landlord are both "careless"—the former because of his closeness to nature; the latter, culpably, because of his remoteness. The peasant is tree-like, ivy-covered, with a face which "bears too much / Of Nature's impress" to be worldly (lines 576–77). He ages, like a tree, through summer and winter. The landlord, on the other hand, merely binds nature by money—"holds the land in fee." Here Wordsworth adapts the line "Which after held the sun and moon in fee" from Milton's twelfth sonnet,[42] referring to Apollo's and Diana's divine power over the orbs dedicated to them. Thus, though carefully unspecific, he implies a critique of the godlike capriciousness of a landowner who resembles Beaumont as he was at the time of the Boultbee case—a rentier absentee who neglected his paternalist duties. But he contains this criticism by *The Excursion*'s structure, in which the sketch is just one vignette subsumed with a larger conservative moral disquisition and in which the point of view is that of a representative of the established rural order—the Pastor—who is identified, even at the price of a cozy condescension, as a better-educated, more reflective, and wiser interpreter of that which the inarticulate Peasant symbolizes:

. . . "in truth"
(Said the good Vicar with a fond half-smile)
"I feel at times a motion of despite
Towards One, whose bold contrivances and skill,
As you have seen, bear such conspicuous part
In works of havoc; taking from these vales,

One after one, their proudest ornaments.
Full oft his doings leave me to deplore
Tall ash-tree sown by winds, by vapours nursed,
In the dry crannies of the pendent rocks;
Light birch, aloft upon the horizons edge,
Transparent texture, framing in the east
A veil of glory for the ascending moon;
And oak whose roots by noontide dew were damped,
And on whose forehead inaccessible
The raven lodged in safety.—Many a ship
Launched into Morecamb bay, hath owed to him
Her strong knee-timbers, and the mast that bears
The loftiest of her pendants; Help he gives
To lordly mansion rising far or near;
The enormous axle-tree that turns ten thousand spindles,
And the vast engine labouring in the mine,
Content with meaner prowess, must have lacked
The trunk and body of its marvellous strength,
If his undaunted enterprise had failed
Among the mountain coves . . .
. . . .
. . . the JOYFUL ELM,
Around whose trunk the lasses dance in May;—
And the LORD'S OAK—would plead their several rights
In vain, if He were master of their fate.
Not one would have his pitiful regard,
For prized accommodation, pleasant use,
For dignity, for old acquaintance sake,
For ancient custom or distinguished name.
His sentence to the axe would doom them all!
—But, green in age and lusty as he is,
And promising to stand from year to year,
Less, as might seem, in rivalship with men
Than with the forest's more enduring growth,
His own appointed hour will come at last;
And, like the haughty Spoilers of the world,
This keen Destroyer, in his turn, must fall.

(lines 605–54)

Here the peasant competes with the landowner as "master of [the trees'] fate": his skill and energy harvest them for industry, but he is bound by others' ownership of the woods that he fells for their profit. He is also bound by his very closeness to the landscape: obedient to its laws like the forest, he too will fall.

The passage is as ambivalent about the peasant as it is about the landlord. This ambivalence results from the strain placed upon Wordsworth's Tory endorsement of rural paternalism by his sympathy with the laborers whose "undaunted enterprise" was exploited for their own "fee" by the landowners. But it results too from his attempt to incorporate a response to industrialization. The peasant was not only providing oaks for the navy that was protecting Britain's trade, but also supplying timber for the mills and mines that were enriching manufacturers and landowners. The peasant's timber felling is shown to replace the organic growth and decay of nature with the exponential mechanism of technological capitalism. This mechanism is portrayed as a disproportionate growth that perverts the nature of nature. It is measured in the revolutions of a single "axle-tree / That whirls (how slow itself!) ten thousand spindles"[43]—machinery powering a mill full of the new cotton-spinning jennys that the Luddites were trying to smash around Coleorton. Supplying this mechanistic transformation of labor, the woodsman is, like Boultbee and Taylor, an exploiter of resources for industry on a new, worrying scale—a "Destroyer," checked only by the death that he, tree-like, will himself suffer.

Kinship with nature is here sustained upon a death that prevents commercial and industrial exploitation from denuding the vale of its communal landmarks. The Pastor takes an anxiously ecological perspective, hoping that nature is reactive and limits the power of human enterprise to destroy it. But this nature also serves an ideological imperative: it is necessary for the Pastor (and Wordsworth) to imagine the peasant's death so that they can retain their faith in their ideal society—one of Georgic agriculture governed by the landed gentry in which commercial and industrial exploitation of the earth is held in check. If the peasant felled timber at will, there would be no Georgic ceremony symbolizing this ideal society, no trees providing "veils of glory" for the aesthetically sensitive, no Maypoles for village sports, no Lord's oak to make visible the ancient power of the local landowning family. Wordsworth's Pastor saves himself from this vision but only by associating commercial and industrial exploitation with a peasant whom he can first naturalize and then show to be subject to the natural law of death.

Beneath this strategy is an anxiety not just about the rapacity of the peasant and the industrialists he symbolizes, but also about the landowners—since landlords who consulted only their "fee" licensed, rather than checked, this exploitation (Lonsdale, as well as Beaumont, licensed extensive mining on his estates). Traditional rural society, and the ceremonies and arts that symbolized it through the Georgic, were under threat from both sides, as "getting and spending" spread capitalism from the metropolis. *The Excursion* was Wordsworth's uneasy response.

Poems *1815*

In an influential discussion, Geoffrey Hartman argued that the Romantic nature lyric was born when Wordsworth liberated from its material context a genre of poetry originally intended to be marked on an object in the landscape.[44] The "nature-inscription" was typically supposed to be written on a plaque, or a seat, or a stone; after Wordsworth's intervention, this "lapidary" deixis was left behind, replaced by the poem's accentuated reference to "the meditative mind" of the poet himself (p. 223). "Romantic poetry," Hartman concluded, "transcends its formal origin in epigram and inscription and creates the modern lyric" (p. 229). The Coleorton inscriptions suggest that this transcendence was of Hartman's rather than the poet's making, for, as texts, they make their meaning in the tension between their two scriptorial media—stones erected in Beaumont's garden and *Poems* 1815, a London-issued print collection. In the garden, they are marked stones as well as writing; seen from a distance they form parts of an array of objects encountered in the landscape—a pattern formed through the juxtaposition of natural and cultural things—trees, mounds, rocks, seats, steps. Thus the inscription is an object in a material context as well the conventional and ideal means of signification that is writing.[45] In the printed book, the inscription is read silently; it communicates ideally but is nonetheless a typographic pattern in relationships with the white paper around it, with other arrays of type elsewhere in the book, and with other books and print media.[46] There is no simple transcendence to pure mind or pure, arbitrary writing.[47] It is in the tension within this material immateriality—unique, specific, and local on one hand, and transferable and portable on another—that Wordsworth's poetry arises, for it is the effort to bear with, if not resolve, the tension that makes him write and rewrite. Efforts at resolving it in one direction or other seemed unsatisfactory and lead to further efforts to acknowledge, as multiple possibilities, both the material and immaterial contexts.

Poems 1815 certainly acknowledged both contexts, for Wordsworth included the section "Inscriptions," which, placing the Coleorton poems of 1811 alongside older inscriptions from *Lyrical Ballads*, epitomized the whole collection as a publication dedicated to Beaumont yet at the same time tested that dedication. On the one hand, the Coleorton inscriptions were so placed in the volume as to allow the poet to express, but also contain, anxieties about the politics of landscape to which his dedication to a landowner newly committed him. The disembodied voice of the classical inscription, terse and formal to fit the limited space and monumental setting of a stone tablet in a garden, allowed Wordsworth to distance himself from the narratorial position. Whereas in 1814 he gave the story of the woodsman to the Pastor, in 1815 he spoke impersonally. On the other hand, he surrounded the poems set in his patron's estate with Lakeland verse, so that their alignment with the landowner's perspective was placed in dialogue with the point of view taken in other, more leveling work. This more leveling work was in fact older (deriving from *Lyrical Ballads*) but was not printed as such: what dated from 1800 and what from 1811 was not marked out: by this means, present and past positions were juxtaposed, without any clear temporal progress being revealed.[48] Tensions were acknowledged and explored by this arrangement, but their resolution was not required. Nevertheless, the strong reference to the material context of monuments in Beaumont's garden brought anxieties about labor, poetry, and memory home to issues of property—to a nature owned by and portrayed for landowners and patrons.

The first poem in the section derived from 1800. It was "Written with a Slate-pencil, upon a Stone, the largest of a Heap lying near a deserted Quarry, upon one of the Islands at Rydale." The last, also a lyrical ballad, was "Written with a Pencil upon a Stone in the Wall of the House (an Outhouse) on the Island at Grasmere." Second was an 1811 poem, "Written with a Slate-pencil, on a Stone, on the Side of the Mountain of Black Comb." There then followed four Coleorton inscriptions also begun on the coast in summer 1811: "In the Grounds of Coleorton, the Seat of Sir George Beaumont, Bart. Leicestershire"; "In a Garden of the same"; "Written at the Request of Sir George Beaumont, Bart. and in his Name, for an Urn, placed by him at the Termination of a newly-planted Avenue, in the same

Grounds"; and "Inscription for a Seat in the Groves of Coleorton." In effect, the section was organized to present a series of reflections on gentlemen's landscaping: the Coleorton poems are framed by Lake District verses; thus the reader's encounter with Wordsworth writing for and as Beaumont is shaped by an older Wordsworth writing for himself. However, as the reader moves through the section, the poems on Coleorton alter the perspective on the already-read Rydal and Black Comb inscriptions. A dialogic relationship between poems aligned with different places and different times is achieved—a relationship that serves to express (if not resolve) in spatial terms, tensions about labor, class, patronage, and poetic independence. Arrangement across the pages of the book displaces social and political anxiety, producing a Wordsworth far less deferential to Beaumont than he was in the dedication to the volumes or in his 1811 letters: the poet admonishes the patron as much as he monumentalizes him, his family, and his estate.

The first inscription opens the section with a rebuke to a landowner. "Sir William" desisted from building a "Pleasure-house" on Rydal island when he discovered "a full-grown man might wade, / And make himself a freeman of this spot / At any hour he chose" (lines 6, 8–11; 1815, II, pp. 283–84). Unable to exclude other people, the gentleman lost interest, leaving "the quarry and the mound" of stones as "monuments of his unfinished task" (lines 12–13). This is the poet of *Lyrical Ballads*, sympathizing with the "freeman" against the landlord and regarding the landlord's desire to turn the place into an exclusive playground as an "outrage." What remains from Sir William's capricious abandonment of his project are the signs of work—a quarry and a mound of dressed stone. Poetry is affiliated with this worked stone rather than with the summer house: its radical rebuke is inscribed on the never-laid "corner-stone / Of the intended Pile" (lines 15–16). Worse still than Sir William's abandoned pleasure dome are the new holiday houses. The poem warns the reader not to become the kind of incomer who, enchanted with the place's beauty, burns to possess it for himself. Such visitors ravage its very essence, hewing "Out of the quiet rock the elements / Of [the] trim mansion destin'd soon to blaze / In snow-white splendour" (lines 29–31). Quarrying is despoliation when carried out to satisfy acquisitiveness and vanity—to indulge playful show rather than local need. That local need is a matter of habitation rather than leisure, at a level still more basic than the human: the "little Builders" are the linnet and the thrush who make the quarry their home and the robin who "hop[s] from stone to stone" (line 35). These birds, like the voice inscribed on the stone, "dwell" in the place; they stand for the poet, who never himself appears: the stony inscription we are reading is offered as the voice of the spot—of the rock and of the peaceful "slow-worm" who suns himself upon the rock (line 34). The animal and mineral naturalize what is, between the lines, a social critique on behalf of laborers, shepherds, and farmers (known as "freemen" in local parlance), of the gentry, and of acquisitive capitalism. Voicing the stone, rather than taking a subjectivized narratorial position, Wordsworth makes this critique appear as the elements disclosing them-selves—the genii loci—rather than the controversial and refutable opinion of a particular person or class.

The poem gives radicalism weight, framing the inscriptions that follow with a politics of nature that is certainly not aligned with the gentleman's point of view. Yet the seeds of Wordsworth's rapprochement with the land-owning classes are discernible in it. Sir William is no sooner admonished than excused because he was "bred in this vale, to which he appertained / With all his ancestry" (lines 22–23). Local tradition saves him; Words-worth's real animus is against encroachment on his peaceful vale by new wealth from outside.

The second poem, written eleven years later, appears also to be about varieties of labor and their claim properly to belong to a place—the place, again, being the Lake District. Once more, the poet uses the classical motif of addressing the passing traveler; again he tells that traveler an emblematic tale of an incomer who aims to subject the spot to his own rule. Whereas Sir William wanted to build a fancy pleasure-house on the island, here a "geographic Labourer"—one of the Ordnance Survey's cartographers—aims to use the hilltop to survey the area, "With books supplied and instru-ments of art, / To measure height and distance" (lines 15–16; 1815, II, pp. 285–86). Although this technological process allows him "many a glimpse . . . / . . . of Nature's processes" (lines 18–19), it is finally inadequate to comprehend them. Without warning, the surveyor finds himself en-shrouded in "total gloom" (line 27) on the summit, his map invisible. Dark-ness eclipses the power of his instrument-aided scientific vision. Thus the inscriber-poet, eliding his own subjectivity and speaking from the fellside seat, makes the mountain bear witness to its own power to overwhelm abstract systems of knowledge: Black Comb will not be plotted and triangu-lated. "Visitants," whether "boisterous" or mathematical, will not "molest" it by rendering its essential nature—its blackness—transparent (lines 7, 8).

Enlightenment science meets its match at the hands of a place that is not, like the Rydal island, the dwelling of small and vulnerable animals but of sublime clouds that overwhelm the human.[49] Again though, the poet uses the inscriptional form to elide his own point of view: his words, disembodied, represent nature writing back against human vanity, empowering him by implication.

The inscription for the mountain Black Comb was drafted while Wordsworth was writing epistles and inscriptions for Beaumont, but not then sent to him. In its published context in *Poems* 1815, it sends him a coded message. The first two inscriptions, both in blank verse, both offering symbolic narratives, frame the Coleorton poems that follow within arguments about property and power. Both rebuke gentlemen, whether knights or surveyors, who seek to impose a non-local, exclusive control of nature. Both use their material context—their existence as writing on stone fixed in the landscape—to give the poet, who never appears as himself, the authority of the genius loci; he is able to record on an object in the landscape and thus to summon in words the landscape's ability to erase human efforts. He has a language of power beginning before and ending beyond himself: his inscriptions are also invocations. Thus, after the oracular ending of the Black Comb poem, the closed couplets, decorous litotes, and garden scenery of "In the Grounds of Coleorton" seem like a diminution in scale in favor of a tamed scene and a decorous art. Yet the domestic opening soon gives way to a discussion of art and poetry:

> The embowering Rose, the Acacia, and the Pine
> Will not unwillingly their place resign,
> If but the Cedar thrive that near them stands,
> Planted by Beaumont's and Wordsworth's hands.
> One wooed the silent Art with studious pains,—
> These Groves have heard the Other's pensive strains
>
> (lines 1–6; 1815, II, p. 287)

If poet and painter jointly plant a tree to adorn Beaumont's grounds, acting as equals rather than as patron and beneficiary, the tribute that follows seems more like a put-down. Taking advantage of the detached view that belongs to the genre, Wordsworth portrays himself among the Coleorton trees—here a classical grove rather than the woods that had been "almost entirely" chopped down by Boultbee. Looking on as if a neutral observer, he rates his own art highly—the groves have received his song—while implying that Beaumont is a less-than-natural painter.

Nature and Art coincide—but not for art's sake. Wordsworth's claim on his own behalf, justifying his turn to a more artificial, more formal poetry than that of *Lyrical Ballads*, is, implicitly, a new aesthetic for him. It is also a power bid, enabling him to trump Beaumont the painter and to, as it were, paint over the fact of his need for Beaumont's money. Wooing with studious pains, Beaumont is an assiduous, zealous, but suffering suitor, neither spontaneous nor natural and not necessarily successful. Wordsworth is his superior as an evoker of nature and is thus confident to portray their relationship not as one of patronage, but of purely aesthetic exchange:

> Devoted thus, their spirits did unite
> By interchange of knowledge and delight
>
> (lines 7–8)

Rhyme enforces the harmony claimed in these lines. Wordsworth successfully puts his mouth where Beaumont's money is, creating alluring visions of spiritual sharing that flatter his patron without seeming to, since, speaking as the successful nature-poet, he patronizes his patron's lesser prowess even as he praises him. It is an artful maneuver, achieved by control of the classical inscription's formal possibilities and by the arrangement of poems within the section; it had not been so marked when Wordsworth had sent the poem to Beaumont in a letter.

After so confident a self-authorization from a distance, Wordsworth can assume the reader's assent to the exhortation of nature that follows:

> May Nature's kindliest powers sustain the Tree
> And Love protect it from all injury
>
> (lines 9–10)

Already the auditor of Wordsworth's pensive strains, nature seems unlikely to be deaf to this plea. Wordsworth is in rhetorical control, but with little of the humility of the alignment, in his 1800 verse, with birds and slow-worms or of the awed sense of nature's power present in the Black Comb poem. Instead, Wordsworth simply appropriates that power on behalf of art, imagining the tree sheltering not Beaumont but a future painter or poet in its shade and being

> Not mindless of that distant age renowned
> When Inspiration hovered o'er this ground,
> The haunt of Him who sang how spear and shield
> In civil conflict met on Bosworth Field;
> And of that famous Youth, full soon removed
> From earth, perhaps by Shakespear's self approved,
> Fletcher's Associate, Jonson's Friend beloved.
>
> (lines 17–23)

These words, set in stone under the sheltering cedar, constitute a self-fulfilling prophecy. They make the reader who sees them on the spot imagine the presence of John and Francis Beaumont, thus becoming the repository of renown of which the poem speaks—and justifying the dedication of the entire *Poems* 1815 to Beaumont as the latest in a noble family of artists and writers. The inscribed words cause this process to occur each time the stone is perused; nature is thus made to renew tradition by repetition: description of the past is also a manual for its mental perpetuation. It is a recipe for a making over of place into imagination—and imagination into place—that hinges on locality. It cannot work for a reader of the printed version, distant from Coleorton, in the way it does for one deciphering the stone in situ. History, the poem shows, is a product of poet, place, and peruser: it is made and remade locally in text and song.

The problem with the particular claim, however, is that "inspiration" did not hover over "this ground": the Beaumont poets did not live at Coleorton but out of sight at Grace Dieu. The poem is economical with the truth in its desire to endow Beaumont's new park, via the poet's ability to stimulate the reader's imagination, with an inspiring poetic heritage. While a tribute to that park, like the inscriptions at Hagley and the Leasowes, it is still more a tribute to the power of the poet: he is able to legislate for future poets by recalling a past in which, thereby, he is incorporated. The poet is the master, not the landowner, for the poem demonstrates that the endowment of a place with meaning—with history, with tradition—depends on the enchantment of words. That enchantment, however, depends on the poet overlooking the unfitness of the ground: Coleorton's lack of poetic heritage and its still-visible history of industrial exploitation are paid no regard. The sympathy for labor present in the 1800 Rydal inscription is notably missing. This overlooking is aided by the tighter classical form—the poem approximates much more closely the inscriptions that actually were carved onto stone, being shorter, while its couplets advertise its formality and slow the reading experience to a crawl. Monumental stasis replaces the developmental narrative that, in the Rydal and Black Comb poems, is enabled by the blank-verse effusion.

The next inscription further develops Wordsworth's strategy of mastering his patron by juxtaposing old and new inscriptions and thus placing independent poet alongside patron. Entitled "In a Garden of the same," the piece is the one that was written for the niche that Wordsworth, his wife, and sister scooped out of the bank in the Coleorton winter garden. That niche was supposed to evoke the cathedral and priory stalls associated with Grace Dieu and John and Francis Beaumont—a seat for the poet as spiritual contemplant. And the poem is shaped to resemble the niche, a small, tight, irreducible object, carved in stone that will survive when greater monuments, and Beaumont's garden, have been destroyed by time:

> OFT is the Medal faithful to its trust
> When Temples, Columns, Towers, are laid in dust;
> And 'tis a common ordinance of fate
> That things obscure and small outlive the great:
> Hence, when yon Mansion and the flowery trim
> Of this fair Garden, and its alleys dim,
> And all its stately trees, are passed away,
> This little Niche, unconscious of decay,
> Perchance may still survive.—And be it known
> That it was scooped within the living stone,—
> Not by the sluggish and ungrateful pains
> Of labourer plodding for his daily gains;
> But by an industry that wrought in love,
> With help from female hands, that proudly strove
> To shape the work, what time these walks and bowers
> Were shaped to cheer dark winter's lonely hours.
>
> (1815, II, p. 289)

In context, the inscription dramatizes, by virtue of the paradox that the insignificant outlasts the great, the superiority of niches, medals, and the inscriptions they bear (including this one) to gardens, trees, and mansions. The inscriber-poet is thus more time-resistant than, and therefore superior to, the landowner, though less wealthy and monumentalized in the present day. And this is reinforced by the fact that readers of *Poems* 1815 are encountering the inscription not in situ on stone, but perhaps years later—in 2018 for instance—on paper. The poem exploits its two material contexts—the garden and the book—to justify an assertiveness, derived in part from its repetition of this theme from the earlier poems in the section, that it had not possessed in its 1811 letter context. It also has a Cowperian focus on decay and loss—a late, death-obsessed view from which the niche is valued because it offers a time capsule of innocence to a narrator haunted by experience: it is "unconscious of decay." Wordsworth again exploits the third-person disembodied voice of the inscription to put poetry and the poet—implicitly himself—before the patron without directly saying so. The form allows him to fulfill the commission of dedicating verse to Beaumont's estate while egotistically taking the ground for himself and his art.

Not just egotistically, but pompously. When Wordsworth contrasts the "industry that wrought in love" with the "sluggish and ungrateful pains / Of labourer plodding for his daily gains" he suggests that the niche builder, and the inscriber of the niche poem, is above demeaning paid labor; he is neither a literary nor a literal hack—no "sluggish and ungrateful" miner, quarryman, or gardener "plodding for his daily gains." From the poet who made the bodily labor of Michael, working stone by hand, and of the Solitary Reaper, cutting wheat with a sickle, a sign of unalienated authentic being, the casual dismissiveness of these lines, as much as the gap they open between poetic pains and field work, is startling. The niche is a sign in stone of a newly asserted class difference proved by exemption from writing for money, an exemption enabled at Coleorton by Beaumont's generosity. Labor is revalued in terms of affection rather than economics. Yet, economics are nevertheless hinted at, since Wordsworth's phrasing cuts two ways: while it sounds condescending toward the Coleorton workers, who are less fortunate than he, it nonetheless draws aside the idealizing curtain of the Georgic. This is no place of happy swains singing as they work, but one of dehumanizing bodily drudgery ("plodding for his daily gains" describes men in terms often used for beasts—perhaps the horse plodding round and round the same circle to turn the gins that worked the pumps at the local mines).

The estate is briefly glimpsed as a place of class resentment: "sluggish and ungrateful" suggests, however unsympathetically, workers who go slow because they feel exploited. Hostility between worker and master is implied, although the local riots of unemployed miners and the Luddite machine-breaking are not mentioned. Wordsworth dramatizes the tensions in his position: he explicitly values leisure and unmonetarized labor, taking the landowner's dismissive point of view of beast-like wage laborers, but implicitly raises questions about the cause of their dehumanization and resentment. They may be sluggish because they are exhausted by toil and plodding because they are not motivated by the pittance they are paid. But not just the laborers: Boultbee and Taylor, onetime stewards and engineers who had reason to resent Beaumont's ungratefulness for their labor, are also ghosts at this pleasure ground. Wordsworth finds the garden haunted by the social tensions arising from labor relations even as he tries to find a recess within it that is exempt from those tensions—a withdrawal within a withdrawal. He displays what, perhaps, he would be reluctant explicitly to admit: his verse performs his conflicting loyalties and his remaining reluctance to simply model the landowner's point of view. It triumphs, as if despite its author, over naked ideology and models a way of thinking in which independence takes the form of critical reserve and anxious distance.

For reserve and distance, the next inscription substitutes exhortation and ventriloquism. "Ye Lime-trees, ranged before this hallowed Urn, / Shoot forth with lively power at Spring's return" it begins, before proceeding in Beaumont's voice to urge the newly planted trees in his garden to form a "darksome Aisle;— / Like a recess within that awful Pile" (St Paul's Cathedral) housing the tomb of Beaumont's mentor Reynolds (lines 1–2, 5–6; 1815, II, p. 290). As in the niche inscription, Wordsworth focuses the view on a recess within an enclosure. The inscription speaks from a funerary urn within an arbor within a garden. The aim is to defy time's destruction of reputation by making a place (a poem-place) so withdrawn that it seems exempt from larger forces—social and temporal. This context, and the formal evenness of the couplets, monumentalize Beaumont's affection for Reynolds, giving personal feeling the dignity of impersonal tribute.

Inscription VI, "For a Seat in the Groves of Coleorton," turns outward from Beaumont's park toward Grace Dieu. If read in situ, as it still can be, this poem calls the visitor not just to look to "yon eastern Ridge" but also to overlook the fore and middle ground—mines, furnaces, beam engines, "meagre" cottages (1815, II, p. 291). The "ivied Ruins," "erst a religious House" (lines 4, 5) are not actually visible from the park; they can be "seen" only by an act of imagination for which the inscription calls and which, once made, imports them into the perspective of the reader standing at Coleorton. Imagination transcends space, endowing Coleorton with spiritual credibility by association with the distant priory. It transcends time also, conferring poetic authority on the present spot by association with the former Grace Dieu inhabitant, Francis Beaumont:

> There, on the margin of a Streamlet wild,
> Did Francis Beaumont sport, an eager Child;
> There, under shadow of the neighbouring rocks,
> Sang youthful tales of shepherds and their flocks;
> Unconscious prelude to heroic themes,
> Heart-breaking tears, and melancholy dreams
> Of slighted love, and scorn, and jealous rage,
> With which his genius shook the buskined stage.
>
> (lines 9–16)

A playground for a youthful poet, Grace Dieu's pastoral innocence is the natal territory, the *fons et origo*, of the heroic verse of Beaumont's adulthood—just as in *The Prelude* Wordsworth had claimed the banks of the Derwent were for him. Here, though, the ground of inspiration can be claimed only vicariously, through a maneuver that imports it, via another's poems, mentally to a place—Coleorton—where it has never been. There were no streams at Coleorton, and there was insufficient water, Wordsworth discovered in 1807, to create one in the winter garden. There were few shepherds too, and so, breaking the imaginative spell no sooner than it has been uttered, the inscription turns away to the late, disillusioned view that stems from hindsight:

> Communities are lost, and Empires die,—
> And things of holy use unhallowed lie;
> They perish;—but the Intellect can raise,
> From airy words alone, a Pile that ne'er decays.
>
> (lines 17–20)

The universality and inevitability of decline, loss, and death become the moral lesson of the poem; Beaumont's new "Pile" is implicitly as vulnerable to destruction as the old Beaumont mansion Grace Dieu. Again, it is the mental memorial created by writings such as this inscription that endures: self-reflexivity is here, and throughout the section, the means by which the poet resists, and indicates his resistance, to time and thereby demonstrates his value to, and superiority over, his patron. The worth of Wordsworth's words is that they build to last, floating free of the stone and the page that decay. The poet, even if removed and dependent on others' preceding mediations (Reynolds' pictures, the Beaumonts' poems, classical inscriptions, the Coleorton garden), is Beaumont's best architect, landscape gardener, and steward: his unpaid labor gives the landowner and his family a life beyond themselves. Beaumont, readers cannot help but feel, has been warned as well as flattered. Wordsworth is no obsequious and anxious seeker of preferment, no mere celebrant of his patron's achievements and possessions. He creates lasting, because ideal, memorials: Beaumont needs his words. However, the buried anxiety in this conception of poetry is that, floating free, it becomes unstable, facile.

Wordsworth's anxious resistance to free-floating words is enforced by the context. The last poem in the section reverts to Grasmere. "Written with a Pencil upon a Stone in the Wall of the House (an Out-house) on the Island at Grasmere" takes the reader beyond the gentleman's estate; it does not invoke celebrated painters, monumentalize landscape gardens, or pay tribute to mansions. The outhouse is a "homely Pile," a "rude" building that is the construction of a village from which the poet writes:

> the poor
> Vitruvius of our village, had no help
> From the great City; never on the leaves
> Of red Morocco folio saw displayed
> The skeleton and pre-existing ghosts
> Of Beauties yet unborn, the rustic Box,
> Snug Cot, with Coach-House, Shed and Hermitage.
> (lines 6–12; 1815, II, pp. 292–93)

It is a real rural building, the poem insists, rather than a classically educated architect's fantasy of rusticity commissioned by a landowner. The classical aesthetics of Beaumont's art, and of the couplet inscriptions Wordsworth dedicated to him, suddenly seem remote (the luxuriousness of the classical is established by the expensive red Morocco book binding). This inscription is not a gentleman's commission for a plaque in a park but a villager's commentary on a barn—the poem poses as graffiti. The alteration in Wordsworth's social and poetic stance is thrown into sharp relief: his Coleorton voice is undercut by his Lakeland determination to speak from a position of community with ordinary villagers. What distinguishes the outhouse, it turns out, is that is gives shelter to the houseless beasts: "to these walls / The heifer comes in the snow-storm, and here / The new-dropped lamb finds shelter from the wind" (lines 13–15). In summer the poet comes too, sharing the place with the sheep—a pastoral community described plainly, without the usual idealizations of classical pastoral: the "sheep / Panting beneath the burthen of their wool / Lie round him, even as if they were a part / Of his own Household" (lines 22–25). From this leisured viewpoint, the poet sees "fair sights" and "visions of romantic joy" (line 29). His art is enabled by his retreat from social hierarchy into a lowly cattle shed. This is a far cry from the patronage relationship with Beaumont and from the distanced view of "plodding" laborers to which that relationship gives rise; yet, it has something in common with it: retreat. The Grasmere poet lying among sheep on an island resembles Francis Beaumont at Grace Dieu among the lambs on the river bank. Withdrawal, the inscriptions indicate, is necessary for poetic composition; only the mode of withdrawal and the status that it confers change. By 1811 and 1815, the retired poet is not a villager but a gentleman, and he resembles not a vagrant but a monk. And he no longer labors for his own needs, whereas in 1800 the poet rows to the island in a "Barge, up-piled / With plenteous store of heath and withered fern, / (A lading which he with his sickle cuts / Among the mountains,)" (lines 17–20). For the island poet, the inspiration that comes from leisured dwelling in a rural shelter is founded on his own self-sufficient labor, not on a patron's beneficence.

Ending on the poet's visions, the section uses the arrangement of poems in sequence on the printed page to elevate the figure of the writer—the writer of these very inscriptions—above that of the patron whose lands are being commemorated. As a sequence, the *Poems* 1815 section "Inscriptions" thus reveals Wordsworth's consistent endowment of the poet with authority, whether by revising the pastoral, the Georgic, or the inscription itself. But the poet is nonetheless an unsettled figure: while the *Lyrical Ballads* inscriptions align him, in a radicalized pastoral, with the humble birds and beasts, the Black Comb inscription associates him with the powerful natural sublime. The Coleorton poems make him variously the official recorder of

Beaumont history and monumentalizer of the new landscape park. Their adoption of the distanced view and disembodied voice typical of classical inscription allows Wordsworth's divided class loyalties and political perspectives to be overlooked. Wordsworth positions the poet as a loyal servant working for a grateful master but elides the factors that made loyal stewardship and due recognition increasingly rare. His inscriptional labor is mystified as an aesthetic exchange, and the exploitation of both place and people is neglected, only to recur in occasional ambiguous phrases that hint at the dehumanizing effects of the mining and quarrying from which Beaumont made the fortune that enabled his munificence. These phrases indicate the persistence of a viewpoint that recognizes class resentment, even if laborers are now viewed from afar. Meanwhile, the poems consistently declare the superior ability of the poet's (this poet's) art—even if secondary to and remediative of his patron's house, garden, statues, and paintings—to know nature and to survive time's destructive power. In this respect they express, even as they explicitly defer to Beaumont, a self-assertive confidence that Wordsworth derives from his skilled labor with words. Between the chiseled lines, Wordsworth's poetic relationship with Beaumont (at least as presented in print in 1815 as opposed to the letters of 1811) is not so different from Boultbee's and Taylor's: pride in his own self-sufficient skill—a skill that the landowner needs—makes him unable to conform successfully to the paternalist terms in which such relationships with landowners were traditionally organized in terms of the mutual duties of master and servant, lord and steward. The eighteenth-century Georgic in which rural paternalism was formulated is strained to the breaking point by the effort to comprehend these changed relationships within its terms. At the root of the change was industrial capitalism, enriching landlords although despoiling their lands, empowering their stewards as entrepreneurs while exploiting laborers as wage slaves. Wordsworth, the steward's son and the onetime spokesman for exploited rural labor, could not, however distanced and controlled his Georgic inscriptions, avert his attention wholly from either the empowerment of the servant or the degradation of the farmhand. Framing his Coleorton poems within the Cumbrian inscriptions, with their adoption of a power derived from an unenclosed, unsurveyed, ungardened, and unplanned nature and with their endorsement of bodily labor as a form of virtue, he puts in question the alignment of the poet with the landowner and leaves his position in doubt—anxiously cultivating an independence within the very medium that declares his affiliation. His new, later poetry is no departure from the old, early verse but neither is it an organic out-growth of it. Instead, as arranged in print in 1815, it is made to appear as a tense duplicity. Neither Coleorton nor Cumbria is simply confirmed or denied; neither is free of the other, but the leveling pastoral and empowering sublime of the Lakes has the first and last words.

PART II

Spots of Space

Materializing Memory

HERE I AM CONCERNED WITH the formal and generic innovations by which the post-1814 Wordsworth attempted to make poetry an adequate witness to the complex and often troubling production of the present by the past. Chapter 3 discusses the memorial—the name Wordsworth gave to many of the numerous poems he wrote as a tourist. The memorial was a development of the autobiographical recollections of self interacting with nature that appear in *The Prelude* as "spots of time." *The Prelude*, of course, was to have been the personal introduction to the more public and general *Recluse*. That poem was never completed; the memorials, however, fulfilled a similar aim. As *spots of space*, they emerged from seeking afar what the childhood land of the Lakes provided at home, a significant place in which the past could be retrieved. Their distance was significant, for it changed the nature of the past recovered, and thereby, the nature of the poetry. The memorials were testaments to visitable sites that provoked the traveling poet to recollect a history of public as well as private significance. In doing so, he articulated them in time (in both the content and form of his verse)—making space significant as place, as a *spot*—both material and textual, in the act of renewing cultural memory.[1] He, as it were, *spotified* geography into history—not only to foster the growth of his own mind but also for locals and visitors—a not necessarily united community that might come together as it shared the past that Wordsworth re-presented in his verse.[2] The memorials, that is, turned *The Prelude's* memorialization outward: spots became foci for a land and for its inhabitants. They thus offered the formal commemoration that, as Wordsworth argued in his "Essays upon Epitaphs," it was the poet's task to perform for the people. Wordsworth became through them a public, as well as private, poet, writing of nature not to escape history but to recall and reflect upon it. History included the history of poetry insofar as Wordsworth invoked previous poeticizations of the place.

Highly self-conscious, the memorial was a dispassionate record of an encounter with a historically significant place in which what was seen to be at stake was history itself—the place's mediation and remediation by oral tradition and written text, not least Wordsworth's own remediation. Many of the memorials were of places encountered in tours of Scotland, written in conscious self-differentiation from the romanticization of the past in the ballads and songs of Walter Scott and in James Hogg's popular pseudo-medieval poems.[3] They took their cue from Burns[4] in respecting the past's difference from the present and pondering the issues of power and appropriation involved in claiming to speak, in a modern, published text, for an oral culture that survives, if at all, in versions and fragments altered over time and by print. Indeed, the memorials act as correctives to what Wordsworth diagnosed as a sentimentalization of history—a heritagization of the past—among his contemporaries. Instead of such sentimentalization, he showed, the poet should bear witness to history as the recollection of the past in diminished form. It is not revived trailing clouds of glory, nor is it irrevocably lost or transcended into an ahistorical imagination discovered by private engagement with an ahistorical nature, as McGann influentially argued of the earlier work.[5] It is repeatedly reproduced in more partial and more fragmented stories, in which diminution as well as revival is inscribed.

The memorials emerged from literary rivalry: they are revelatory of the importance in the Romantic period of the contest to define the meaning of the past as it was transmitted in the traditional cultures of countries colonized by England. This contest is not yet over, and the poems are still powerfully resonant today. They alert us to the dangerous enchantments of cultural nationalism, not least to the retrospective glamorization of violence. Survivors as well as conquerors may be diminished and degenerated by the experience of colonial war, Wordsworth suggests, and poets should look dispassionately at their own medium before celebrating the "last of the race" as a founding hero of the independence struggle.[6]

Wordsworth embraced the role of national poet; nevertheless, he also continued producing poems that recollected encounters with places of personal, rather than public, significance—poetic heirs of "Tintern Abbey" and *The Prelude* "spots." In Chapter 4 I discuss one of these, from 1820 and 1827. "Enough of Climbing Toil" exemplifies a post-1814 turn from the solitary effort to ascend to commanding heights that had driven much of Wordsworth's earlier verse. Like many of the later landscape poems, it projects a mode of writing beyond the pursuit of spots of time, a working-out of what it is to be the poet who has written of them without wanting to relive them or generate new ones. My analysis of it has the larger purpose of altering critical debate about recollection as a central part of Wordsworthian poetics. Exploring the scriptorial practices of the

Wordsworth household, in which his wife, sister, and sister-in-law produced, stored, and retrieved manuscripts, I show that Wordsworth's
poetic memory was already textualized.[7] It materialized on paper
inscribed and curated by his helpers, whence it was retrieved and incorporated into (or, as) new poetic manuscripts—a collage technique. In other
words, the remembered experience is not prior to writing, or to textuality,
or to others: "Wordsworth" the experiencing narrator of "Enough of
Climbing Toil" is the product of the outsourcing of memory to a remote
server operated by his female coworkers. The women of the scriptorium
guarantee his ability to "enshrine the spirit of the past" not just because
they were present on the occasions he looks back toward, but also because
they can lay their hands on the old pieces of paper on which they had
written out those occasions.[8] Acknowledging this, indeed thematizing it
both formally and semantically, Wordsworth is able to contemplate his
long-term poetic dependence on his loved ones in a way he never had
before. He is also able to acknowledge his debts to older writers, alluding
to classical and eighteenth-century poets so as to place himself in a poetic
fellowship; renunciation of the solitary striving to be a "prophet of imagination" allows him to relax the anxious struggle to master Milton's style.
Pacé Harold Bloom, this relaxation does not lead to flaccidity but to generosity and to an embrace of nature as a place whose multiplicity is articulated in a text that incorporates fragments of many prior texts—his own
and others'. Memory is thus built into the poem's structure: it is visible
as a textual process involving the transcription, preservation, and reuse
of manuscripts. Wordsworth thereby acknowledges the communal and
material process that is omitted in *The Prelude*, where the past is said to
return mentally to the solitary Wordsworth and only then to be recorded
in verse. This, then, was construction by salvage rather than organic form:
"Enough of Climbing Toil" is the product not just of revision of old texts
into newer versions but of new building with used materials (each of
which bespoke the social context of its first composition and transcription).

The collage method was not just a matter of personal poetic history
becoming form, for it was a response to a contemporary event that made
the nature of history a topical question. Geologists' excavation of a Yorkshire cave made public a past of deep time, showing that the earth itself
comprised strata of fossilized bones. Wordsworth's later poetry of
memory responded to this discovery as a layered assemblage of poetic

fragments from his past manuscripts. Poetic form, that is, was modified in response to contemporary scientific discourse about prehistory (as depicted in newspapers and journals). The later Wordsworth responded to new understandings of the past with formal innovation, as well as by explicit reference.

Chapter 3

Memorials of Scott-land, 1814–33

This chapter explores the development of a new, revisionary genre in Wordsworth's later career, relating it to his competition with contemporary poets whose textual imitations of oral poetry—rural songs and ballads—became far more popular than his own, although his own had preceded them. The poets in question were Scottish, and the revisionary genre—the tourist memorial—developed when Wordsworth visited Scotland and, as a consequence, tried to make the culture of Scotland's historical past appear differently on his pages from its appearance in their volumes. The Scottish tours in question were those of 1814, 1831, and 1833, building on that of 1803, because it was by the time of these later visits that the Scottish poets had become voices to be reckoned with—popular and respected authorities in whose printed volumes the vanishing oral culture of the clans was thought to be collected.

The poems that Wordsworth wrote during and after these tours evince the gradual transformation of his earlier ballad style by the adoption of the perspective of the visiting outsider writing a tour journal in verse, rather than the villager supposedly speaking or singing from within a local culture. Self-evidently texts rather than textualized songs, they are the productions of an English visitor emulating, yet also differentiating himself from the resident Scots poets—Macpherson, Scott, Hogg—who were highly influential on his conception of the poet's role in the British (rather than English or Scottish) nation. They demonstrate the effect of Wordsworth's ambivalence about what he called the "balladism" of Macpherson, Scott, and Hogg, revealing both his desire to share their popularity by adapting the forms in which they versified Scottish history and his suspicion of the kind of history they constructed. This suspicion caused him uneasily to compete with, then create an alternative to, their sentimentalization of aristocratic chivalry. His alternative—the tourist memorial—was both formally and thematically a way of revising the modernization of tradition achieved by the Bard of the Highlands (Ossian), the Wizard of the North (Scott), and the Border Minstrel (Hogg). The memorial was the erstwhile lyrical balladeer's textual reworking of the oral ballad as it appeared in bardism and minstrelsy—a restatement (rather than outright rejection) of what he viewed as the pseudo-medieval textualization of the Scottish past as preserved in tale, song, and legend. It involved countering Scott-ish poetry by a revision of the use of local legend and superstitious tradition made by Burns (and in some of Hogg's tales). Honoring Scottish culture through Burns rather than Macpherson and Scott, Wordsworth attempted to make his own verse its conduit to the present, modern day. A key aspect of his attempt, I argue, was his textual manifestation of the natural sounds characteristic of the Scottish landscape—the sounds of wind, water, birds—in rhymes, echoes, and rhythms. This sonic reproduction became a token of his authority as a poet able to speak the place's nature, despite the fact that he was a visitor and not a native member of the oral community from which its songs and ballads emanated.

A hybrid of traditional forms and dispassionate contemporary witness, the tourist memorial casts the cold eye of a detached visitor on historical violence and its local and national legacy. It problematizes, rather than sentimentalizes, the poet's relationship to the literary and personal past. I say "memorial," but in fact Wordsworth gathered memorials into sequences: by moving from place to place in poem after poem, he aimed to offer disenchanted perspectives not available to those who only vied to be the authentic mediator of their spot and its history.[1] Circumspect about the appropriation, in contemporary print, of the voices that transmit local story and historical lore, Wordsworth placed limits on the poetic impulse to imagine the past into new textual life. Countering Scott's practice, he became anti-Romantic in that he borrowed the forms used in border romances but broke with Scott's assumption that historical trauma can be repaired by adapting into a love story the traditional genres that told of that trauma. Wordsworth's take on Scottish tradition does not have a happy ending for participants or poet: at its best it is not only a critique of the foundation of national identity on the sentimentalization of place and past but also an acutely unsentimental account of the effects of war on its survivors. Wordsworth becomes in these poems, a remarkable—shocking—poet, when he is pushed by rivalry to resist the conventional consolations used to assuage pain as nobility and to rehabilitate suffering as heroism. His resistance, I shall argue, includes resistance to his own Romantic impulse—so strongly marked in the *Prelude* "spots of time"—to show temporal loss as redeemable by poetic recollection. In the memorials of the Scottish tours, the past remains recalcitrant because it is public and disputed, rather than personal and (apparently) recuperable. The vexed questions that history poses to representation lead Wordsworth to investigate what is at stake in his desire to imaginatively renew it—even as he attempts the renewal.

Rival Balladeers in the Press

Behind the tourist memorials by which Wordsworth responded to Macpherson, Scott, and Hogg was a decade and longer in which Wordsworth had seen their ballads, songs, and romances win popularity and respect while his own sold poorly and were reviewed harshly by Scots journalists. The *Edinburgh Review*, the most influential journal of the day, had attacked *Lyrical Ballads* as early as 1802, in a review of Southey's *Thalaba*. But it was in 1807 that it devoted a whole review to one of Wordsworth's publications, damning *Poems, in Two Volumes* by suggesting that it showed Wordsworth as a "bad imitator of the worst of his former productions." Of the 1803 tour poem, "An Address to the Sons of Burns, after visiting their Father's Grave," the *Edinburgh* declared "Never was any thing . . . more miserable."[2] Treating Wordsworth's ballads as childish nonsense, the journal rejected his credentials as a poet of the common people and as poet of Scotland.

About Scott, the *Edinburgh* was initially skeptical. Reviewing *Marmion* in 1808, Francis Jeffrey perceptively saw that the poem was not a revival of Scots ballads and romances so much as a hybrid: "To write a modern romance of chivalry, seems to be much such a fantasy as to build a modern abbey, or an English pagoda."[3] The poem was a piece of kitsch, a pseudo-antique—a view that Wordsworth shared, for on 4 August 1808 (MY, I, p. 264) he wrote to Scott distinguishing his own romance *The White Doe* in "composition, both as to matter and manner" from *Marmion*. By 1810, however, the *Edinburgh* was extolling Scott's ballad romance *The Lady of the Lake* for the very qualities that the lyrical balladeer had thought were his own pioneering achievements: "He has made more use of common topics, images and expressions, than any original poet of later times; and, at the same time, displayed more genius and originality than any recent author who has worked in the same materials."[4] With Scott's poems achieving critical respect, and selling by the tens of thousands, Wordsworth felt himself usurped. By 1812 he was assenting "to the observation 'that the secret of Scott's popularity is the vulgarity of his conceptions, which the million can at once comprehend.'"[5]

Wordsworth's relationship with Scott was complex, including approval and admiration as well as envy. Yet ungracious remarks about Scott's poetry were common in Wordsworth's circle, and what was especially disliked were the characteristics it shared with Macpherson's Ossian—minstrelsy and bardism: the mediation of the past through idealized, invented poet-figures who were imagined singing ballads and romances for a feudal lord. The minstrel associated the ballad with the aristocratic culture of chivalry; he dissociated it from the common people, past and present. He allowed Scott to serve up the past as pageantry, a performance of the antique, with himself in the place of the minstrel and his readership in the place of the lord and the clan. And the minstrel related local historical legends transformed into action-packed narratives that were antique in style yet modern in sentiment. As chivalric love stories, they turned history into romance; contemporary productions manufactured to seem old, they also contained a commentary on the production and reproduction of the past in legend, song, and verse. They were, in Susan Stewart's term, "distressed"—new works presented with a patina of age.[6] They turned the places in which they were set into "Scottland": a romantic region imbued both with historical tradition and poetic inspiration. In Ian Duncan's words, "romance" was "modern culture's construction of a symbolic form prior to itself."[7] The past's difference, its strangeness, was acknowledged only to be paraded as a show, preventing it from challenging contemporary values. Conversely, Scott also remodeled some aspects of it so that they resembled aspects of the present that he wanted to position as their descendants: among these was violence, which he represented as noble and chivalric.[8] Romanticizing war, Scott made Scotland's history heroic, a matter of bravehearts and true heroes, rewriting the past in the terms of the honor code of present-day officers and gentlemen (and romanticizing that code in the process—a useful service for a nation at war with revolutionary France). Wordsworth thought this rewriting a trivializing glamorization of the past to serve the fashionable taste of the present.

At least some of Wordsworth's dislike had to do with the representation of an oral culture in modern print. Macpherson's and Scott's work, he found, collapsed cultural difference, even as it appeared to honor it, by too easily assuming that old songs and ballads—and the specific world-experiences they codified—could be mimicked in his own modern, printed songs. The work lacked responsibility: it did not, as Wordsworth himself had in poems such as "The Solitary Reaper" and "The Discharged Soldier," consider the proper limits of the poet's right to write about those who could or did not represent themselves in writing.[9] For this reason, Macpherson's and Scott's ballads and songs were too smooth: a textual surface of pseudo-medieval motifs substituted for a harder imaginative assessment of the poet's position as a would-be interpreter of a culture whose orality was a sign of its cultural and historical difference. And Scott was too presidential in his deployment of historians', antiquarians', and editors' authority-devices: he used a carapace of prefaces, notes, and frame narratives to estab-lish his written text as the place where the elusively oral poetic past was reliably corralled.

Wordsworth's was a minority view: Ossian was a success all over Europe; Scott sold by the tens of thousands among the English middle and upper classes who found its version of Scots dialect and culture lite enough not to be deterred from both reading it silently and reciting it aloud. The prime minister himself performed it at breakfast. Wordsworth, skeptical of the poetry and envious of its popularity, did not. What he did instead was try to write his own Scott-ish poetry, more respectful of the cultural speci-ficity and human difference of the oral culture it represented by textual means. Scott sent Wordsworth back to the border ballad; he returned him to the updated ballads of Percy; he made him redefine what he thought good in modern ballads. And he prompted him into a change of style—in competition and emulation. While denigrating Scott's romances to friends, Wordsworth imitated them, striving to turn local legend into sentimental romance in his own region—the Lakes and Yorkshire—as Scott had for Scotland. His 1807 bardic romance "Song at the Feast" borrowed Scott's hallmark device of placing a chivalric romance within the frame of a medie-val minstrel's performance—borrowed it only, in Maureen McLane's words, "to kill it"[10]—rejecting the idealization of the poet as a bard singing of his feudal lord's warlike deeds. His 1807/1815 narrative romance, *The White Doe of Rylstone*, followed Scott's recipe of focusing on the divided loyalties of families and lovers in an era of civil strife, yet turned from the battle scenes beloved of Scott to a meditation on suffering. The poem, which Dorothy had hoped would save the family finances, failed. Depressed by the hostile reviews and dismal sales of the 1807 *Poems, in Two Volumes*, Wordsworth lost confidence and withheld the piece from the press for eight years; when it did reach print it won him neither respect nor money.[11] By summer 1814 it had become clear that he would secure neither a reputation nor a living, whether as the lyrical balladeer of 1800 or the romancer of 1807. He would not be, as he had hoped, the Scott of England—the people's choice as national poet, revered for his renewal of the old ballad tradition. The question this left him was a fundamental one: if not a balladeer and romancer, then what kind of poet was he, in the public's eyes and his own—and more specifically, in what form could he explore his abiding concerns with the local, present, and past? The Coleorton inscriptions, invoking poetic ancestors and updating classical form, were one answer, but not all his poetry could be in this genre and about that place. His great project, *The Recluse*, was stalled and, without Coleridge's friendship, in abeyance. *The Prelude*, its preface, would not be published in his lifetime. Alienated from the public, resentful of reviewers, snide about Scott's poems—however much he respected him personally—Wordsworth, with *The White Doe* withdrawn from the press, pinned his hopes for reputation on *The Excursion*. But he was gloomy even about the prospects of this work on the current literary market, although it was markedly different from Scott's popular romances and his own unpopular ballads: "I shall be content if the Publication pays its expense, for Mr. Scott and your friend Lord B. flourishing at the rate they do, how can an honest *Poet* hope to thrive?" (MY, II, p. 148).[12] Not only Scotland, but also Britain as a whole, now seemed to him Scott-ish ground, glibly made over into shallow textual versions of its local and historical oralities.

The 1814 Tour: Scott-ish Ground

On 18 July 1814, with his wife Mary and his sister-in-law Sarah Hutchinson, Wordsworth headed north to Scotland for a summer holiday. The trip was a return to what had once been fertile ground. Wordsworth had toured Scotland with his sister Dorothy in 1803; he now wanted to share with Mary and Sarah places that, when he had shared them with his sister, had stirred him into some of his finest lyrics.[13] In addition, far more so than in 1803,

Scotland was not his poetic territory alone. Then, Ossian and Burns were on the scene as poets of Scottish landscape and identity; now, not only Scott but also James Hogg spoke for Scottishness from Yarrow, Ettrick, and the borders.

The tourists went to Moffat, to New Lanark and the Falls of Clyde, to Glasgow, then up Loch Long to Luss on Loch Lomond, where, at the end of July, they visited the islands near the lake's western shore. From Stirling they went to Edinburgh, and on 1 September back west to Traquair, in the borders, where they met Hogg, who conducted them to Yarrow in the company of Dr. Anderson—the venerable compiler of the anthology *Anderson's British Poets*, on which Wordsworth had long relied. They went next to Abbotsford; Scott was away but they were welcomed by his wife and daughter.

After their return home, Wordsworth began to put the trip on paper. By the end of November he had drafted "Yarrow Visited," a ballad, prompted by the day spent with Hogg, that recalled his 1803 stay with Scott and that alluded to a number of the ballads collected in the *Minstrelsy of the Scottish Border*. This poem was published in the 1815 collected edition of Wordsworth's verse, where it has a relationship not just with Scott but also with Hogg as the local collector of the traditional Yarrow ballads it invokes and as a contemporary poet enjoying some popularity. Hogg was a rival as well as a still more local representative of Yarrow and its ballads than was Scott. He was also a different class of man, and poet, from Scott, and this should have recommended him to the lyrical balladeer. Hogg was no Edinburgh lawyer but a shepherd and small farmer—exactly the kind of person Wordsworth had idealized when writing of the Lake District. Hogg wrote from a rural tradition in which ballads were still sung, in a rustic language taken from the vernacular of his fellow rural lowlanders. Poems such as "The Witch of Fife," "Kilmenie," and "The Abbot Mackinnon" were not sentimental chivalric romances but ballads in Scots, rather than standard English. Wordsworth read them in autumn 1814 in Hogg's collection *The Queen's Wake* (1813). He thought them much the best in a volume that "does Mr. Hogg great credit," though tellingly he found it "disfigured" in its "intermediate parts" by "false finery" (MY, II, 169). By "intermediate parts" he had in mind the Scott-ish elements of the volume—in which individual ballads and songs were presented as the works of a group of bards assembled to praise Mary Queen of Scots as she arrived in Scotland, from France, in 1561 (Scott, too, had presented various ballads in *The Lay of the Last Minstrel* as works of a group of minstrels). Wordsworth disliked the minstrelizing apparatus but admired the ballads that vocalized the supernatural beliefs of the local people.[14] Hogg's supernatural poems spoke in contemporary rustic dialect, as Wordsworth's own lyrical ballads aimed to do. They would help Wordsworth to a reformulation and relocation of his own ballad style in the tour poems he drafted over the next few years, as I shall show later in this chapter. Their immediate effect was felt in "Yarrow Visited," the ballad Wordsworth wrote in September and November 1814, recalling the day on which he had explored the valley in Hogg's and Anderson's company.

"Yarrow Visited" is a memorial—a memento of a tourist's visit to a spot that itself commemorates the historical past, as rendered in songs and ballads that told of a lover's murder, at the riverside, by the brothers of the Yarrow girl he loved. Wordsworth's own past, and past poetry, was also invoked: he had written of Yarrow before, and the 1814 poem alludes to that writing (writing that had itself echoed an earlier ballad tradition). It is a text—as many of the poems derived from the 1814 tour would be—in which retrospect and revision take the form of allusion, allusion both verbal and formal. A text of return to an earlier poem that was itself allusive, it is a restatement of Wordsworth's own poetic past and, beyond, of the context alluded to then. It updates the 1803 tour poem "Yarrow Unvisited," in which Wordsworth had justified leaving the valley unseen so that it would remain a place of imagination. Unseen but heard—unseen, indeed, because heard. In "Yarrow Unvisited" Wordsworth had declared himself at home in Yarrow sonically, though visually estranged, because he both quoted Yarrow ballads and echoed their meter and rhyme:

> Be Yarrow Stream unseen, unknown!
> It must, or we shall rue it:
> We have a vision of our own;
> Ah! why should we undo it?
> The treasured dreams of times long past,
> We'll keep them, winsome Marrow!
> For when we're there, although 'tis fair,
> 'Twill be another Yarrow!
>
> (lines 49–56; 1815, II, pp. 16–19)

These echoes—particularly that of the strongly marked feminine rhymes, "Yarrow"/"marrow"/"harrow"/"sorrow," that the Yarrow ballads and songs employed—foregrounded Wordsworth's lyricism as a borrowing. Not only did they invoke words and cadences, moreover, but also tunes. Songs such as "Braw Lads" (Burns), "The Dowie Dens of Yarrow" (collected by Hogg; published by Scott),[15] "The Braes of Yarrow" (written by William Hamilton, published by Percy),[16] and "Rare Willie Drowned in Yarrow" (published by Allan Ramsay)[17] were so well known that the airs to which they were sung were heard in the head when the texts—or even just the hallmark rhyming words—were seen (just as occurs today for "Jerusalem" and "Amazing Grace"). Wordsworth was, as it were, formally sampling previous Yarrow songs so that their trademark harmony and melody sounded in his own—an effect so intense that the reader does not only replay their emphases and chimes in his head ("subvocalizing" the written text into an oral one[18]) but also infers their tunes. If the Yarrow valley, then, is poetic ground, Wordsworth need not see it because it sounds as if he were there: its music sings from his allusive writing.

So it was in "Yarrow Unvisited." In 1814, however, Wordsworth records his tourist trip, asking whether the visual experience of being there that he now depicts disrupts the imaginative engagement that previously depended, when he had never visited, on his sonic echoing of the local song tradition. The 1814 poem portrays his restless and fruitless search, as a passer-by, for the exact spots in which the events narrated by those local songs occurred: responding to his own earlier poem, it asks whether imagination's hallowing of unvisited ground can survive the mundane reality. How might a visiting poet sing, or can he sing at all, of a place already existent so long, and so significantly, as a purely imaginary visual form and sonic trace? Belatedly on the scene from which he had turned aside in 1803, would he not only fail to make it live up to his projection, but also retrospectively despoil that projection—its free-floating lyric ideality now and forever brought down to earth? Changed utterly? Wordsworth copes with this possibility by expanding the range of his poem's allusions. The words of Scott's *The Lay of the Last Minstrel* are invoked; so are those of John Logan's "The Braes of Yarrow" (perhaps an act of homage to Wordsworth's companions; Hogg had praised Logan in *The Queen's Wake* and Anderson had included "The Braes," and a biography of Logan, in his *British Poets*).[19] And it is not only the invocation of other poets' words, but also of their rhythms, rhymes, and tunes, that allows Wordsworth to cope with the disappointment of seeing the dreary place he had previously only imagined. "Yarrow Visited" is more lyric than ballad, more music than narrative, more sound than sense, so insistently do its feminine rhymes foreground its own formality:

> O that some Minstrel's harp were near,
> To utter notes of gladness,
> And chase this silence from the air,
> That fills my heart with sadness!
>
> Yet why?—a silvery current flows
> With uncontrolled meanderings;
> Nor have these eyes by greener hills
> Been soothed, in all my wanderings.
> And, through her depths, Saint Mary's Lake
> Is visibly delighted;
> For not a feature of those hills
> Is in the mirror slighted.
>
> A blue sky bends o'er Yarrow vale,
> Save where that pearly whiteness
> Is round the rising sun diffused,
> A tender hazy brightness;
> Mild dawn of promise! that excludes
> All profitless dejection;
> Though not unwilling here to admit
> A pensive recollection.
>
> Where was it that the famous Flower
> Of Yarrow Vale lay bleeding?
> His bed perchance was yon smooth mound
> On which the herd is feeding:
> And haply from this crystal pool,
> Now peaceful as the morning,
> The Water-wraith ascended thrice—
> And gave his doleful warning.
>
> Delicious is the Lay that sings
> The haunts of happy Lovers,
> The path that leads them to the grove,
> The leafy grove that covers:
> And Pity sanctifies the verse

That paints, by strength of sorrow,
The unconquerable strength of love;
Bear witness, rueful Yarrow!

(lines 5–40; 1815, II, 20–23)

Here "flower of Yarrow" alludes to the song of that name by William Hamilton, published by Anderson, and the water-wraith to Logan's "Braes of
Yarrow," while the "sorrow"/"Yarrow" rhyme echoes the entire local song
tradition. Thus it was re-sounding that enabled renewal. Echoing the
rhymes of previous Yarrow songs has the effect of calling up a tradition,
materializing the work of harmonizing that is always performed by rhyme
but that usually stays in the background of readers' minds. Here it is so
obtrusive that it becomes the poem's subject as much as its narrative is,
and the point of this is to demonstrate, in writing—and on the silent pages
of print—that Wordsworth, though a visiting stranger, has joined the vocal
harmony, the choir, that *is* Yarrow—a choir that aims, in its keening
rhymes, to echo the original lament of the local girl bereaved by her lover's
murder. The repetition of the name, Yarrow, that stands for the place
(before it is visited and after) aims to let one see, on the page, the sound of
harmony—to show to the eye the melody of song. Thus to see Yarrow is
not just to go to a place where, in tradition, tales repeat a girl's lament, it
is also to receive the harmony that makes Yarrow what it is—to see all the
previous ballads and songs that depend on the chime of "Yarrow" with
"sorrow." Thus Wordsworth claims admission to the group of songwriters
who can invoke, even in the silence of print, the ballad tradition that is the
place's cultural identity. He claims a place in a song community that is not
confined to Yarrow's distant past (now supposedly revived in antiquarian
print), but that is still extant, as is proved by the songs of Hogg, Logan,
Hamilton, and Burns that it echoes. In other words, Wordsworth is able to
renew his lyric vocation, his ability to turn place into poetry—when challenged by the failure of the visual real to match the imagined ideal, when
confronted by other poets' prior claims, and when driven by critical hostility to doubt his ballad style—by *harping on*—alluding formally to the Yarrow sound or Yarrow beat—and thus effecting his lyric participation in the
place as song. In doing this he emulates Hogg as a local poet who could
claim to be a living member of the oral community from which the song
arose, not by making a claim for local knowledge (as he did in the Lakes)
but by sonic alignment with the poem-sounds that had, by tradition, come

to seem characteristic of the community and the place. At the same time, he emulates Scott, the editor of the collection of border ballads that included some of the Yarrow songs, as the contemporary reproducer of the song tradition in print. Unlike Scott, however, he does so without a paratext that presents his words as those of a medieval minstrel or ancient bard: in order to represent his own subjective experience as a visitor, his poem eschews the paraphernalia of the antique that Scott uses to demonstrate authenticity.[20] Where Scott and, to a lesser extent Hogg, presented a vocal concert in print by allotting different ballads and songs to different members of a historical group of imaginary bards and minstrels, Wordsworth did not. "Yarrow Visited" is a modern lyrical ballad, claiming in the here and now an ability to articulate, without falsification, the oral expression of a rural culture in words that will circulate in a London-published book. The sonic invocation of border songs—tunes as well as rhymes and rhythms—is the key to this ability: Yarrow's prior existence in oral poetry emplaces Wordsworth's writing, allowing a transference that he had not been able to achieve in his 1803 tour poem "The Solitary Reaper," in which he was unable to understand what the highland girl sang. The visiting tourist, that is to say, needed an interpreter in order to overcome his foreignness; a song tradition accessible through texts, as at Yarrow, acted in that enabling role.

Scotch Reviewers and Wordsworth's Alienation from the Ballad and Romance, 1814–20

"Yarrow Visited" was the first of the poems to stem from the 1814 tour. Several others, however, emerged more slowly because Wordsworth lacked an enabling tradition to help him write of the place visited without being reminded of his disabling foreignness. Three poems did, however, reach print in 1820 in a collection that heralded what would become a staple of his later career—it was named after a sequence of poems that invited readers to follow the poet on tour. The River Duddon established Wordsworth as a tourist poet, and although the Lake District was the main place visited, it also contained three Scottish tour pieces: "The Lament of Mary Queen of Scots," "The Brownie's Cell," and "Composed at Cora Linn, in Sight of Wallace's Tower." These poems were of varied kind. They reveal Wordsworth's desire to appear as a poet of Scottish tradition and the difficult genesis of a new genre in which he could do so (the poems were named as memorials in 1827).

The desire and the difficulty were intensified at the end of 1814 and in 1815, when Wordsworth met further setbacks that troubled his relationship with Scottish poetry and criticism, and thus with Scotland as a place he could lyricize. By the end of 1814 he was aware of Jeffrey's review of *The Excursion* in the *Edinburgh*, which damned not just his new poem, but his old ballad poems too:

> This will never do. It bears no doubt the stamp of the author's heart and fancy; but unfortunately not half so visibly as that of his peculiar system. His former poems were intended to recommend that system, and to bespeak favor for it by their individual merit;—but this, we suspect, must be recommended by the system—and can only expect to succeed where it has been previously established. It is longer, weaker, and tamer, than any of Mr. Wordsworth's other productions; with less boldness of originality, and less even of that extreme simplicity and lowliness of tone which wavered so prettily, in the Lyrical Ballads, between silliness and pathos. . . . The case of Mr. Wordsworth, we perceive, is now manifestly hopeless; and we give him up as altogether incurable, and beyond the power of criticism.[21]

The condescension rankled: in letters Wordsworth called Jeffrey a "coxcomb" and "Aristarchus" (MY, II, pp. 179–80). Sales were bad: by June 1815 a mere 291 copies had been purchased—hence Wordsworth's need for Beaumont's gifts and Lonsdale's patronage.[22] Wordsworth was left embittered—resentful of Jeffrey, alienated from the bookbuying public (from "taste"), and envious of Scott, who continued to win praise and make money. He became prickly and defensive, prone to sour remarks about the faults of fellow poets who were more successful than he. One of these was Hogg, whose *Queen's Wake* had gone through several editions and whom Wordsworth coupled with Scott in a petulant reference to the "insupportable slovenliness and neglect of syntax and grammar, by which James Hogg's writings are disfigured." Such faults were "excusable in him from his education, but Walter Scott knows, and ought to do, better. . . . They neither of them write a language which has any pretension to be called English." Hogg is "too illiterate to write in any measure of style that does not savour of balladism" (MY, II, 179–80). If this comment was hypocritical coming from a poet notorious for his ballads and who had just written a ballad that invoked Scott's and Hogg's ballads, its snobbish unfairness reveals how stung Wordsworth was by Jeffrey's argument that the lofty blank-verse *Excursion* was still "weaker and tamer" than the lyrical ballads he had already dismissed as childish and simpleminded. Wordsworth now wanted to be recognized as a poet of importance who wrote in the grand tradition of Milton; he regretted an association with balladry and rusticity that dragged him down in reviewers' eyes. In the face of these regrets, his decision, that spring, to publish his long-withheld ballad-romance *The White Doe of Rylstone* was at once a perverse act of defiance and a last, desperate bid for success—a declaration that he could write in Scott's genre without the glib solecisms in language, plot, and characterization that reviewers had noted in *The Lord of the Isles*, Scott's latest romance about Scotland's heroic past, which had appeared at the start of January. That poem, introduced by a latter-day "minstrel" from the Tweed and Ettrick, sold out an edition of 15,000 within the month.

Wordsworth preceded the publication of *The White Doe* with an embattled attempt to shape the reception of his poems that, again, hinged on the genre of the ballad and its lyricization of place and past. Scotland and Scottland were at the heart of this attempt. Published in March, the "Essay Supplementary to the Preface" not only attempted to lift readers out of their current tastes and not only anticipated an appreciative posterity to compensate for the uninterested public, but also tried to lay down criteria for the proper development of traditional ballads and songs. Wordsworth regretted the modern and sentimental manners that characterized Percy's exercises in the genre, but he reserved his spleen for Macpherson and Ossian—synecdoches for Scott-land (Sir Walter being too much a personal friend to be criticized by name).

> All hail, Macpherson! hail to thee, Sire of Ossian! The Phantom was begotten by the snug embrace of an impudent Highlander upon a cloud of tradition—it travelled southward, where it was greeted with acclamation, and the thin Consistence took its course through Europe, upon the breath of popular applause.
>
> Having had the good fortune to be born and reared in a mountainous country, from my very childhood I have felt the falsehood that pervades the volumes imposed upon the world under the name

of Ossian. From what I saw with my own eyes, I knew that the imagery was spurious. In nature everything is distinct, yet nothing defined into absolute independent singleness. In Macpherson's work it is exactly the reverse; everything (that is not stolen) is in this manner defined, insulated, dislocated, deadened,—yet nothing distinct. It will always be so when words are substituted for things. To say that the characters never could exist, that the manners are impossible, and that a dream has more substance than the whole state of society, as there depicted, is doing nothing more than pronouncing a censure which Macpherson defied. (*Prose Works*, III, 77)

Clouds, phantoms, dreams: Ossian, the Scots bard, here represents the lack of precision and consequent lack of vitality not just of Macpherson's fakes, but of the minstrelizing of a "whole state of society" to which Scott and even Hogg had subjected tradition. Hogg, who had been personally slighted by Wordsworth when visiting Rydal, saw as much, recognizing that the *Essay* was an exercise in self-assertion that created an opposition to Scots balladeers where once there had been tribute. He told John Murray that the literary world "was laughing immoderately at Mr. Wordsworth's new prefaces which certainly excel all that ever was written in this world in egotism, vanity and absurdity."[23] Wordsworth's ulterior motive, to supplant the Scots as poets of rural tradition and as national bards, was all too transparent; it produced a reversion to national and nationalist stereotypes. Where the border ballads had once seemed a local tradition, crossing national boundaries, an English/Scots divide was now drawn.

A Poetic Proxy: Wordsworth's Defense of Burns

If the "Essay Supplementary" seemed a nadir in Wordsworth's relationship with the reading public and the reviewers who influenced it, nevertheless matters got worse at the year's end. Asked for his opinion about a new edition of James Currie's biography of Burns, Wordsworth composed a defense of the poet that excoriated both the biographer and the reviewers who, having read the biography, criticized Burns's character. Chief among these reviewers was Jeffrey who, in the *Edinburgh*, had written:

But the leading vice in Burns's character, and the cardinal deformity, indeed, of all his productions, was his contempt, or affectation of contempt, for prudence, decency, and regularity; and his admiration of thoughtlessness, oddity, and vehement sensibility;—his belief, in short, in the dispensing power of genius and social feeling, in all matters of morality and common sense. This is the very slang of the worst German plays, and the lowest of our town-made novels, nor can anything be more lamentable, than that it should have found a patron in such a man as Burns, and communicated to many of his productions a character of immorality at once contemptible and hateful.[24]

Jeffrey had also remarked that Burns's characters, however immoral, were preferable to the "hysterical schoolmasters and sententious leechgatherers" of the Lake school (p. 276)—a sideswipe that Wordsworth did not forget.

In Burns's defense, Wordsworth exacerbated his own alienation from the versions of Scottish culture created by Jeffrey and by Scott. In defending the poet against his detractors, he was pushed into defining how, using traditional forms and vernacular diction, he might turn place and past into a historical poetry that was opposed to the versions of Scotland now in vogue but could not be dismissed, as his poems had hitherto been dismissed, as feeble-minded balladry. Burns became, in effect, the proxy of a restored Wordsworth, a precursor whose cultural prestige, if Wordsworth could but redeem it from the aspersions being cast upon it, sanctioned the practice of writing about Scotland without a pseudo-medieval, fake-chivalric romanticization of tradition.[25] Burns's modern lyrics, ballads, satires, and songs, Wordsworth argued, were self-conscious explorations of traditional beliefs rather than naive, or faux naive, expressions of those beliefs. They were not would-be revivals of the lost past but critical representations of the past's persistence in present-day culture.[26]

To exemplify his argument, Wordsworth discussed Burns's liking for spirits, in both senses of that word. That Burns wrote poems which celebrated the effects of strong liquor was not evidence of the deplorable vices of the private man, but part of a strategy designed to let the reader occupy the believing minds of his rustic characters, who drunkenly "see" the spirits they have been raised to believe in—witches, fairies, kelpies, selkies, brownies. "Not less successfully," Wordsworth remarked,

> does Burns avail himself of his own character and situation in society, to construct out of them a poetic self,—introduced as a dramatic personage—for the purpose of inspiriting his incidents,

diversifying his pictures, recommending his opinions, and giving point to his sentiments. His brother can set me right if I am mistaken when I express a belief that, at the time when he wrote his story of *Death and Dr. Hornbook*, he had very rarely been intoxicated, or perhaps even much exhilarated by liquor. Yet how happily does he lead his reader into that track of sensations! and with what lively humour does he describe the disorder of his senses and the confusion of his understanding, put to test by a deliberate attempt to count the horns of the moon! (*Letter to . . . Burns*, p. 24)

Burns's drunkard narrator is a persona constructed to allow the reader to entertain imaginative play—to share the creative transformation of the perceived world; though comic, this process is liberating. And though it does not demand belief in kelpies and other traditional spirits, it allows readers to share the mindset of one who does—or does sufficiently for his drunken imaginings to take their form. As the narrator of "Address to the Deil" tipsily confesses,

> When thowes dissolve the snawy hoord,
> An' float the jinglin' icy boord,
> Then water-kelpies haunt the foord,
>   By your direction,
> And 'nighted trav'llers are allur'd
>   To their destruction.
>
> An' aft your moss-traversin Spunkies
> Decoy the wight that late an' drunk is:
> The bleezin, curst, mischievous monkies
>   Delude his eyes,
> Till in some miry slough he sunk is,
>   Ne'er mair to rise.

(lines 67–78)[27]

Kelpies, spunkies, brownies: the tipsy narrator sees the world in the forms provided by traditional supernatural belief. As Burns explained in a letter included in his biography—a letter read by Wordsworth—a woman friend of his mother's had "the largest collection in the county of tales and songs concerning devils, ghosts, fairies, brownies, witches, warlocks, spunkies, kelpies, elf-candles, dead-lights, wraiths, apparitions, cantraips, giants, inchanted towers, dragons, and other trumpery.—This cultivated the latent seeds of Posey; but had so strong an effect on my imagination, that to this hour, in my nocturnal rambles, I sometimes keep a sharp look-out in suspicious places; and though nobody can be more sceptical in these matters than I, yet it often takes an effort of Philosophy to shake off these idle terrors."[28] In another letter Burns suggested that such brownies, bogles, and witches were the forms in which his writerly inventiveness materialized. Addressing his fellow poet Cunningham, he asked,

> But what shall I write to you? "The Voice said, Cry: & I said, What shall I cry?" O thou Spirit! Whatever thou art, or wherever thou makest thyself visible. Be thou a Bogle by the eerie side of an auld thorn, in the dreary glen through which the herd-callan maun bicker in his gloamin route frae the fauld! Be thou a Brownie set, at dead of night, to thy task by the blazing ingle, or in the solitary barn, where the repercussions of they iron flail half affright thyself, as thou performest the work of twenty of the sons of men ere the cockcrowing summon thee to thy ample cog of substantial brose![29]

Thus Burns writes of himself writing, self-reflexively portraying his art as the transformation of his correspondent into a spirit. Cunningham becomes an imaginary being of his literary creation—a creation shaped, however, by folk belief. Burns self-mockingly places his writing within a cultural tradition of supernatural beings while maintaining a distinction between himself and credulous cottagers. Writing in the vernacular, adapting oral song and ballad form, Burns offers a version of Scots traditional culture at once more playful and more serious than Scott's analogous version of vernacular forms. He is neither an antiquarian editor collecting past minstrelsy for historical reasons nor a literary imitator of a naive peasant balladeer but a self-conscious artist who playfully reflects upon the relationship of his imagination to the supernatural tales among which he grew up, tales in which the "brownie" figured large.

Building on Burns: Wordsworth's Brownie, 1816–20

Having formulated his thoughts about Burns and in so doing restated his ideas about imagination's relationship to local folk beliefs, Wordsworth was able to write about Scotland in new terms. Neither the ballad nor the minstrel romance, but the memorial: a remodeled lyricism drawing on models provided by Scott and Hogg and yet differentiated from them via a revision of Burns's self-conscious examination of the relationship of supernatural belief to historical action and poetic creativity.

The poem in which this redevelopment first came to fruition was "The Brownie's Cell," a memorial of Wordsworth's 1814 visit to a place that was itself a memorial of historical events, supernatural beliefs, and his own past engagement with Scotland. In August, on that 1814 tour, he, his wife, and sister-in-law had visited the islands in Loch Lomond; it is on one of these that the poem is set. But the island had previously been the object of admiration when the Wordsworths had visited in 1803. Dorothy, passing by in a boat, had been fascinated by glimpses of a ruined tower, noting that "I wanted much to go to the old ruin, but the boatmen were in a hurry to be at home. They told us it had been a stronghold built by a man who lived there alone, and was used to swim over and make depredations on the shore,—that nobody could ever lay hands on him, he was such a good swimmer, but at last they caught him in a net."[30] The poem picks up this tale, investing the island as seen in 1814 with the 1803 memory; as such it is a return to territory evoking a personal history as well as a local story. Doubly a memorial, it is, I want to suggest, one of Wordsworth's more profound poems about memory, story, and history, though a strange and riven one that exhibits his not-entirely-achieved struggle to develop a post-lyrical ballad style. It is a meditation on tradition and its perpetuators—bards, prophets, tale-tellers—that is also an unsentimental meditation on historical violence and its traumatic after-effects.

Wordsworth composed the poem sometime between 1816 and 1820 and prefaced it, on publication in the *River Duddon* collection, with a note: "suggested by a beautiful ruin upon one of the islands of Loch Lomond, a place chosen for the retreat of a solitary individual, from whom this habitation acquired the name of 'The Brownie's Cell.'" This "beautiful ruin" still exists: it is a broken tower on the northernmost island of Loch Lomond (Ellan I Vow) and was a stronghold of the Macfarlanes during that clan's involvement in the religious wars of the seventeenth century. The country around Lomond was associated with Scott; so were Scottish ruins. And Scott had discussed the "brownie"—a spirit that haunted houses, streams, and waterfalls and could be seen by those with second sight—in the notes to his *Minstrelsy of the Scottish Border*. In the manner of an antiquarian amused by quaint primitive beliefs, Scott recounted stories, probably derived from Hogg, of brownies on the Tweed and at Ettrick.

On Scott's ground, Wordsworth differentiated his poem from Scott's antiquarianism. His poem is grim where Scott's are glamorous about both war and the beliefs to which war gives rise. It begins by using imagery redolent of the wasted landscapes that form the setting for trauma in *Macbeth* and *King Lear*. It depicts medieval Scotland as a forbidding wilderness, peopled not by chivalric heroes but by recluses, solitaries, and hermits—men who have turned away from their earlier active lives. As in *The Excursion*, the *White Doe*, and the 1811 hermitage inscription (see Chapter 2), Wordsworth imagines religious retirement as an aspect of belatedness—a self-reclusion. Here it is a retreat from previous experience of military action in the remote fastnesses of an unwelcoming, penitential landscape:

> To barren heath, and quaking fen,
> Or depth of labyrinthine glen;
> Or into trackless forest set
> With trees, whose lofty umbrage met;
> World-wearied Men withdrew of yore;
> (Penance their trust, and Prayer their store;)
> And in the wilderness were bound
> To such apartments as they found,
> Or with a new ambition raised;
> That God might suitably be praised.
>
> > (lines 1–10; *Duddon*, pp. 104–9)

Having offered this wide-angle landscape shot of the past, the poem moves, in the second stanza, to a close-up of the hermitages of such reclusive men—not so much huts or hovels as a tree house or nest, as if the former warrior has utterly gone back to nature: "High lodged the Warrior, like a bird of prey; / Or where broad waters round him lay" (lines 11–12). But Wordsworth then brings himself and the reader up short in a moment of deixis: the here and now, presenting itself, changes his view:

> But this wild Ruin is no ghost
> Of his devices—buried, lost!
> Within this little lonely Isle
> There stood a consecrated Pile;

Where tapers burn'd, and mass was sung,
For them whose timid spirits clung
To mortal succour, though the tomb
Had fixed, for ever fixed, their doom!

(lines 13–20)

This "wild Ruin," we take it, is the "beautiful ruin" referred to in the poem's headnote—the building known as the brownie's cell. Wordsworth pictures it not, at first, as a solitary's den but as an outpost of organized religion—a place of civilized spirituality, a chantry chapel where services were held and prayers sung for the souls of those in purgatory. As such, it is reminiscent of the cells and oratories to which he had likened his poems in 1814—and to those of Grace Dieu abbey, that, in 1811, he had portrayed as the seat of the Beaumont poets.

Unlike Grace Dieu, the chapel was ruined by violence. The clan Macfarlane having taken the side of the Stuart kings in the 1640s, Cromwell's occupying army destroyed their strongholds. The next stanza compresses this destruction, which Scott might have made the subject of an entire romance, into a few lines so unspecific that it is not clear whether Wordsworth is describing it or an earlier, legendary attack.

Upon those servants of another world
When madding Power her bolts had hurled,
Their habitation shook;—it fell,
And perished—save one narrow Cell;
Whither, at length, a Wretch retir'd
Who neither grovell'd nor aspir'd:
He, struggling in the net of pride,
The future scorned, the past defied;
Still tempering, from the unguilty forge
Of vain conceit, an iron scourge!

(lines 21–30)

The retired "wretch" is no peaceful contemplant, spiritually purified by solitude. Sheltering in the fragments of the bombed-out building, he is beyond hope and expects no improvement. Trapped by pride, he is isolated and obsessed; he fantasizes about violent revenge. He is a Byronic figure, an embittered Romantic refugee defying past defeat, scorning future compromise—a product of war and its destruction of civilized community, for whom endurance is a form of defiance. Proud and conceited, he is a scourge who may chastise himself as much as the age he defies.

The next two stanzas expand on the refugee's story. It turns out that he is a survivor of a brave, formerly honest, latterly treacherous, clan:

> Proud Remnant was he of a fearless Race,
> Who stood and flourished face to face
> With their perennial hills;—but Crime,
> Hastening the stern decrees of Time,
> Brought low a Power, which from its home
> Burst, when repose grew wearisome;
> And, taking impulse from the sword,
> And, mocking its own plighted word,
> Had found, in ravage widely dealt,
> Its warfare's bourn, its travel's belt!
>
> (lines 31–40)

Behind these words are the clan Macfarlane's reputation for raiding, thieving, and feuding. In 1594 it was denounced by the Scots government for robbery and murder; in 1603 the Macfarlanes and Macgregors attacked the clan Colquhoun at Glen Fruin, slaughtering hundreds, including clerical students who were innocent bystanders. Again, however, Wordsworth does not detail the events; his purpose is not to dramatize or glorify war, but to examine, in cold blood, its human costs. In the first stanza a religious community is lost; here the clan's bravery, honesty, and honor are corrupted from within. Once "face to face" with "their perennial hills"—in, that is, an open and equal relationship of emplacedness, of dwelling—they turn to crime from boredom with peace, break their oaths, and ravage the surrounding area. "Taking impulse from the sword" portrays this local raiding as an abandonment of self-command that leaves the clan in thrall to the material world. The clansmen let themselves be led on by their own weaponry rather than uphold signs of civilization (adhering to "plighted word" requires conformity to an abstract principle embodied only in the ideal realm of language).

The stanzas are notable for their invocation of, and deviation from, the romantic myth of the clan warrior and the survivor bard promoted by Scott and by Macpherson.

All, all were dispossess'd, save Him whose smile
Shot lightning through this lonely Isle!
No right had he but what he made
To this small spot, his leafy shade;
But the ground lay within that ring
To which he only dared to cling;
Renouncing here, as worse than dead,
The craven few who bowed the head
Beneath the change; who heard a claim
How loud! yet liv'd in peace with shame.

(lines 41–50)

Last of his race to adhere to the old ways, Wordsworth's refugee does not
bow the head; he will not swear allegiance to the new dispensation and
accept the clan's subordination to centralized law and government. He is a
vestige of an older feudal Scottish past, conquered but hanging on in a new
era, and as such brings Ossian, son of Fingal, to mind—a remnant who
maintains the proud values of his extirpated clan, and the primitive heroism it represents, alone. But whereas Macpherson establishes this figure
nostalgically, so as to lament a departed era of manly valor, an authentically
Scots past of nobility and independence, Wordsworth is critical.[31] His survivor's proud defiance of compromise is said to be daring and exceptional
—an act of lone bravery—but is also questioned. Not only is the clan whose
values he maintains shown to have been treacherous and criminal—
responsible for and even deserving of its own doom—but his own vigil is
also brought into doubt.

From year to year this shaggy Mortal went
(So seemed it) down a strange descent:
Till they, who saw his outward frame,
Fixed on him an unhallow'd name;
Him—free from all malicious taint,
And guiding, like the Patmos Saint,
A pen unwearied—to indite,
In his lone Isle, the dreams of night;
Impassion'd dreams, that strove to span
The faded glories of his Clan!

Suns that through blood their western harbour sought,
And stars that in their courses fought,—
Towers rent, winds combating with woods—
Lands delug'd by unbridled floods,—
And beast and bird that from the spell
Of sleep took import terrible,—
These types mysterious (if the show
Of battle and the routed foe
Had failed) would furnish an array
Of matter for the dawning day!

(lines 51–70)

The survivor responds to defeat by compensatory dreams that give him prophetic power and allow loss some significance, perhaps apocalyptic. Eliding Ossian with St John the Revelations prophet, Wordsworth here gives a psychosocial explanation of the causes of prophecy. He anthropologizes it, rather than recreate it uncritically, even as he summons its power. Prophetic writing is the response of a disturbed, desperate war victim to defeat and to the destruction of the community that had given his world structure and meaning. It is wild and sublime but not necessarily reliable or true. Wordsworth's list of its typical images gives it graphic scope but also removes its specificity; he also shows that it is the record of the dreams of a shaggy, world-renouncing mortal, given "import terrible" by the "spell" of sleep—the stuff of nightmare rather than the word of God or voice of History. If the prophet-survivor is the conscience of his defeated people, that conscience is under pressure: he is so isolated that what he sees may be only the visions of one spellbound by dreams. If he is enchanted, Wordsworth is not: the poet's perspective is disillusioned, if not unsympathetic. It is historicizing, demythologizing, and anti-Ossianic.

In keeping with this anti-Romantic narrative, the next stanza is no more than tentative about the brownie superstition:

How disappeared He?—ask the Newt and Toad,
Inheritors of his abode;
The Otter crouching undisturb'd,
In her dank cleft . . .

(lines 71–74)

If the refugee seer is popularly believed to have been metamorphosed into the water animals that haunt the island ruin, if the newt and toad are brownies or kelpies embodying his spirit, the poet does not positively say so. His question is not a ringing endorsement of local supernaturalism, for even if the animals could answer that he is reincarnated in them, this would leave the prophet reduced to a skulking beast. The "dank cleft" and the otter are, as an inheritance from the Scottish past, a far cry from the romantic ruins and singing minstrels of Scott's Newark Castle and Melrose Abbey. The now-ruined tower had begun as a spiritual place; it ends as a site of superstition. The brownie's cell is small, slimy, and silent; it discloses a Scotland of defeat, retreat, and reduction rather than a glorious past of chivalric warriors and thrilling battles. Visiting this place rather than the monuments glamorized by Scott with the aura of past romance, Wordsworth suggests that to see Scotland unsentimentally, as does the tourist who is off the beaten track and unswayed by national pride, is to know loss, suffering, extinction—the myths with which locals have endowed ruins bespeak a cultural memory of flight and of respect for those given wisdom as seers by their survival. But Wordsworth questions whether isolated endurance does bring wisdom and insight, resisting the tendency to rewrite bardic solitariness as hermitic truth. As such, the refugee is a corrective to Scott's and Ossian's romantic nationalism.[32] He is also a self-corrective: like the Solitary in *The Excursion*, he represents Wordsworth's warning to himself of the dangers involved in simplistically endorsing the perspective of sublime egotists who live alone in nature. He is, thus, an embodiment of the later Wordsworth's critical distance from the figure of the poet as "prophet of nature" that he had promulgated in *The Prelude* and his earlier lyrics—much to the derision of critics. That figure is not now rejected but is placed in historical and poetical context—as if resisting Scott's and Macpherson's minstrelizing of tradition gave Wordsworth disillusioned hindsight into the process of romantic mythologization by which he had formerly created his own poetic stature.

"The Brownie's Cell" adopts a highly unusual stanza that appears nowhere else in Wordsworth's oeuvre but that is reminiscent of the unusual stanzas Hogg utilized. It is distinct from, though related to, both the common meter stanzas of many old ballads and the pacy verse forms employed by Scott. It is intensely lyrical—consisting of five rhyming couplets—and unexpectedly asymmetrical. It opens by means of an iambic pentameter first line that signals a break, being longer than the ballad meter tetrameter lines that follow it, though joined to them by rhyme. Thus the ease and evenness that couplets normally produce is interrupted by the extra foot—an asymmetry that brings form to readers' attention and that delays the narrative flow. Each new stanza is visually and metrically marked as a separate stage. The form renders the subject matter—the historical events that occurred on the island in the loch at different periods—as a series of distinct, though similar, steps. The reader, conscious of the line's modulation—the falling away from the pentameter and its reassertion in each new stanza—is slowed, forced to scrutinize each one distinctly and to infer connections between them that are not explicitly made. Thus, though they are related, each acts as a distinct memorialization of a stage in the mediation of events by historical tradition. As in *The White Doe*, this slow and reflection-inducing form is a marked contrast to Scott—a means of making readers steadily contemplate relations between causes and effect, events and consequences, rather than hurry toward an action-packed climax.

Hogg's unusual stanzas appeared not only in *The Queen's Wake*, which Wordsworth admired, but also in a work directly concerned with war's effects on survivors, with superstition, and with brownies. *The Brownie of Bodsbeck* (1818) concerned the hunting down of the Covenanters—dissenting Scottish Protestants who refused to conform to church authority even when persecuted by the government and pursued by the army. Hogg's tale thus connected the brownie tradition with Scots history seen as a matter of religious and colonial repression. It is prefaced by a dedicatory poem to the Duchess of Buccleuch that presents Hogg's credentials as a local minstrel, able to sing of "what Scotland had, and now has not" because historical tradition has been handed down to him orally, on the scene, in the form of supernatural tales:

> And had'st thou lived where I was bred,
> Amid the scenes where martyrs bled,
> Their sufferings all to thee endear'd
> By those most honour'd and revered;
> And where the wild dark streamlet raves,
> Had'st wept above their lonely graves,
> Thou would'st have felt, I know it true,
> As I have done, and aye must do.
> And for the same exalted cause,
> For mankind's right, and nature's laws,

The cause of liberty divine,
Thy fathers bled as well as mine.

Then be it thine, O noble Maid,
On some still eve these tales to read;
And thou wilt read, I know full well,
For still thou lovest the haunted dell;
To linger by the sainted spring,
And trace the ancient fairy ring
Where moonlight revels long were held
In many a lone sequester'd field,
By Yarrow dens and Ettrick shaw,
And the green mounds of Carterhaugh.
. . . .
Such scenes, dear Lady, now no more
Are given, or fitted as before,
To eye or ear of guilty dust;
But when it comes, as come it must,
The time when I, from earth set free,
Shall turn the spark I fain would be;
If there's a land, as grandsires tell,
Where Brownies, Elves, and Fairies dwell,
There my first visit shall be sped—
Journeyer of earth, go hide thy head!

(lines 85–160)[33]

Wordsworth's ten-line couplet stanzas bear some resemblance to the twelve-line couplet stanzas Hogg uses here. Versifying the brownie tradition, Wordsworth used it, as Hogg did, as a local myth connected with historical violence—a tradition produced by the need of ordinary villagers to keep their sympathies with hunted religious fugitives secret and to preserve, in disguised form, the memory of those who had died for their proscribed beliefs. Hogg's tale honored these needs, if not the fanaticism to which they led. It concerned itself with a comparison between religious and superstitious belief, suggesting that they are shaped by similar social and political circumstances—not least by repression. It was Hogg's model that Wordsworth used, without the minstrel persona. "The Brownie's Cell" offered in verse what *The Brownie of Bodsbeck* sought in prose: a localized romance to contrast with Scott's romances and Macpherson's bardic nationalism in tracing the superstitions of the place to the unexorcized historical trauma that was their origin. In this respect Wordsworth found in Hogg a model he could use to think through the questions posed his art by the two Scots Romantics by whom he was most troubled.[34]

If the brownie's cell turns out to be no romantic ruin, then "The Brownie's Cell" is no Romantic poem. It is, rather, an anti-Romantic poem —one that conjures a Romantic scenario and methodology, only to place them in disenchanting contexts. A lyric memorial rather than pseudo-medieval romance, it is self-reflexive, as a memorial of Wordsworth's visit to a poet-prophet's memorial, a memorial where history's residue is present both in material form (a ruined tower) and in folklore (a local story engendered by place). It is a poem of belated witness: Wordsworth reports not the events but their successive displacement into after-effects on fugitive survivors, as reported later by a guide. He attests not to the thing itself— the past made present as in a spot of time—but the thing successively diminished as it is displaced into other forms. This is a process of remaindering—a process of discounted, reduced reproduction, in fragments and relics, material and cultural. Wordsworth is a spectator of and commentator on this process, rather than the *Prelude* poet who recollects a past of his own making or the Scott-ish poet who presents history anew as if it were happening now. Lateness is built into this position as a matter of a relative lack of power, an acceptance of imagination's inability to restore what has occurred or to repair damage caused. Distance is also built into it: away from his home ground, holidaying in others' poetic territory, Wordsworth stood far enough aside to be able to tell a story that put himself and his art in doubt. "The Brownie's Cell" continued his skeptical departure from the romanticization of the sole self to a more impersonal poetry in which it is civilized community, in the form of traditional institutions rather than oral tradition or solitary seeing, that maintains meaning and value against the depredations of time and history.

This departure is not fully achieved in the poem as originally written (although, as we shall see, it is attempted in the reworked ending Wordsworth composed in 1831). The original ending does, nevertheless, turn aside from the mythologization of the survivor as a prophet and from the romanticization of Scottish history as nostalgia for feudal society. Mid-stanza, Wordsworth corrects his imagination, averting his mind's eye from the dank cleft and from oral tradition's memorialization of the last vestiges of clan culture:

> but be thou curb'd,
> O froward Fancy! mid a scene
> Of aspect winning and serene;
> For those offensive creatures shun
> The inquisition of the sun!
>
> (lines 74–78)

Wordsworth turns from dark to light, from death to life. The island around the ruined tower and dank cleft is in full flower. Nature repairs historical violence and its traumatic aftermath, replacing solitary endurance with an enlivening spirit of Fancy that elicits a sensual and fertile response:

> And in this region flowers delight,
> And all is lovely to the sight.
>
> Spring finds not here a melancholy breast,
> When she applies her annual test
> To dead and living; when her breath
> Quickens, as now, the withered heath;—
> Nor flaunting Summer—when he throws
> His soul into the briar-rose;
> Or calls the lily from her sleep
> Prolong'd beneath the bordering deep;
> Nor Autumn, when the viewless wren
> Is warbling near the BROWNIE's Den.
>
> (lines 79–90)

The den does not have to be seen as the last residue of a Scottish history tainted by crime, treachery, and war. Looking around rather than peering within, the visiting poet views it as part of a revival—surrounded by nature's delightful and social creativity. But the significance of this way of seeing cannot be delivered by Scottish superstitions and traditions. Wordsworth opts instead for an Ovidian mythology in which the world is organized by the metamorphosis resulting from desire and love, rather than by the remaindering produced by war and trauma. He now sees not the residue of Scottish violence and suffering, but a nursery for the pagan god of fertility—a place so lush that it is fit to shelter the divine embodiment of nature's power:

> Wild Relique! beauteous as the chosen spot
> In Nysa's isle, the embellish'd Grot;
> Whither, by care of Libyan Jove,
> (High Servant of paternal Love)
> Young Bacchus was conveyed—to lie
> Safe from his step-dame Rhea's eye;
> Where bud, and bloom, and fruitage, glowed,
> Close-crowding round the Infant God;
> All colours,—and the liveliest streak
> A foil to his celestial cheek!
>
> (lines 91–100)

Nysa's African isle was a hideout in which Amalthea and Bacchus, her son by Jove, were secure from the revenge of Jove's jealous wife Rhea. It was a fabled place whose luscious vegetation echoed Jove's potent promiscuity—a fit locale for the infant god of fertility, frenzy, and wine. A most unScottish place when used to illustrate an island in Loch Lomond, and a decidedly literary one, deriving from classical myth and from the neoclassical poetry of Pope and Milton. In *Paradise Lost*, Eden is said to be still more beautiful than "that Nyseian Ile / Girt with the River Triton, where old Cham, / Whom Gentiles Ammon call and Lybian Jove, / Hid Amalthea and her florid son / Young Bacchus from his stepdame Rhea's eye" (IV, 75–79). Ending with an allusion to classical myth rather than to Scottish superstition or bardic tradition, Wordsworth rejects solitary reclusion from the world in favor of delight in a nature driven by sexuality. This is an unexpected turn, unparalleled in the Scots ballads and traditions he began the poem by invoking. But it is not uncommon in Wordsworth's poems of 1814 and later, which often turn to Ovid and prefer Fancy to Imagination (see Chapters 4 and 5 for examples). It is a development of the move made in *The Excursion* that so inspired Keats in *Endymion* and reveals Wordsworth countering his own desire to embrace the role of hermitic prophet in the wilderness. It is also, I think, a response to what he valued in Burns—not by way of imitation but through evocation of a poetic consciousness finding in supernatural belief a form in which to contemplate its own fertile creativity. Burns treated Scottish tradition in this way when in "Tam O'shanter" and "Address to the Deil" he occupied the tipsy mind of a narrator seeing the world through drunken eyes. Wordsworth had approved of this strategy in 1816, and though he turns from the brownies and kelpies seen by Burns to Greek myths as portrayed by Milton, he nonetheless makes the island the nursery of the god of drunkenness: where Burns puts Tam, Wordsworth puts Bacchus. Both embody the creative playfulness and transformation of perception that result from sensual indulgence. Wordsworth's term for this was "poetry of the fancy," and here it is used to summon a way of being (and instance a way of thinking and writing) that embraces variety and change, so as to highlight the dangers of self-consciously cultivating a prophetic imagination.[35] "The Brownie's Cell," in other words, both ponders and sketches a poetic alternative to the "prophet of nature" role that Wordsworth sought in and by *The Prelude*. The alternative seems necessary because, disenchanted, he sees in Scottish history that imagination may be a self-authorizing seduction: its rhetorical power may arise from and compensate for historical defeat but it does not thereby necessarily utter truth or allow change.

The bacchic and Ovidian was a mode of which Wordsworth rapidly became wary. When he looked back on the poem in 1843, he was quick to play up its Protestant piety and to differentiate it from Burns:

> The account of the "Brownie's Cell" and the Brownies was given me by a man we met with on the banks of Loch Lomond, a little above Tarbert, and in front of a huge mass of rock, by the side of which, we were told, preachings were often held in the open air. The place is quite a solitude, and the surrounding scenery very striking. How much is it to be regretted that, instead of writing such Poems as the "Holy Fair" and others, in which the religious observances of his country are treated with so much levity and too often with indecency, Burns had not employed his genius in describing religion under the serious and affecting aspects it must so frequently take.[36]

Here, Wordsworth's poem is shown to have stemmed from sources similar to those that engendered Burns's flights of imagination—villagers' tales; it will, however, supplement a lack in that imagination and thus enact a critique. Burns's "Holy Fair" was a satire that gently mocked the vanity of open-air preachers and the less-than-pious motives that many of the congregation had for meeting. Its indulgent portrait of ordinary folk using the religious occasion as an opportunity to exchange gossip, discuss business, and flirt with the opposite sex bespoke a modern Scotland far removed from the puritan intensity—not to say Protestant fanaticism—of its relatively recent past. Visiting the site of a prayer meeting, Wordsworth, as he sees it from the viewpoint of 1843, replaces Burns's skepticism about spirituality with an examination of the relationship between religion and superstition. Where Burns was jocular, he was sober about the creative effects of past and place on people's imaginations. The 1842 "Brownie's Cell" imagines a local spirit inhabiting a place, as Burns had done, but the poem is a corrective as well as a homage to the vivifying and playful imagination that created, and is the subject of, poems such as "Address to the Deil." Whereas in Burns, kelpies, selkies, brownies, and the devil himself are addressed with humorous bravado as incarnations of the poet's imaginative playfulness and are taken seriously only by superstitious old women, country wives, drunkards, and freemasons, in Wordsworth imaginative belief is not to be a matter of jocularity. He would have readers share, for the space of the poem, the local belief in spirits so as to see that belief—whether superstitious legend or religious doctrine—as the residue of the extraordinary historical events that once occurred at the place. The supernatural turns out to be a traditional form of memorialization of events that cross the boundary of life and death. Thus "The Brownie's Cell" renews the lyrical ballads project, but in a self-consciously historicized form made possible by Wordsworth's position as a visiting tourist rather than a rooted local. The mobile perspective that the traveler possesses allows a disenchanted and comparative understanding of how, why, and when belief occurs and flourishes. Wordsworth offers an archaeology of belief in order to trace the development of historically informed awe, whereas Burns aims to leave readers reveling in his playful enjoyment of the ability that imagination gives him to conjure spirits in poetry without believing in them as the local people do.

Such was the later Wordsworth's reflection on his old piece. It is not the perspective of the poet who published it in 1820, but, despite his omission of the poem's pagan ending, it does indicate that it was motivated by the need to respond to and differ from the kinds of poeticization of history and legend then prominent in Scotland. Just as he eschewed the ballad and romance genres, he turned to classical myth as an answer to Burns's playful imagination and as an alternative to Scott's and Macpherson's romanticization of the oral tradition. Recoiling from a history he portrayed as a chain of displacements of trauma and from a commemoration he depicted as a tradition of honoring isolated remnants whether or not their isolation made them authentically representative, Wordsworth turned from a human past to a natural present of growth and fertility. Thus he signaled his departure from Scott-land and his determination to lyricize Scottish places and past in new poetic forms and modes—even if he had to import a Mediterranean mythology to do so.

"The Brownie's Cell" is the best of the 1814 memorials. It is the piece in which Wordsworth probed most carefully into the meaning of tradition, the nature of commemoration, the pitfalls of romantic nationalist history, and, beneath it all, the destructive and traumatizing effects of war, both on its immediate victims and on those who follow them in a culture whose past is dominated by violence, feuding, destruction, and defeat. Wordsworth demythologizes the glorifications of that past offered by his contemporaries; his is altogether a more unorthodox, more disturbing, and more serious a representation of history than theirs. He is, in fact, a profound poet of war and of the trauma of war.

The Tourist Memorials of 1827

The turn to the lyrical memorial from the autobiographical effort to regain lost time, and from the rendition of rustic orality in the ballad, was more still more strongly made in Wordsworth's next collection, the *Poetical Works* of 1827. Here, the 1814 poems were first grouped as a separate section under the "memorial" and "tour"-poem banners. Wordsworth added "Effusion, in the Pleasure-Ground on the Banks of the Bran, near Dunkeld" and "Yarrow Visited" and, significantly, gave them a title— "Memorials of a Tour in Scotland, 1814." The title drew attention to memory, branding the poems as tourist souvenirs, snapshots returning to many-times-visited spots; it thus revised the 1803/1807 "Poems Written During a Tour of Scotland." The 1827 Wordsworth was interested in foregrounding return and retrieval.

"Effusion, in the Pleasure-Ground on the Banks of the Bran, near Dunkeld" derived from a return to a commemorative site that Wordsworth had visited in 1803. On that first occasion, Dorothy had recorded that the River

Bran was accessed via "a small apartment, where the gardener desired us to look at a painting of Ossian, which, while he was telling us the story of the young artists who performed the work, disappeared . . . flying asunder as if by the touch of magic, and lo! we are at the entrance of a splendid room, which was almost dizzy and alive with waterfalls" reflected "in innumerable mirrors upon the ceiling and against the walls."[37] William's poem amplifies Dorothy's distaste, objecting to the "pantomime" "scene, fantastic and uneasy / As ever made a maniac dizzy" with "baubles of theatric taste" (lines 34, 27–28, 120). Wordsworth sees the staging as a cheap trick that trifles both with nature and the visitor; it is evidence of a commercialized, degenerate taste that turns the place and its history into pageantry and performance:

> Vain Pleasures of luxurious life,
> For ever with yourselves at strife;
> Through town and country both deranged
> By affectations interchanged,
> And all the perishable gauds
> That heaven-deserted Man applauds;
> When will your hapless Patrons learn
> To watch and ponder—to discern
> The freshness, the eternal youth,
> Of admiration sprung from truth;
> From beauty infinitely growing
> Upon a mind with love o'erflowing;
> To sound the depths of every Art
> That seeks its wisdom through the heart?
>
> (lines 105–18; 1827, III, pp. 68–74)

Recoiling from the scene, Wordsworth defines his own aesthetic of unadorned simplicity (an aesthetic embodied in the simple rhyming couplet form). He does so by turning to a hermit's retreat. Not only does this retreat represent spiritual quiet and focused concentration—the opposite of the frenetic display on the River Bran—but it also provides an example of how to memorialize the past. It is "guarded" by a plain statue in commemoration of a knight who, after the hermit's death, had intervened to prevent the monks of Fountains Abbey removing the hermit's body so as to display it as an object of veneration—a visitor attraction for pilgrims.

Memorials of the Scottish past, Wordsworth concludes, should be of similar kind. Whereas the viewing house on the Bran had exhibited the figure of Ossian on a painted board that was whisked aside to reveal the reflected waterfall, a proper Scottish art would embody his haunting spirit by carving out a statue from the cliffs bordering the river:

> Then let him hew with patient stroke
> An Ossian out of mural rock,
> And leave the figurative Man
> Upon thy Margin, roaring Bran!
> Fixed, like the Templar of the steep,
> An everlasting watch to keep;
> With local sanctities in trust,
> More precious than a Hermit's dust;
> And virtues through the mass infused,
> Which old Idolatry abused.
>
> (lines 84–93)

There would be no trickery, no performance to such a statue; if it seemed to come to life, this would be solely because the forces of nature played over it:

> What though the Granite would deny
> All fervour to the sightless eye;
> And touch from rising Suns in vain
> Solicit a Memnonian strain;
> Yet, in some fit of anger sharp,
> The Wind might force the deep-grooved harp
> To utter melancholy moans
> Not unconnected with the tones
> Of soul-sick flesh and weary bones;
> While grove and river notes would lend,
> Less deeply sad, with these to blend!
>
> (lines 94–104)

Sound rather than sight: here Wordsworth's preference for the wind's moans and the grove's and river's notes reveals that he wants to found his own poetic authority on his ability to articulate the sounds of nature. These sounds are more authentically local, and therefore more reliably represent-able, than either the songs of Ossian himself or the pleasure-ground specta-cle. The songs are probably manufactured fakes, neither genuinely old nor local; the spectacle is a hall-of-mirrors showground trick. Both reveal the ways in which even the most traditional, specific, and rooted aspects of a place can be virtualized. Too easily represented in other media and then circulated as a commodity uprooted from its local context, Ossian in songs, in print, and in picturesque spectacle is unreliable—the figure of an art that lacks weight because it glories in its own ability to float free of its spatiotemporal origins. An unmoored signifier, it ignores history in his-tory's name. The statue, by contrast, depends on local processes: fixed, stalwart, and voiced by the motions of nature, it represents one of Words-worth's aspirations for his own art, an aspiration built upon his unease that he is, in fact, a tourist making a brief stay and, rather than a local bard, a visiting writer committed to circulating the place in the visual medium of print published in London—the metropolitan center of the theatricality that he now sees on the Bran. In other words, the picturesque viewing station, importing an urban culture of tricksy visual mobility to the coun-try, pricks Wordsworth's anxious conscience about the participation of his own writing in that culture. Imagining a local statue that roots Ossianic song to the spot is wish fulfillment meant to assuage that conscience, but it remains a fantasy and Wordsworth is left discomfited, unsure of where he and his writing stand. "I mused," the poem ends, "and, thirsting for redress, / Recoiled into the wilderness" (lines 127–28).

Recoil dramatizes the problem of poetic memorialization of tradition—of, therefore, past poetry. It is a self-reflexive quandary, as well as a gesture of rejection at the trivialization of a historical site. It is a gesture that links the "Effusion" with "The Brownie's Cell" as one of a series of reflections on the problems of memorialization attendant on the poet's own position as a contemporary visitor writing for print rather than an ancient local singing on the spot, as a visitor also committed to a poetic ideal of orality and to the writing of ballads and lyrics, and as a man steeped in the songs and ballads of the Scottish tradition who regards current Scots' trivializa-tion of that tradition as a minstrelized, sentimentalized, romanticized show. On the Bran, finding no resolution of these pitfalls, he turns back to the wilderness: on the banks of Loch Lomond he turns forward to a natural fertility sexualized by Greek mythology; he cannot, in the face of his tran-sience and the predominance of trivialization, embody Scotland, present and past, as its national poet, only criticize those who are currently fashionable and propose alternative routes to theirs. In this respect, the genre of the tour sequence offers an advantage to compensate for Wordsworth's lack of locality and orality: by moving from place to place in poem after poem, it enables the poet to offer perspectives not available to those who only vie to be the authentic mediator of their spot and its history. They know not the Bran, Cora Linn, and Lomond—they know not Scotland, Wordsworth implies, who only Scotland know. He may not know it either, but in demystifying others' representations of its places and past, he demonstrates the dangers of claiming—on behalf of tradition, on behalf of the nation—to embody Scottish history and identity.

Rememorialization of the Memorial: The Brownie in 1831 and 1835

In 1831 Wordsworth visited Scotland again, returning to Yarrow and the Tweed and bidding farewell to an ailing Scott who, having suffered a stroke, was departing for Italy in a vain attempt to restore his health. The encounter left Wordsworth elegiac and retrospective in "Yarrow Revisited," the parting gift he drafted on his return from the tour and sent to Scott. It was now that he was moved both to become more personal in his poeticization of place and to set out a manifesto of poetry as memorialization:

> And what, for this frail world, were all
>   That mortals do or suffer,
> Did no responsive harp, no pen,
>   Memorial tribute offer
> Yea, what were mighty Nature's self?
>   Her features, could they win us,
> Unhelped by the poetic voice
>   That hourly speaks within us?
>
> Nor deem that localised Romance
>   Plays false with our affections;
> Unsanctifies our tears—made sport
>   For fanciful dejections:
> Ah, no! the visions of the past
>   Sustain the heart in feeling

Life as she is—our changeful Life,
   With friends and kindred dealing.

(lines 81–96; YR, pp. 3–8)

These lines articulate a late, retrospective poetic, a response to the pressures that time places upon the aging writer. Localized romance—envisioning the past, if not recovering it whole, in poetry—sustains meaning, preserving the self in a remembered community of loved ones when those loved ones leave, sicken, and die.

"Yarrow Revisited" gave its name to a collection of 1835, published after Scott's death, in which localized romances were moved to the fore. The volume included two Scottish tour sequences, each of which featured poems that responded to places Wordsworth had visited previously. These poems reflected on the effect of a visited place having been visited many times before; they also responded to old poems written about the same spots years earlier. The sequences were thus doubly retrospective and revisionary, revisiting Wordsworth's textual past as well as his touristic route. Effectively an archive of Wordsworth's past poetic visits, they were in dialogue with the kind of poet he had been in 1814 and 1803, recontextualizing old work, self-reflexively presenting temporal loss and memorial as textual as well as experiential affairs. Wordsworth measured the passing of his life and the lives of his friends by checking, in print, one textualized spot against another.

One of the poems featured in the sequence deriving from the 1831 tour was "The Brownie," a sonnet that is a response, or even an alternative ending, to "The Brownie's Cell." Wordsworth's headnote alerts readers to its 1814 origins, although not to the earlier poem:

> Upon a small island not far from the head of Loch Lomond are some remains of an ancient building, which was for several years the abode of a solitary individual, one of the last survivors of the clan of Macfarlane, once powerful in that neighborhood. Passing along the shore opposite this island in the year 1814, the author learned these particulars, and that this person then living there had acquired the appellation of "The Brownie."

"How disappeared he?" Ask the newt and toad;
Ask of his fellow men, and they will tell

How he was found, cold as an icicle,
Under an arch of that forlorn abode;
Where he, unpropp'd, and by the gathering flood
Of years hemm'd round, had dwelt, prepared to try
Privation's worst extremities, and die
With no one near save the omnipresent God.
Verily so to live was an awful choice,—
A choice that wears the aspect of a doom;
But in the mould of mercy all is cast
For Souls familiar with the eternal Voice;
And this forgotten Taper to the last
Drove from itself, we trust, all frightful gloom.

(YR, p. 22)

The sonnet's opening line is taken from the earlier poem, but what follows rejects the bacchic paganism of 1820 in favor of belated historical witness. The newt and toad had represented possible metamorphoses, but Wordsworth no longer pursues either Scottish or Greek myths of reincarnation and the fertile transformation of one life-form to another. The beasts will not answer as to the brownie's fate, but "fellow men" will: and the poet is a witness of their witness, a memorial of memory. Local tradition, in 1831, is more confidently invoked than in 1820, because it has no miracles to report, only a grim process of solitary aging and decline, an occupation of a locale that amounts to a form of emplacedness. The place's history and meaning are embodied in its self-supporting ("unpropp'd") hermit: his form of dwelling is also a mode of being toward death. Wordsworth now imagines a cold pastoral indeed, with no trace, as formerly, of nature's annual return to life or of man's prophetic power. Nature is inimical in this perspective: the lake surrounding the island features not in its own right but as a metaphor for encroaching time ("by the gathering flood / Of years hemm'd round," lines 5–6). The brownie is no longer exemplary for any past deeds or visions but because his solitary endurance so starkly wills as a choice what most people merely suffer without insight: he is a paragon of death-directed being in time.

Wordsworth is not Sartre, however strongly he anticipates him. He invokes a religious mercy that is available after death ("But in the mould of mercy all is cast / For Souls familiar with the eternal Voice," lines 11–12). Yet this mercy is to be found, if found at all, via a stark, austere duality.

There is temporal man and there is an "eternal voice": Wordsworth does not mention the redeeming Christ or even a fatherly God. The eternal, as voice, seems rather to be an abstraction and mystification of the judgmental orality that Wordsworth seeks for himself as a poet reporting (deciding) on his character's fate. He voices his own discourse as God—in so many words. If this voice is, on the surface, more conventional than in 1820, speaking in Judeo-Christian terms rather than embracing paganism, it is nonetheless, underneath, less hopeful about spiritual rebirth and natural vitality. Indeed, for a renowned nature poet, it is astonishingly world-renouncing. But it is arresting: that is to say, the 1831 poem aims to put a stop to the potentially endless chain of substitutions endorsed in 1820. Speaking confidently as a reliable reporter of reliable witnesses, it controls the textual remaindering in which "The Brownie's Cell" mediated history (brownie = chapel > tower > ruin > cell; or = monk > clansmen > survivor > newt > otter > Jove the sex god > Bacchus the god of drunken frenzy). Endless insemination and dissemination—an Ovidian natural/textual pairing—is repressed in 1831's formally constrained and carefully truncated text. The eternal voice is final.

Only it is not final. Having spoken for and as that voice, Wordsworth at once climbs down from this hubristic personification of his textual presence. He ends, instead, on a note of inconclusive tentativeness: "And this forgotten Taper to the last / Drove from itself, we trust, all frightful gloom" (lines 13–14). Who, here, has forgotten the taper? The hermit or the fellow men or the reader? "We trust" tacitly admits doubt, highlighting the limits of the poet's witness: he and his informants do not—cannot—know the dying solitary's emotional condition or his state of enlightenment, still less his fate after death. The poem's move to consolation and to judgment is turned aside: the past remains a place we take on trust, but what we trust is not clear, given the attenuation of the Christian God to a voice (saying what?).

If the 1831 poem is ambivalent in its own textual logic, it is still more so in its effect on the 1820 text, because, of course, it cannot cancel the 1820 ending, only present an alternative to it—a limitation that undoes the finality it would assert. Both poems continued to appear separately in Wordsworth's collections: the metamorphic paganism and the austere existentialism remained in play, challenging each other. 1831 is a later, but not the last, word—a problematic situation given that whether there is, or should be, a last word is the issue the poems dramatize in their scrutiny of history and poetry. The dialogue between the two versions prevents either being, any more than the local legends are, the final culmination of the process of substitution that passes memory through time. It reveals that the poet's view shifts with departure and return and shows that retrospect does not necessarily produce a more complete perspective, just a different one— and in this respect it undoes the illusion Wordsworth worked so hard to achieve when revisiting old haunts in "Tintern Abbey" and recollecting former spots in *The Prelude*. The tour-poem dialogue deconstructs these earlier, Romantic poems (seen now, though not in his lifetime, as his central oeuvre), because it replays them from a position—formal as well as temporal—of irredeemable lateness. Visit, departure, and revisit, and therefore absence and difference, as well as re-presence, are built into the pairing. So is rewriting, but return and revision do not cancel and are not canceled by the original text. It is, then, the process of representation as remaindering—as the production of related differences that cannot be collapsed into continuity or oneness—that his poems comment on and themselves enact, and in this they align themselves, as printed texts published away from the locality, with local oral tradition as a series of often contradictory substitutions rather than an unbroken stream of historical witness. The past is another country, and vice versa, but it is memorializing writing that repeatedly presents it as such.

Rewriting the Oral: Wordsworth's Ossian—1827, 1833, 1835, 1845

After 1820, the tour sequences that dominated Wordsworth's publications were often reconstructed for subsequent editions and later collections so that they featured poems written at different times and published years before. They were, in effect, memorial archives that juxtaposed the different responses to a place he had made on different visits, giving those responses the appearance of temporal simultaneity under the flag of a tour made in a particular year. The verse of 1824 and 1827 appeared in 1845 as that of an 1833 experience: immediacy was an illusion constructed in print rather than an autobiographical claim. Faithfulness to temporal experience—keeping to time—was now openly an effect of bookmaking, a means, on paper, of assembling poems so that thematically similar though temporally different responses to a place were brought into dialogue on an equal footing. "1833" (first published in 1835) was a fabrication and could be seen by informed readers to be so; as a consequence it could not be presumed to succeed to "1803" (first published in 1807) and "1814" (first published in 1827). Rather than a temporal arc, with its inevitable connotations of passage from innocence to experience, youth to age, and foresight to hindsight, Wordsworth's tour sequences presented zones of interaction within and between which old texts, printed as if new, pressed their claims on new ones. Early and late stood alongside each other as works of an equal moment as the reader went back and forth in the volumes and pages of Wordsworth's publications. Behind this development was the need of an older poet with a long career behind him to set his work in order, for his own sake and to impress a public that had ignored his early verse, by re-presenting his old poems—reviving them as if new so as to bring them into interaction with those more recently written rather than relegating them to the past.

"Written in a Blank Leaf of Macpherson's Ossian," one of the finest of the memorials, is a case in point. This poem revisited previous memorials of the mythical bard—not only "Effusion . . . Bran" (where Ossian was to be commemorated by a statue on the riverbank) but also the "Essay Supplementary" (where Ossian was attacked as a fake and a bad poet of place) and the 1803 tour poem "Glen-Almain; or, The Narrow Glen" (where Ossian is symbolized by a peaceful and secluded valley). In dialogue with these earlier texts, "Written in a Blank Leaf" makes the mediation of place, and poetic song, an issue at the level of form as well as content. It was written (probably) in 1824 and published in 1827 as a Poem of Sentiment and Reflection rather than a tour poem; in 1845 it was repositioned in the sequence of poems deriving from Wordsworth's 1833 tour of Scotland (a sequence first published in 1835). This repositioning drew attention to the fact that the sequence was an artifact constructed and reconstructed for publication—a print genre containing poems composed at different times that only posed as a record of verse responses to a single journey. It belied the Romantic poetic of immediate response to nature: it was clearly not in any organic sense the product of a "spontaneous overflow of powerful feelings, recollected in tranquillity" (LB, p. 756).

In the 1845 reconstruction of the "1833" sequence, "Written in a Blank Leaf" appeared after two sonnets prompted by returning, later, to a previously toured and versified spot. In "On Revisiting Dunolly Castle," Wordsworth found the eagle that had formerly been chained to its battlements, and that he had apostrophized in an 1831 poem, gone. Imagining it liberated, or dead, he consoled himself that a mosaic picture of an eagle on the floor of the castle memorialized the bird and the fierce and brave Scottish history the bird symbolized:

Effigy of the Vanished—(shall I dare
To call thee so?) or symbol of fierce deeds
And of the towering courage which past times
Rejoiced in—take, whate'er thou be, a share,
Not undeserved, of the memorial rhymes
That animate my way where'er it leads!

(lines 9–14; 1845, p. 354)

Here the "effigy" of the eagle is an image of Wordsworth's own art: his "memorial rhymes" are akin to it in their mediation of place and past, hence they pay tribute to it—memorializing the memorial, remediating the mediation. So, Wordsworth implies, memory is perpetuated by art. However, in the very next poem, this implication is questioned. "The Dunolly Eagle" reveals that the bird, having been freed from its perch by a storm, had not flown off to crag or clouds but to the castle dungeon, where he now lived "kennelled and chained" (line 7). The majestic bird of prey, scared of freedom, had become a willing captive, immured in a castle that was itself a relic of Scotland's lost independence, ruined after its clan chiefs' involvement in the civil wars that resulted from the seventeenth-century revolution in England. The eagle represented the perversion of liberty into slavery; Scotland's present offered a memorial of tyranny and of broken spirits, rather than recalling a past of chivalry and bravery:

Balanced in ether he will never tarry,
Eyeing the sea's blue depths. Poor Bird! even so
Doth man of brother man a creature make
That clings to slavery for its own sad sake.

(lines 11–14; 1845, p. 354)

Placed after the Dunolly sonnets, "Written in a Blank Leaf" is read as part of a debate about memorials in various media, and the reliability of the mediations of history that they effect. Its very title alerts us to these issues, because Macpherson's printed book of Ossian's oral songs was a cause célèbre for its forgery of the past. Macpherson, notoriously, never produced manuscript evidence to demonstrate the true antiquity of the poems he printed, and they had not survived, either, in oral tradition. Wordsworth had derided him as a faker in the "Essay Supplementary" on these grounds and also because his lyricization was lacking in the distinctness and vitality associated with ancient poets who responded directly to nature. Thus to publish a poem called "Written in a Blank Leaf of Macpherson's Ossian" was to highlight the problems of authenticity surrounding print and to dramatize the vagaries of transmission from voice to script.[38] Wordsworth's poem, that is, was a printed text posing as a piece of manuscript marginalia inscribed on another printed text which was itself supposedly a publication of the collected manuscript fragments that survived an ancient oral poet. Inscribing the blank page, Wordsworth alludes to the absence of handwritten pages behind Macpherson's printed text and thus to the incompleteness and unreliability of its mediation of "Ossian's" lyricization of the Scottish past. But this allusion also, willy nilly, emphasizes that Wordsworth's own poem is a printed text and only notionally a manuscript inscription; it only gesturally supplements Macpherson's volumes by compensating for their lack of the writer's hand. Wordsworth's poetry—all poetry—it follows, is shown to have a complex and not necessarily reliable relationship to the medium of its dissemination; all mediation involves alteration. Alteration, however, is not to be feared; in Wordsworth's eyes, Macpherson's sin stems from his inability to admit that a lossless transmission of the remote original is not possible. Not desirable either, since "fragments of far-off melodies," "caught upon a fitful breeze" can charm his soul without his "coveting the whole" (lines 2, 1, 3). The sounds and sights that fleetingly cross the poet's consciousness, in a particular place and time, are, he suggests, taken up as fragments of song. And this shaped oral response itself undergoes partial remediation—not just as writing, but also as manuscript and as print. Thus, in print that pretends to be a manuscript transcription of speech (as if self-reflexively contrasting his verse's playfully multiple media-affiliations with Macpherson's rigid dependence on temporal progression from voice to manuscript to publication), Wordsworth apostrophizes Macpherson's book:

What need, then, of these finished Strains?
Away with counterfeit Remains!
An abbey in its lone recess,
A temple of the wilderness,

Wrecks though they be, announce with feeling
The majesty of honest dealing.

(lines 11–16; 1845, pp. 354–55)

The Wordsworthian context invoked here is the chantry chapel that became
the brownie's cell and the ruined Grace Dieu and Bolton Abbey—
fragmentary remains of sources of spiritual and poetic power. The point is
that such diminished remnants, admittedly partial, are plain tokens of the
losses that the original sustains through time; as such, they enable "honest
dealing"—a poetry that accepts that partiality and fragmentation are attendant upon its mediations of the source, rather than one that fakes that
source's complete retrieval.

As he continues, Wordsworth paradoxically both addresses Ossian's
spirit—as if it could hear and speak—and doubts that it can be found
within language, since Macpherson has so falsely put words in its mouth
that its true discourse is almost impossible to discern. If it can be found, it
will be in "shattered and impaired" fragments of speech or writing and via
the "memorial claim" of places that traditionally call it to mind (line 21).
Here Wordsworth is in dialogue with his 1803 tour poem "Glen-Almain;
or, The Narrow Glen," in which commemoration by local tradition seems
relatively unproblematic. Visiting the glen—a calm, austere, secluded
recess—Wordsworth was then surprised to find it associated with Ossian
since, given his martial poetry, that poet should, he naively thinks, be linked
with a turbulent, disturbed, harsh place. Traveling further into the glen, he
revises his opinion and accedes to the local custom, learning how and why
local memorialization works:

The separation that is here
Is of the grave; and of austere
And happy feelings of the dead:
And, therefore, was it rightly said
That Ossian, last of all his race!
Lies buried in this lonely place.

(lines 27–32; 1807, II, pp. 16–17)

Interacting with this poem, "Written in a Blank Leaf" focuses memorialization and mediation as Wordsworth's central poetic concern—in Scotland and further abroad. More than the texts it was published alongside,

however, the poem makes "Ossian" a figure of a specifically linguistic problem:

> Spirit of Ossian! if imbound
> In language thou may'st yet be found,
> If aught (intrusted to the pen
> Or floating on the tongues of men,
> Albeit shattered and impaired)
> Subsist thy dignity to guard,
> In concert with memorial claim
> Of old grey stone, and high-born name
> That cleaves to rock or pillared cave
> Where moans the blast, or beats the wave
>
> (lines 17–26)

Here, the name "Ossian" endures better, is less lost in translation, when inscribed onto the landscape by memorial tradition than when written into a book. But even here inscription is subject to further mediation. The name "cleaves to rock" and cave but is then reflected in the sounds of the sea rebounding from that rock and of the wind funneling through that cave. Nevertheless, sounds, although fleeting, moan and beat; they are more powerfully present mediators than tongues or pages, and if this seems like Wordsworth's familiar attempt to bypass culture and portray poetry as a direct overflowing of nature, it is nonetheless complicated by the fact that this particular poem advertises its cultural status as, problematically, printed verse in a publication of Wordsworth's that pretends to be a handwritten note in a book of Macpherson's. As in "The Brownie's Cell," transmission is a process of metamorphosis into diminished forms— remaindering. A poem cannot long escape its own implication in this process, hence Wordsworth's sudden need to arrest it by summoning an external authority:

> Let Truth, stern arbitress of all,
> Interpret that Original,
> And for presumptuous wrongs atone;—
> Authentic words be given, or none!
>
> (lines 27–30)

The optative mood of the verb "let" makes the poet into truth's usher, or less modestly, her taskmaster. She works upon his word, for she is a creation of it, a verbal goddess existing only as poetic allegory. Wordsworth claims the authority to make her present, make her interpret, and make her atone for forgery; he summons her as a timeless solution to the endless remediation of the original in which human discourse, being timebound, participates. She will produce either perfect clarity and perfect recovery— lossless rendering of original words—or silence. Yet she is an impossible fantasy, and he knows it, for she is a poetic figure—as a personification— that he uses to imagine a language that would, effectively, put an end to figuration. Absolute originality and authenticity would preclude the transformations effected by poetic language. "Truth," then, militates against the very discourse in which Wordsworth invents her: she represents his desire to bring words to book (finally), to end his writer's frustration that they "slip, slide, perish, / Decay with imprecision, will not stay in place, / Will not stay still"[39]—a slipperiness that unscrupulous poets such as Macpherson take advantage of.

No sooner said than undone. Wordsworth turns away from the fantasy of final judgment and perfect authenticity to a lament for, that is also an acceptance of, the world in which poets' lyric tracing of nature's evanescence alters and decays over time and is retrieved in fragments, if at all.

> Time is not blind;—yet He, who spares
> Pyramid pointing to the stars,
> Hath preyed with ruthless appetite
> On all that marked the primal flight
> Of the poetic ecstasy
> Into the land of mystery.
> No tongue is able to rehearse
> One measure, Orpheus! of thy verse;
> Musaeus, stationed with his lyre
> Supreme among the Elysian quire,
> Is, for the dwellers upon earth,
> Mute as a lark ere morning's birth.

(lines 31–42)

Musaeus may be inaudible to mortals, but morning does come and larks do then sing. Resurgence remains a possibility.

Faced with time's depredations on their song, poets are heroes. To commit to making poems, Wordsworth's metaphors suggest, is to undertake an existential quest or to undergo trials: it is to "survive / Privation," like the brownie:

Hail, Bards of mightier grasp! on you
I chiefly call, the chosen Few,
Who cast not off the acknowledged guide,
Who faltered not, nor turned aside;
Whose lofty Genius could survive
Privation, under sorrow thrive[.]

(lines 53–58)

What results from this winnowing by time and the word is an affirmation that memorialization depends on love. The mighty bards are remembered, in translation, because they "a plenitude of love retained" (line 66). Their translation, however, is not from "original" song to manuscript to print; it is from human voice to the sounds and sights of nature as figured by the imagination of fellow locals:

Ye lingered among human kind,
Sweet voices for the passing wind,
Departing sunbeams, loth to stop,
Though smiling on the last hill top!
Such to the tender-hearted maid
Even ere her joys begin to fade;
Such, haply, to the rugged chief
By Fortune crushed, or tamed by grief;
Appears, on Morven's lonely shore,
Dim-gleaming through imperfect lore,
The Son of Fingal; such was blind
Maeonides of ampler mind;
Such Milton, to the fountain head
Of glory by Urania led!

(lines 69–82)

Here Ossian is redefined as the consoling voice, the loving form, heard and seen by subsequent generations in his and their country. Neither textual, nor oral, he is instead an imaginary figure / figure of imagination, a fleeting and fragmentary materialization of minds taught by traditional lore to articulate their troubles and needs in words handed down from the past in the place they inhabit. He is the presiding figure of their localized romance—their love of country—as Homer and Milton were in their places, and it is as such, rather than by the production of authentic texts that perfectly transfer song to manuscript to print, that poets live—and matter. This reimagined Ossian is, of course, a figure of Wordsworth's poetry, a haunting presence brought into being by this verse and as a personification of it. He is also a sign of the poet Wordsworth wanted to be—a figure, however imperfectly formed, in the minds and hearts of the people: posterity's compensation for the public's reluctance to buy his publications.

To escape print and paper was an impossible Romantic fantasy, and "Written in a Blank Leaf" both indulges and undermines it. It is both a song of partial retrieval and a text of remediation. Self-canceling, it dramatizes the impossibility of making an authentic representation of the original and of being a true embodiment of its poet-bard, showing poetry's memorialization of place and past to cycle repeatedly through orality, writing, and print, all of which articulate and none of which comprehend the trace of nature's sounds which disappear across space and through time. There is no escape from this situation—no escape, therefore, from history as a series of displacements and diminutions despite the fantasy of an appeal to eternal judgment. Only by escaping language altogether, and appearing to the mind's eye and ear as a ghostly figure of its locally sourced creativity ("Dim-gleaming through imperfect lore"), might displacement and diminution be avoided. But this localized creativity is itself dependent on an upbringing in the oral and textual tradition through which the ancient poetry is passed down. There is no immediate access, no transcendence of the timebound structuring of imagination by language: Ossian in 1827 and 1845 is not what he was—whatever he was.

In its dialogue with the Scottish poems that surround it in Wordsworth's books—poems both earlier and later—"Written in a Blank Leaf" is a tour de force. The clarity and economy with which it delivers sweeping historical overviews is astonishing. It is the mark of a later poet whose technique is so honed by practice that all inessential elements of style have been eliminated: nothing flashy; no fripperies. Central concerns about the purpose and persistence of poetry are rendered in a style whose lyricism is intensified by its compression of meaning. It is not paraphrasable, for it is a way of thinking through the purpose and persistence of poetry that can only be made in poetry, notwithstanding poetry's slippage, in time and space, from song to writing to print. Yet it is not a poem attempting formal finality: it ends with an exclamation, rather than a statement, hailing a Milton who is approaching, but has not yet reached, the source of inspiration. It is journey rather than arrival—an unconcluded conclusion that leaves poet and reader still traveling, still in dialogue with the other tour poems that aim to lyricize place and past even as they question how lyricization arises and how it should be continued down the years. Ossian—met here as a figure interacting with the Ossians Wordsworth constructed in 1803/1807 at Glen Almain, in 1815 in the "Essay Supplementary," and in 1827 near Dunkeld—is a synecdoche of Scotland and Scott-land, a figure of the searching questions that Scottish tours posed to Wordsworth's art and of the genre, the poetic memorial, that he constructed as an alternative to the versions of place and past offered by Scott, Macpherson, and Hogg. That genre, as exemplified here self-reflexively and as written and rewritten on the banks of Loch Lomond, is altogether a more serious and profound engagement with history than that of contemporary romancers and balladeers. One of Wordsworth's finest achievements, it is a dark poetry—a poetry of decay, diminution and death, of remnants and remainders, of fragmentary memorials and partial survivals; a poetry in which lateness and retrospect is the textual product of revisiting[40] and rewriting.

Chapter 4

Textual Strata and Geological Form

The Scriptorium and the Cave

In this chapter I offer a case study of memorialization, in contexts both private and public, as it worked in one, remarkable poem—the blank-verse nature piece "Enough of Climbing Toil." First published in the *River Duddon* collection of 1820, it reappeared, much revised, as a Poem of Sentiment and Reflection in the 1827 *Poetical Works*. A description of a fell walk made in the company of Wordsworth's sister Dorothy, it was a companion poem to the "Ode to Lycoris," a meditation on poetry and its relationship to landscape, time, and memory passing into evening ("Lycoris" meaning "twilight").[1] It is much concerned with what became major themes of the post-1820 years: loss, memory, and adaptation to the diminished.

The 1827 poem was a composite text, built up not just of lines written for the 1820 publication but also of fragments first penned in 1799 and 1800. I discuss this formal incorporation of manuscript fragments to ask some questions about the organization of knowledge as a textual practice in Wordsworth's later writing. I show that his use of manuscripts, and his preparation of the poem for print, are far different from the account of poetic creativity he gave in the Preface to *Lyrical Ballads*. Nor does his practice produce anything much like the organic form that many critics saw as the hallmark of Wordsworthian Romanticism. In "Enough of Climbing Toil," the poem is not the product of a prior mental process. Recollection is an already-textualized process,[2] dependent on a family archive of old manuscripts that were transcribed and collated by a female scriptorium— the wife, sister, and sister-in-law scribing away like so many monks or nuns.[3] These manuscripts were then retrieved and cut up, sometimes

literally, more often by the transcription of passages.[4] The detached fragments were then assembled—collaged almost—into the new poem. Thus
"Enough of Climbing Toil," a poem about memory, also materializes memory as a process of textual retrieval and reassemblage, being pieced together
from old pieces; it was a matter of cut and paste rather than imaginative,
mental revisiting of internalized experiences or verses known by heart.[5] The
poem also thematizes what it shows formally: that for the later Wordsworth,
recollection was not a self-sufficient process of reviving the past (spots of
time) in mind, or even in composition, but instead occurred via a prosthe-
sis. Dorothy takes the function, as Mary and Sarah did elsewhere, of being
an external hard drive, as a living repository of past experiences and as a
curator of an archive of manuscripts where the memory is lodged, allowing
retrieval and reuse in new poems which thereby themselves become archival repositories of memory. The process, moreover, is circular because in
"Enough of Climbing Toil" the incorporated manuscript fragments are
about Dorothy and Mary as repositories of meaning.

If circular, "Enough of Climbing Toil" also suggests that Wordsworth's
organization of memory was sometimes a less self-enclosed process than,
when reading *The Prelude*, many critics have thought. Revision was not
always a self-recycling process of revisiting old events and old poems and
revising them in relation to his latest position.[6] When Wordsworth republished "Enough of Climbing Toil" in 1827, he made major changes in
response to texts from beyond his family scriptorium. These changes re-
oriented the poem; they also improved it. But they were made because his
technique of textual self-retrieval was challenged by new textual knowledge
from outside his spatiotemporal remit. The lively print culture of the 1820s
presented Wordsworth, in newspapers, journals, and books, with news suggesting that extinction was at the heart of nature—that the earth presents a
layered archive of specimens of the lost and dead: fossils. The new geology
assembled fragments of the past—as Wordsworth himself did to win back
lost time—but retrieved only specimens of the dead and vanished. Wordsworth responded to this by adding a new section to his poem: a portrait of
a cave, with fossilized deposits from the extinct past. This portrait is in part
a figure of the poem's own textual history; it suggests that the textual deposits of the past can be reviewed, like the fossils in the rock, but neither
renewed nor reanimated. The cave of poetic memory, in the poem and as
the poem, does not formally recollect the past in toto, nor relive it, but
displays it compressed in fragments *as past*. This procedure suggests that

for the late Wordsworth, poetry does not recover the growth of the self so much as shore fragments against the ruins of the organic self made by time.[7] It works by assemblage rather than organic unity, and by archaeologizing rather than endless pursuit. It performs neither the quest of *The Prelude* nor the moralizing of *The Excursion* but instead attempts a laying-to-rest of the search upon which Wordsworth has been, and can still imagine himself being, engaged.[8]

Throughout my discussion, Wordsworth's relationship with his sister Dorothy, and with the feminine as he conceives it, will be in focus. "Enough of Climbing Toil," I suggest, achieves a subtle modification of Wordsworth's earlier gender politics. Alluding to "Tintern Abbey," it revises the way of speaking of and for Dorothy elaborated in that famous poem, in the direction of a more companionate discourse in which Wordsworth values his companion because she possesses a separate self. Using old fragments about Dorothy in a new context radically recontextualizes them, placing their original poeticization of her in doubt. To be sure, Wordsworth still wants her to embody the spirit of nature for him, but he now seeks her consent, entreating her to act in this way, rather than, as in "Tintern Abbey" defining her as an empty vessel filled by the spirit of nature. This is partly a matter of age: acknowledging loss and decay, he can no longer confidently assume that the feminine (women, or nature herself) exists to assist his prophetic voice. He now needs Dorothy because she embodies a past—a textual as well as lived past—that he cannot sort, by acts of poetic recollection, into a grand narrative or perfect order. The late Wordsworth prefers entreaty to command, and acknowledgment to assumption: the result is to allow Dorothy her separate identity and to articulate his own vulnerability.[9] He needs her to be whom she may or may not choose to be in order to be who he needs to be: his identity is conditional upon hers, but hers is not within his power, though it might respond to his behest. Here, that is to say, Wordsworth's delicate articulation of the loving, long-term sibling relationship includes equality and need; it is far different than formulations of it as subordinative and silencing made by, among others, Anne Mellor and Marlon Ross.[10] One of my purposes here is to extol, as well as to uncover, its delicate wisdom of experience.

The Poem of 1820: Revising Milton

Intensely revelatory of private experience, the poem was nevertheless crafted and recrafted for a readership that already knew Wordsworth's earlier work. Thus, when first published, "Enough of Climbing Toil" was a shorter and lesser poem than it later became. It was a blank-verse, present-tense narrative of a local encounter, in the manner of "Nutting" and two poems written in 1816 and 1817 (the period when "Enough of Climbing Toil" was first worked up for publication)—"A little onward lend thy guid-ing hand" and "To Miss — on her first ascent of Helvellyn":

> Enough of climbing toil!—Ambition treads
> Here, as in busier scenes, ground steep and rough,
> Oft perilous, always tiresome; and each step,
> As we for most uncertain gain ascend
> Toward the clouds, dwarfing the world below,
> Induces, for its old familiar sights,
> Unacceptable feelings of contempt,
> With wonder mixed—that Man could e'er be tied,
> In anxious bondage, to such nice array
> And formal fellowship of petty things!
> Oh, 'tis the *heart* that magnifies this life,
> Making a truth and beauty of her own!
> And moss-grown alleys, circumscribing shades,
> And gurgling rills, assist her in the work
> More efficaciously than realms outspread,
> As in a map, before the adventurer's gaze,
> Ocean and earth contending for regard!
> Lo! there a dim Egerian grotto fringed
> With ivy-twine, profusely from its brows
> Dependant;—enter without further aim;
> And let me see thee sink into a mood
> Of quiet thought—protracted till thine eye
> Be calm as water when the winds are gone
> And no one can tell whither. Dearest Friend!
> We two have known such happy hours together
> That, were power granted to replace them (fetched
> From out the pensive shadows where they lie)
> In the first warmth of their original sunshine,
> Loth should I be to use it; passing sweet
> Are the domains of tender memory!
>
> (*Duddon*, pp. 102–3)[11]

Even at first reading, the poem is unusual: beginning in mid ascent with an exasperated exclamation, it presents a poet who is exhausted and grumpy rather than awed and inspired. Wordsworth is tired of climbing and tired of the prospect view that in so many eighteenth-century poems offered a position of authority. This is not the poet who finds, on Snowdon summit or in an Alpine pass, that standing on top of the world leads to intimations of apocalyptic power. He rejects the map-like aerial view because it gives a false elevation, divorcing the viewer from involvement with the small things that shelter us at ground level.[12] Endearment, he suggests, is a result of familiarity magnifying the close-at-hand rather than of inherent sublimity: we are attached to "moss-grown alleys, . . . / And gurgling rills" (lines 13–14) rather than to mountains or extensive prospects. The crucial metaphors are derived from visual technologies: an aesthetic of magnification is preferred to one of survey, the close-up view to the cartographic plan. Truth and beauty, it emerges, as if Wordsworth were in dialogue with Keats, are subjective, created by our visual (imaginative) transformation of our long-lived experience of a place. To imply this was to revive in a newly oppositional context a theme that had occupied Wordsworth earlier—in "Nutting" and *Home at Grasmere*, for instance—that the spirit is nurtured when sheltered by nature, as well as when encountering its disturbing power. Here, though, it is less a matter of "as well" than of "instead." At the same time, he places the onus more firmly on the human than he once had done: "Oh, 'tis the *heart* that magnifies this life," he says, echoing Coleridge's "in our life alone does nature live" ("Dejection: an Ode," line 48) rather than reaffirming his own argument that it is the "beautiful and permanent objects of nature" which educate the spirit (LB, pp. 743–44). The poetic mode for this argument is the "fancy," as in "The Brownie's Cell" and "The Haunted Tree" (see Chapters 3 and 5; the poem derives from the same manuscript drafts as the latter). Here again, as in those other poems of this period, Wordsworth seeks to supplant the poetry of imagination that he had, as recently as 1815, declared to be the highest kind. Now he is concerned about its costs, both to the poet who seeks vatic power through it and to his companions.

The poem first appeared in the *River Duddon* volume, the first major publication in which Wordsworth explicitly dwelt upon the Lake District as a ground for his own selfhood, and selfhood more generally. The volume was the first of Wordsworth's many later publications giving a tour of local places, enshrining their historical as well as personal value, taking stock of what it is to be English—a bid to be a national poet in a landscape changed by time and death. It features a sequence of poems that become, in this context, meditations on the varied ways in which self-knowledge is engendered by encounters with a long-dwelt-in landscape. "Enough of Climbing Toil" is one of these. Overall, the volume is explicitly topographical, aimed at the increasingly popular market for guidebooks to the Lakes, many of which incorporated extracts of loco-descriptive verse and engravings.

We know that Wordsworth thought very carefully about the order in which his poems should be printed. Thus it is no coincidence that "Enough of Climbing Toil" appeared immediately after the "Ode to Lycoris" (*Duddon*, pp. 99–101). The ode is the meditation of "a bard of ebbing time, / And nurtured in a fickle clime" (lines 10–11) who sees in the autumnal scene a reminder that "we nearer draw to life's dark goal" (line 53) and who wishes, in consequence, to restate the importance of his relationship with an aging Dorothy/Lycoris, for it is by so doing that he can imagine seizing, as a shared experience of life's renewal, the remaining signs of spring. Thus "Enough of Climbing Toil" is conditioned by the reader's prior experience of a poem that accepts belatedness only to find the value of the sibling relationship increased by that acceptance. It is shaped, too, by the ode's inscribing of Dorothy, as companion, addressee, and muse, into a rural scene that is present to the poet's senses and that prompts a train of reflection. But while the ode is in rhymed stanzas, and thus a self-evidently *poetic* organization of the sentiment springing from a particular place and time, "Enough of Climbing Toil" is, by contrast, "plainer and more emphatic" (LB, pp. 743–44), a narration that approximates in-the-moment speech although its Miltonic blank verse is also informed by that of "Tintern Abbey" and *The Prelude*.

The 1820 text of "Enough of Climbing Toil" modifies the Miltonic, power-seeking strategies of Wordsworth's Snowdon and Simplon verse. The first seven lines echo Satan's admission (in Book IV of *Paradise Lost*) that "ambition threw me down" (line 40) when, thinking that "one step higher / Would set me highest" (lines 50–51). In Wordsworth's 1827 text, the allusion is more evident still, for there "uncertain gain" (1820) becomes "uncertain recompense," echoing Satan's confession that instead of giving God thanks ("easiest recompense," line 47), he had striven to gain his "bright eminence" (line 44) for himself. The effect of these allusions is to color the struggle for the commanding heights with Satan's admission of ingratitude, perversity, and guilt. Wordsworth now adapts Milton's critique of his antihero's rebellious course rather than deriving from that course (and from the verse that energizes it) an endorsement of his own assumption of authority. This was to place one of his oldest poetic strategies in doubt; to put aside, if not to reject or deny, one of the chief Wordsworthian routes to power, pausing his solitary ascent to sublimity. Uncertain rather than abundant recompense.

The adaptation of Milton's critique was not a simple process. A manuscript draft of lines not included in the 1820 "Enough of Climbing Toil" shows Wordsworth striving to absorb the Miltonic vocabulary into his Lakeland setting.[13] This draft circles around the key terms Milton applied to Satan: "recompense," "reproach," "envious"; it also, however, borrows from Milton's treatment of the angel Michael: images of "tower'd Palace high" and "pomp / Of sea and land contending for regard" echo *Paradise Lost* Book XI, in which the angel shows Adam the world from a mountain summit. Unlike Adam, Wordsworth's viewer is a Lakeland shepherd, an embodiment of goodness and immune to the temptation offered by the prospect view because he is intent on more humble matters (the daily-encountered small things to which we are tied and endeared). The shepherd thus opens the way for Wordsworth to "gaze / On a small flower retaining at my feet / Its long lovd aspect." Concentration on the "the meanest flower that blows" prevents pride and envy.[14]

The manuscript draft was perhaps too long-winded for adoption. The published poem certainly offers a more concentrated formulation of the hill climb and its meaning, with the Miltonic allusions more subsumed. The effect is still to criticize the satanic struggle for power, even before Wordsworth directly declares that the view from above produces "unacceptable feelings of contempt" for the world below (line 7). Striving for the mountain-top perspective is now an uncertain and self-deluding slog as likely to produce contempt as it is wonder.

What had happened? Why this rewriting of the treatment of landscape that Wordsworth had made in "Tintern Abbey" and *The Prelude*? Part of the answer is provided by the poem's addressee. Dorothy was now an old companion and a woman of middle age rather than the youthful, recently reunited figure of 1798. The implicit gender and sexual dynamic of the poem is accordingly different. This difference has an effect upon Wordsworth's use of poetic models: he makes a decorous allusion to a classical site, writing "Lo! there a dim Egerian grotto fringed." Egeria, as described by the historian Livy and the poet Juvenal, dispensed advice to King Numa Pompilius in her cave-like grotto outside Rome. Wordsworth invokes her here to precipitate a sudden departure from the patriarchal struggle upon which he has been engaged. In Egeria he finds a female conduit for his experience of nature and for his expression of that experience. He thus turns abruptly away from a past struggle to master Milton's discourse and inherit the power of his hero, via an unexpected classical reference that obtrudes on a poem that had hitherto showed no sign of invoking Latin sources. Moreover, the classical reference comes via an eighteenth-century poet whose work is less concerned with power than Milton's: Joseph Warton, whose "The Enthusiast; or, The Lover of Nature" first likens the poet's imagination tapping into nature's secret powers to Numa being confided in by Egeria:

> As to a secret grot Ægeria stole
> With patriot Numa, and in silent night
> Whisper'd him sacred laws . . .
>
> (lines 21–23)[15]

The borrowing displaces Wordsworth's satanic tussle for power. Here he self-sponsors his verse by drawing upon Warton's vision of a benignant nature willingly disclosing its secrets without violence. The resultant change in tone highlights an eighteenth-century neoclassical, rather than seventeenth-century Protestant/Hebraic, model of poetic inspiration and a modified attitude to nature—the cave rather than summit is the place where wisdom is discovered. Thus Wordsworth urges Dorothy to "enter without further aim" the Egerian grotto, renouncing the climb in favor of the unexpected and half-hidden recess, whence there is no commanding prospect (line 20). Accepting a new limit to one's aims, it seems, is the key, for it precipitates a social relationship to nature in companionship with, rather than paternalism over, a woman (however benevolent).

The relationship does not require a complete renunciation of Milton, since the Wartonian intertext prompts Wordsworth to call upon other aspects of *Paradise Lost* than its articulation of satanic usurpation. Warton's Egerian cave takes him back to Milton's description of Eve reminding Adam how she was created as a "like consort to thy self."

> That day I oft remember, when from sleep
> I first awak't and found my self repos'd
> Under a shade of flours, much wondring where

And what I was, whence thither brought, and how.
Not distant far from thence a murmuring sound
Of waters issu'd from a Cave and spread
Into a liquid Plain, then stood unmov'd
Pure as th' expanse of Heav'n; I thither went
With unexperienc't thought, and laid me downe
On the green bank, to look into the cleer
Smooth Lake, that to me seemd another Skie.

(Paradise Lost, IV, 49–59)

Wordsworth's cave, then, is the literalization of what Christopher Ricks calls a summoning of benignant influence, "a retrospect that opens up a new prospect,"[16] Warton's expressions of love and tenderness making it possible for Wordsworth to access a side of Milton that he had previously neglected. In his next lines, he writes as tenderly of Dorothy as Milton does of Eve, but his cave is a fount of female experience rather than of innocence. Unlike Egeria, however, Wordsworth's cavewoman will not dispense advice; rather, she will register the trace of the passing of spirit:

And let me see thee sink into a mood
Of quiet thought—protracted till thine eye
Be calm as water when the winds are gone
And no one can tell whither.

(lines 21–24)

Nature, and Dorothy registering it, is here represented as a presence marked by absence, a calmness that comes into being because of the passing of what disturbs, as in water abandoned by the evanescent winds. The present becomes apparent—or comes to be—because the activity of the past, though gone, is refracted in it. Here it is significant that Wordsworth writes "no one can tell"; he accepts thereby that nature's powers are ungraspable and unsayable. A satanic struggle to reach a height from which these powers can be commanded will be of no avail; they will escape language, being manifest and traceable not in the poet's imagination but in Dorothy's "quiet thought," a mode of being and seeing that does not bring forth utterance. Even there, it is only the trace of the past that is summonable. By comparing Dorothy's eye to water abandoned by the wind, Wordsworth does not inscribe nature's powers into her—does not find them to be embodied by her—but instead writes her as the being in whom appears the present's dependence on the disappearance of the past, which nevertheless lingers as a significant absence.

Here Wordsworth finds a new vocabulary and scenario to restage an old concern, a concern now seen with hindsight rather than experienced for the first time: a concern about the limits of his own poetic telling. He reformulates what is, for instance, implicit in "To Joanna," the realization that the fleeing away of the world leaves language in a temporal regress, always pursuing an elusive goal of total re-present-ation of what lapses. This is the case, at least, unless, accepting the hopelessness of the pursuit, the poet acknowledges that what can presently be, and presently be said, is already marked by a past that cannot be traced to its origin and destination. This acknowledgment is what he calls upon Dorothy, in her quiet and calm eschewal of language, to show him and thus grant him a language of accep- tance. Her human otherness, her individual difference from himself, her self-absorption are recognized: she cannot be governed by his patriarchal words. Through her, he will learn to transform, from the altered perspective of age, the poetic struggle for mastery of self and world that is, at root, a struggle to control time and space through language. It is Dorothy's long familiarity as his nearest and dearest of kin that fits her for this role. He knows her of old but sees her anew outside the cave, and this prompts him to a different kind of linguistic act—that of urging her to respond to his need for a trace that brings the present into being as marked by the absence of the past. So he uses a verbal mood that summons the world to his plea: "Let me see thee," he says, calling Dorothy to occupy a role of his choosing between nature (water and winds) and himself (viewer and poet). This is a form of saying that precipitates action—a linguistic interference in, rather than representation of, the world, since, within the world that the reader imagines in response to the poem, Wordsworth's invocation does indeed bring Dorothy to the mind's eye in the terms he chooses. In the imaginary space of the poem, "Let me see" is a self-fulfilling entreaty that calls up the being Wordsworth wishes for. And this calling-up is aided by non-verbal means too: the dash before "protracted" separates what follows from "Let me see," thereby turning the vision of Dorothy's "eye / . . . calm as water when the winds are gone" into a semi-detached, observed state rather than, as it grammatically ought to be, just a wish yet to be fulfilled. By disrupting the poem's metrical and syntactical organization of time, the dash also ges- tures toward the temporal dislocation and detached attachment of past to present that Wordsworth is illustrating in the winds/water image. It marks, in fact, a pause that is silent but noticed, where a sound (word) might be but is not, a metrical beat registered though nothing is said.

By bringing into imagined being the sister he invokes, Wordsworth aims to redeem his poetic power by changing the terms on which it operates: displacing the opposition between viewer and viewed, poet and nature (time/space), words and world. Henceforth in the poem Wordsworth, entreating and calling on Dorothy, is also dependent upon her since she, by virtue of the continued silent presence he urges her to provide, reassures him that the past, though lost, leaves its mark as the present. The corollary of this is that his words still have purchase though they cannot arrest time and distance. The "me," of "let me see thee," it turns out, is "dependant" on the "thee." Thus the poem concludes with a tender declaration whose affectionate tone is far from that of its beginning. William feels united to Dorothy again; as in "Tintern Abbey" he is empowered by what he conceives as her non-linguistic way of being and feels endeared, both to her and to nature—the very feeling that his restless desire to be at the top had endangered. He is buoyed by the memory of previous occasions in which she had embodied the spirit of nature for him but does not want to relive those occasions, accepting their place in memory rather than trying to defy the natural passing of time by making them live again: "We two have known such happy hours together / That, were power granted to replace them / . . . / Loth should I be to use it; passing sweet / Are the domains of tender memory!" Accepting loss and enjoying peace, rather than pitting himself against the order of time and space, he ends the poem having learned, like Numa, the consolation of companionship that depends on letting another (another person / another time) be as they are. The echo is now not of Satan's ambition: Wordsworth finds himself permitted to discover in Dorothy, as Milton's Adam does in Eve, that "what seemed fair in all the world, seemed now / . . . in her contained" (*Paradise Lost*, VIII, 472–73), and as Warton's Numa finds in Egeria's "whisper'd" laws. The present poem draws on the past without eclipsing it, finding contentment in accepting its belatedness. Milton's and Warton's tenderness can be heard in Wordsworth's words: the poets are companions in the verse just as the couples they portray.

Such is an account of the poem as it appeared in 1820, a strange piece in that its Miltonic beginning, which engages with the other poems in the Duddon volume that endorse Wordsworth's solitary assumption of power in nature's high places, is contradicted semantically, stylistically, and in its gender politics by its neoclassical and Miltonic ending. It is as if Wordsworth chose a self-canceling procedure, having found a source of inspiration more effective for his stage of life than the egotistical and satanic one that had once been so vital to him. But the shift, mid-poem, is sudden and the change rapid: the verse hurries to its unexpected conclusion without having explored in depth the causes for its change of direction—as if Wordsworth were himself surprised by his own shift in perspective. The Egerian cave is a brief reference, its significance barely sketched in. The reader is left confused: the poem seems to record the initial lurch of an abrupt refocusing caused by the sudden realization that one no longer wants what one had wanted for so long.

The Poem of 1827: Sonic Sources

It was perhaps his sense that the poem was too swift to carry the emotional weight he wished it to bear that led Wordsworth to revise it heavily. He had a further incentive too: his 1827 *Poetical Works* were a statement of a mature poet collecting his poems for posterity. By this time Wordsworth knew that his verse would never sell well and that the market for poetry had collapsed. A collected edition might interest purchasers who were not prepared to buy all the individual volumes that had appeared since his 1815 *Poems*. And it would demonstrate his achievement, for the present and the future, as a multi-volume overall survey of his career. In these circumstances, it was worth revising to ensure readers would judge him as he now wanted to be judged. A publishing strategy now dovetailed with Wordsworth's constitutional habit of revising his past poems. And so he revised "Enough of Climbing Toil" so that when Longman republished it, it was far more substantial, with a new section describing the cave:

> The umbrageous woods are left—how far beneath!
> But lo! where darkness seems to guard the mouth
> Of yon wild cave, whose jagged brows are fringed
> With flaccid threads of ivy, in the still
> And sultry air, depending motionless.
> Yet cool the space within, and not uncheered
> (As whoso enters shall ere long perceive)
> By stealthy influx of the timid day

Mingling with night, such twilight to compose
As Numa loved; when, in the Egerian grot,
From the sage Nymph appearing at his wish,
He gained whate'er a regal mind might ask,
Or need, of counsel breathed through lips divine.

Long as the heat shall rage, let that dim cave
Protect us, there deciphering as we may
Diluvian records; or the sighs of Earth
Interpreting; or counting for old Time
His minutes, by reiterated drops,
Audible tears, from some invisible source
That deepens upon fancy—more and more
Drawn tow'rd the centre whence those sighs creep forth
To awe the lightness of humanity:
Or, shutting up thyself within thyself,
There let me see thee sink into a mood
Of gentler thought, protracted till thine eye
Be calm as water when the winds are gone,
And no one can tell whither. Dearest Friend!
We two have known such happy hours together
That, were power granted to replace them (fetched
From out the pensive shadows where they lie)
In the first warmth of their original sunshine,
Loth should I be to use it: passing sweet
Are the domains of tender memory!

(lines 19–51; 1827, IV, pp. 251–53)

The main addition occurs in lines 19–41, which transform 1820's passing reference to the "Egerian grotto" into an in-depth exploration of a cave that, it turns out, is both a portal to a spot of time and a figure for the poem's own layered textual history, which, like the cave wall, exhibits buried fragments of the past. Since that past is bound up with Dorothy—it is with her he will enter the cave; it is she who is depicted in the poetic fragments reassembled in "Enough of Climbing Toil"—then the cave also opens a space for pondering her significance. It offers Wordsworth a twilight zone in which he can image to himself his present relationships to his past and to the most fundamental sources of his art: the pursuit of nature's and his own temporal and spatial origin and the dependence of that pursuit on a female companion who preserves his memory in the form of a textual archive that she brings to life by being. The cave functions as a material analogue of textual extinction and archival renewal—a figure of the challenge time poses to Wordsworth's art and of his poetry's dependence on Dorothy as curator and performer.

If the cave is a figure of the poem's textual history and a testing ground for Wordsworth's art, it is also—and this does not become explicit but is nevertheless vital—an actual cave jointly discovered by William and Dorothy in the past or, more probably, a compendium of caves. The text echoes the first lines of *The Excursion*, which describe the view from "the front / Of some huge cave, whose rocky ceiling casts / A twilight of its own, an ample shade" (*Excursion*, I, 10–12). But it also revises manuscript fragments that date from 1799/1800 and that mention a cave: "while in the cave we sat, thy face / Was still as water when the winds are gone / And no one can tell whither."[17] Near Grasmere is Helm Crag, a fell Wordsworth climbed many times, and in "To Joanna" (1800) he mentions the cavern near its summit. He also visited the Yorkshire show cave—Yordas—in 1800 and depicted it as a visual spectacle in *The Prelude*. But whichever cave—if any single cave—inspired the passage, its differences from Yordas are instructive. The 1827 cave is a place where hearing outweighs seeing, a place where daylight is a "stealthy influx" and twilight dimness reigns (line 26). Rather than Yordas's spectacular sights, this cave offers faint "sighs of Earth"— "audible tears"—emanating from "some invisible source" (lines 34, 37). A place of secret disclosure rather than open spectacle, elusiveness rather than revelation, the 1827 cave is more mysterious than the cave briefly mentioned in the 1820 text, for although it still puts Wordsworth in mind of the Egerian grotto, it now resembles Numa's cave in its secretive mixture of day and night. The emphasis is upon the evanescent sonic passage of the cave's counsel, which is not spelled out but "breathed through lips divine" (line 30): the nymph inspires by breathings rather than tells in words, and the mystery is intensified because her lips are described but not her face.

Strictly speaking, nothing in the cave is described thoroughly. This lack is not just a matter of the difficulty of discerning things in the gloom. It is also a question of grammar. Wordsworth's presentation of the cave takes the form of an entreaty, being governed by the hortative phrase "let that dim cave / Protect us" (lines 32–33). He then envisages what he and Dorothy would do were they in the cave that he is actually inviting her to enter.

The cave scene, in other words, is not a depiction of but a fantasy about an experience that may not yet have occurred. Yet if a fantasy, it nevertheless comes to seem real as the hearer/reader registers its details and creates an imagined scene in response to them. As a result, the cave is strangely suspended between description and fantasy, its imagined presence established but simultaneously under question. It is a place of uncertain status in which what seems to be an in-the-moment experience may be only the conjectural present conjured up by the poet's inviting words. In this respect, the cave resembles the real/imaginary lakes and sandy shores of "Frost at Midnight," Wordsworth having borrowed Coleridge's techniques for giving an apparent reality to what he simultaneously shows is an imaginary encounter that is summoned by the poet's words and offered as a gift to his companion.

If one of those techniques involves the use of verbal moods and grammatical constructions that eschew the normal means by which language structures time, another involves shifting the burden of mimesis toward sound. Wordsworth imagines the cave as a place in which he and Dorothy may become interpreters of the sighs of the earth itself, "counting for old Time" (line 35)—taking, that is, time's measure in their breaths and in the beats of the verse lines. Theirs would be a secret communication wherein human codes find their derivation from nature's motions, articulating them, telling seconds and minutes from water drops. This would be more than mere numbering: the phrase "audible tears" animates the sound of the drops falling from the cave roof, treating them as if they were signs of sorrow. Thus by personifying as well as numbering them, William and Dorothy, in Wordsworth's imagined scenario, will give them meaning and value. Something else here too: tears are silent, seen and not heard, so by attributing audibility to them Wordsworth creates an uncanny transfer of the visual to the aural. The cave seems a place of unfathomable transformations of the elements and the senses. To enter will be to sound its depths, to take its measure by attuning the eyes to its shadows and the ears to its noises, which re-sound in human utterance. It will be to intuit a dark inscape where one overhears nature's secret inarticulate sounds—and turns them haltingly into words. The cave is, as the Egerian allusion suggests, a fount, an omphalos, an oracle for poets, since turning sounds into words is, for Wordsworth, their prophetic gift. A feminine source, the cave is the place where the earth itself becomes counselor—the fount of articulate language, in which the evanescent spirits of nature are apprehended.

Such the scenario seems to be. Under the surface, however, matters are not so simple—and the male poet not an acknowledged, worldly, legislator of a feminine, inarticulate fount. In 1827 the cave is a more elusive sound-stage than in 1820: its counsel is now too evanescent to formulate as a series of laws or doctrines; its breathings turn out to require a different measure. Just as, in the imagined world presented by the poem, the cave is a recess in which one steps aside from toil and ambition, so too in the syntax, the cave description suspends the temporal progress of the verse: forward motion is lost in a parenthesis ("As whoso," line 25), in an analogy ("As Numa," line 28), in unusual verbal moods (the hortative "Let that dim cave"), and in accumulated alternative scenarios that may or may not be mutually exclusive ("or the sighs of Earth / Interpreting; or counting for old Time," lines 34–35). Then there is the piling-up of phrases and prepositions that leaves grammatical and spatial relationships unclear in the lines "from some invisible source / That deepens upon fancy—more and more / Drawn tow'rd the centre whence those sighs creep forth" (lines 37–39). What does "deepens upon fancy" mean? That the source recedes, or becomes more profound, as fancy tries to apprehend it? Or is fancy itself being deepened by the effect of the cave upon it? What exactly is being drawn to the center—tears, fancy, the source? And where is the center—the center of the earth, or of the cave, or the self? We cannot be sure, and our uncertainty turns attention to the language as a medium: grammar and syntax seem stretched to breaking point as Wordsworth reaches for a formulation of nature's forces that may lie too deep for (audible) tears—or for words. Language buckles as it tries to make meaning from what lies beyond its grasp. And as sense disarticulates, spatiotemporal relations blur—the receding center retreats from knowledge; the feminine oracle cannot simply transfer it to the enquiring poet, however worthy his words.

Several critics have argued that death lies at the heart of the nature which Wordsworth would penetrate to its core and that it is his fear of and fascination with it that causes him to recoil into the depths of his own mind.[18] "Enough of Climbing Toil" suggests a related but less final risk outlined by Frances Ferguson:[19] that Wordsworth might have no magic spell powerful enough to open nature's ultimate origin and that, when entered, the cave might bespeak another, deeper, inaccessible source where final meaning might lie. In this case, language would not be able to name, or call up, a firm foundation for itself; the foundation would retreat before the poet. As in Plato's cave, the poet would be left interpreting fleeting shadows of a source that could not be penetrated, formulated, or sounded. Wordsworth would measure in the cave not only his desire to summon the world to his words, but also its resistance to that desire, its elusive otherness—an otherness revealed in the slow and inexorable processes that have turned living beings into stone. It is a place to be petrified, where one can only hope briefly to bring one's own articulations into time with its endless reiterations. In this cave, both the material world and the world of language remain, be they ever so close, ultimately un-united, just short of the stability that would come from things' full presence in the words that call them up and tell them out. The risk here is an infinite regress in which the poet's words conjure up an abyss—a risk charted by Geoffrey Hartman, who traced Wordsworth's pursuit of the ground of being through language—an unending search for the receding founding word.[20] Hence in classical myth, caves are the places where oracular words stand in where the world is not—where it opens itself but offers no beginning and end.

What is left, now more sharply marked by meaning's effacement, is rhythm or measure: Wordsworth's last mimetic recourse lies in the measuring of sound. Not, that is to say, measuring by recording, but by performing—matching the rhythms of human activity to those of the earth. Measuring a sonic trace whose nature lies beyond sense is a deepening experience of nature's ungraspability; thus earth's sighs "awe the lightness of humanity" (line 40), making the cave a place of unknowing, prompting a salutary endarkening that is at the same time a taking up of weight. Nevertheless, such taking up, such measuring, endorses one vital aspect of verse: its sounding line becomes a way of telling (counting, beating) what cannot be told (explained). Here, it is implied, poetic lines are, more than metaphorically, numbers. Wordsworth takes up the sounds of the earth in verse whose measure is that of earth's repeated sighs, achieving this by the repetition of rhythmically similar phrases that metrically suggest the repetition of sighs, tears, and strata—the patterns of earthly action—that they describe. The phrases "deciphering . . . records," "or . . . Interpreting," "or counting . . . minutes," "by . . . tears," "from . . . fancy," echoing each other, arrest the poem's syntactical and metrical linearity, as if the cave's pulses hypnotize the visitors into a time that is too long-term in its turns and returns for teleology to be sustained. Thus it is by a sonic and rhythmic echoing of natural sound in verse lines that Wordsworth would find a harmony and thus an unknowing knowledge of, or unformulable participation in, nature.[21]

The cave's challenge to Wordsworth's retrieval of time and organization of space had a particular cause, as is suggested when he pictures himself and Dorothy "deciphering as we may / Diluvian records" (lines 33–34) as if they were geologists, reading in the strata evidence of the flood. This is an allusion by which the personal meanings of the caves explored by the siblings in 1799–1800 are overwritten by a more public context: a sensational discovery made by two Yorkshire quarrymen who, in 1821, found that a tiny aperture in a hillside in Kirkdale led them into a cave. When the Oxford geologist William Buckland was called in, he unearthed, under layers of silt and gravel, hundreds of fossilized bones—broken and chewed and from extinct species of elephant, rhinoceros, hippopotamus, and hyena. In 1822 Buckland announced his findings in the Royal Society's *Philosophical Transactions* as "An Assemblage of Fossil Teeth and Bones." This paper was then discussed in the *Quarterly Review*. The *Quarterly* article was in turn extracted in provincial newspapers such as the *Bury and Norwich Post*, 6 November 1822, which declared that Buckland had thrown more light on "the history of the planet we inhabit" than "the most brilliant imagination had, in preceding ages, been able to discover." In 1823 Buckland capitalized on the publicity by publishing a book, *Reliquiae Diluviae*. Here, he made the cave a key to understanding the deep history of the earth, publicizing the fact of mass extinction more widely than ever before. So "completely," he said, "has the violence of that tremendous convulsion destroyed and remodeled the form of the ante-diluvian surface, that it is only in caverns that have been protected from its ravages that we may hope to find undisturbed evidence of events in the period immediately preceding it."[22] Churchmen protested: Buckland had ignored Biblical chronology and suggested that God the creator let whole species die out.

Wordsworth altered "Enough of Climbing Toil" in reference to the furor Kirkdale caused, for his phrase "diluvian records" is Buckland's key concept, used in his book as the English version of its title. It is clear, too, that Wordsworth saw Kirkdale as a troubling challenge not just to his view of nature and time but also to his time-defying poetic method—his way of writing by retrieving past texts that bespoke different eras in his past life. The strata uncovered at Kirkdale cave showed the earth to be an archive of specimens of the past that cannot be retrieved other than as fossils of former life that is now not just dead but extinct. As such they stand against Wordsworth's family archive of texts—objects written years earlier—which can be assembled into new wholes, giving them a new use and new, as it were, life—recycling the past into the present. Kirkdale's dead letter versus Grasmere's renewal by assemblage. Wordsworth bears the weight of this cave lore as he hears the song of the earth as sighs and "audible tears," the cries of petrified past generations that he cannot relieve.

It is to be remembered, though, that "Enough of Climbing Toil" retains an alternative to both looking at and being in the abyss of time—and that alternative is not to rebound into the sublime freedom of the poet's own mind. Now, in 1827, Wordsworth prefers a more social and less solipsistic means of bearing the pressure of his quest for intimations of originating spirit, and in this way he sets aside his past. In effect, he brackets the exploration of the cave by offering it as an imagined scene that does not have to become an experienced reality, however strongly it seems to place the siblings there. He stands outside the entrance imagining what he and Dorothy might find *if* they go in, keeping one foot on the cold fellside, on terra firma, where he and his sister remain in the light of day even as they peer in at the cave's mouth. Thus the pair might escape immersion in the abyss that is conjured up as a possibility, leaving the cave as a road that is glimpsed—imagined but not irretrievably taken into nature and the self—so as not to take the risk of again plunging into vertiginous depths. As in other late poems, Wordsworth first steps toward, but then aside from, a spot of time lest the present compete with or renew the past and thereby undo its primary, founding significance.[23]

Dorothy (as Wordsworth conceives her) does not, like the poet, respond to the cave by deciphering and interpreting, for she will not speak or tell the "mood" into which the cave makes her sink. Instead, he urges, she will simply let her thought be visible: "shutting up thyself within thyself, / There let me see thee sink into a mood / Of gentler thought" (lines 41–43). Hers will be a response of embodiment rather than utterance, an enclosure of an enclosure, for if the cave is an enclosure whose meaning is not declarable, Dorothy will humanize it by herself becoming an enclosure. In achieving this embodied secrecy, she will stand in for the cave, rendering it a little less alien, and therefore a little less unreadable—becoming an Egeria by virtue not of speech but of "gentler thought," which is discernible in her if only by contrast with past agitation of spirit—"calm as water when the winds are gone, / And no one can tell whither" (lines 44–45). This phrase lays to rest the cave's inarticulate natural forces (or spirits in motion): the awesome sighs, audible tears, and reiterated drops are subsumed in and quietened by it. If their source and meaning cannot be traced, they are at least held, poised and enfolded in the woman who has come to be as she is because they have worked upon her.

Wordsworth's treatment of Dorothy recalls, but also modifies, the role he gives her in "Tintern Abbey" (LB, pp. 116–20). There he confidently entreats nature to work openly upon her, so that she may focus its forces and make them available to him after the event.[24] Aged twenty-eight, Wordsworth found it easier to assert that nature could be incorporated in memory and caught again from Dorothy's eyes (which are "wild" rather than "calm," as in 1827). He feared absence from Dorothy but did not fear the evanescence of the nature-spirits that were present in her: the "gleams / Of past existence" (lines 149–50) were catchable from her eyes; her mind was a "mansion for all lovely forms" (line 141). In "Enough of Climbing Toil" she embodies a present built on a past known only in its absence. It is an elusive, self-withdrawing source that can neither be commanded nor directly entreated (he urges Dorothy to "Let me" rather than urging the moon and mountain winds to "let" themselves play upon her). This is a major change in perspective, which exhorts Dorothy for permission to let him see her now as once she seemed, treating her as a separate self whom he wishes to relate to and draw upon, rather than guide. He is no longer Numa to Dorothy's nymph; she does not disclose nature's source and secrets by her embodiment of its cavernous depths so much as embody its secrecy. There's a letting be, an acceptance of the limitedness of recall and the elusiveness of nature. Like the cave, memory is shadowy, a recess of temporal and spatial distance—it is neither a mansion of lovely forms nor a map-like prospect laid out beneath the viewer. It is enclosed and private: Wordsworth cannot tell what Dorothy is thinking.

The Strata of the Poem

This, though, is not the poem's final word on memory. "Enough of Climbing Toil" incorporates in its very form the poetry of Wordsworth's past, for it includes fragments written long before and revised many times even before they appeared in this new context. Like the cave, it reveals, to those who know how to decipher, a history of layers. Indeed, the cave, as added to the poem in 1827, is to an extent a figure of the poem's textual history, a history in which, of course, Wordsworth's poetic past is deposited. The strata visible in the cave wall and the secret sounds heard from the earth represent textual strata too deep, too old, and too elusive to be set straight—fragments that might once have found their place in *The Recluse* but that were now redolent of the failure of that grand attempt to place spirit, nature, and society in philosophic order. The effect of assembling these fragments in the new, published, poem of 1827 was to encode in the poem traces of past events and past verse that could be known fully only to the poet and his intimate circle. "Enough of Climbing Toil" has a private, secret form that is inseparable from its public one: its lines, for those in the know, resound with their past, however present the tense in which they are written. But they do not retrieve that past completely; they are fragments of it, traces of memory, and of whole poems, which bespeak loss as well as recollection—mementos, tokens. They suggest on a formal level that the poet creates not an organic unity of past and present self, but a collection of fragments, a pieced-together self, a remaindered textuality in which Wordsworth finds consolation and acceptance, freeing himself from the struggle to fuse past and present, self and world—not rejecting that struggle but bracketing it as a quest he no longer has to perform.

The poem's key episode appeared first in 1799–1800 manuscript fragments that were produced by his female transcribers and were published, in altered form, as "Nutting." Wordsworth wrote thus:

> While in the cave we sate this noon
> Oh! what a countenance was thine come here
> And rest on this light bed of purple heath
> and let me see thine eye
> As at that moment, rich with happiness
> And still as water when the winds are gone
> And no man can tell whither.
>
> (LB, p. 547)

These lines suggest that the cave was already by 1799–1800 a spot of time, a precious experience valued for its transformation of Dorothy into a heightened version of herself. This transformation is doubled when it is Dorothy transcribing the experience into manuscript (the manuscript becomes a token of her hand in producing her brother as a poet by producing a textualization of herself). On the previous manuscript folio, the Wordsworths tried out another version in which the cave is a place where the evanescent motions of the outside scene are traced in Dorothy's body:

> While in the cave we sat thou didst o'erflow
> With love even for the unsubstantial clouds
> And silent incorporeal colours spread
> Over the surface of the earth and sky.
>
> (LB, p. 302)

Revising the lines as if unsatisfied by them, Wordsworth uncoupled Dorothy's reaction from the cave, as if to make use of her state of embodied joy independent of the occasion that gave rise to it. Thus in the longer "Nutting" narrative, he removed the cave but kept the description of Dorothy's eyes (see LB, pp. 305–7). Then, sometime between 1800 and 1802, he worked the lines into the fragment "Travelling/This is the spot":

> This is the spot:—how mildly does the Sun
> Shine in between these fading leaves! the air
> In the habitual silence of this wood
> Is more than silent; and this bed of heath
> Where shall we find so sweet a resting-place!
> Come! let me see thee sink into a dream
> Of quiet thoughts,—protracted till thine eye
> Be calm as water when the winds are gone
> And no one can tell whither.—My sweet Friend!
> We two have had such happy hours together
> That my heart melts in me to think of it.
>
> (LB, p. 307)

These lines, written down by Dorothy and Mary, were of great solace to Wordsworth. He had Dorothy read them aloud to him through the night of 4 May 1802 to ease the anxiety caused by the composition of "Resolution and Independence." Thus she retrieved the poem from the manuscripts she and Mary had written and stored, and performed the version of herself she had collaborated in inscribing. She spoke aloud what she bespoke—bespoke because she wrote his words down, archived them on paper, and then retrieved them from the page he could not bear to look at. A repository of textual memory, she became a redeemer of the loss of presence that textuality memorializes. The performance was thus doubly symbolic of what Dorothy meant to him: a nurturing companion in nature and a collaborator in textualization whose calm presence produced a kindly, companionate verse that reassured him of human love. Wordsworth revived that performance again in 1817 or 1818, when he had the "Travelling" manuscript brought out again and took it over into the first manuscript version of "Enough of Climbing Toil":

> Here let us rest—here, where the gentle beams
> Of noontide stealing in between the boughs
> Illuminate their faded leaves;—the air
> In the habitual silence of this wood
> Is more than silent; and this tuft of heath
> Deck'd with the fullness of its flowers presents
> As beautiful a couch as e'er was framed.
> Come—let us venture to exchange the pomp
> Of widespread landscape for the internal wealth
> Of quiet thought—protracted till thine eye
> Be calm as water when the winds are gone
> And no one can tell whither. Dearest Friend!
> We two have had such blissful hours together
> That were power granted to replace them (fetched
> From out the pensive shadows where they lie)
> In the first warmth of their original sunshine,
> Loth should I be to use it. Passing sweet
> Are the domains of tender memory!
>
> (*Shorter Poems*, pp. 251–52)

This new/old manuscript fragment was in turn revised, probably in 1817–18, the outcome of these revisions being the 1820 text of "Enough of Climbing Toil."

By 1820, and still more by 1827, the long history of past uses of the key phrases on Dorothy's eyes, the cave, and nature's calmness had created a formal memory within the poem, had made it an archive of manuscript fragments about Dorothy that had been transcribed and stored by Dorothy, Mary, and Sarah and retrieved by them for this new use. The effect of this is to encode within the poem the paradoxical persistence and diminution of the past, because since the incorporated phrases derive from fragments, they speak of incompleteness, of the lack of the whole they might have been part of. They are rearticulated in a different context—a whole, finished poem—but not thereby utterly deprived of their bespeaking of their past lack of completion, or of the dependence of Wordsworth's poetic recollection—so vital to his identity—on the storage and retrieval of written paper. His memory was externalized and textualized in a material archive in order to be available for later internalization through the assembly of that archive into texts that appear to be in-the-moment narratives of present experience. Beneath that appearance, the assembled fragments make the 1827 "Enough of Climbing Toil" a mini-archive derived from the larger manuscript library at Rydal Mount: they are, as it were, spots of text that are not revived in wholeness or relived but that stand silently within this new text, which thus defers to them without bringing about their restitution in all their original shape. They repeat at the formal level what was witnessed in the cave with regard to sound: they are an elusive presence that cannot be fully recovered from its origins. A perceptive remark by Peter Larkin is relevant here. The late Wordsworth, he says, "admits that the present moment may be threateningly unique, that a climax, almost by definition, cannot continue on the same level—a post-climactic sphere must be consolidated in some way, even by inviting meditation on loss, old age or on death, the pure past. Such an after-dimension is part of the constitution of any heightened occasion in Wordsworth's poetry, but it also calls for a working out, or for a literalization, which can only be carried on in terms of the relations between discrete, and chronologically disparate, texts."[25] "Enough of Climbing Toil" is a post-climactic text invoking, without trying to repeat, old spots of time and without trying to find new ones. It is a late, twilight poetry that develops past work but is not a triumphant revision of it or a finishing of the unfinished. The incorporated fragments are, like the sighs of earth in the cave, traces/sounds that Wordsworth can re-sound, but he cannot thereby capture the (incomplete) wholes they came from: the past they testify to is a retreating source. Nevertheless, it is a past rearticulated in Wordsworth's own old words: what is lost or half-retained is his own and his female companions' who have experienced, transcribed, stored, and retrieved it. Both loss and continuity are configured and accepted in this textual remaindering.

Wordsworth concludes with an insight that tenderness and sweetness depend upon loss and lapse and with a turning to Dorothy that is enabled by this insight. He feels with her not because he knows nature through her, but because she re-presents in herself the past incidents (and verses) that betoken incompleteness of knowledge, the inevitability of loss, the necessity of vulnerability, and the separateness of selves. She bespeaks, in silence, all he has written about her—all the words she has transcribed and read aloud, including these very words. Being there, new in the old words of "Nutting," she makes the poet's song live because she does not sing it; its survival, in a world in which time destroys breath, depends on silent, secret materiality: Dorothy as embodiment of textual archive, the word made flesh. Thus she shelters him as poet, finding and giving a deeper version of the shelter that Wordsworth invokes earlier in the poem when wanting "moss-grown alleys, circumscribing shades" and a protective cave.[26] And so the poem ends with no triumphant restitution but with a significant departure from Wordsworth's earlier poetics: here the poet cannot—nor does he want to— retrieve the past alone and make it live again. Instead, he is both unsettled by loss and accepting of it, both rueful and resigned—he is determined to value the feeling of endearment that comes from knowing that he has shared with Dorothy a past that cannot be made present but that has nevertheless made the present what it is. The spots of time remain closed, but the poetry they enabled remains, a testament to them, if in fragments. This is the poetry of a man salvaging what he can from a manuscript archive that, as a memory storage and retrieval system, counters time's depredations even as the verse inscribed in the manuscripts acknowledges those depredations. For that reason, retrospective as it is, it is also the expression of a discovery that the textualization and curation of his memory among his beloved female transcribers enables him to acknowledge dependence on another human, even if that human embodies what has passed and what cannot be known.

PART III

The Politics of Diction

I hold that the mission of poetry is to record impressions, not convictions.
Wordsworth in his later writings fell into the error of recording the latter
. . . so do many poets when they grow old.
—Thomas Hardy, notebook, *Life and Work of Thomas Hardy*, p. 408

IN THIS SECTION I AIM to counter the many critical verdicts that convict the later Wordsworth of stylistic ossification.[1] Rather than a trend toward ever-increasing declamation and authoritarianism, the post-1814 career reveals a poet who could, at any time, be provoked into innovation by force of circumstances. The particular circumstances I explore here are rivalry with younger poets influenced by his earlier diction, combined with political and social controversies. In Chapter 5 I show how—finding his nature poetry emulated by Byron and Keats, who took it in a sensualized and sexualized direction he wished to disavow—Wordsworth wrote new poems that set out a Burkean sexual politics in contrast to an Ovidian nature of desire, rape, and metamorphosis. They were, however, colonized by the language they strove to correct: Wordsworth became a more Ovidian poet than he had ever been as he borrowed from the charged diction of Keats's "Hymn to Pan." Echoing Keats, the patriarch was surprised by boy—discovering, despite himself, that his poetic child was father of the man.

Fifteen years later, as I reveal in Chapter 6, the conservative, later Wordsworth, the "lost leader"[2] who had supposedly sold out to a corrupt establishment, published the most explicitly critical, not to say radical, writing of his entire career. *Yarrow Revisited* (1835) contained a long prose attack on the new Poor Laws; it also included verse condemnations of slavery. The trigger for this unexpected outburst was the *Corn Law Rhymes* of the Sheffield manufacturer Ebenezer Elliott—Wordsworthian landscape verse and lyrical ballads voicing, in the "real language of men," the anger and passion of the poor in the industrial towns. Wordsworth was galvanized by this latter day use of his 1790s' poetry: it pushed him to write new political verse of his own that tried to match Elliott's righteous anger but to channel it in a less revolutionary direction. If this was a corrective of a follower's work it was, as with the Keatsian Wordsworth of 1820, a corrective that became influenced by it. Wordsworth found himself testifying to a lifelong radicalism and attacking the government and aristocracy to which many thought him beholden: his political language gained a vehemence it had not possessed since 1798, if then. What is revealed here is that, contrary to the critical assumption that as Wordsworth aged he became reactionary, his poetry was renewed by dialogue with younger poets. What is also shown is that to the second generation of Romantic poets he was not just a forbiddingly sublime voice from the past, encountered on paper—a voice both admired and resisted—he was also a living poet, still writing, with whom one might have a dialogue and whom one might influence. Understanding this, and Wordsworth's stylistic renewal, enlarges our received picture of both his work and Romantic periodicity.[3]

Chapter 5

The Erotics of Influence

Wordsworth as Byron and Keats

The Excursion brought Wordsworth admirers in the next generation, none more so than Keats. And it was in reaction to this admiration that Wordsworth included in the *River Duddon* collection of 1820 a nature poem that significantly modified the gender and sexual politics of his past nature poetry. Derived from the same manuscript fragments as "Enough of Climbing Toil," "The Haunted Tree" addressed a long-beloved woman and member of his household scriptorium—his wife, Mary.[1] Like "Enough of Climbing Toil," it showed an older poet tempering the self-assertion that had formerly positioned women as his helpmeets. More surprisingly, it also featured echoes and allusions to the work of younger poets who imitated his style—Byron as well as Keats. These suggest that Wordsworth became Byronic in answer to Byron and Keatsian in rivalry with Keats—a father rebuking sons who presumed to be his partners yet modifying his style to answer the challenge of a new generation's Wordsworthianism. Part of what was at stake was the question of how properly to allude: on which elements of Ovid's sexualized nature should the contemporary nature poet call? The resultant poem was a departure from the nature poetry of earlier years and an intervention in the sexual politics and poetics of the day. It reveals not Hardy's poet listing his convictions, but Keats's poet exploring sensuality by reviving the mythology of the classics.

*   *   *

"The Haunted Tree" is an evocation of a particular oak tree on an exposed ridge at the top of Rydal Park—the picturesque, enclosed landscape owned by the Le Flemings, a long-established family of wealthy gentry who lived in Rydal Hall, the large mansion near Wordsworth's home. The park was a private playground, an aesthetically ordered landscape garden, a visible manifestation of the wealth and taste of the landowners. It was not open to locals; however, Wordsworth, as a friend of Lady Le Fleming, had permission to walk there. This scenario resembled those of Coleorton, where Wordsworth was Beaumont's poet, and Yardley Chase, where Cowper wrote of oak trees owned by the Earl of Northampton. In the poem Wordsworth calls on his Beaumont inscriptions, on "Yardley Oak," and his own "Yew Trees" as he ponders the tree's symbolic import. He also makes it an arbor for a pastoral comedy of love, with Ovidian antecedents and Burkean implications, that forms a dialogue with the Orientalist and Hellenistic poems of Keats and Byron. And since Keats's and Byron's language was, in 1819 and 1820, itself implicated in a scandal that threatened to unseat ministry and monarchy—to trigger, no less, revolution—then "The Haunted Tree" was also an intervention in cultural politics, however quiet and retired it first appears.

Here is the opening of the poem as published in 1820:

> THOSE silver clouds collected round the sun
> His mid-day warmth abate not, seeming less
> To overshade than multiply his beams
> By soft reflection—grateful to the sky,
> To rocks, fields, woods. Nor doth our human sense
> Ask, for its pleasure, screen or canopy
> More ample than that time-dismantled Oak
> Spreads o'er this tuft of heath: which now, attired
> In the whole fulness of its bloom, affords
> As beautiful a couch as e'er on earth
> Was fashioned; whether by the hand of art
> That Eastern Sultan, amid flowers enwrought
> On silken tissue, might diffuse his limbs
> In languor; or, by Nature, for repose
> Of panting Wood-nymph weary of the chace.
>
> (lines 1–15; *Duddon*, pp. 157–58)

The scene is beautiful, peaceful, pleasing, sensual; the spot seems remote from injustice, let alone from political controversy. The clouds do not blot out the sun and turn the day chilly; they multiply its brightness and soften its warmth. "Soft," "grateful," "pleasure": the diction emphasizes relaxed enjoyment—even the oak, being "time-dismantled," is a figure of softened power rather than undiminished authority, and it offers shelter, affording a beautiful couch for a walker to rest in peace.

It is Wordsworth's simile that takes the poem in an Orientalist direction and first introduces sexual politics to the local spot. The "Eastern Sultan" (line 12) transports the reader from the Lakeland heath to an Ottoman pleasure garden where the Sultan reposes on a silk-covered divan (an ottoman)—although Cowper's tapestry-covered sofa, embroidered with flowers, may also be in the background.[2] Wordsworth's vocabulary, unusually, lingers on sensuality: the Sultan's body "diffuse[s]," he says with a telling lexical choice, as if the too too solid flesh has been turned to smoke or scent—perhaps, we infer, after smoking fragrant opium or dallying with a harem-girl. Suddenly, we seem to be in the world of Byron, whose Eastern Tales, often set in Ottoman-ruled Greece, had caused a sensation because of their poetic evocations of Orientalized sensuality. In July 1819 the sensation was redoubled and, for Wordsworth, made uncomfortably personal, when the first cantos of the newly published Don Juan proved to contain a risqué attack on him. Byron presented his own poetry as a manly alternative to the namby-pambyness of Wordsworth's Lake poetry. He used Oriental figures to image himself as one who preferred sexual conquest to Wordsworthian solitude-in-nature: "By solitude I mean a Sultan's (not / A Hermit's), with a haram for a grot" (Don Juan, canto I, line 696; BPW, V, p. 36). He had previously portrayed Orientalism as "the only poetical policy" (BLJ, II, p. 68) guaranteed to achieve commercial success; now he offered it as a sexually frank style in contrast to Wordsworth's primness. He insulted Wordsworth as "crazed beyond all hope" and alluded to his nature poetry when he imagined Juan wandering

> by the glassy brooks,
> Thinking unutterable things; he threw
> Himself at length within the leafy nooks
> Where the wild branch of the cork forest grew;
> There poets find materials for their books,
> And every now and then we read them through,
> So that their plan and prosody are eligible,
> Unless, like Wordsworth, they prove unintelligible.
>
> (Don Juan, I, line 1635; I, lines 720–27; BPW, V, pp. 74, 37)

Don Juan did more than joke at Wordsworth's expense. It included an erotic fantasy in which the young hero, washed ashore on an Greek island governed by a pirate, meets the pirate's daughter, Haidée, "the greatest heiress of the Eastern Isles," "and like a lovely tree" (II, 1017, 1020; BPW, V, pp. 128–29). Dressed by Haidée in Turkish clothes, Juan becomes the object of her desire and, when her father leaves the island on a voyage, the couple make love (II, 1505–12; BPW, V, p. 148). The poem's knowing glamorization of youthful—and especially female—sexuality disturbed Wordsworth, who referred to the "despicable quality of the powers requisite for [its] production," adding, "I am persuaded that *Don Juan* will do more harm to the English character, than anything of our time; not so much as a Book;—But thousands who would be afraid to have it in that shape, will batten upon choice bits of it in the shape of Extracts." He bemoaned the fact that the close association of its publisher with Byron had prevented the *Quarterly Review* from defending the threatened "English character": "every true-born Englishman will regard the pretension of the Review to the character of a faithful defender of the Institutions of the country, as *hollow*" (MY, II, p. 579). For Wordsworth, Byron's popularity epitomized a worrying tendency in the nation to prefer sensual extravagance—the kind of pleasures Byron associated with a sultan—over obedience to proper authorities and to the poetry that defended them.

In 1819 and 1820 this worrying tendency was more than usually evident in the very father of the nation, the monarch. George IV, who after many years as Prince Regent became king in 1819, had been notoriously profligate, both sexually and financially, since his youth. In 1818 Wordsworth worried that George's extravagance and that of the other princes, at a time of poverty and protest, undermined support for the Tories, who supported Church and King. And this extravagance seemed truly Oriental: George spent £155,000 on adding pagodas, minarets, domes, and Indian columns to Brighton Pavilion. Thousands were spent on a succession of mistresses, while his estranged wife, Caroline, toured Europe, having numerous affairs. She returned to England in 1820, and Lord Liverpool's Tory ministry, acting on George's instigation, had her "tried" before the House of Lords, attempting to produce enough evidence of her sexual misdemeanors to enable it to deny her the title of "queen." The trial caused public outrage; for a period of months it seemed as if there might be a revolution against the tyrannical king and the ministry that tainted itself by supporting him. A crowd outside the house of the Duke of York viewed Caroline as a victim of George's "Oriental" despotism, shouting "We like princes who show themselves; we don't like Grand Turks who shut themselves up in their seraglio."[3] Radical and laboring-class protest was accompanied by opposition from middle-class women, who clearly understood that the affair had implications for the sexual politics of the nation. An address to the Queen from the "Ladies of Edinburgh," printed in *The Times* on 4 September, noted: "As your majesty has justly observed, the principles and doctrines now advanced by your accusers do not apply to your case alone, but, if made part of the law of this land, may hereafter be applied as a precedent by every careless and dissipated husband to rid himself of his wife, however good and innocent she may be; and to render his family, however, amiable, illegitimate; thereby destroying the sacred bond of matrimony, and rendering all domestic felicity very uncertain."[4] Cartoonists portrayed the threat that George's actions posed to family and legitimacy by turning his penchant for Oriental decoration against him: one depicted him as a Chinese potentate surrounded by his concubines.[5]

Given the personal, poetic, and political controversies that surrounded Orientalism and especially the sexual conduct of sultans, it is telling that Wordsworth should have referred to an "Eastern Sultan" in his poem about a Lakeland tree. He did not usually include such figures in his celebration of English landscapes; the Sultan took him far beyond his normal subject matter and diction. He included the Oriental potentate, I suggest, because he wished to indicate by allusion that his nature-poem was an antidote to Orientalist sexual politics, as practiced by the Regent and promoted in the work of Byron and other poets of the younger generation.

The poet of the younger generation most given to languorous sensuality was Keats. The words "languor" and "silken," very rare in Wordsworth's verse, feature in Keats's second collection, *Endymion*, a copy of which was owned by Wordsworth, who also heard Keats recite the "Hymn to Pan" in December 1817.[6] On that occasion Wordsworth offended Keats by declaring the poem a "pretty piece of paganism."[7] The remark was especially galling because Keats's hymn arose from his admiration for Wordsworth's fanciful picture of pagan nature in *The Excursion*:[8]

> The Traveller slaked
> His thirst from Rill or gushing Fount, and thanked
> The Naiad.—Sunbeams, upon distant Hills
> Gliding apace, with Shadows in their train,

Might, with small help from fancy, be transformed
Into fleet Oreads sporting visibly.
The Zephyrs, fanning as they passed, their wings,
Lacked not, for love, fair Objects whom they wooed
With gentle whisper. Withered Boughs grotesque,
Stripped of their leaves and twigs by hoary age,
From depth of shaggy covert peeping forth
In the low vale, or on steep mountain side

(IV, 867–78; Excursion, pp. 154–55)

In "The Haunted Tree," Wordsworth's unusually Keatsian diction suggests that he adopted from Keats the sensual language that Keats had developed from *The Excursion*'s vision of Greek nature as a playground of love[9]—a place of zephyrs wooing and of "shaggy covert[s]" where satyrs lurk. Wordsworth's description of an arboreal couch where the Sultan, "amid flowers enwrought / On silken tissue, might diffuse his limbs / In languor" (lines 12–14) evokes Keats's description of Endymion entering

A chamber, myrtle wall'd, embowered high,
Full of light, incense, tender minstrelsy,
And more of beautiful and strange beside:
For on a silken couch of rosy pride,
In midst of all, there lay a sleeping youth
Of fondest beauty

(Endymion, lines 390–95)[10]

The association of "languor" with a "heath" also uncannily echoes Keats's woodland scene, itself indebted to Wordsworth's earlier poems:

From languor's sullen bands
His limbs are loos'd, and eager, on he hies
Dazzled to trace it in the sunny skies.
It seem'd he flew, the way so easy was;
And like a new-born spirit did he pass
Through the green evening quiet in the sun,
O'er many a heath, through many a woodland dun,
Through buried paths, where sleepy twilight dreams
The summer time away.

(Endymion, lines 67–75)

Not only does Wordsworth's diction echo Keats's, but his classical similes also allude to *Endymion* only to revise its celebration of pagan sensuality. "The Haunted Tree" compares the shady heath to a spot prepared "by Nature, for repose / Of panting Wood-nymph, weary of the chase" (lines 14–15). A few lines later, Wordsworth suggests that the tree emits a strange creaking sound "As if (so Grecian shepherds would have deemed) / The Hamadryad, pent within, bewailed / Some bitter wrong" (lines 25–27). Hamadryads, as Eric C. Walker points out, appear nowhere else in Wordsworth's verse and are rarely found in either English or classical literature. They do appear, however, in the work of Keats's mentor Leigh Hunt[11] and in the very "Hymn to Pan" that Wordsworth had belittled, where they are exotic ingredients in Keats's celebration of a nature governed by uninhibited sensuality:

> O thou, whose mighty palace roof doth hang
> From jagged trunks, and overshadoweth
> Eternal whispers, glooms, the birth, life, death
> Of unseen flowers in heavy peacefulness;
> Who lov'st to see the hamadryads dress
> Their ruffled locks where meeting hazels darken;
> And through whole solemn hours dost sit, and hearken
> The dreary melody of bedded reeds—
> In desolate places, where dank moisture breeds
> The pipy hemlock to strange overgrowth;
> Bethinking thee, how melancholy loth
> Thou wast to lose fair Syrinx—do thou now,
> By thy love's milky brow!
> By all the trembling mazes that she ran,
> Hear us, great Pan!
>
> (lines 232–46)

Here Keats's Pan has a palace among the trees, the roof of which "overshadoweth" the world below; Wordsworth's "overshade" (a word he had never used before) may be an allusion to it.

If Wordsworth echoes Keats, he does so in order to differ from him. Wordsworth's hamadryad is confined within the tree, lamenting a bitter wrong: classical nature, the poet implies, contains violence and regret. Not so in the "Hymn to Pan," where the hamadryads are the object of Pan's voyeuristic desire and the whole palace is devoted to passion and fecundity, seemingly without either self-restraint or ill-consequence (lines 247–78). Keats's cornucopia is poetic as well as natural—a matter of grammar and syntax that allows the listing of each appealing natural image without requiring the reader to choose between the alternatives. We can have—see, smell, touch, taste—it all. For Wordsworth, however, this unbridled sensuality was a free-for-all: young Keats's Greek world was, at best, callow and, at worst, dangerously akin to Byron's Ottomanized endorsement of uninhibited desire and liberated sexuality. Wordsworth had no wish for twenty-something admirers to write poetry of such a kind in his wake. According to Haydon, Wordsworth's displeasure when he heard the Hymn stemmed from the fact that his "puling Christian feelings were annoyed."[12] From Wordsworth's own point of view, it was the implication that sensuality could be indulged without emotional pain and moral consequence that was naive and dangerous. It is a lesson for a young pretender that Wordsworth encodes in "The Haunted Tree": his oak, that is to say, is haunted by ancestral voices bewailing violence just as Kubla's pleasure dome proved to be. These, as we shall see, are the voices of those—usually women—who pay the price of a world that works on the principle of unrestrained male sensual desire.

Wordsworth's argument with Keats was an argument about the Lake poets' legacy. In 1817, Leigh Hunt had touted Keats and Shelley as members of a new school that was improving on the Lake poets, who had been "revolutionists" but had gone "to an extreme, calculated rather at first to make the readers of poetry disgusted with originality."[13] Keats, then, was positioned as a poet able to build successfully on the flawed revolution that Wordsworth had abandoned. But to Wordsworth, Keats was a young pretender whose romanticized nature turned classical sources and his own verse into an excuse for licentiousness. "The Haunted Tree" provided a corrective account of nature's significance in which allusion to texts both modern and ancient—Cowper, Burke, and Ovid—enacted a relationship with the past that was not only different from but a rebuke to Keats's. Wordsworth effectively returned Keats's verse to Ovid's in order to demonstrate that a nature governed by the unbridled expression of sensual desire produces pain, violence, and rape as much as love. The hamadryad bewailing some bitter wrong almost certainly alludes to Ovid's tale of Erisichthon, who chops violently into an aged oak that is sacred to Ceres, to the chagrin of her wood nymphs. The tree bleeds and a voice from within cries out (in Dryden's translation):

A *Dryad* I, by *Ceres'* Love prefer'd,
Within the Circle of this clasping Rind
Coeval grew, and now in Ruin joyn'd;
But instant Vengeance shall thy Sin pursue,
And Death is chear'd with this prophetick View.

At last the Oak with Cords enforc'd to bow,
Strain'd from the Top, and sap'd with Wounds below,
The humbler Wood, Partaker of its Fate,
Crush'd with its Fall, and shiver'd with its Weight.

The Grove destroy'd, the Sister *Dryads* moan,
Griev'd at its Loss, and frighted at their own.
Strait, Suppliants for Revenge, to *Ceres* go,
In sable Weeds, expressive of their Woe.

(lines 1177–89)[14]

It is worth noting that in "The Haunted Tree" Wordsworth uses the word "coeval" for the first time in his poetry (the oak has "coevals in the sheltered vale," line 35). This echo of "coeval grew" suggests that he most likely had Dryden's translation in mind when using Ovid to remind Keats that pagan nature metamorphoses by violence—and should therefore not be indulged but instead controlled by a self-restraining masculinity.

Self-restraining masculinity had political as well as sexual implications. Wordsworth's haunted tree stood for a version of English manliness that was significant in the public sphere. Burke, as we saw in Chapter 1, had used the oak as a symbol of the kind of authority that was proper for, and native to, British government: the people were "great cattle reposed beneath the shadow of the British oak."[15] Here the oak served to naturalize Burke's vision of politics: a growth of English soil, it suggested that the constitution was rooted in the heritable property of land, was ancient, was slow to change and grow, was organic rather than constructed, and was protective of the subjects who sheltered beneath it. Those subjects included women: the constitution demanded chivalry from the men it rewarded with power; it was their duty to protect the propertyless who were necessarily powerless.

Burke indicted Warren Hastings, the governor of the East India Company, for acting like an Oriental despot when, rather than extending his chivalric protection to the Begums of the Nawab Wazir of Oudh, he let his soldiers loot their zenana.[16]

A significant element of the British, rather than Eastern, authority of Wordsworth's oak is its agedness: it is "time-dismantled" (line 7), its vigor diminished and canopy reduced by the passing of the years. Decay and diminution, however, were essential elements of the iconographic tradition in which oaks embodied a vision of English authority. It was as a hollow shell, shorn of its branches, that Cowper's Yardley Oak configured the wisdom of age that is inseparable from loss. And it was as an ancient tree that, in lines written in 1820 or after, Wordsworth depicted Burke the elder statesman, making him an embodiment of the English constitution that he had compared to an oak:

> I see him,—old, but vigorous in age,
> Stand like an oak whose stag-horn branches start
> Out of its leafy brow, the more to awe
> The younger brethren of the grove . . .
> While he forewarns, denounces, launches forth,
> Against all systems built on abstract rights,
> Keen ridicule; the majesty proclaims
> Of Institutes and Laws, hallowed by time;
> Declares the vital power of social ties
> Endeared by Custom; and with high disdain,
> Exploding upstart Theory, insists
> Upon the allegiance to which men are born.
>
> (*The Prelude* (1850), VII, 519–30)

Burke had himself argued for the merits of age in a governor. He suggested that the effective ruler tempered the naked exercise of paternal power so as to rule not only through fear and awe but also through the willing acquiescence of the ruled. Burke identified the grandfather as being a man of this kind because his awesome authority is softened by the decrepitude that comes with the years. The aged grandfather could be admired and loved as well as feared and obeyed: he was beautiful as well as sublime.[17]

Wordsworth's tree is an oak of this grandfatherly kind, a grandpaternal presence that is symbolic in its "time-dismantled" state. Now decayed, it is an oak of protective assurance rather than threatening assertion. And, as a metonym for the poet, it defines Wordsworth himself as such a male, whom age has not so much wearied as rendered chivalrous. Thus, unlike a sultan in his pleasure garden or a Greek god pursuing a nymph through an oak grove, Wordsworth can offer to his lady the ground at the tree's foot, despite its exposed position, as a place she (rather than the Sultan) can rest in comfort. Such is his confidence in the sheltering nature of the tree—in the symbolic English masculinity which it represents—that he can subsume troubling intimations in social generosity: "O Lady" he says, "approach." This is a decorous invitation rather than an abrupt instruction or passionate demand; it stems from his conviction that the ghosts of the female victims of male (sexual) despotism are laid to rest in the tree.

> O Lady! fairer in thy Poet's sight
> Than fairest spiritual Creature of the groves,
> Approach—and, thus invited, crown with rest
> The noon-tide hour:—though truly some there are
> Whose footsteps superstitiously avoid
> This venerable Tree; for, when the wind
> Blows keenly, it sends forth a creaking sound
> Above the general roar of woods and crags;
> Distinctly heard from far—a doleful note!
> As if (so Grecian shepherds would have deem'd)
> The Hamadryad, pent within, bewailed
> Some bitter wrong. Nor it is unbelieved,
> By ruder fancy, that a troubled Ghost
> Haunts this old Trunk; lamenting deeds of which
> The flowery ground is conscious. But no wind
> Sweeps now along this elevated ridge;
> Not even a zephyr stirs;—the obnoxious Tree
> Is mute; and, in his silence, would look down
> On thy reclining form . . .
>
> (lines 16–34)

Wordsworth is sure the Lady will not be troubled by the ghosts lurking in the tree—still less be subjected to the same violent pursuit that the nymphs suffered—for he knows better than the locals who superstitiously avoid the creaking oak, their "fancy" imagining it to be haunted. Yet how sure is he?

He does not dismiss the ghost stories out of hand, for such stories represent a sensitive response to nature's power akin to his own intimations. Perhaps they are contemporary Lakeland versions of the classical belief in nature-spirits. He is ambivalent: his syntax becomes indirect and the rhetoric self-canceling: the litotes "Nor is it unbelieved" (line 27) leaves it undecided as to who exactly of the locals might entertain at least a half-belief in ghosts. And that half-belief, once declared, taints the peaceful spot with the knowledge of past "deeds of which / The flowery ground is conscious" (lines 29–30) (whether these deeds really happened or are just fancies). To put this another way, the poem raises the possibility of the defloration of the ground (and of the Lady), as if Wordsworth, so often the intimator of troubling forces within nature, feels at least a residual affiliation to the local—and classical—beliefs in ghosts and deities that haunt the tree with strange fits of passion. His language betrays him, suggesting that he remains drawn toward an anthropomorphic relationship that ostensibly he would banish from the local scene to the pagan past. The word "obnoxious" (line 32) is a case in point: meaning principally "vulnerable to harm," 'subject to authority," it also meant, as it still does, "harmful." It appears in *Paradise Lost*, where its ambiguity reveals the fallen Satan's vulnerability and his harmfulness as he enters Eden ready to tempt Eve: "Who aspires must down as low / As high he soared, obnoxious first or last / To basest things" (IX, 169–71). Here the Miltonic allusion makes one of the ghosts haunting the tree satanic: it invokes, indirectly, the tree of knowledge in Genesis and Wordsworth's yew trees. The oak, and the lady who lies in its shade, remain potentially vulnerable to the harmful spirit of Satanic desire. The tree-poet who wishes for a safe and social ground for Englishman and woman must keep the ghosts of both Greek (carnal) and Hebrew (Biblical) knowledge safely confined within, for they cannot be ignored—the sexuality upon which all nature depends always, it seems, contains the potential for violence and destruction.

Violence, destruction, and, at least implicitly, sexuality had been significant in Wordsworth's own early poetry, vital, in fact, to his intimate engagement with the Lakeland treescape. In "Nutting" and in *The Prelude*, when pillaging hazelnuts and bird nests he had violated the woods and had, in the process, won revelations of its dark spiritual power, albeit in the form of rebukes and hauntings. He could not turn his back on such violence and rapine now, when a middle-aged paternal figure representing the woodland as a calm retreat, without registering a residual temptation to believe that nature-spirits are brought forth by man's violent desire. Ovid, if not Keats, remained compelling, not least because, as *The Excursion* passage that Keats admired reveals, Wordsworth continued to see a poetry of fanciful play as an alternative to the dangerous seductions of playing the role of imaginative prophet in the wilderness (see my readings of "The Brownie's Cell" and "Enough of Climbing Toil" in Chapters 3 and 4). Ovidian tales were also examples of the legends and lore by which people expressed their relationship with their locality. Thus, he also invoked Ovid elsewhere in the Duddon volume to relate his own rendition of Cumbrian locality to classical tales recording the Greek myths—myths born of people's translation of their love of place into narrative.[18]

Allusions to his own and his friends' earlier poems of love and peace help to limit the persistence of past violence. The lines "it sends forth a creaking sound / (Above the general roar of woods and crags) / Distinctly heard from far—a doleful note" (lines 22–24) echo Coleridge's "This Lime-Tree Bower My Prison," in which the senses "keep the heart / Awake to Love and Beauty" and the "last rook" "flew creaking o'er thy head, and had a charm / For thee, my gentle-hearted Charles, to whom / No sound is dissonant which tells of Life" (lines 63–64, 74–76; CPW, I, i, pp. 353–54). By revising Coleridge's lines, Wordsworth invokes the community-in-nature expressed in the writing of the Somerset period. He summons up a loving conversation poem, making a beautiful appeal to feminine sympathy, rather than a self-assertive raid upon the fells, cliffs, and groves. Wordsworth invokes spousal and sibling verses, rather than songs of conquest and rapine. Addressed to Mary, "The Haunted Tree" seeks to subsume his youthful lust for nature within, and to replace the immoral routes taken by his poetic successors with, a circle of men, women, and nature that renews the poetic circle of his youth in a new, paternalist form.

In the remaining lines, Wordsworth sets out a vision of this renewed circle—a vision of the kind of love he would now elicit from nature. He would confine the dangerous voices of lament, while not ignoring their occupation of the ground. By so doing, he would render it safe it for the Lady to approach. He would control nature by his written art, redeeming it and himself from an affiliation to the threatening violence of male desire, in favor of a decorous and chivalric eroticism. His time-dismantled tree, despite its lonely elevated position, would not be, as was "the one blasted tree" on the misty pass in *The Prelude*, a location of "visionary dreariness" (XI, 378, 311) where nature becomes an abyss of death. It would be, instead, a place where a poet might express desire by polite entreaty, seeking a lady's confidence by preparing the (peaceful) ground. Here Wordsworth's tree is decidedly Burkean, that of a powerful male entranced by the female that he shelters. The sublime softened by the beautiful. Since the whole scene is imagined *for* the Lady, it acts, at the same time, as a gift to her in which offers of a more intimate relationship are encoded, a courteous but knowing discourse of courtship.

In the poem's very last lines the focus changes from the single tree on the ridge to several oaks that grow below, by the river. These valley trees

> in the sheltered vale
> Seem to participate, the whilst they view
> Their own far-stretching arms and leafy heads
> Vividly pictured in some glassy pool,
> That, for a brief space, checks the hurrying stream!
>
> (lines 36–40)

These trees do not look down on a resting lady; they look down on their own reflections. This self-reflexive looking allows them a momentary self-image, "vividly pictured" in a still pool that arrests "the hurrying stream" of time and space. Vivid though it is, however, the privileged picture that these waterside trees together gain of themselves is potentially narcissistic (in Ovid, of course, Narcissus was changed into a waterside plant). It is less permanent and less social than the reconciliation of sublime and beautiful, and of male and female, that is available to the tree-poet and the Lady. Solitary self-observation is here firmly relegated below the more bracing relationship possible if one risks the more exposed spot on the ridge, where the tree may be assaulted by violence both natural (wind) and human (desire). Wordsworth chooses the more difficult place (a place that for him contrasts with Keats's lowdown bowers and Byron's enclosed harems). Asserting himself to make the spot safe for a loving partnership, he takes the risk of violence (both past and present) upon himself, as a knight should for his lady. This chivalric position is paternalist: protective, gentlemanly, Burkean. The oak's location in the private park of the local landowner is germane to this vision: the poem not only sets out a more appropriate masculinity for the governing gentry and aristocracy than that of Lord Byron and the King, but also suggests how that masculinity should be both derived from and symbolized by the land they own. Since landownership was the basis of their wealth and power, the poem was effectively repairing the ideology that justified their domination of economics and politics, insofar as that ideology was expressed through landscape gardening and literature (cf. the Coleorton inscriptions).

And yet "The Haunted Tree" is not simply a restatement of conservatism; it is also a validation of poetic play—of the mythmaking that stems from fiction's ability to transform the known world into one of pretense. Wordsworth asks his Lady—and his reader—to re-imagine their relationships to each other by pretending that the human is embodied in the natural. Narrator and Lady, poet and reader, can then meet in a land safe for courteous play. It is a poetic land in which one encounters the human as if it were natural and the natural as if it were human—a dreamy land of representation poised between self and other, subject and object, power and love, violence and peace, sight and sound. It is a land, Wordsworth suggests, in which poetry must make men live lest the solitary man, like a despotic ruler or pagan poet, hear in all things only his own violent desire, see only his own beloved self. It is an anti-Keatsian, anti-Byronic land, avowedly English rather than Orientalist, but one governed by a naturalized paternalism. To love nature, Wordsworth shows, involves remaking it in our own image—and that image changes with age. The Prospero-poet writes the world with all the skill and art he has accumulated over the years. He writes it with erudition and with enlightenment. Alluding, he raises, only to banish, or try to banish, the ghosts that remain of his power-seeking past—and the power-seeking animation of nature represented by Ovid and the myths Ovid poeticized. But he also banishes the rough strife of youth, which appears to him as a threat to the world that is under his spell. And as for that spell, it is powerful still, renewed by its allusion to past spells, but it is power seeking rest and peace, content to look, converse, and reflect. Within it, calm and controlled as it is, traditional hierarchies and inequalities are remade but not changed utterly.

Published in a volume named after a cherished spot—the Duddon valley—"The Haunted Tree" demonstrates that by 1820 Wordsworth wished to be read as a poet who placed specific spots within a national landscape construed historically and geographically but also sexually and poetically—this construal being both personal and public (cf. "The Brownie's Cell" in the same volume: see Chapter 3). The poem suggests that for the later Wordsworth spots of time—and space—were vital, but not in the same way they had been in his youth. The places where and times when nature uncovered its inner powers are not lost: the ghosts are not exorcised. They still haunt Wordsworth: he still encounters them in the rocks, stones, and trees of his local landscape. But he now works to lay them to rest, turning aside from the need to pursue them to their sources, in favor of an affirmation of a human companionship that is facilitated by (and itself facilitates) a peaceful relationship to nature. For this turning aside to be meaningful, it has to occur with a companion who knows what the spot has previously meant, who has co-made the spot in that she has written it out in manuscripts and retrieved it from them. As in "Enough of Climbing Toil," when validated by her, he can turn aside—with and to her—from the need to wrest from the place its inner secrets. Only with a companion—a woman—who shares his past in her memory archive can Wordsworth redeem (his) nature from possession by the ghosts of his own, and other males', pursuit of its being. The older Wordsworth needed more than ever before to find himself with and through long-beloved women. He needed their imagined witness, he needed their embodied memory, and he needed their manuscript curation to be able to raise the ghosts of his past and then cope with the consequences of having done so. That is why so many of his late poems are not only poems of allusion to his own and others' texts but also poems that prefer companionship to solitariness and exchange a landscape of power for one of vulnerability.

Chapter 6

Wordsworth and Ebenezer Elliott

Radicalism Renewed

In 1835 Wordsworth published, in *Yarrow Revisited*, some of the most explicitly political writing of his entire career. In both verse and prose, he intervened in current affairs with an unprecedented directness. Gone was the caution that had, in the 1790s, led him to suppress his letter to the Bishop of Llandaff and in 1807 to delay his pamphlet on the Convention of Cintra so that, by the time it appeared, it was outdated. Moreover, what he had to say in poems entitled "Humanity" and "The Warning," and in a twenty-six-page prose postscript on the Poor Laws, was not the kind of endorsement of the established order that his allegiance to the arch-reactionary Earl of Lonsdale led readers to expect. Hazlitt, Shelley, and Byron, had they still been living, would have been surprised to read the poet whom they regarded as having abandoned the cause of liberty attacking "reckless laws, in conformity with theories of political economy, which, whether right or wrong in the abstract, have proved a scourge to tens of thousands" (YR, p. 329). Wordsworth reinforced this critique by quoting from "The Female Vagrant" lines that showed poverty as a matter of social injustice: "Homeless, near a thousand homes they stood, / And near a thousand tables pined, and wanted food" (YR, p. 328). This was to revive the radical verse that had led him to be called a Jacobin, and that verse was matched by new poetry that was equally Jacobinical in that, rather than viewing poverty as the effect of the lower orders' immorality or of the natural scheme of things, it diagnosed it as the terrible result of a commercial system defended by law:

                                                                    rules
Fetched with cupidity from heartless schools,
That to an Idol, falsely called "the Wealth
Of Nations," sacrifice a People's health,
Body and mind and soul; a thirst so keen
Is ever urging on the vast machine
Of sleepless Labour, 'mid whose dizzy wheels
The Power least prized is that which thinks and feels.

                    ("Humanity," lines 87–94; YR, pp. 295–300)

The poor were "in a state of wretchedness," Wordsworth continued (YR, p. 328), and the new Poor Law—blaming them for their poverty, removing support for impoverished workers, and forcing paupers into workhouses—was an abdication of the nation's responsibility to its people.

Wordsworth's diagnosis was radical, but his remedy was not. "The Warning" attacked campaigners who in speeches and writings tried to politicize—in his view, inflame—the people (YR, pp. 255–62). Wordsworth may have resented the system that impoverished laborers, but he was afraid of the consequences of their politicization, although his own verse tends toward that very politicization. His fear is shown by his imputation of "slanderous tongues" (line 113) to the leaders who aim for the very reforms he had once supported: universal suffrage and social justice. Behind his fear are his knowledge that the poor have cause to be wrathful and his interpretation of the French Revolution as the manipulation of mob rule by demagogues. In the face of this fear, he has no political solution to recommend for the injustices he so graphically protests. Instead, he refers the legitimately angry laborers to God:

Oh may the Almighty scatter with his grace
These mists, and lead you to a safer place,
By paths no human wisdom can foretrace!
May He pour round you, from worlds far above
Man's feverish passions, his pure light of love[.]

                                                    (lines 131–35)

This pious hope is a cop-out designed less to calm the people's resentments or answer their needs than to excuse Wordsworth of the demagoguery he attributes to others who make the poor aware of the political injustice they suffer. It stops his revived radicalism short, although it does not invalidate it.

In this chapter I investigate a hidden context for the revived radicalism and the stopping short that characterize *Yarrow Revisited*. I explore one of the reasons a poet so keen in 1815 to live down his notoriety as a Jacobin should have jeopardized his recently achieved respectability by attacking the political system that benefited his readers and his patrons. He did so, moreover, only to rebuke the radical leaders with whom the attacks linked him. Poets do not normally include political essays in their collections, but Wordsworth was evidently strongly aroused. What aroused him was not just current public debate (he had, after all, published no writing about the 1832 Reform Bill although vehement in his dislike of it in private) but also a personal, poetic relationship that troubled him to the core. This relationship, like that with Keats examined in Chapter 5, exhibited an anxiety of influence not from but upon another poet. In this case the anxiety concerned not the sexual politics but the labor politics of his follower's verse. The follower was Ebenezer Elliott, from the industrial town of Sheffield—a man born into the manufacturing classes who, after a childhood working in a foundry had denied him formal education, made himself both a factory owner and a poet, having been encouraged to improve his verse by Southey, with whom he had corresponded since 1809.

Elliott had published poems before, but he appeared in startling new guise in 1831 as the author of the *Corn Law Rhymes*—poems protesting that the tariff on imported wheat, which protected the profits of British landowners, had raised the grain price beyond the means of the laboring classes. Laborers tilling the land, their wages too low to afford bread, effectively starved amid fields of plenty. Elliott's volume recruited *Lyrical Ballads* for a political cause; it was both a tribute to Wordsworth's radical poetry of 1798 and a rebuke to the poet he had more recently become. Wordsworth, whose patron Lonsdale strongly supported the laws, had encountered Elliott's volume by early 1832,[1] passing it on to Southey and commenting (in 1836), "None of us have done better than he has in his best, though there is a deal of stuff arising from his hatred of existing things. Like Byron, Shelley, &c., he looks on much with an evil eye. . . . Elliott has a fine eye for nature. He is an extraordinary man."[2]

The *Corn Law Rhymes* was extraordinary indeed. It begins with a preface, decisive in judgment, aggressive in tone, which echoes Wordsworth's Preface to *Lyrical Ballads* when it declares that "any subject whatever in which man takes interest, how ever humble and common-place it may be, is capable of inspiring high and true poetry."[3] Like Wordsworth, Elliott admires Burns as a poet of the people; however, he is more direct and more decided in arguing that poetry and politics are united: "all genuine poets are fervid politicians," he asserts (p. v), citing Shakespeare and Milton. He adds to Wordsworth's vindication of the poetry of the common man a contempt for the beneficiaries of a social and political system that enriches the aristocrat and the gentleman and impoverishes the rustic and the mechanic: "And is it of no importance what a man of the middle class— hardly raised above the lowest, thinks—when the lowest are beginning to think? To Sir Thomas Bread-tax Pauper, Lady Betty Pension, and all the great and small vulgar, my opinions may be the ne plus ultra of impropriety; but, believing as I do, that the Corn Laws have a direct and rapid tendency to ruin my ten children and their country, with all its venerable and venerated institutions, where is the wonder if I hate the perpetrators of such insane atrocities?" (p. vii). Passion in poetry is justified as the righteous indignation of a man who speaks for a class that has suffered under laws that enrich the landowner at the laborer's expense.

The *Corn Law Rhymes* spoke to, as well as for, the laboring classes: it sold for ninepence, a price laborers could afford; *Yarrow Revisited*, by contrast, cost nine shillings. Elliott addressed both the "lowest" and their so-called superiors, ending his preface by printing wholesale the "Declaration of the Sheffield Mechanics' Anti-Bread-Tax Society"—a laborers' union he had helped create. This declaration was an expression of laboring class solidarity, a consciousness-raising politicization designed to let the governing classes know that the workers were now a collectivized mass who would no longer tolerate their exploitation:

Convinced that the mechanics are the only body of men in this country sufficiently independent to oppose, with any chance of success, the host of corruptionists who are feeding on our labour, and, at the same time, limiting the market for our productions; trusting also that we shall speedily be joined by every wise and good mechanic in the empire, and supported by the yet undebased portion of the middle class of our countrymen, if any such there be,— We, the Sheffield Mechanics' Anti-Bread-Tax Society . . . declare, That, as we cannot escape from the consequences of the Cornlaw, (except by causing it to be repealed, or by emigrating with our heart-broken wives and children) we will, by all the legal means in our power, oppose the horrible . . . Corn law; and never remit in our exertions until the monopoly of the first necessary of life be utterly destroyed. The case of our oppressors, as stated by themselves, furnishes unanswerable reasons why we ought no longer to maintain them in their present character of palaced paupers. They say they cannot live without alms. If the assertion be true, why do they not go to the workhouse for their pay as other paupers do? If it be not true, why are they not sent to the tread-mill for obtaining money under false pretences? (pp. 3–4)

He concluded with a message of warning for the rich: parliamentary reform had better be enacted, for the Society, which had suspended its operations when the Reform Bill was announced, was capable of mustering "at least five hundred thousand adult males! . . . Should the Reform Bill disappoint our just expectations, . . . it may yet be necessary to array a Political Union of all the plundered against all the thieves."[4]

Elliott's thinly veiled threats of public disorder placed him directly at odds with Wordsworth, who, in private, opposed parliamentary reform because he feared it would precipitate class revenge, as revolution had in France. Yet Wordsworth did not dismiss Elliott for his radical rhetoric, although he complained about "his hatred of existing things."[5] Evidently, he was energized by, as well as disgruntled about, Elliott's intensely topical politicization of the *Lyrical Ballads*' poetic manifesto. The *Corn Law Rhymes* put this politicization into practice on the lines of such ballads as "The Mad Mother" and "The Complaint of a Forsaken Indian Woman." "Song," for instance, is spoken by a girl to a dying father, his wife and baby having already died of poverty:

And their mother, who sank
   Broken-hearted to rest;
And the baby, that drank
   'Till it froze on her breast;
With tears, and with smiles,
   Are waiting for thee,
In the beautiful isles
   Where the wrong'd are the free.

Go, loved one, and rest
 Where the poor cease to pay!
To the land of the blest
 Thou art wearing away.
But the son of thy pain
 Will yet stay with me,
And poor little Jane
 Look sadly like thee.

     (lines 17–32; *Corn Law Rhymes*, p. 23)

Verbally and thematically indebted to Wordsworth, Elliott's ballad evokes a
more specific and more urban setting—the poverty of the industrial town. So
does "The Death Feast," a macabre ballad evoking "We Are Seven," "The Mad
Mother," "The Thorn," "The Female Vagrant," and "The Last of the Flock":

My brother John work'd hard, and tried
 To smile on Jane and me.
But work grew scarce, while bread grew dear,
 And wages lessen'd too;
For Irish hordes were bidders here,
 Our half-paid work to do.
Yet still he strove with failing breath
 And sinking cheek, to save
Consumptive Jane from early death—
 Then join'd her in the grave.
His watery hand in mine I took,
 And kiss'd him till he slept;
O, still I see his dying look!
 He tried to smile, and wept!
I bought his coffin with my bed,
 My gown bought earth and prayer;
I pawn'd my mother's ring for bread—
 I pawn'd my father's chair.
My Bible yet remains to sell,
 And yet unsold shall be;
But language fails my woes to tell—
 Even crumbs were scarce with me.

I sold poor Jane's grey linnet then—
    It cost a groat a-year;
I sold John's hen, and miss'd the hen,
    When eggs were selling dear:
For autumn nights seem'd wintry cold,
    While seldom blazed my fire,
And eight times eight no more I sold
    When eggs were getting higher.
But still I glean the moor and heath;
    I wash, they say, with skill;
And workhouse bread ne'er cross'd my teeth,—
    I trust it never will.
But when the day on which John died
    Returns with all its gloom,
I seek kind friends, and beg, with pride,
    A banquet for the tomb.
One friend, my brother James, at least,
    Comes then with me to dine;
Let others keep the marriage-feast,
    The funeral feast is mine.
For then on him I fondly call,
    And then they live again!
Tomorrow is our festival
    Of death, and John, and Jane.
Even now, behold! they look on me,
    Exulting from the skies,
While angels round them weep to see
    The tears gush from their eyes!
I cannot weep—why can I not?
    My tears refuse to flow:
My feet are cold, my brain is hot—
    Is fever madness?—No.
Thou smilest, and in scorn—but thou,
    Couldst thou forget the dead?
No common beggar courtsies now,
    And begs for burial bread.

              (lines 11–68; *Corn Law Rhymes*, pp. 32–34)

These poems represent the most successful reworking of Wordsworth's lyrical ballad style: like their models, they are saved from sentimentality by their concentration on the specifics of common people's poverty—in this case, urban rather than rural. Elliott was close enough to his speakers to focus on the exact, colloquial detail, but it was from Wordsworth that he learned to do so.

If Wordsworth was impressed by Elliott's mastery of his ballad style, he nonetheless singled out for praise a more complex piece entitled "The Ranter." This poem tells of a Sheffield preacher called Miles Gordon, a Primitive Methodist. A solitary, he lodges with a widow and her children; his domestic kindnesses to this poor family establish his virtue. But he is also a man who puts his natural piety into social action, and this wins him the loyal following of the exploited workers, to whom he preaches about the love of nature and the need for equality, mixing scripture and politics. His "words of truth" bring his laborer followers out of doors to hear his Sunday sermon in the open air, on the moors above the manufacturing town Sheffield. Elliott, in fact, addresses readers on his behalf, including us in the energized congregation:

> Up, sluggards, up! the mountains one by one,
> Ascend in light; and slow the mists retire
> From vale and plain. The cloud on Stannington
> Beholds a rocket—No, 'tis Morthen spire!
> The sun is risen! cries Stanedge, tipp'd with fire;
> On Norwood's flowers the dew-drops shine and shake;
> Up, sluggards, up! and drink the morning breeze.
> The birds on cloud-left Osgathorpe awake;
> And Wincobank is waving all his trees
> O'er subject towns, and farms, and villages,
> And gleaming streams, and wood, and waterfalls.
> Up, climb the oak-crown'd summit! Hoober Stand
> And Keppel's Pillar, gaze on Wentworth's halls,
> And misty lakes, that brighten and expand,
> And distant hills, that watch the western strand.
> Up! trace God's foot-prints, where they paint the mould
> With heavenly green, and hues that blush and glow
> Like angel's wings; while skies of blue and gold
> Stoop to Miles Gordon on the mountain's brow.

Behold the Great Unpaid! the prophet, lo!
Sublime he stands beneath the Gospel tree,
And Edmund stands on Shirecliffe at his side;
Behind him, sinks, and swells, and spreads a sea
Of hills, and vales, and groves; before him glide
Don, Rivelin, Loxley, wandering in their pride
From heights that mix their azure with the cloud;
Beneath him, spire and dome are glittering;
And round him press his flock, a woe-worn crowd.

(lines 66–93; Corn Law Rhymes, pp. 7–8)

This magnificent passage might well be what Wordsworth thought of as Elliott's "best": it displays complete mastery of the interrelation of imagery, exclamation, syntax, and rhyme to create a visualization of places that, with gathering urgency, come to center on the preacher. Elliott harnesses the techniques of eighteenth-century prospect poetry to the Miltonic verse sentences of Wordsworth's nature poems; he echoes *The Excursion* and "To Joanna" in invoking the names of local hills to place Gordon at the center of his region and his people. The preacher stands aloft between shore and shore, earth and sky. All are united by the poet's spellbinding exhortation, a prelude to his own inspiring sermon: climactic and sublime, indeed.

It is *The Excursion*, the Wordsworthian poem Elliott praised most highly,[6] to which "The Ranter" most strongly responds. The themes, topoi, and diction are all derived from Wordsworth's portrait of a reclusive former preacher who retreats from public commitments to a mountain cottage and instructs his audience on the open fell. What Wordsworth's Solitary has to teach is his experience of the shared excitement of being part of a radical movement:

<blockquote>
If busy men
In sober conclave met, to weave a web
Of amity, whose living threads should stretch
Beyond the seas, and to the farthest pole,
There did I sit, assisting. If, with noise
And acclamation, crowds in open air
Expressed the tumult of their minds, my voice
There mingled, heard or not. The powers of song
I left not uninvoked; and, in still groves,
</blockquote>

Where mild enthusiasts tuned a pensive lay
Of thanks and expectation, in accord
With their belief, I sang Saturnian rule
Returned,—a progeny of golden years
Permitted to descend, and bless mankind.
—With promises the Hebrew Scriptures teem:
I felt their invitation; and resumed
A long-suspended office in the House
Of public worship, where, the glowing phrase
Of ancient inspiration serving me,
I promised also,—with undaunted trust
Foretold, and added prayer to prophecy;
The admiration winning of the crowd;
The help desiring of the pure devout.

(*Excursion*, III, 753–75)

Looking back, the Solitary attributes his embrace of the role of political agitator as much to the mutual excitement of speaker and audience as he does to French revolutionary principles. But he has come to distrust his ability to inspire communal activism by the power of oratory. Political prophesying, he reflects, led him to extreme views and dangerous company. Disillusioned, the Solitary now regards his political sermonizing as having been not only a futile but also a self-serving process into which he was lured by his enjoyment of popular admiration. He turns away from politics, and from preaching, in bitter regret. His auditors hope to heal his consequent depression by advocating an active love of nature as a therapeutic alternative to the dangerous liaisons of radical campaigning. The Solitary's moorland home will be a nest of local attachment, leading to spiritual transcendence, rather than a height from which to spread visions of social justice and political reform.

"The Ranter" is in direct opposition to the quietism of *The Excursion*. Elliott rewrites the Wordsworthian moor as a place not remote from, but essential to, political engagement. Hoober Stand, Keppel's Pillar, and Shirecliffe are accessible to the laborers of Sheffield—at least on the one day a week they are free from labor. These are unenclosed lands that offer a liberty not experienced in the laborer's workplace or home; they are vantage points that let the worker look down upon the landed estate of the aristocrat (this is to reverse the topographical hierarchy of the prospect poem in which the view from the top is the property of the landowner, master of all he surveys). Commanding heights, the moors allow preacher and congregation to see the patterns of economic injustice spread across the lands below; they also empower a freedom of speech. From the natural pulpit they provide, Gordon, the preacher, foments his listeners' class resentment, calling down scriptural wrath on the heads of the ministers and aristocrats who have thrown away Englishmen's liberty in the interests of their own profit:

> Oh, we were great, magnanimous, and free,
> And pillage-purchased—yet unsold, unbought;
> Bread-tax'd, and Peterloo'd, and parish paid,
> And Cadi-Dervised—therefore most devout;
> Unplunder'd, undegraded, unbetray'd,
> And Sidmouth'd, Oliver'd, and Castlereagh'd!—
> (lines 166–71; *Corn-Law Rhymes*, p. 11)

He treats the Christianity of politicians such as William Wilberforce as pious fraud, asking his flock to see themselves as worse off than the colonial slaves whom the Evangelicals were campaigning to emancipate and proselytize:

> Pious they are, cool, circumspect, severe;
> And while they feel for woes beyond the wave,
> They laud the tyrants who starve millions here:
> The famish'd Briton must be fool or knave,
> But wrongs are precious in a foreign slave.
> Their Bibles for the heathen load our fleets;
> Lo, gloating eastward, they inquire, "What news?"
> We die, we answer, foodless, in the streets,
> And what reply your men of Gospel-views?
> Oh, they are sending bacon to the Jews!
> Their lofty souls have telescopic eyes,
> Which see the smallest speck of distant pain,
> While, at their feet, a world of agonies,
> Unseen, unheard, unheeded, writhes in vain.
> (lines 172–85; pp. 11–12)

In effect, "The Ranter" reconnects Wordsworth's Solitary with his rejected past: Elliott makes him again a radical preacher and in the process aligns

The Excursion with the Jacobin poetry that Wordsworth (and Coleridge) had written in the 1790s. "The Ranter" is both a tribute and an act of critical revision, repoliticizing the nature poetry that had once also been reformist poetry by again voicing the complaints of the poor, and attacking religious cant, as Wordsworth had done in *Lyrical Ballads.*

The poetry Wordsworth wrote after encountering the *Corn Law Rhymes* reveals how profoundly stirred he was by Elliott's radical reworking of his verse. The ranter Miles Gordon haunted his imagination to the extent that when he came to write the epitaph of Charles Lamb, in 1835–36, he borrowed the key phrase used to establish the goodness of the ranter. Voicing the feelings of the widow who will survive Gordon's death, Elliott wrote, modifying Psalm 106,

> But they shall meet again—that hope is sure;
> And, oh! she venerates his mind and heart,
> For he is pure, if mortal e'er was pure!
>
> (lines 27–29; p. 6)

Wordsworth, in turn, speaks of Lamb on behalf of his "widow"—the recurrently disturbed sister with whom Lamb had lived to save her from a life in a madhouse. Voicing her point of view, Wordsworth says, "Oh he was good, if e'er a good man lived."[7] This phrase is the climactic statement of the epitaph, the moment when the commemorative poem finally breaks into simple exclamation. Wordsworth concentrates the emotional impact by contracting Elliott's phrase and rendering it as direct speech.

In fact, the epitaph for Lamb plays out Wordsworth's ambivalence about Elliott's modification of *The Excursion.* Wordsworth draws on Elliott's idealization of Gordon as an updated version of the Solitary, but he does not include Gordon's politics. Like Gordon's, Lamb's acts of domestic charity assure his "widow" that he will go to heaven where she will be reunited with him. Lamb, Wordsworth tells his sister, has gone "To the blest world where parting is unknown" (line 131). In death as in life, Lamb becomes the man the Solitary might have been if he could have been content, as Lamb is said to have been, with a life of "quiet sequestration!" (line 121) shared with a companion—a "*dual* loneliness" (line 128). In fact, the Lambs had lived quite a social life, regularly entertaining friends; moreover, Lamb had engaged with social, if not political, issues in his publications. Wordsworth's insistence on Lamb's sequestration bespeaks his own wish to idealize the virtue of reclusive domesticity over and against political engagement. The Solitary, after Elliott's response to *The Excursion*, is reincarnated, and cured, as Lamb-with-sister; he is, however, still kept away from active involvement in the public sphere.

If Wordsworth's Lamb remained "gentle," secluded from political commitment of Gordon's kind, Wordsworth was less restrained in his own person, rediscovering an explicitly radical voice for the first time in thirty years. In "Humanity" (drafted 1829–30, revised 1835) he echoed the argument that there were slaves in England, shaming the mine and factory owners (many of them aristocrats—including his patron Lonsdale) who opposed measures designed to alleviate the exploitation of women and children in mills and collieries:

> Shame that our laws at distance should protect
> Enormities, which they at home reject!
> "Slaves cannot breathe in England"—a proud boast!
> And yet a mockery! if, from coast to coast,
> Though fettered slave be none, her floors and soil
> Groan underneath a weight of slavish toil,
> For the poor Many . . .
>
> (lines 82–88)

The argument that not only did the law, to its shame, allow slavery abroad but also effectively condoned it at home had long been made in prose by Cobbett, the reformist journalist whom the Tories most hated. In making it in verse in which political points were sharpened by rhyme, Wordsworth allied his poem with Elliott's rhyming "rant" on the subject[8]—an unlikely association for a government office-holder and one that implied he had been moved to rediscover an underlying radicalism by this unexpected protégé whose political poems renewed his 1798 poetic achievement and exposed his more recent quietude.

This rediscovered radicalism was unmistakable in the prose postscript, where Wordsworth not only criticized the assumption of the Whig reformers who drafted the Poor Law Amendment Act that those receiving parish relief were feckless and that the stigmatization of pauperism would reduce their numbers, but also returned to the Paineite revolutionary language of "rights," rather than the Burkean conservative emphasis on duties. There was, he stated, "a right in the people (not to be gainsaid by utilitarians and economists) to public support when, from any cause, they may be unable to support themselves" (YR, p. 326). Thus, relief of poverty was not a matter of pity and charity but a basic right of the citizen established by his or her membership of the nation. This was the language of Jacobinism rather than that of Tory paternalism.

Wordsworth's diagnosis may have been Jacobinical, but he stopped short of endorsing radical campaigns. In "The Warning" he responds to the *Corn Law Rhymes* by attacking the leaders of laboring-class protest as "headstrong": they dizzy themselves and their followers with vain and specious dreams of plenty:

> Or, bound by oaths, come forth to tread earth's floor
> In marshalled thousands, darkening street and moor
> With the worst shape mock-patience ever wore;
> Or, to the giddy top of self-esteem
> By Flatterers carried, mount into a dream
> Of boundless suffrage, at whose sage behest
> Justice shall rule, disorder be supprest,
> And every man sit down as Plenty's Guest!
> —Oh for a bridle bitted with remorse
> To stop your Leaders in their headstrong course!
>
> (lines 121–30)

"Bound by oaths" keys Wordsworth's critique to Elliott's text, which had published verbatim the resolution of the oath-taking Sheffield Mechanics' Anti-Bread-Tax Society. "Darkening street and moor," meanwhile, evokes the scene of radical instruction in "The Ranter" (the moor, filled with light, that was itself a response to the moors that featured in "Resolution and Independence" and *The Excursion*). Wordsworth depicts the united workers as an ominous presence, as if reacting to the threatening tone in which Elliott reminded parliament of their united strength en masse.

That Wordsworth was disturbed by Elliott's development of his poetry becomes still more apparent in the postscript, where he takes up Elliott's charge that the poor are slaves only to redefine the word by suggesting that, when they join unions, they give up their individual will and become enslaved to their demagogue leaders. This was to differ widely from his endorsement of the church as an institution in which the individual, through liturgy and custom, participated in a mass organization. The church, Wordsworth argued, united the nation—all classes—geographically and historically (as I discuss in Chapter 7). Labor unions, because they represented the interest of only one class, threatened mob rule. He was unable to accept their democratic basis because he was wedded to a society in which royalty and aristocracy maintained the governing interest. The Church of England symbolized and perpetuated such a society.

Wordsworth follows his anti-union remark with a long quotation from the unpublished *Prelude* so as to vindicate himself as a poet who has always spoken for (and hopes to speak to) the poor personally—testifying to their individual humanity and right to human dignity without attempting to agitate them into revolution. The passage is a remarkable instance of a writer responding to pressure by taking a stance. One of the frankest declarations of independence in Wordsworth's entire oeuvre, it is aimed on the one hand at Elliott, who took his work in a radical direction he distrusted, and on the other at the Tory anti-Jacobins, who suspected him of revolutionary views. It suggests that autobiography, however apparently independent, was necessarily articulated in a political context. Wordsworth's *Prelude* imagination is now shown, under pressure from Elliott and the times, to have been political, although not partisan:

> It was with reference to thoughts expressed in verse, that the Author entered upon the above notices, and with verse he will conclude. The passage is extracted from his MSS. written above thirty years ago: it turns upon the individual dignity which humbleness of social condition does not preclude, but frequently promotes. It has no direct bearing upon clubs for the discussion of public affairs, nor upon political or trade unions; but if a single workman—who, being a member of one of those clubs, runs the risk of becoming an agitator, or who, being enrolled in a union, must be left without a will of his own, and therefore a slave—should read these lines, and be touched by them, the Author would indeed rejoice, and little would he care for losing credit as a poet with intemperate critics, who think differently from him upon political philosophy or public measures, if the sober minded admit that, in general views, his affections have been moved, and his imagination exercised, under and for the guidance of reason.

> Here might I pause, and bend in reverence
> To Nature, and the power of human minds;

To men as they are men within themselves.
How oft high service is performed within,
When all the external man is rude in show;
Not like a temple rich with pomp and gold,
But a mere mountain chapel that protects
Its simple worshippers from sun and shower!
Of these, said I, shall be my song; of these,
If future years mature me for the task,
Will I record the praises, making verse
Deal boldly with substantial things—in truth
And sanctity of passion, speak of these,
That justice may be done, obeisance paid
Where it is due.

(YR, pp. 347–48; cf. Prelude (1850), XIII, 224–38)

The Prelude is summoned to demonstrate Wordsworth's consistency as a poet who addresses the common man individually rather than communally. In this context, it is proof of both his humanitarian opposition to the commercial system that impoverished laborers and his distance from writers and speakers like Elliott who agitate for reform.[9] The self-citation—of a poem that Elliott could not modify because it remained unpublished—is a self-authorization designed to show that Wordsworth had neither, as Hazlitt and Shelley contended, abandoned radicalism nor given license to the "ranting" harangues of mass audiences that the Corn Law Rhymer developed from his work. It is a strategy produced by his need to reclaim an earlier, radical version of himself because that version was being reworked in a still more radical form by a poet whose discipleship he admired too much to reject. The lyrical balladeer now declared his essential poetic solidarity with the poor and intervened in political debate on that basis. Elliott had brought the radical Wordsworth out of the closet.

PART IV

Late Genres

IN YOPIE PRINS'S DEFINITION, the practice of Historical Poetics comprises the study of the way poems have been "read through the generic conventions that make up the history of reading poetry."[1] In Simon Jarvis's formulation, it entails the recognition that "the (historical) truth content of works of art is to be sought precisely in their technical organization, which, far from being a transhistorical frame for the work of art, is instead its most intimately historical aspect."[2] Marjorie Levinson has noted that part of the history refracted in formal change is the history of the form itself.[3] In this section, I take these statements as watchwords for a critical methodology that aims to examine form, prosody, and genre as they are adapted in particular poems in particular times and places—a methodology that implies a historicized account of how poetry was understood when it was first produced and consumed.

I commence with a discussion of the genre Wordsworth favored most often in his later years—the sonnet. If, in his later blank-verse landscape poetry Wordsworth produced new kinds of form as he responded to new views of history (see "Enough of Climbing Toil," in Chapter 4), in the sonnet sequences he assembled in the 1820s, '30s, and '40s he produced new kinds of history in response to his need for form. The *Ecclesiastical Sketches* and "Sonnets on the Punishment of Death" align the traditional process of sonnet writing with the incarnation of eternal law in the historical institutions of church and state. They identify the authority that, by its observation of formal and prosodic conventions, accrues to poetic form with the absolute order of divine truth as manifested in the fallen world. Hubristic, arrogant, and authoritarian, these sonnet sequences are products of Wordsworth's need for a lasting foundation for the intimations of immortality that his poetry fleetingly discovered: the perfection glimpsed by virtue of the formal dance of words is reified as the eternal mediated, across history, in the doctrine, liturgy, buildings, and lore of the church. The poet's need for form shapes his view of history: the church (and even the divine that the church represents) is a figure of his need for and delight in poetic order. As such they represent his desire to make his art serve the cause of social cohesion, in the face of political unrest from the laboring classes that he thought threatened revolution. Not just in what they said but in the way they said it, his sonnets would recall readers in the middling and upper classes to an intimation of the church's ideological role, historically and geographically, in reconciling class interests—as people of all ranks participate in its rituals, knowing their ancestors had done so in the same spot. In this way a revitalized church—revitalized parochially and by poetry—would be a bastion against the mass meetings and proto-unions that Ebenezer Elliott endorsed in the 1830s.

This is not the whole story, however, for the later Wordsworth also wrote many poems that aligned his poetry-making with cultural forms stemming from pagan worship of a polysemous, metamorphic nature. So pressing did sonneteering make the issue of form that, as William H. Galperin shows, it brought the tension between these alignments to a head, without allowing more than provisional resolution.[4] Thus it reveals that the nature of the central conflict driving Wordsworth's poetry had shifted since its massive formulation in the 1805 *Prelude*. It was no longer a conflict between nature/history and the imagination, but one in which poetry was affiliated to historical institutionalizations of absolute law on the one hand and, on the other, to the circles and cycles of a fertile nature.

The problem of lateness is that the forms and genres guiding the poet's hand and that are redefined in the process are not simply those of past poets but also his own—both those he chooses to use once more and those he eschews. To be late in one's career makes this choice one that is in part about renewing or departing from earlier work—a choice complicated by the fact that this earlier work is not solely the author's own, for it has been published and so defines him in readers' minds, shaping their expectations. Wordsworth's negotiation of these pressures is the subject of Chapter 8, in which I discuss his Evening Voluntaries, published from 1835 onward. These poems are a release of the pressure to reconcile form and history, and individual and institution, that vexed Wordsworth in his sonnet sequences and worried him as he contemplated the destruction of social cohesion. I explore them as formally innovative hybridizations of the "conversation" poem that he and Coleridge had pioneered with late seventeenth- and early eighteenth-century landscape verse. This hybridization enabled Wordsworth to depart from his own past work rather than merely repeat it. It gave him a blend of freedom and order flexible enough to shape evocations of evanescence that ride on the traces and rhythms of time passing—of sound and sight fading into silence and darkness—so as to steer them toward the imagined possibility of continuation. They are poems of lateness, using all the aging Wordsworth's accumulated poetic skill to make their anticipation of ending disclose delay. Acceptance rather than defiance is the predominant note, an acceptance expressed as participation in and harnessing of a landscape manifested as a stage of sonic traces, after-images, and residues. Edward Said's words on Adorno describe the mood, though not the method: "Lateness is a thing in its own right, not a premonition or obliteration of something else. Lateness is being at the end, fully conscious, full of memory, and also very (even preternaturally) aware of the present."[5] The method is an extraordinarily subtle manipulation of sound effects, imagery, grammar, tense, and mood. It is all the more original for the fact that, like the poems' themes, it is a transformation of Wordsworth's earlier style and that of the elder poets he had departed from in the 1790s, having been influenced by them in the 1780s—poets such as Wither, Langhorne, Finch, Gray, Young, and Collins. It is a revival of eighteenth-century landscape poetry that makes it new, deploying its signature tropes, couplets, and topoi—borrowing phrases too—yet turning it toward an articulation of lateness and oncoming death that, accepting diminution since the poems of youth, forges a language both to contemplate and defer the end.

Chapter 7

Narrow Cells and Stone Circles

Sonnet Form and Spiritual History

Between 1820 and the end of his life, Wordsworth wrote more than three hundred and fifty sonnets. Sequences such as *The River Duddon* and "Sonnets on the Punishment of Death" made the sonnet the preponderant genre of his later career. *Ecclesiastical Sketches* (1822), a sequence of 102 poems, later expanded to 132, made the sonnet thematically as well as chronologically late, a means of articulating spirituality as the product of a tradition—an institution indeed—that had developed continuously out of a distant past. That institution was the church, and Wordsworth returned to it in the sonnet sequences of 1831 and 1833, when he devoted poems to particular abbeys, cathedrals, and chapels that he encountered on his tours. Church history and church architecture were, by the end of his life, his most frequent and lasting preoccupations as a sonneteer. In portraying the church in this way, the sonnets develop the themes of *The Excursion*; they are also a substitute for *The Recluse* that Wordsworth never finished, because they suggest how personal spirituality may take public shape. In Marjorie Levinson's trenchant formulation, the poetry "sketches an inclusive, processual, morphologically indeterminate continuum. . . . This is the place where individual psychic life and social being are innocent again and lie down with each other."[1]

But while several commentators have examined the ideological import and argumentative coherence of Wordsworth's church "sketches,"[2] fewer have considered why they are sonnets—what is the connection between sonnet form and church subject?[3] After all, Wordsworth could perfectly well have upheld the social and cultural importance of the church, as a historical manifestation of divine law, in blank verse as he had in *The Excursion*. Why choose the compact form of the sonnet to do so? Was it merely coincidental that after he began attending church service regularly, giving his voice to the communally spoken words of the 1662 prayer book, he also began writing religious sonnets, the form practiced by Herbert and Milton? In what follows I argue that Wordsworth wrote more and more church sonnets because the church, as a historical institution and as holy buildings, became a materialization of his own devotion to traditional poetics. The church became a figure for the activity of turning inchoate thought and feeling into the kind of public verse that accrued authority by conformity to historical literary form. I shall argue, further, that it was ultimately too limiting and authoritarian a metaphor and that Wordsworth, chafing at the commitment to it, supplemented it with non-Christian, less institutionalized analogies for his creative process (the Evening Voluntaries are examples; see Chapter 8). Some of these were natural—the energies of winds and waters, for example—as we might expect of the poet of "Tintern Abbey" and *The Prelude*; more unexpectedly, some of them were pagan and feminine.[4] He attempted, but was unable satisfactorily, to assimilate these analogies into his alignment of the process of sonnet writing with the church. He remained more divided than he could admit, but these divisions were the productive tensions that drove him to keep writing, to keep attempting resolutions. They made him, as Peter Manning has suggested, at best a maverick churchman and tepid Christian, despite the sheer extent of poetry he devoted to supporting ecclesiastical orthodoxy.[5]

The Sonnet's Narrow Room

Wordsworth began aligning sonnet form with architectural form as soon as he became interested in its history—in 1802, when he encountered Milton's sonnets (which used the Petrarchan structure and rhyme scheme but ran the argument from the octet into the sestet). At this stage he merely developed the meaning of "stanza" ("room"). Milton's sonnets, he wrote, have "an energetic and varied flow of sound crowding into narrow room more of the combined effect of rhyme and blank verse than can be done by any other kind of verse I know" (EY, p. 379). By this remark he seems to have meant that the metrical language that seems, for lack of end rhymes, especially flowing in the blank verse of *Paradise Lost* gains an increased pressure in the sonnet because of the restricted form and tight rhyme scheme. This was a timely interpretation for Wordsworth to make, since his own "flowing" blank verse had recently been dismissed by Jeffrey, the leading critic, as slack and formless. Confining its movement within the sonnet's terseness, on the Miltonic model, might redeem his reputation and give him the authoritative public voice Jeffrey had denied him. In 1803 he published Miltonic sonnets in a national newspaper, exhorting his countrymen to revive England's past greatness. In 1805 his interest in the form was renewed when he translated some of the Petrarchan sonnets of Michelangelo and remarked how "much meaning has been put . . . into so little room" (EY, p. 628). Petrarchan form, with its strictly limited number of rhymes, was a particularly demanding, but also stimulating, enclosure: "'twas pastime to be bound / Within the Sonnet's scanty plot of ground" he declared in the "Prefatory Sonnet" to the 1807 *Poems, in Two Volumes* (lines 10–11; I, p. 101).

It was in that same sonnet—in strict Petrarchan form—that he first identified the "narrow room" with the church. "Nuns fret not at their Convent's narrow room; / And Hermits are contented with their Cells," he began, and concluded that he would be

> Pleas'd if some Souls (for such there needs must be)
> Who have felt the weight of too much liberty,
> Should find brief solace there, as I have found.
>
> (lines 12–14)

Wordsworth imagines the sonnet as a small space of retirement from the demands of freedom, one in which spiritual succor is produced by willing submission to restriction ("the prison, unto which we doom / Ourselves, no prison is," lines 8–9). He imagines it, too, as being rather like the Ruined Cottage: "four naked walls / That stared upon each other!" (*Excursion*, I, 30–31)—the four walls being the two quatrains (which he usually rhymes *abba abba*) and the two tercets (combinations of *c* and *d* rhymes). The rhyme scheme, as well as the traditional argumentative structure, makes the poem a piece of architecture, built of two sets of similar sides, restricting the poet's freedom but powerfully symmetrical. That restriction, moreover, is more than self-imposed: the nuns and hermits are content because they participate in a historical institution by which their choice is given cultural meaning; the sonneteer, likewise, submits himself to the historical institution of Petrarchan and Miltonic sonnet form, by which his verse is given cultural value.

"Too much liberty" refers both to poetics and politics. By 1803, as I argued in Chapter 1, Wordsworth's horror at the common people's pro-French sentiments alienated him from their speech, his model for his experimental lyrical ballads. By then, he had also been attacked in print for the "effusions" he had written after Coleridge's example, poems that lacked rhyme to point line ends aurally and visually and that eschewed the predetermined structure of historical genres such as the ode and the epitaph. The poet of such different poetic forms as "The Last of the Flock" and "Tintern Abbey" was under pressure on both fronts. His revolutionary poetry was, according to reviewers, a manifestation of Jacobinical politics; his poetic innovations showed disrespect for established canons of taste and revealed his contempt for the conventional readership for poetry. The poems' freedom from traditional poetic form revealed both his willful egotism and his desire to pander to the uneducated lower classes in an effort to radicalize them.[6] In this context, Wordsworth's characterization of his turn to sonnet writing as an escape from the weight of liberty to the solace of institutional confinement is a declaration of conformity to established institutions, not least the established institution of literary tradition, parallel to the one he made at Coleorton (as explored in Chapter 2). Joseph Phelan summarizes the matter: "The heavily rule-governed Petrarchan or 'legitimate' sonnet becomes an iconic representation of the poet's own freely chosen confinement; both his acquiescence in the rules of form and his minor creative infractions of them acquire an almost immediate moral and political resonance, reinforcing or counterpointing the poem's explicit discussion of the relative merits of liberty and submission to authority."[7]

In the 1807 sonnet, the nuns and hermits are two examples among several of people happy to exchange liberty for confinement: Wordsworth also instances students, spinsters, and weavers. By 1820, however, it is largely contemplants and clerics, dedicated to the church, who shape the metaphor. Wordsworth came to religion neither by a conversion to doctrine nor by an engagement with the Bible, but by local attachment. His belief centered upon the parish church as a present-day but also historical place in which villagers had, for centuries, found form, in service and in ceremony, for their griefs and wants. Going to church was one of those customs and manners that, as Burke had argued, united a nation by perpetuating, as shared culture, historical and geographical continuity. It was, for this reason, unlike the associations that represented one class's interests at the expense of others (manufacturers' cartels and laborers' unions). Wordsworth depicted manners in these Burkean terms in the prefatory poem to the Duddon sonnet sequence of 1820, using his favorite metaphor for sonnet form:

> Hail ancient Manners! Sure defence,
> Where they survive, of wholesome laws;
> Remnants of love whose modest sense
> Thus into narrow room withdraws[.]
>
> (lines 55–58; *Duddon*, p. 116)

The sequence then observes the persistence of ancient manners in the human settlements that are to be found in the narrow valley that surrounds the River Duddon. At the heart of these settlements, and thus of the manners that familiarize "wholesome laws," are the village churches. Pressing his materializing metaphor home, Wordsworth names individual sonnets after these holy places. "Seathwaite Chapel," building and poem, materializes "truth's holy lamp":

> SACRED Religion, "mother of form and fear,"
> Dread Arbitress of mutable respect,
> New rites ordaining when the old are wreck'd,
> Or cease to please the fickle worshipper;
> If one strong wish may be embosomed here,
> Mother of LOVE! for this deep vale, protect
> Truth's holy lamp, pure source of bright effect,
> Gifted to purge the vapoury atmosphere
> That seeks to stifle it;—as in those days
> When this low Pile a Gospel Teacher knew,
> Whose good works formed an endless retinue;
> Such Priest as Chaucer sang in fervent lays,
> Such as the heaven-taught skill of Herbert drew,
> And tender Goldsmith crown'd with deathless praise!
>
> (*Duddon*, p. 20)

If religion gives form to humans' fickle fear and love, the local representative of that form, shining in the vapory "deep vale," is the "low Pile"—the
narrow, simple church from which the pastor spreads good works. Commemorating the place, the poem's "narrow room" configures the chapel's
microcosmic materialization, in the here and now, of religion's past: it is
the son to its mother.[8] Commemorating the parson, and invoking previous
parsons celebrated by poets, Wordsworth justifies his poem as part of a
literary tradition that creates, from lowly churchmen, moral exemplars. He
renews this tradition in words just as Seathwaite's curate, "Wonderful"
Walker, renews the role of pastor by his deeds. He renews it by form too:
the sonnet is a small and traditional edifice, perpetuating the Petrarchan
model, using only four rhymes and breaking from octet to sestet—the latter
justifying by historical example the apostrophic address of the former
("SACRED Religion").[9] The authority of tight, enclosed form gives the poet
confidence to invoke the amorphous and transcendental, to call it into his
presence.

   In 1822 Wordsworth followed the Duddon sonnet sequence with
another, Ecclesiastical Sketches, which took as its point of departure a local
church building. The poems originated, Wordsworth noted, when he took
a walk with George Beaumont to see the plot of ground on which a new
church was to be erected, Beaumont's response to a parliamentary campaign to spread Anglicanism to the deprived and potentially rebellious
laboring classes (and Coleorton, as we saw in Chapter 2, had been the scene
of machine-breaking protests by laborers who preferred their own radical
associations to clerical institutions).[10] Wordsworth was inspired to trace the
"holy River" of British Christianity, as he had traced the real river Duddon,
from its sources to the present (line 10; Sonnets, p. 139). This metaphor for
the sequence suggested an analogy between ecclesiastical history and his
own verse—the flow of metrical language that was itself a development of
the historical medium developed by Shakespeare and Milton from Chaucer
(and meter, Wordsworth had argued, gave pleasure precisely because of its
historical associations with past poems).[11] Tracing it, however, was less a
matter of reproducing a continuous flow of Christianity in the continuous
stream of his verse than one of building "Cells [and] Oratories"—small
discrete poems whose restricted form mirrored that of church buildings
(Excursion, p. 38). Size mattered. In the 1820s Wordsworth was compul-
sively drawn to sonnet writing because it was manageable: the addictive
process of shaping inchoate thoughts and feelings into controlled literary

form could be completed in an hour or two—a stark contrast to the philosophical epic *Recluse*, which he had been laboring unsuccessfully to formulate since the late 1790s (and that had itself originated with the idea of
tracing the course of a brook). Sonnets' small-scale demands offered relief
from the uncomfortable "Liberty" (line 6, sonnet 1, *Ecclesiastical Sketches*;
Sonnets, p. 138) of generating an original structure for a larger blank-verse
poem, yet if they were in this respect an acknowledgement of diminishing
powers and of the failure of ambition, they could nonetheless, when joined
into a sequence, fulfill some of the grander aims of *The Recluse*. Building
on traditional lines, they recast the poet's individual spiritual intimations
in terms of institutions, literary and ecclesiastical, by which human crafts-
men have, using forms sanctioned by history, shaped their understanding
of the spiritual. Thus sonnet 24 in the sequence, "Saxon monasteries,"
images itself in terms of "quiet Fortresses" and "sacred Towers" (lines 3, 8;
Sonnets, p. 152), places whose confining form creates and symbolizes a spiritual intensity that prompts the secular to perform good works.

The conflation of literary and ecclesiastical tradition is formally present
throughout the *Ecclesiastical Sketches*; in places it also appears as a theme,
as in a sonnet on King Canute being enchanted by the song emanating
from Ely Cathedral:

A PLEASANT music floats along the Mere,
From Monks in Ely chaunting service high,
Whileas Canute the King is rowing by:
"My Oarsmen," quoth the mighty King, "draw near,
That we the sweet song of the Monks may hear!"
He listen'd (all past conquests, and all schemes
Of future vanishing like empty dreams)
Heart-touch'd, and haply not without a tear.
The Royal Minstrel, ere the choir was still,
While his free Barge skims the smooth flood along,
Gives to that rapture a memorial Rhyme.
O suffering Earth! be thankful: sternest clime
And rudest age are subject to the thrill
Of heaven-descended Piety and Song.

(*Sonnets*, p. 156)

Church and state are united by music, the point of origin being the building that holds and concentrates spiritual energies. The minstrel's rhyme harmonizes with the church music and is, a note informs the reader, still extant. By evoking its presence, Wordsworth makes his own rhyme its descendant—part of a tradition. Thus a new sonnet is a new chapel built in the familiar style, as "New Churches" indicates:

> BUT liberty, and triumphs on the Main,
> And laurelled Armies—not to be withstood,
> What serve they? if, on transitory good
> Intent, and sedulous of abject gain,
> The State (ah, surely not preserved in vain!)
> Forbear to shape due channels which the Flood
> Of sacred Truth may enter—till it brood
> O'er the wide realm, as o'er the Egyptian plain
> The all-sustaining Nile. No more—the time
> Is conscious of her want; through England's bounds,
> In rival haste, the wished-for Temples rise!
> I hear their Sabbath bells' harmonious chime
> Float on the breeze—the heavenliest of all sounds
> That vale or hill prolongs or multiplies!
>
> (*Sonnets*, p. 199)

Beaumont's building project and Wordsworth's poetry writing, the poem suggests, both channel "sacred Truth" so that it fertilizes a nation recently given over to commercialism and imperialism. They confine spirituality within narrow limits, so that it irrigates the land and propagates "temples": these then become sources of music that are remediated by "vale and hill." The sonnet thematizes the conditions of reception its author sought for it: the church bells, backed by the chiming rhyme scheme, ring out a fantasy of poetic song (patterned articulation: metrical sound) as an extant tradition,[12] focusing and focused by nature in every locality—received and redoubled by "England's bounds." And the song is one with a social purpose: it reunites the nation as a spiritual rather than a capitalist or military entity.

The exemplification of the public role for this idealized "song" depends upon subscription to an institutionalized form. The sonnets' verbal authority relies not on their expression of what the poet already thought, or on their resolution of an inner debate (as in Shakespeare's, Donne's, and Herbert's religious sonnets), but on their arrival at a statement lent such power by conformity that it seems a magisterial, and therefore generally valid, pronouncement. "Mutability" is an example:

> FROM low to high doth dissolution climb,
> And sinks from high to low, along a scale
> Of awful notes, whose concord shall not fail;
> A musical but melancholy chime,
> Which they can hear who meddle not with crime,
> Nor avarice, nor over-anxious care.
> Truth fails not; but her outward forms that bear
> The longest date do melt like frosty rime,
> That in the morning whitened hill and plain
> And is no more; drop like the tower sublime
> Of yesterday, which royally did wear
> Its crown of weeds, but could not even sustain
> Some casual shout that broke the silent air,
> Or the unimaginable touch of Time.
>
> (*Sonnets*, p. 197)

Paradoxically, this "frosty" rhyme does not melt since, even as it multiplies examples of dissolution, the sonnet formally sides with an immutability based on the return of sound. The *a* rhyme (or something closer to it than a half-echo) appears not just at lines 1, 4, 5, and 8, as is normal in Petrarchan form, but also at lines 10 and 14. A still stricter conformity than is required by literary tradition enforces the argument.

In the fifteenth sonnet of Part 3 of the sequence, renewal of sound represents the revival of the customary practices that connect people with their ancestors: "graceful rites / And usages, whose due return invites / A stir of mind too natural to deceive" (lines 2–4; *Sonnets*, p. 196). Decking the church with holly before Christmas, as previous generations had done, endears parishioners to the institution and links its calendar to the continual renewal of nature, the green holly symbolizing spring in midwinter. Here church and sonnet are time capsules, preserving the past and anticipating the future. In "Old Abbeys," too, former holiness is retrievable from decline and ruin, a salutary lesson for an aging poet facing his own decline:

MONASTIC Domes! following my downward way,
Untouched by due regret I marked your fall!
Now, ruin, beauty, ancient stillness, all
Dispose to judgments temperate as we lay
On our past selves in life's declining day:
For as, by discipline of Time made wise,
We learn to tolerate the infirmities
And faults of others, gently as he may,
Towards our own the mild Instructor deals,
Teaching us to forget them or forgive.
Perversely curious, then, for hidden ill
Why should we break Time's charitable seals?
Once ye were holy, ye are holy still;
Your spirit freely let me drink and live!

(Sonnets, pp. 197–98)

This sonnet sounds a significant undertone because it implies that discovering one's feelings in the forms offered by tradition is easier when these forms are ruined, because they then image "infirmities" rather than demand strict adherence to rule. Ruined abbeys confine less with dogma and ritual than intact ones. The tolerant, time-chastened poet of "life's declining day" prefers a "narrow room," "cell," or "hermitage" that he can view for the spirit it once fostered, without enquiring too closely into, or living in the shadow of, the "hidden ill" that it also produced. In formal terms this implies that Wordsworth is not utterly content with the figuration of sonnet writing as church building and of sonnet form as monastic restriction. Form is more forgiving, more nourishing, when its strict regularity is a little broken by time. This implication is not, however, one that Wordsworth takes further in the *Ecclesiastical Sketches*, for he is too committed there to the sonnet/church alignment, which after all justifies his own practice as a poet working for the nation's good by reconnecting it to the historical traditions and institutions that formed, and inform, its common culture. The sequence is thus braced, but also limited, by its structuring metaphor—unable to realize the virtue of doubt, dissent, and dispute in its version of church history.

Taken as a whole, *Ecclesiastical Sketches* suggests that, if sonnet writing appealed to Wordsworth because observance of tight, traditional structure and rhyme produced a verbal authority both formally and by association with past sonnets, it also enticed him because it permitted an authoritarian identification of formal observance with truth. In many sonnets in the sequence, verbal authority is taken for moral and political authority. An impersonal voice, given weight by form, pronounces didactically, but the pronouncement is not the resolution of a moral or historical debate in which opposing arguments are pondered. The poem lacks tension, immediacy, and drama; its certainty is unearned—it is too ex cathedra (ironically, since the doctrine of papal infallibility is one of the ecclesiastical developments Wordsworth does criticize). As Barbara T. Gates points out,[13] too many of the sonnets are too tight, too cellular, too closed to allow doubt or to include the vagaries and contentions out of which the Church of England arose. The sequence neither debates the poet's own struggles of faith nor dramatizes the religious crises that fundamentally shaped the church; it glosses over the theological arguments of the Reformation and almost entirely omits the Civil War and Commonwealth. The "narrow room," village chapel, and monastic cell are too isolated and too static to allow the sequence to articulate historical struggle; it functions instead as a series of isolated snapshots, which are "abruptly" separated from each other (as Wordsworth himself feared). It becomes apparent that he is not interested enough in the how and why and when, in cause and effect, to be a historian, and his architectonic metaphor—the holy river—remains too gestural to compensate for this deficiency. For this reason the sequence does not overcome the problem of creating a large-scale poetic structure in which to deal with historical events and to create a public narrativization of the relation of man to nature and to spirit; the issue that dogged the unwritten *Recluse* persisted. The sequence remains a testament to Wordsworth's yearning for, rather than a continuous realization of, a present whose embodiment of the past is palpable in the forms it adopts.

Rather than a coherent presentation of Christian history in Britain, the *Sketches* offered a partial response to a current affair. Both in what they said, and by their very existence as a renewal of a traditional form associated with the Protestant sonnets of Milton, Donne, and Herbert, Wordsworth's sonnets stood against the campaign to repeal the laws that prevented Roman Catholics from holding office or attending university. In the 1790s Wordsworth had supported this campaign; in the 1820s he was vehement in his opposition to it, fearing that the presence of Catholics in parliament and the army would encourage the disenfranchised and discontented poor to rebel. It would disrupt the Anglican Church's central place as the historical institution binding the English together as a cohesive, Protestant nation. Revolution and anarchy would result.

Wordsworth's alarmism was shared by Southey and Coleridge, although they too had supported Catholic emancipation in the reformist 1790s. But it seemed, to many of their friends, irrational, reactionary, and absurd. It stemmed from the former Jacobins' anxious need to distance themselves from the revolutionary causes they had once espoused as well as from a genuine fear that the "lower orders," angry at their impoverishment by the current social system and morally debased by it, would be a vengeful mob of sans culottes if manipulated by a newly empowered Catholic demagogue. At the same time, Wordsworth was well aware that the current social system, for all its ills, supported him and his fellow poets in their vocations. He was able to spend his time writing poetry, and to earn respect for so doing, because he was supported by Lonsdale and Beaumont, men who derived their status and wealth from their families' influence in parliament. In this context, the publication of poems idealizing the church's ideological role in ensuring local and national order was a self-defensive and self-interested act, as well as an intervention in a social and political issue. That these poems were sonnets was significant too: the sequence revealed Wordsworth to the public as a traditionalist—an upholder of a historical form and a respecter of order. The sonnet sequence bespoke an exemplary program of almost daily literary self-discipline. Each was an exercise in movement from free thought to historical form, an act of self-definition by submission to rule, ranged against what Wordsworth saw as the disruptive forces of political and religious reform. And the sonnet, as a learned Renaissance form that required an education to be appreciated, was affiliated with the established social order. It was a genre that sat comfortably with the enfranchised middle and upper classes, in contrast to the ballads and songs of villagers and mechanics that Wordsworth had once imitated, and was unlike the blank-verse, open-ended conversation poems such as "Tintern Abbey" that most educated readers found egotistical and idiosyncratic. This form conformed: it enacted commitment to traditional order as well as endorsing tradition thematically.

In 1829, Catholic emancipation passed into law; anarchy did not follow. Wordsworth's alarmism proved ill-founded; his *Ecclesiastical Sketches* lost their topicality. Still fearful of political reform, he was nevertheless, as church and state continued untoppled and as his own way of life went on peacefully, able to remodel his understanding of sonnet writing as conformity to a narrow, institutionalized form best represented by the cell, oratory, and chapel. The undertone of discontent at so strict a formalization of his creative process that is discernible in "Old Abbeys" now began to appear more explicitly: the didactic church-builder let himself canvas more liberal and secular metaphors for his writing. Both the power of the church metaphor and the canvassing of others are apparent in the 1831 sonnet "Composed in Roslin Chapel During a Storm," about which Wordsworth noted

> We were detained by incessant rain and storm at the small inn near Roslin Chapel, and I passed a great part of the day pacing to and fro in this beautiful structure, which, though not used for public service, is not allowed to go to ruin. Here this Sonnet was composed. If it has at all done justice to the feeling which the place and the storm raging without inspired, I was as a prisoner. A painter delineating the interior of the chapel and its minute features under such circumstances would have, no doubt, found his time agreeably shortened. But the movements of the mind must be more free while dealing with words than with lines and colours; such at least was then and has been on many other occasions my belief, and, as it is allotted to few to follow both arts with success, I am grateful to my own calling for this and a thousand other recommendations which are denied to that of the painter.[14]

While not ruined like the old abbeys, Rosslyn Chapel was not in current use—Wordsworth was able to be the sole occupant of the place, enjoying its beauty without the presence of priest or religious service. It imposed no doctrine or ritual upon him. We know that he sometimes composed his verse orally, under his breath, while walking: here, then, the "pacing to and fro" in the deserted chapel channels his verbal creativity. Its walls are not simply inconveniences, but necessary limits, the presence of which creates the verbal and syntactical measure needed for the heightened language that is poetry. The sonnet is thus portrayed as the outcome of the author's compositional motion, a poem returning on itself because of the constraints of form. In a mutual reinforcement of form and subject matter, poetic occasion and achieved poem, the chapel's walls produce the metrical, stanza, and rhyme conventions of the sonnet that depicts the chapel's walls.

Nevertheless, the note also registers Wordsworth's impatience, declaring him a prisoner. He is no monk, resigned to a retired life in an institution, but a traveler who finds that confinement generates a productive tension, so long as it is not protracted. He will leave, but even while he remains, he is inspired not by simple restraint but by the fact that the narrow chapel allows the storm entrance. The sonnet comes to be as an articulation of an opening of the institution to external energies, so that what results is a hybrid of culture and nature, combining the energies of the human and nonhuman.

> THE wind is now thy organist;—a clank
> (We know not whence) ministers for a bell
> To mark some change of service. As the swell
> Of music reached its height, and even when sank
> The notes, in prelude, ROSLIN! to a blank
> Of silence, how it thrilled thy sumptuous roof,
> Pillars, and arches;—not in vain time-proof,
> Though Christian rites be wanting! From what bank
> Came those live herbs? by what hand were they sown
> Where dew falls not, where rain-drops seem unknown?
> Yet in the Temple they a friendly niche
> Share with their sculptured fellows, that, green-grown,
> Copy their beauty more and more, and preach,
> Though mute, of all things blending into one.
>
> (YR, p. 12)

As in *The White Doe of Rylstone* and "The Brownie's Cell," Wordsworth is energized by a historical form that embodies constraint but has been rent and torn so that irregularities are possible and the constraint is not uniform or absolute. Here, the chapel is a place where culture and nature meet and meld: the roof, though proof against time, is thrilled (pierced) by the organ music, rising from within, which is also the sound of wind entering from without. The "live herbs" growing in the interior grow alongside "green-grown" stone statues. This chapel is a porous form, and the sonnet composed in it is porous too, in the respect that it does not end with a couplet or conclusive rhyme but with a half rhyme. The expected pattern is not completely fulfilled, and the poem finishes on a note of slight dissonance— the sound of in-conclusion—and this echoes Wordsworth's suggestion that the chapel is an enclosure with apertures that allow inside and outside, nature and culture, to interact and copy each other. Sonnet form and chapel form image each other—narrow cells rent enough by time to admit energies that originate outside the institution, ecclesiastical and literary. The image of the rent enclosure, it follows, is a figure of poetry's emergence neither from restriction nor from freedom but from barriers broken through—form de- or reformed.

An Orbicular Body

Writing to Alexander Dyce in 1833, Wordsworth abandoned the "narrow room" figure of sonnet writing. Turning from the rectitude of chapel and church as architectural localizations of historical (and ultimately eternal) form, he declared, "Instead of looking at this composition as a piece of architecture, making a whole out of three parts, I have been much in the habit of preferring the image of an orbicular body,—a sphere,—or a dew-drop" (LY, II, pp. 604–5). While it may seem unsurprising that a nature-poet should think of his poems as having organic form, the comment also hinted at an affiliation that is more unlikely: the spherical patterns made by humans. This affiliation is discernible in a few of the Duddon sonnets and *Ecclesiastical Sketches*, although it is subsumed within the larger characterizations of the poems as a river and as a series of cells. In the 1830s Wordsworth gave it more weight, even to the extent of dramatizing a conflict between square and circle as the forms, and between holy church and pagan temples as the institutions, which his poetry adopted and developed.

In a remarkable sonnet of 1818, Wordsworth associated himself as a poet of place—the Duddon valley—with pagan priests. He read signs of the divine in nature and patterned that nature so that it modeled the priests' prophetic role.

> A DARK plume fetch me from yon blasted Yew,
> Perched on whose top the Danish Raven croaks;
> Aloft, the imperial Bird of Rome invokes
> Departed ages, shedding where he flew
> Loose fragments of wild wailing that bestrew
> The clouds, and thrill the chambers of the rocks,
> And into silence hush the timorous flocks,
> That slept so calmly while the nightly dew

Moisten'd each fleece, beneath the twinkling stars:
These couch'd mid that lone Camp on Hardknot's height,
Whose Guardians bent the knee to Jove and Mars:
These near that mystic Round of Druid frame,
Tardily sinking by its proper weight
Deep into patient Earth, from whose smooth breast it came!

(*Duddon*, p. 19)

Here the yew tree on which the raven perches is not just a symbol of death but also a reminder of the destruction wrought by invading Vikings, who bore the sign of the raven on their shields. As Wordsworth knew, Donnerdale is full of places with Norse names—nearby Ravenglass being one. The dale also discloses a still-older invasion: the call of the predatory eagle wheeling over the valley "invokes" Roman conquest and the cries of fear and suffering which that conquest brought. Observing and overhearing these avian signs, the poet is more an augur than an ornithologist: like a Roman or Druid priest, he reads the place's inner meaning in the birds' appearance (hence "A dark plume fetch me"). What it means, it seems, is a history of paganism—a religion built on the interpretation of nature rather than on the divine Word. This religion, like the predatory eagle that represents nature in the poem, is one that includes violence and terror.[15]

The sonnet turns in its seventh line: moving from birds to buildings, Wordsworth shifts from animate signs to inanimate relics and from violence to peace. At Hardknott Fort, where the invading Romans once made obeisance to their cruel and martial gods, sheep now find calm rest, moistened by dew, lit by stars. Nature is peaceful and favorable; the military building, in its ruined state, is a shelter rather than the stronghold of an occupying army. It no longer signifies the Romans' violent suppression of the native Celtic religion, a religion still discernible in "that mystic Round of Druid frame," the Swinside stone circle (known locally, Wordsworth notes, as "sunken church"). Here the stones are being reabsorbed by the rocky earth from which they were raised. The stone circle connotes the depths—spatial and temporal—of a patient nature that imperceptibly accepts into itself the effortful works of man. Given time and place, Wordsworth suggests, the patterns made by humans as they try to interpret their world of space and time are laid to rest in nature, whence they can be invoked, without fear, by the sensitive observer. To put this another way, the poet responds to his strange meeting with the ancient stone circle, both natural and human as it is, by taking a perspective so local and so long that he can conjure up the place's Celtic history, retrieving it from its near obliteration by the invading Romans. He calls his own voice into poetic form by summoning the prophetic forms of the past from the ruined temple that survives, acknowledging their violence but confident that this violence is now laid to rest. To do so is to align his poetry with historical materializations of spirituality that are opposed to the Christian church—they are manifested not in chapels, doctrines, or liturgies but in forms of worship that are part natural, part cultural: birds' feathers and cries, arrangements of local stones that focus the rotations of sun, moon, and stars. In this thematic context, the sonnet's Petrarchan form seems more circular than square: the *b* rhyme returns in the second quatrain, and the final tercets' symmetrical formats ensure the regular return of both individual rhyme sounds and the rhyme pattern: *cdc ede*.

Wordsworth published the Swinside sonnet in his *River Duddon* collection of 1820. It was followed there by a sonnet on one of the churches in the valley—"The Kirk of Ulpha"—in which square and circle, ecclesiastical and pagan, are both present as characterizations of sonnet form.

THE KIRK OF ULPHA to the Pilgrim's eye
Is welcome as a Star, that doth present
Its shining forehead through the peaceful rent
Of a black cloud diffused o'er half the sky;
Or as a fruitful palm-tree towering high
O'er the parched waste beside an Arab's tent;
Or the Indian tree whose branches, downward bent,
Take root again, a boundless canopy,
How sweet were leisure! could it yield no more
Than mid that wave-washed Churchyard to recline,
From pastoral graves extracting thoughts divine;
Or there to pace, and mark the summits hoar
Of distant moon-lit mountains faintly shine,
Sooth'd by the unseen River's gentle roar.

(*Duddon*, p. 32)

Land and sea, mountain and valley, burial and divinity, churchyard and starry sky: Wordsworth locates a meeting of extremes in this "pastoral" Eden via another "rent"—a gap allowing interpenetration between different determining forms. The church is no narrow room of institutional discipline; the poet, in fact, does not enter it. The churchyard, not the church itself, is the focus, as the place where present and past lie next to each other and where form is sufficiently torn for the physicality of death to be translated to "thoughts divine." It is poetry, Wordsworth suggests, that effects this translation: the sonnet thematizes itself in the scene. Thus the kirk in the lonely valley is said to be as "welcome" as a star shining through black cloud or as a palm tree in a desert. The kirk focuses; it bespeaks light and fertility in a wasteland or empty space. It is emphasized as singular—but paradoxically this emphasis is an effect of its having been moved through two analogies. And the palm tree then transforms into a banyan, the Indian tree whose branches root themselves and grow further trunks—a moving, spreading tree encompassing more and more land and whose center constantly changes. With this image, Wordsworth offers an analogy for poetry as an analogizing process that, proteus-like, invents new forms of likeness that in turn spawn others and change the terms of the initial comparison as they grow (the sense of change reinforced by the fact that "canopy" is only a half-rhyme for "eye" and "high"). And of course the analogies are Orientalist: the Arab in the desert changes Donnerdale into the world of the *One Thousand and One Nights*—a fantasy world wherein story has the power to transform space and time; the Indian tree reroots/routes the kirk into the nature of Hindu scripture in which the growth of exotic plants is the love life of gods and goddesses. Wordsworth is remarkably unanxious about these Eastern analogies for the writing process; he pictures the poet reclining, idly "extracting thoughts divine" from the graves—as if his thought-process, banyan-like, Hinduesque, expresses the divine principle as part of nature's metamorphic reincarnation of the dead. This is poetry in/as motion—the conversion of spiritual singularity and the Anglican kirk into a natural multiplicity that is both an achievement and an incarnation of poetic metamorphosis.

Wordsworth is unanxious because of his sonnet's orbicular form. The shining star and moonlit mountains betoken wider circumferences, circling the earth, that are reached through the "rent" that opens both the local valley and its poetic representation to the beyond. They are figures of the transformation of emplacedness that the poet "marks" on the page to articulate a nature of proliferating cycles concentered by the church. The poem images a virtuous circle of nature and culture in mutually locating orbicular relationship—the whole scene a round reflection in the pilgrim's eye imaging and reflecting the star's distant orb (itself imaged as a reflection of the human by the phrase "shining forehead"). Reflections of reflections, circle upon circle: the surrounding summits, beyond them the moon, beyond that the stars that at least seem to turn through the sky. These concentric horizons are the containing instantiations of the poem's tendency to thematize its own poetic form as a process of turn and return in which the singular is made multiple. They are, as it were, the visible envelope of an alignment of sonnet writing with self-regenerating natural growth. Far more remote, and thus less restrictive, than the walls of the sonnet-cell, they allow room for the articulation of metamorphosis but assure that this process has formal and natural limits—a return upon itself rather than a disappearance into flux.

The larger question posed to Wordsworth by the exhilarating transformations of "The Kirk of Ulpha" is whether the poet can always discover, in his articulation of nature, formal limits to the analogizing process. The figure of the rent, the tear, opening the narrow cell to proliferating circles in fact replays the central question of the origin and end of his poetic calling, the question played out in *The Prelude*, of whether poetic imagination leads to an abyss of endless proliferation (orbs as remoter and remoter orbits) by unstoppably converting things to the airy nothings they are said to resemble, or whether "rocks and stones and trees"—the material world—act as a reliable, tactile anchor. It is his ambivalent commitment to and fear of the former that leads him both to portray it as a violent as well as prophetic insight; it is his need to control it that leads him, in *The Excursion* and still more in the *Ecclesiastical Sketches*, to dedicate himself formally to a historical institution in which restraint and limit are passed down as a communal legacy and thus familiarized. That dedication, though, is not made by denial of the commitment to poetry as metamorphosis, for that commitment is too strong and too omnipresent to be denied. Wordsworth attempts instead to show metamorphosis being subsumed within the historical institution that he wants to identify with the formal limits of his art: a rent, a tear that opens but does not destroy the building. For this reason *Ecclesiastical Sketches* begins with stone circles in pre-Christian Britain as the poet searches for the original fountain from which British, and later Christian, spirituality sprang.

II. CONJECTURES
Where lies the ground in Albion that was blest
With the first gushings of that sacred Well?

What song of Bard, O mighty stream, can tell
The origin what Pinacles attest?
Did holy Paul, a Wanderer in the west,
As some have taught, awhile in Britain dwell
And call thy fountain forth by miracle
And with dread signs thy nascent stream invest?
Darkness surrounds us; seeking we are lost
'Mid shade unpierceable of Druid groves,
Shades that enwrap the majesty unhewn
Of Temples—still preserved in mountain coves
Entire, and seeming perfect as the Moon
Before her wane begins, on heaven's blue coast.

(*Sonnets*, pp. 139–40)

This sonnet—here in an early draft—answers its own call for a "song of Bard" to bring origins to light when no written record exists. Self-founding in the name of ancient poets, it arrives at a prophetic vision to end the darkness that surrounds historical enquiry into prehistoric spirituality. The poet leaves the shady groves behind, emerging into the moonlight, finding his bearings by viewing the Swinside stone circle. His sight is clarified because the circle transcends time's obliteration of records (it is "preserved" "entire"), because it unites culture with nature (its rocks are "unhewn," like those of the mountains that shelter it), and because its circularity matches that of the mountain cove that houses it and the full moon that shines upon it. Here Wordsworth alludes to Lake District folklore that identified stone circles as temples to a lunar goddess who patterned time into monthly cycles (in *The Excursion*, IX, 705, he named this female deity Andates, after the victory goddess invoked by the female warrior Boudica during her resistance to the Roman conquest).[16] The circle, and the sonnet that comes round to it in its final lines, are pagan reflections of the pattern-making of a female nature, based on orbicular return rather than linearity—time as shaped space; multiplicity rather than the singular patriarchal Word. The final, beautiful, image lays to rest the syntactical maziness of the long preceding sentence: Wordsworth, it seems, has found what he was restlessly searching for. The (stone) circle is an adequate origin for British spirituality, a perfect form that transforms the Cumbrian shore into the coast of heaven. Natural supernaturalism, created by ancient Britons, recreated by a modern one: a bard who is a silent, sensitive witness, a sole observer receiving intimations rather than a poet-leader of a clan.

But Wordsworth did not publish this version of the sonnet, because its natural supernaturalism aligned his art so closely with the circles and cycles of a feminine lunar paganism that did not "square" with the prescribed forms of the church. The following sonnet, in its published form, certainly corrected this concentric alignment, for it rehearsed the view of the antiquarian Edward Davies that the Celtic Britons had preserved fragments of the patriarchal religion of the ancient Hebrews only for their Druids to corrupt this religion into one of human sacrifice at their stone circles (Wordsworth had previously poeticized Davies in *The Prelude*).[17]

> III. TREPIDATION OF THE DRUIDS
> SCREAMS round the Arch-druid's brow the seamew—white
> As Menai's foam; and toward the mystic ring
> Where Augurs stand, the future questioning,
> Slowly the Cormorant aims her heavy flight,
> Portending ruin to each baleful rite,
> That, in the lapse of seasons, hath crept o'er
> Diluvian truths, and patriarchal lore:
> Haughty the Bard: can these meek doctrines blight
> His transports? wither his heroic strains?
> But all shall be fulfilled;—the Julian spear
> A way first open'd; and, with Roman chains,
> The tidings come of Jesus crucified;
> They come—they spread—the weak, the suffering, hear;
> Receive the faith, and in the hope abide.
>
> (*Sonnets*, p. 140)

Here the setting is Anglesey, last stronghold of the Druids after the Roman invasion. The "mystic ring" is a generic reference to a stone circle, rather than to the specific, encounter-based, portrait of the previous sonnet. Avoiding personal confrontation with the uncanny stones, Wordsworth is able to replace his earlier poetic affiliation to a pagan, lunar, feminine, natural supernaturalism by a conventional narrative of historical progress, but at the cost of endorsing violence in the name of Christianity. The "haughty" bard, with his prophetic transports and heroic song, will, in time, be humbled by the "meek doctrines" of Jesus—but at the spear-point of

Christian Romans. The diction is euphemistic and anodyne: thus Wordsworth avoids the awkward questions that picturing the Romans' slaughter and enslavement of Celts would have posed to his justification of Christian meekness. He also avoids considering his own position as a self-proclaimed bard and "prophet of nature" (*Prelude* (1805), XIII, 442), as if blind to the irony of the poet of *The Excursion* extolling a culture that destroys native poets and their heroic song. Wordsworth's willful effort to depict native spirituality as a history of a righteous progress from the pagan patternmaking that images a cyclical nature to an increasingly correct Christian enlightenment fails: it is too forced; he cannot square the circle.

Sonnet V fudges Wordsworth's divided loyalties between ecclesiastical and rectilinear and pagan and orbicular, reusing the motif of darkness that he had included in his draft of Sonnet II.

V. UNCERTAINTY

DARKNESS surrounds us; seeking, we are lost
On Snowdon's wilds, amid Brigantian coves,
Or where the solitary Shepherd roves
Along the Plain of Sarum, by the Ghost
Of silently departed ages crossed;
And where the boatman of the Western Isles
Slackens his course—to mark those holy piles
Which yet survive on bleak Iona's coast.
Nor these, nor monuments of eldest name,
Nor Taliesin's unforgotten lays,
Nor Characters of Greek or Roman fame,
To an unquestionable Source have led;
Enough—if eyes, that sought the fountain-head
In vain, upon the growing Rill may gaze.

(*Sonnets*, pp. 140–41)

Again, Wordsworth alludes to stone circles but does not depict an encounter with any of them in particular, thus keeping his affiliation to their uncanny form under control. The "Plain of Sarum" is the location of Stonehenge; Iona's coast features prehistoric, as well as early Christian remains; Taliesin was a Welsh bard of the era of Llywarc Hen, discussed in Sharon Turner's *History of the Anglo-Saxons*, which Wordsworth was using as source material. The "characters of Greek or Roman fame" may refer to

Druidic runes or to inscribed Roman altar stones. Wordsworth does not say; he canvases many sources but does not engage with any of them, so as not to disturb a narrative presented as a continuous organic flow.

Sonnet X effects a reconciliation and represents the final attempt in *Ecclesiastical Sketches* to subsume within a linear narrative of church history an orbicular poetry modeled on bardic, Celtic natural supernaturalism.

> X. STRUGGLE OF THE BRITONS AGAINST THE BARBARIANS
> Rise!—they *have* risen: of brave Aneurin ask
> How they have scourged old foes, perfidious friends:
> The Spirit of Caractacus defends
> The Patriots, animates their glorious task;—
> Amazement runs before the towering casque
> Of Arthur, bearing thro' the stormy field
> The Virgin sculptured on his Christian shield:—
> Stretched in the sunny light of victory bask
> The Host that followed Urien as he strode
> O'er heaps of slain;—from Cambrian wood and moss
> Druids descend, auxiliars of the Cross;
> Bards, nursed on blue Plinlimmon's still abode,
> Rush on the fight, to harps preferring swords,
> And everlasting deeds to burning words!
>
> (*Sonnets*, pp. 144–45)

Here Wordsworth implies that cultural advancement is driven by a mono-theistic and teleological, rather than pagan and cyclical, religion. Temporal progress depends on bards and Druids—poet-prophets who have by now espoused Christianity, who use their verbal art to muster violence against the enemies of Christian lands. Aneurin, as Turner's *History* shows, was a bard of Rheged, the sixth-century northern Celtic realm of which Cumbria was part. Urien ruled some or all of it, possibly in conjunction with Llywarc Hen. Celebrated in bardic poems by Taliesin, Urien, like Arthur, fought against the Anglo-Saxons, as their predecessor Caradoc ("Caractacus") had fought the Romans five hundred years before.[18] Crucially, however, Urien and his northern Celts were now Christian, allowing Wordsworth to incor-porate their valor in his progressive narrative. Free from doubt and division about his affiliation to the relics of paganism, he reclaims the bardic role as a heroic one, echoing Taliesin's poems like a latter-day bard himself. He is vicariously excited by imagining a culture in which poets fought as well as wrote, winning "everlasting" fame in battle. His own "burning words" passionately appropriate Christian Celticism on behalf of British patriotism. His rhymes, meanwhile, are less cyclical than is often the case: unusually, Wordsworth ends with a couplet, a conclusive gesture that also means that the last rhyme-sound is only heard at the poem's very close. Finality, rather than return, is enforced.

By incorporating Druids and bards into his history of the church, Wordsworth makes an institution take over the role that, in the Duddon sonnets, is played by the builders of stone circles. The patterned monuments that testify to worship of a cyclical nature are portrayed as flowing into the holy river of Christianity, a river glimpsed from the narrow rooms and cells of specific historical materializations; they appear little and brief by comparison with the religion's continuous and ancient history. Bards and druids play small but significant parts in this story; they are assimilated; it moves on—moves on, only to recur from time to time, as a lingering inclination toward a poetry allied to natural cycles of proliferation and metamorphosis. This inclination is apparent in one of the later *Sketches* in the sequence, "The Liturgy":

> Yes, if the intensities of hope and fear
> Attract us still, and passionate exercise
> Of lofty thoughts, the way before us lies
> Distinct with signs—through which in fixed career,
> As through a zodiac, moves the ritual year
> Of England's Church—stupendous mysteries!
> Which whoso travels in her bosom, eyes
> As he approaches them, with solemn cheer.
> Upon that circle traced from sacred story
> We only dare to cast a transient glance,
> Trusting in hope that Others may advance
> With mind intent upon the King of Glory,
> From his mild advent till his countenance
> Shall dissipate the seas and mountains hoary.
>
> (*Sonnets*, pp. 194–95, 1845 text)

In likening the rituals of the ecclesiastical year to the zodiac, Wordsworth's analogy becomes distinctly unorthodox and even unchristian. The zodiac is a means of interpreting the changing appearance of the night skies caused by the orbits of the planets and the moon; it was originally pre-Christian and retained its associations with non-Christian astrology in the Romantic era. It is a conceptualization of the starry sky imaged in "The Kirk of Ulpha" and in the Swinside sonnet in the circular forms of nature and pagan culture. Here too, "that circle" upon which "We only dare to cast a transient glance" does not, despite Wordsworth's qualification "traced from sacred story," chiefly derive from the Bible. The sun may have been a symbol of the Son, but it was also the object of pagan rituals; Wordsworth's image of "others" advancing toward it cannot but liken the Christian's relationship with God to members of a nature-worshipping religion. Stone circles, Davies argued, were used by such worshippers to view the sun's appearance from within representations of the diurnal round and of the return of solstice and equinox. Wordsworth's depiction of the approach to God is much closer to them than to the Christian attending divine service within the walls of the Anglican parish church: it prefers circle to square, nature to institution, and noticeably elides Son—the incarnate Messiah—in Sun. Wordsworth has little need of a personal God it seems; his poetry-making process is his god, and, when he allows it to, it allies him with the pagan and orbicular even when he tries to subsume them within the ecclesiastical and rectilinear. The process of using images, forms, and rhymes over long spans too frequently seems cyclical and polysemous for him to rest content with allying his art with ecclesiastical history's slow but steady progress toward orthodoxy. Once the orbicular analogy is introduced, it inevitably links his poetry with organic, if not pagan, forms. The sonnet is itself such a form since, although strictly Petrarchan in rhyme scheme, all the lines ending on the *c* rhyme have an extra syllable produced by the feminine endings ("story," "glory," "hoary"): thus Wordsworth deviates from traditional form and strict pentameter. The sonnet is a slightly elliptical, wandering orb—as are the orbits of many of the planets through the zodiac.

The circular, and pagan, historicization and monumentalization of art is what Wordsworth's poetry at its most radical aims to found itself upon. Thus the following lines, intended for an ecclesiastical sonnet, apply to his own writing just as strongly as they do to the Swinside stone circle:

And thus a Structure potent to enchain
The eye of Wonder rose in this fair Isle;

Not built with calculations nice and vain
But in mysterious Nature's boldest style,
Yet orderly as some basaltic Pile
That steadfastly repels the fretful main.

(Sonnets, p. 205)

Here the "Structure" is both stone circle and poem. It rose, it seems, of its own accord—a natural growth of the soil, imaging its island origin (Britain is imaged as a stone "Pile" encircled by "fretful main"). The "Structure" then enchains the round "eye of Wonder" to itself (a chain is composed of linked circles). Natural yet orderly, it is an organic form. It is a patriotic one too: the structure steadfastly repels disturbance from outside the fair isle from which it sprang. The lines are a self-authorizing, wish-fulfillment fantasy by which Wordsworth imagines himself as the acknowledged legislator of his country (if not the world). Stone-circle sonnets, it suggests, configure Wordsworth's understanding of the sources and purposes of his art.

Copying the One Paternal Mind

The conflict as to the source and nature of authority that was precipitated by the sonnet form reached its apogee in the 1841 "Sonnets on the Punishment of Death." In this sequence Wordsworth puts the state in the position that the church had formerly occupied in order to oppose the arguments of liberals that the death penalty should be abolished. The state, enacting the penalty on certain occasions, becomes the historical institution that realizes the eternal—Death—in time. It carries out, at intervals, a power that mostly it holds in reserve, and this occasional enactment provokes penitence (among the condemned) and obedience (within the general population).

What is a State? The wise behold in her
A creature born of time, that keeps one eye
Fixed on the Statutes of Eternity,
To which her judgments reverently defer.
Speaking through Law's dispassionate voice the State
Endues her conscience with external life
And being, to preclude or quell the strife

Of individual will, to elevate
The grovelling mind, the erring to recal,
And fortify the moral sense of all.

                                        (IX, lines 5–14; *Sonnets*, p. 874)

Here Wordsworth's linguistic authority is clearly identified with legal and social authority: the sonnets formally and verbally enforce the death penalty as a form of punitive sublime. It is of himself, as a public poet, as well as of the state "Legislator," that Wordsworth speaks when he says, "As all Authority in earth depends / On Love and Fear, their several powers he blends, / Copying with awe the one Paternal mind" (IV, lines 4, 6–8; *Sonnets*, p. 871). In a gesture saved only by its impersonal expression from revealing a breathtaking arrogance, Wordsworth has the sonnet writer and government minister "copy" not the elusive traces of nature, but the authoritarian mind of God. This assertion represents the final development of the configuration of poetic form in terms of a "narrow room." Subsumed in Wordsworth's poetics at a subverbal level, this configuration now sustains an apotheosis: prosodic order legitimizes governmental authority as an image of the divine perfection—a reification of the power of rhythm and rhyme if ever there was one. Wordsworth, as Sharon Setzer notes, uses the form that he had, in 1807, termed a "prison" into which he willingly doomed himself, as a means of idealizing the imprisonment and execution of others. Having "so thoroughly internalized the structural forms of the sonnet . . . that they had come to govern the structure of his thoughts," he changes "an instrument for . . . self-discipline into an instrument for defending the State's power to discipline and punish."[19]

How to reconcile the "death" sonnets with sonnets such as "The Kirk of Ulpha"? Largely, Wordsworth used different collections to publish different kinds of sonnets that embodied contrasting understandings of his poetic power. He increasingly did not attempt to reconcile them—and this evinced a failing energy, an acceptance that he would not press himself too hard to arrive at a coherent understanding of "the hiding-places of [his] power."[20] But for all this reluctance—perhaps a necessary reluctance in that, if he understood clearly, his motivation to write might have lapsed—he admitted that he could not rest content with an authoritarian identification of poetic form with a punitive, patriarchal word.[21] At the end of "Sonnets upon the Punishment of Death," he placed an "Apology," for his didactic formality and assumption of authority. This apology looks, as Milton once had done, to wider, more formally relaxed new pastures. In the process, it gives a brief insight into his creativity as a process of generating passionate discourse by finding barriers to resist.

> THE formal World relaxes her cold chain
> For One who speaks in numbers; ampler scope
> His utterance finds; and, conscious of the gain,
> Imagination works with bolder hope
> The cause of grateful reason to sustain;
> And, serving Truth, the heart more strongly beats
> Against all barriers which his labour meets
> In lofty place, or humble Life's domain.
>
> (lines 1–8; *Sonnets*, p. 877)

This was to half-admit that Wordsworth needed, or even sought out, issues to define himself against—that the causes he espoused were instrumental for his writing, rather than mattering in and for themselves. Having made this tacit admission, he was able to lay down his burden of certainty and accept that others might differ from him but that they could set aside their differences and unite as fellows who trust in God's wisdom and providence:

> Enough;—before us lay a painful road,
> And guidance have I sought in duteous love
> From Wisdom's heavenly Father. Hence hath flowed
> Patience, with trust that, whatsoe'er the way
> Each takes in this high matter, all may move
> Cheered with the prospect of a brighter day.
>
> (lines 9–14)

The "brighter day" might well be in heaven. Wordsworth's humble and hopeful note is that of a man conscious of his vulnerability to mortality: it stemmed not just from thinking of prisoners condemned to death, but also from his increasing exposure to the death of friends and loved ones. Wordsworth the sonneteer, in what he saw as the evening of his life, was changed by Wordsworth the elegist.

Chapter 8

Evanescence and After-Effect

The Evening Voluntaries

Yarrow Revisited was the most varied and daring of Wordsworth's later collections. As well as the post-Elliott political poems, it contained two sonnet series that memorialized tours and a section of longer poems, which were announced as belonging to a new genre, that explored the unexpected perspectives brought on by age. Lateness, the latter suggested, allowed a coming to terms with forms of vitality and insight that, although self-consciously "after" those enjoyed in the past, were not simply retrospective. These poems were "Evening Voluntaries"—named after the improvised music played in church before and after evensong: music, that is, which could follow any form the organist chose. The Voluntary is both apart from the liturgy, in the freedom granted the organist, and a recognized part of it. To call a poem a Voluntary indicated that it praised God's creation in traditional manner, and thus perpetuated a historical practice through which worship had taken place, but without having to conform to established poetic or liturgical forms. This provision for individual freedom within the rituals of the community came to symbolize a displacement of the tensions that Wordsworth experienced in the 1830s, when, to his disillusioned eye, radical protest threatened to bring anarchy to the streets of Britain while the institutions of the state—parliament and church—refused to recognize the plight of the laboring poor. Having idealized the church's social role in the *Ecclesiastical Sketches*, only to find the clergy uninterested in engaging the laboring classes and the government imposing the New Poor Law, he used the Voluntary as a freer form that escaped, without refuting, his self-imposed mission to make poetic form recommend ideological apparatuses. Significantly, his Voluntaries stood outside the church, even as they invoked the performance of the church organist. By making that invocation, however, they placed within the formal frame of an Anglican art Wordsworth's efforts to bear with oncoming death and to intimate immortality.

The Evening Voluntaries renovated the form and voice of Wordsworth's past verse by adapting those of late seventeenth- and early eighteenth-century nature poetry.[1] Freer in their prosodic structure than the sonnet, they stood at a slight remove from their models. Their untraditional traditionalism allowed Wordsworth to explore—and to dramatize himself exploring—the conflict between allegiance to singular authority and fertile multiplicity that had led him to affiliate sonnet form both to the church and to paganism. They gave him room to meditate on, and articulate a mode of bearing with, being after not only the lost fullness of youth, but also the poetry that first mourned the loss of that fullness. They were a form elaborated so as to, on one hand, achieve precise and delicate evocations of transience, vestige, and after-effect—a verse-scape of traces and echoes—and, on the other, enable deeply serious explorations of perspectives granted to an aging writer, late in his career, with youth distant and death near. At their best they achieve great poetry of old age, of a kind only a highly experienced poet who had come to terms with his art and its forebears could have written. They show Wordsworth's technical brilliance at the organization of syntactical movement in relation to meter and to rhyme; they produce, from the hybridization of the nature-meditation he learned from Cowper and Coleridge with the couplet style of such poets as Finch and Gray, a revitalization of poetic tradition. Wordsworth did not simply hark back to the styles of the past but forged from them a new, flexible form that was uniquely his—conversation poems in couplets. Less nakedly subjective than that of "Tintern Abbey" and the Immortality Ode, whose musings on landscapes at evening it revised, this form, in which conversational flow is checked by rhyme's return, allowed him to hold the personal in reserve and so to find a space-time to put issues in play without the need for hasty resolution. These issues, ultimately, penetrated to the core of his being as a late poet: they concerned age, decline, oncoming death, and the consequent fragility of life. They concerned, too, his changed relationship to his own art and to nature as the source of his poetic vocation. Thus, contemplating a present that required him to bear with decline and loss, he invoked a past (including a past body of his own writing) only to turn that past in a new direction that in some respects rejects his earlier practice. To put it bluntly, an Evening Voluntary was sometimes an anti-, as well as post-, Wordsworthian and Romantic form.

Sight and Sound: The First Voluntary

Wordsworth was prompted to write the Voluntaries in March and April 1833 when visiting his son John, the vicar of Moresby, a village on the Cumbrian coast. The sojourn by the sea was a shift of emotional, as well as physical, ground. The location necessarily called to mind his 1811 stay on the same coast, shortly after which his children Catherine and Thomas had died. The sight of the sea also revived memories of John Wordsworth's 1805 death in the shipwreck of the *Earl of Abergavenny*. At Moresby, death, and memories of bearing death's consequences as a father and brother, was evident on the face of nature.

Initially, Wordsworth found the coastal visit stirring, writing home to say that

> the sea is a delightful companion and nothing can be more charming, especially for a sequestered Mountaineer, than to cast eyes over its boundless surface, and hear as I have done almost from the brow of the steep in the Church field at Moresby, the waves chafing and murmuring in a variety of tones below, as a kind of base of harmony to the shrill but liquid music of the larks above. I took yesterday five minutes of this . . . before going into the Church, and surely it was as good a prelude for devotion as any Psalm, though one of the Moresby female songsters has a charming voice and manages it well. (LY, I, p. 600)

Here, then, the sound of the limitless sea is itself the evening voluntary, the holy music that prepares for worship in church. It was from this mode of thinking about the Moresby experience that the poems developed. They were prompted by the sea song that was a prelude to religious service; often, their movement is modeled on the tides; their sound, on the waves. Sound, indeed, is especially significant to them because they are the creations of a poet from whom the sight of nature had become, all too often, a painful burden; a poet who, afflicted by the bodily infirmities that accrue with age, found that what had once been a metaphor was now coming physically true: "the things which I have seen I now can see no more" (Immortality Ode, line 9). Already in 1832 Wordsworth had complained that sunlight inflamed his eyes and stopped him reading and writing. In a letter written for him by Mary, he ordered tinted spectacles "of a cold bluish tint" to "subdue the glaring light" (LY, I, p. 543). Despite this protection, which turned the yellow blaze of the sun to the blue pallor of the moon, he continued to suffer, noting in January 1835 that his eyes could not "bear strong sun-shine or candle light striking full upon them" (LY, I, p. 23). He was now a nature-poet whom it hurt both to look on nature and to pore over the page. The two interactions on which his vocation depended left him afflicted rather than exalted.

The first of the Evening Voluntaries in *Yarrow Revisited* is an attempt to articulate a mode of evening vision—a way of seeing that avoids the dangers of the fuller light experienced at midday, a way in which sight, diminished, is also renewed by the other senses, a way of sensing. This way involves a turn to the mode of proceeding pioneered in "Yew Trees" rather than that of *The Prelude*. Wordsworth decouples the observation of nature from the observer. The poet does not at first appear in the poem; his responses to the scene, physical and emotional, are not its focal point—their reliability is not foregrounded. Instead, an impersonal narrative point of view predominates. The tone is subdued; the poem adopts the mode of a catalogue in which the aspects of evening—setting sun and approaching night—make difficulty in seeing seem an aspect of the time and place rather than an infirmity of the poet. Evening here is a relief from the quest to see and, by seeing, to seize the spiritual powers animating self and world. A list rather than a quest narrative about the dawning intimations of immortality, the poem is a means of diversion not just from pains of vision but also from the burden of the visionary. Diversion entails revision; it is a matter of style as well as focalization: Wordsworth eschews the blank verse of his earlier nature poetry and of *The Prelude*, returning instead to the rhyming couplets and generic figures typical of the eighteenth-century poets he had once rejected. At the levels of style as well as subject matter, then, he improvises on traditional motifs: his Voluntary plays upon lateness, making its music from acceptance that it comes after the energies of an earlier time. In this way, it emblematizes the passage of a poetic vocation not as a linear development but as a return, late in the day, to old poets who were themselves thinking back upon on the past. Hindsight (or mostly, in effect, hindsound) revived: the past made present only to intensify pastness.

CALM is the fragrant air, and loth to lose
Day's grateful warmth, tho' moist with falling dews.

(lines 1–2; YR, pp. 161–62)

These opening lines raise the poem's main concern: to evoke, without identifying merely as the poet's subjective case, a state that, though belated—indeed, because belated—can delay time's depredations. "Loth to lose" suggests a reluctance to concede dispossession, a need to articulate space and time so that loss can be imagined as withheld—withholding here effected by the half rhyme that makes "lose" merely an echo of "loth." Withholding is effected also by the registration of evening in transient effects on the sense of touch and smell. These suspend in the air, in the form of warmth and fragrance, what we assume is the narrator's anxious desire to find a means of holding off the disappearance of day—as if evening, if its necessarily diminished qualities can be delicately enough gauged, might function as a reservoir of sensible residues of earlier things (the sun's heat). These residues are also, potentially, renewals because they appeal to senses that are often subordinated to the dominant sense of sight during bright daytime. Warmth and fragrance register to touch and smell more noticeably at twilight as vision dims; evening manifests aspects of day in ways not felt at noon. The air is qualified, however, by a sensible trace of the future: the present participle "falling" makes evening's lapse an ongoing, if as yet unachieved, process; moisture is a hint of the invisible nighttime translation of dry to wet, warmth to cold. This is no Eden, but rather a liminal state in which day and night are both immanent though only in vestigial form, so that it seems possible to hold on to the former while keeping the latter at bay. Dew is a soft and gentle Fall.

When sight suddenly erupts into the poem, it is directive, goal-oriented, and forward-looking rather than immersive, residual, and evanescent:

Look for the stars, you'll say that there are none;
Look up a second time, and, one by one,
You mark them twinkling out with silvery light,
And wonder how they could elude the sight.

(lines 3–6)

Evening's gathering gloom allows unreliable sight to be overcome: undazzled by sunlight, the second look allows the stars to be tallied and marked, fixed in their places. Discernment as a possibility of evening that was impossible back in the day is here the issue—an issue raised not auto-biographically, for the poet has at this point not appeared in his poem, but grammatically, since when the poem commands to "Look," it suddenly turns to a second-person direct address although no companion whom the (anyway absent) poet could be addressing has previously appeared. The reader is disconcerted, left wondering who is being addressed and by whom; he then, for lack of candidates within the poem's imagined scene, puts himself in the addressee's place. But this substitution creates unease too, since a poem that began as a descriptive record of a scene now bids the reader step into the scene as an actor within it. The reader does so, but knows that the command is a fiction that occurs in the silently read writing but not in the experienced moment that the writing purports to document. Thus, even as he steps in, he is pushed out: his attention is drawn to a textual effect and the poem's status as a written document comes to the fore. To "look" is to look at the printed page; it's in seeing these inky characters in an evening poem that you recover your sight of the stars. The poem is revealed as, in its textuality, a magic mirror—or telescope—an aid to vision when vision, unaided by it, is all too fallible. And vision, renewed by an evening text, is a gift given by the writer of that text to its reader, rather than experienced by the poet in his poem. It is no longer that Words-worth sees, or is a seer, in spots of time that his writing retrieves; it is that he writes a spell enabling others to see—see and in turn write (in that they will "mark" the stars onto the skies—the task of accurate notation of nature passed to better-sighted readers than Wordsworth now found himself to be). Being an ageing poet here entails a sharing of the task of re-visioning the world in words.

The next lines turn again to sonic record: an absent third-person narra-tor hears evening as temporal events, rather than a place of crepuscular glimpses. Heard rather than seen, it manifests as a series of aural traces, caught just as they diminish into silence.[2]

> The birds, of late so noisy in their bowers,
> Warbled a while with faint and fainter powers,
> But now are silent as the dim-seen flowers . . .

(lines 7–9)

The triplet, deviating from the overall couplet rhyme scheme, preserves the warble longer than the reader expects, only for the following lines to comment explicitly on sonic patterning:

> Nor does the village Church-clock's iron tone
> The time's and season's influence disown;
> Nine beats distinctly to each other bound
> In drowsy sequence; how unlike the sound
> That, in rough winter, oft inflicts a fear
> On fireside Listeners, doubting what they hear!
>
> (lines 10–15)

The clock perpetuates one note, as if doubling the poem's own protraction of rhyme (its own rhyme and the rhyme of Gray, whose "Elegy Written in a Country Churchyard" the description of the clock echoes). Thus, by reiterating the sound, it retards the temporal progress it exists to register. The effect is one of sonic slowdown: the very distinctness of the beats, all alike, binds them into a "drowsy sequence"—a lullaby that contrasts, in its steady pulsation, with the same sounds heard indistinctly during the rough winter. Then, scrambled by winds and storms, the notes vary so alarmingly in volume and clarity that they lose their identity. They are imagined by "fireside Listeners" as, perhaps, the sound of intruders or ghosts; now, they mobilize a time that is soporific in its calmness. Evening is even-time.

Over the following lines, the poem's genre subtly shifts under the reader's eyes. What seemed to be located in a specific place and time gradually turns into a list of generic characteristics located nowhere or when in particular:

> The Shepherd, bent on rising with the sun,
> Had closed his door before the day was done,
> And now with thankful heart to bed doth creep,
> And join his little children in their sleep.
> The Bat, lured forth where trees the lane o'ershade,
> Flits and reflits along the close arcade;
> Far-heard the Dor-hawk chases the white Moth
> With burring note, which Industry and Sloth
> Might both be pleased with, for it suits them both.
>
> (lines 16–24)

These generic figures and personified attributes are noticeably literary: Wordsworth invokes the form and voice of Gray's "Elegy," Collins's "Ode to Evening,"[3] Mickle's "Sir Martyn," and Anne Finch's "Nocturnal Reverie,"[4] each of which also lists rustic examples of pastoral evenings rather than recount the poet's interaction with an individual place. After the specific in-the-moment command "Look for the stars," this listing is strange: the poem now offers a series of vignettes, but their location is unclear; the specific has, before the reader realizes, drifted into the typical. Again, the reader is gently disconcerted: the status of these figures, whether observed or imagined, is not clear. The shepherd creeping to his bed is here, there, and everywhere—as much a figure of pastoral poems as any real village, let alone *the* real village that the poem led us to expect but failed to describe. Diverting the expectations its opening aroused, the poem substitutes the mind's eye—and other poets' eyes—for the poet's actual eye. The visualized appears as a product of writing, having no real origin, however particular a record the poem seemed to be at its start. By mixing local and general, observed detail and literary figure, in this way, Wordsworth radically reworks, rather than reverts to, his formal models, subverting the convention of generic commentary that is characteristic of the eighteenth-century nature poem. But he also reworks the style of his own earlier subjective quest for intimations of immortality—that of the blank-verse nature effusion (or conversation poem). This reworking may have come about as an older poet's way of compensating for his dimming vision—Gray, Finch, Thomson, and others acting as seeing-eye guide-poets—but what is gained by their use is a new form: the Voluntary, here, is a hybrid of the nature verse of Wordsworth's prime with that of the previous century that puts into question the relation of vision to poetic words. It effects the decoupling of insight from Wordsworth's earlier egotistical pursuit of sublimities. The poet of evening is a poet for whom decline—the decline of the day and the decline of his powers—entails an appeal to the eyes and words of others. His vision comes via allusion, though not allusion to a single "strong" poet with whom he wrestles for individuality but to a collective in which he takes a place.

While it questions sight, the poem also renders temporal experience unstable. The list of generic figures is organized around a contrast between past-participle adjectival phrases and present-tense verbs that suggests time's inexorable power (the shepherd is "bent" and now "creeps"; the bat is "lured" and now "Flits and reflits"). But this schematic past/present contrast is overwritten by verbs indicating other temporal stages too; for example, the shepherd "Had closed his door before the day was done"— here the unexpected pluperfect disturbs the generic present that the poem seemed to be occupying. More oddly, Industry and Sloth are described in the conditional mood, suggesting, as it were, a future possibility rather than uncertainty about the present, only for the present tense to follow, rather than the conditional or future: they "Might both be pleased with, for it suits them both." The effect is not of radical indeterminacy but a mild displacement from the grammatical norm—just enough to render the times when the natural events are happening elusive, and the relations between them uncertain. Evening, here, does not allow the reader to rest in one time zone or move inexorably from past to present: it's now, it's in the possible future, and it's in the recent and in the more distant past, all in the time it takes to read ten lines. Meanwhile, the list structure ensures there is neither progression nor conclusion: a sound as brief and transient as a "burr" is an isolated item held up to the ear, rather than a short-lived aspect of a continually changing sound-world.[5] The ear in question, the list form implies, is that of a naturalist—one whose discourse about nature is an ordered catalogue of the fauna of a locality as revealed by the traces he has learned to interpret (birdcalls; spraint—as in Gilbert White's *History of Selbourne*, a text the Wordsworths liked). This natural history discourse can turn sound to sight: the burring note generates an imagined picture of the dor-hawk chasing a moth. It is a snapshot rather than a movie—whether the bird will catch its prey we do not discover; hawk and moth are suspended in a perpetual present. In this time-out-of-time, opposite interpretations of nature can be indulged without a decision between them having finally to be made: Industry and Sloth might both be pleased with the dor-hawk's burr (presumably because it resembles the grunt of effort or the sound of snoring). Temporal lapse, and thus the logic of acts and consequences, is held in check: this poetic evening may be late in the day, but it wards off its ending.

Having lulled the reader and suspended narrative progress with the catalogue of generics, the poem turns again to the specific and implies a narrator present within a scene: "A stream is heard." This disembodied, passive formulation raises the question, Who is there (where?) to hear?, but as if to answer it, Wordsworth suddenly enters his own poem in the first person for the first time: "I see it not, but know / By its soft music whence the waters flow."[6] This is the heart of the matter: it is only in this confession of

failing sight that he declares himself directly in order to reassert his located-
ness, his ability to know nature, by means of an aural receptivity so acute
it can follow a sound stream to its source and can hear it as harmony and
melody. There is no need, in these circumstances, to present a coherent
visual scene in the poem; it is by tracing, in its prosody and word-sounds,
sonic passages across various sound stages that it articulates evening and
thereby allows the poet to rediscover, despite his limited vision, an assurance of deep participatory knowledge in a nature that is at once here and
now and a flowing out from a remote source.

But this knowledge is not to last in the face of sound's evanescence. The
first-person narrator departs and the poem reverts to the passive, disembodied voice of "Wheels and the tread of hoofs are heard no more." This
reversion both depersonalizes and generalizes the process of loss. It is not
Wordsworth's predicament alone to find his senses unavailing and his
knowledge shrinking as the activities of the day quieten at nightfall; it is,
the narrative voice suggests, an observed fact and as such an admonition
to all:

> One Boat there was, but it will touch the shore
> With the next dipping of its slackened oar;
> Faint sound, that, for the gayest of the gay,
> Might give to serious thought a moment's sway,
> As a last token of Man's toilsome day!
>
> (lines 28–32)

At first glance, these concluding lines draw the sobering moral that all
things come to an end, albeit a calm and gentle end after toil. Not with a
bang but a feather—a feathered oar quietly bringing a journey to rest at the
appropriate time. The shore is a final destination arrived at by a skillfully
regulated diminution of activity: the oar is slackened; the oarsman is not so
much "bent" or "bound" by temporal exigency as moving in rhythm with
it. He, of course, is not mentioned; he is a figure inferred rather than
declared and as such a figure of the absent poet whose boat is this poem
(the poem is thus the "last token" of human life—an emblem showing how
to make way toward the close or to negotiate gradual decline unto death).
And yet, even as the poem slows to the quiet ending that justifies the final
moral exclamation, it creates a counter-current that keeps the boat on the
water, holding finality at bay. Again, this current is a matter of tenses: "one

Boat there was" notes, from an inferred present moment, a completed action in the past: the vessel was, but is no more—a disappearance into the darkness and hush. "But it will touch the shore," immediately following, revives the vessel, unseen, as an imaginary visualization inferred from its sonic vestige, the "Faint sound" that is interpreted as an oar breaking the water's surface. The future tense, "will touch," leaves the action incomplete: the shore is evermore about to be, but never is finally, touched. In the space/time of the poem's scene, ending is anticipated but suspended. And in this suspension what is realized is the temporal freedom of a sonically sustained imagination, recorded in the poem's imagined scene but also manifested in its grammar and prosody.[7]

It turns out that the sonic vestige has not yet been heard: the "next dipping" is yet to occur; it is a scenario that is not recorded but is predicted on the basis of the poet's already-demonstrated ability to imagine with his mind's ear, from his calibrated sensitivity to sonic sequencing, what happens. (Thus, hearing the village clock beat, he pictures villagers' lives bound to time counted out in regular pattern; thus too, hearing the dor-hawk's burr, he visualizes its pursuit of the moth.) Unlike the villagers creeping to bed, however, he is not simply bound to the beats of time as repeated iteration of the same, not merely "bent" in automatic response to the returns of clock chimes, dusks, and dawns. In contrast, he understands time as rhythmic and temporal variation: he intuits enough of the oar strokes' increasingly spaced intervals and diminishing volume to project the sequence forward, to infer its future temporal spacing, and so to predict a visual scene from a sound not yet heard. By knowing that sequence, by articulating it in his own rhythmic words (oar strokes and metrical beats), he frees himself from existing merely in the past and present and makes it possible to imagine the future rather than just "creep" to day's end, "bent" by the "iron tones" of inexorable time's repeated routine. Able to anticipate what "might" happen, even if what he anticipates is a slow, diminishing but inevitable movement toward ending, he puts acceptance of the inevitable on his own terms: it is he (or rather it is his poem speaking for him and so giving the appearance of factual authority that stems from third-person narrative) who "sees" when the boat will reach the shore and tells how time inevitably dims our sight and leads us into darkness—inevitably, but not now, not here, for it is displaced into an imagined, not quite real, moment of forever not-yet-ness. This is an evening voluntary—a shaped sequence of sounds, word-music—shaped on the pattern of natural sounds, unfolding its own pattern into the future.[8] *Organic* form: music improvised after worship.

The co-existence of current and counter-current are emblematized, near the poem's end, by the phrase "give to serious thought a moment's sway." On the one hand, "sway" is read as "rule." So, the "faint sound" is to cause "serious thought" to dominate the thought-time of the otherwise unthinking "gayest of the gay"—to overrule, through a momentary interruption, their heedlessness of temporal lapse and its consequences—to make them, like the poet and his readers, anticipate the end by a temporal internalization of lateness—to place them mentally in the evening. Yet at the same time, "sway" contains a residual counter-meaning of "move slowly or rhythmically backwards and forwards or from side to side" (OED), as when a tree sways in the wind or a boat rocks on the swell of waters, in which case the phrase suggests that serious thought will be given the back-and-forth motion of the unspent, unprogressive moment: it will be swayed upon the pivot of a time that, albeit briefly, is excerpted from temporal lapse, like, perhaps, the boat on the water (see also the meaning of "moment" as "a turning effect produced by a force acting at a distance on an object" [OED]). In this reading, the "gayest of the gay" are given "serious thought" because the "faint sound" attunes their mental processes to the rhythm of a place/time (evening) that suspends linear progress indefinitely. The two readings cannot be reconciled, but neither do they cancel each other out: it is a gentle aporia in which the very anticipation of ending is poised as a thought-experience that, still in the moment, renders progress an always-unrealized inevitability.

Buoyed on the waters? Buoyed on the prosody, since the poem achieves its non-ends not only by semantic aporias and shifting tenses but also by playing against each other (among each other) subtly patterned articulations of temporal experience. Many of these counter the readerly expectation (both temporal and aesthetic) of movement from beginning, through middle, to end. Rhyming couplets (unusual for the earlier Wordsworth) function in this way: they return sound on a rapid, as well as regular, basis—not so much the past echoing in the present as a present prolonged by its sonic reiteration. The couplet is an insistent double unit: it appears so often that its presence is both lulling and constantly noticeable; it seems it could be protracted on the same basis forever (as in Erasmus Darwin's verse). Thus it reminds—visually and aurally—that this is poetry and that poetry constitutes a formal control, a sonic patterning, of time. In the meantime, the (mostly regular) iambic pentameter establishes a steady, repeating organization of time into recurring beat patterns (less monotonous than the village clock but just as predictable)—a base rhythm to which the reader becomes attuned, inferring its pulse when, for a while, it is interrupted (overlaid by other stress patterns). Prosodic form, then, is strongly enough marked to be heard and seen as the poem's means of controling time lapse: the same again, rather than a dying fall. Yet the dominant meter does interplay with countercurrents. These make time move on, faster and slower, with the accelerations and retardations of reading that are created by syntax. For instance, while most of the verse lines are end-stopped, suiting the poem as list rather than linear progression, a number do move over the line ends, disturbing the regular, even pattern. Notably, this disturbance occurs when the poem discusses the disruption made by "rough winter" to what in summer evenings is the regular, even, drowsy sequence of clock chimes.

> Nine beats distinctly to each other bound
> In drowsy sequence; how unlike the sound
> That, in rough winter, oft inflicts a fear
> On fireside Listeners, doubting what they hear

(lines 12–15)

"Sound" is enjambed not, as might be expected, to an adjectival phrase, but to a new clause, governing a new verb and beginning with a stressed foot instead of the metrically expected unstressed foot. The reading time stirs to a more urgent motion as syntax is energized by the rendering of complex relations of cause and effect—but this motion itself varies: it slows with the parenthetical phrase "in rough winter," demanding pauses before and after it is arrived at. Speed is faster and slower, though still riding over the iambic pentameter bass: the chime-sequence is dispersed and doubtful, no longer an even, steady, distinct pulse.

A similarly telling effect is produced in the last lines. The unexpected triplet rhyme delays resolution even as the poem, as it appears on the page and in its imagined scene, nears its end. Rhyme enforces meaning: the song remains the same, and "sway" turns out, when the sound recurs in "day," not to be the closing rhyme word of a couplet but the pivot on which "gay" and "day" balance. Likewise, the last line, because it rhymes as do the previous two, is left hanging—the reader's internalization of the already established sonic sequence makes us expect another line to follow and close the couplet. There ought to be something more: the poem remains pointed toward a closure—a lastness—that its recognition of lastness anticipates but does not achieve. The "last token" intimates a passage to an end but is not itself final.

> Faint sound, that, for the gayest of the gay,
> Might give to serious thought a moment's sway,
> As a last token of Man's toilsome day!
>
> (lines 30–32)

This is a new formulation of old concerns; it reworks the kinds of prosody Wordsworth had used in his earliest poems but from which he had broken in the 1790s, thus setting aside the need to pursue as an autobiographical quest the revival of the once-experienced spots of time that was the source of his poetic voice. As the Voluntary moves in and out of imagined scenes, displacing its narrator(s), it produces a series of iterations of voice, more and less personal, de- and recoupling from the self the poet's capacity to articulate sound so that it stimulates a process of mental imaging (imagination). Wordsworth recognizes this voicing as prophetic and admonitory (it provokes "serious thought") but cannot define it as a doctrine or teach it as a lesson.

The Admonitions of Age: On Not Being Byron

The next Voluntary in the section appears a response to this inability, for if it does not presume to say what the human/nature relationship teaches, it does wish to define the terms on which that relationship is possible. In the process, the poem assumes a defensive mode, ossifying the fluidity of the relationship and treating it as an exclusive preserve of which Wordsworth is the gatekeeper. A number of the later poems do this, as Wordsworth attempts to lay down the law in response to critics who disparage his art or to poets who compete with it. In this case, the competitor he has in mind is Byron, whose letters had been published in 1832.

> Not in the lucid intervals of life
> That come but as a curse to Party-strife;
> Not in some hour when Pleasure with a sigh
> Of languor puts his rosy garland by;
> Not in the breathing-times of that poor Slave

> Who daily piles up wealth in Mammon's cave—
> Is Nature felt, or can be . . .
>
> > (lines 1–7; YR, pp. 163–64)[9]

The insistent negatives, coming before the delayed subject, make the reader wait for resolution, while being lectured by an urgent voice. Syntactically as well as semantically, Nature is not easily arrived at. Wordsworth speaks confidently for it, but as a restrictive marshal of its influence. It is partly a matter of sexual politics: he primly lectures the Byronic poet to the effect that nature's "gentle beauty" is not to be captured by "he" who is ruled by "passion craved for passion's sake / Untaught that meekness is the cherished bent / Of all the truly Great and all the Innocent" (lines 10, 12, 13–15). The emphasis on meekness (cf. Matthew 5.5) seems counter-intuitive because, after all the confident listing of restrictions, the narrator seems anything but meek—more like a protocol-obsessed high priest excluding others from the temple.

> But who *is* innocent? By grace divine,
> Not otherwise, O Nature! we are thine,
> Through good and evil thine, in just degree
> Of rational and manly sympathy.
>
> > (lines 16–19)

If "By grace divine, / . . . we are thine" transfers to Nature Methodism's doctrine of free and unrestricted access to God's saving grace, Wordsworth soon imposes a hierarchy, contradicting himself theologically in the process. He asserts that access is not, after all, a matter of God's unknowable grace but a matter of "just degree": some get nearer than others, in proportion to the "rational and manly sympathy" they show. The adjectives perhaps respond to an anxiety that he has overly feminized the relationship with nature as a matter of gentle feeling, lapsing into discourse of sensibility. But they are a defensive reaction, rather than a working-through of the relationship as he had described it—and it remains unclear whether access is governed by the divine, or by human qualities, or by nature's own nature as a gentle beauty whom the passionate and busy man overlooks.

The poem recovers from its tendency to tie itself in knots laying down rules of access when it begins to number blessings and count costs:

To all that Earth from pensive hearts is stealing,
And Heaven is now to gladdened eyes revealing,
Add every charm the Universe can show
Through every change its aspects undergo . . .

(lines 20–23)

Earth, heaven, the universe: the lines build toward a best of all possible worlds in which the nature that relieves sadness and induces happiness is on offer everywhere. The poet imagines a superabundance of charm, whatever the changeable weather, only to crash unexpectedly into the deliberate anti-climax of

Care may be respited, but not repealed;
No perfect cure grows on that bounded field.

(lines 24–25)

This tremendous couplet concentrates the fall and its consequences—and the autobiographical plot of the Immortality Ode—into a microcosm so formally controlled that it attains the status of axiom. Everyone experiences care, in the sense of a known, lived suffering rather than charity. It cannot be avoided; nature cannot heal knowledge, pain, and loss. Wordsworth shows Nature to be fallen and, if not entirely lost, only partly restorative and accessible. It is bounded—hedged or fenced or walled—and although the past participles are not explicitly governed by a declared grammatical subject, the lawgiver, implicitly, must be God. Unnamed, He is the unseen owner who excludes humans as He once banished them from Eden, like a dispossessing, self-enriching landlord enclosing the common land (a current economic activity that Wordsworth had lamented in the 1790s). The full rhymes "repealed"/"field" give this general declaration the authority of finality, while the half-rhymes and echoes—"respite"/"repealed," "cure"/"care"—enact respite, a less-than-whole remedy, a partial remediation. This is the poem's declared insight, its irredeemable realization: the late Wordsworth, here, knows that the ills that flesh is heir to can be borne with, can be accommodated, but cannot be overcome by a paradisal nature, even by the innocent and meek. Poetry cannot renew the hiding places of its power, cannot recollect the hour of splendor by virtue of recalling spots of time—the poet cannot even explore, as he did at huge length in *The Prelude*, the personal quest to do so; that game has already been played. All the more so because the rhymes echo the endorsement of free love in nature that Wordsworth had made in 1798 in "Lines Written at a Small Distance from My House"—only to refute that endorsement entirely:

> Love, now a universal birth,
> From heart to heart is stealing,
> From earth to man, from man to earth:
> —It is the hour of feeling.
>
> One moment now may give us more
> Than fifty years of reason:
> Our minds shall drink at every pore
> The spirit of the season.
>
> (lines 21–28; LB, pp. 63–64)

Alluding to that poem to Dorothy, Wordsworth destroys its optimism: there is now no easy framing of the "measure of our souls" to "the blessed power that rolls / About, below, above" (lines 33–34). But the allusion suggests a reason why Wordsworth should have changed so utterly. It is left undeclared in the poem, but his sister was by 1835, after two years and more of exhausting illness that confined her to the house, an incontinent and demented wreck of her past self, her short-term memory gone almost completely. Wordsworth had reason to know, when he wrote of "lucid intervals," that time could make these very few even among those who loved nature meekly, as Dorothy always had. It is possible, then, that the poem is motivated by finding one's beloved partner an Alzheimer's sufferer. Its method, though, is rightly to leave such occasioning events at a distance, faintly invoked by allusion to past poems, so as to invite readerly reflection on the effects of time rather than indulge self-pity.

The poem's concluding lines sound confident: they make a general pronouncement on behalf of humankind and, indeed, God, setting out the terms on which access to a partial cure is denied or offered. It is important not to be distempered, not to be a Byron who refuses to be humbled by the human predicament:

> Vain is the pleasure, a false calm the peace,
> If He, through whom alone our conflicts cease,
> Our virtuous hopes without relapse advance,

Come not to speed the Soul's deliverance;
To the distempered Intellect refuse
His gracious help, or give what we abuse.

(lines 26–31)

Wordsworth speaks for God: the pronoun "He" is, in effect, a personification of the poem's rhetorical vigor, energized as the verse is by patrolling the boundaries on behalf of almighty law. "He" is the crystallization of the poem's articulation of time and space as restrictions and permissions, the deification of the poetics of a grumpy old man. Wordsworth is far from meek, for by establishing the conditions determining whether care will be respited, he seizes a certain power—albeit restricted—as if speaking God's authority will secure partial visiting privileges to nature's partly curative field. But this power-seeking is also a desperate measure, for it can only delay the specter that deliverance from suffering may not come at all. Grammar and syntax become indirect: qualifications succeed conditionals, and parentheses delay resolution because, when resolution appears, it is in the negative form of God's envisaged non-arrival and refusal to help. Wordsworth defers, but finally arrives at, a remote God—and identifying his poetry as God's interpreter offers only limited strength and no prospect of exemption from His withdrawal/its failure. For all its masterful rhetoric, poetry may lead to no help from nature or beyond, and its power is hollow if it cannot articulate (and thereby bring about) a saving grace. What is missing here is Christ—and Christianity. It is a straight fight between Wordsworth as suffering sinner and Wordsworth as God's spokesman (or God as Wordsworth's poetic power), in which the poem takes both positions.[10] But there's no possibility envisaged of Jesus, the son, as the means on earth of God's amazing grace—nor, indeed, is there any actual encounter with nature, if that is to effect a partial cure. So while the poem begins by reserving nature for those meek enough to appreciate her, it neither offers any evidence of this appreciation nor sustains its argument that a privileged access is possible. Nature is not to be relied upon, and disappears from the poem: even the soul's deliverance (to where is not specified) is uncertain.

Perhaps Wordsworth placed "Not in the lucid intervals" among the Evening Voluntaries in an effort to define the cultural meaning of the kind of poetic exploration that he was making in the larger verse sequence. Telling readers what his purpose was entailed showing them how and why to read nature in verse, as the means of showing them how to be toward nature in life. But nature—nature as a self/world experience happening as (and because) it is represented—is lost in this didacticism. It is objectified, shrunk to a token in an argument. Wordsworth sermonizes about nature's importance but does not trust himself to it—as if to put his thoughts and feelings into play in an encounter would involve a vulnerability he does not want to risk, or as if he's lost his sustaining faith in it—hence the appeal to, or rather the attempt to negotiate with, a power (the divine) who might govern it and everything. The gendering is instructive: Wordsworth wants to act as an interpreter or deputy for a male boss (poetry here narrowly a man speaking to men). Stereotyping nature as a gentle, healing female excuses it from having any independent power or action. Thus he saves faith and avoids blaming her, but at the price of patronizing her: she needs protection by the right kind of man—Wordsworth himself, the steward maintaining her "bounded field," acting in her owner's name, as if God were Sir George Beaumont (see Chapter 2 on Wordsworth's self-positioning as his patrons' steward).

"Not in the lucid intervals" shows that the new hybrid form of the Voluntary could lend itself to didacticism: here the provisional self suggested by the conversational, open-ended form is disciplined by the authority given to statements by couplet rhyme. Despite its formal affiliation to the authoritarian, the poem nevertheless evinces a degree of doubt in nature's power that, if thoroughly admitted, would undermine the sustaining fiction of Wordsworth's earlier poetic oeuvre. It is implicitly a turn from nature and the spatiotemporal exploration of the self in nature—a disenchanted poem indeed, by a poet who had found no remedy for the unjust pain and suffering that comes with age. As the second poem in a sequence, it has the effect of casting doubt on the bearing with evening (the being toward ending) that characterized the first. The Evening Voluntaries, as a formal group, admit not just variety and contrast but also disagreement and conflict. They suggest that to be a poet of twilight is to pitch modes of accommodation to lateness against ways of eluding, or at least deferring, the dying of the light.

Birdsong and Poetic Song: The Third Voluntary

The next poem after this reads as a local exploration of the lack and loss that are only implicitly displayed in "Not in the lucid intervals." It renews the process undertaken in the first Voluntary, a process of elaborating, by hybridizing the conversation poetry of the 1790s with the couplet verse of the previous century, a poetic form and voice able to defer finality by subjecting temporal lapse to the shifting rhythms and time-sense of the verse. It also thematizes this process by offering an evocation of nature that is also a reflection on poetic song—Wordsworth's own and behind it Keats's, Coleridge's, and Milton's. Turning away from Moresby, Wordsworth explores at home, in the sheltered mountain valley in which he lived, the renewed alertness to the transient sights and sounds of evening that he had experienced on the Cumberland coast. These sights and sounds, however, bespeak an absence: they are tokens of a fuller natural and poetic voice that Wordsworth now realizes he lacks. What is absent "By the Side of Rydal Mere" is the Muse—the natural voice that sponsors poetic voice. The absence is not registered at first, for the poem opens with birdcalls, crossing the ear in real time:

> THE Linnet's warble, sinking towards a close,
> Hints to the thrush 'tis time for their repose;
> The shrill-voiced Thrush is heedless, and again
> The Monitor revives his own sweet strain[.]
>
> (lines 1–4; YR, pp. 165–66)

Evening at Rydal takes the form of nature's revival of song and heedlessness of night. But the impersonal narrator knows better:

> But both will soon be mastered, and the copse
> Be left as silent as the mountain-tops,
> Ere some commanding Star dismiss to rest
> The throng of Rooks, that now, from twig or nest,
> (After a steady flight on home-bound wings,
> And a last game of mazy hoverings
> Around their ancient grove) with cawing noise
> Disturb the liquid music's equipoise.
>
> (lines 5–12)

Up to this point, the poem has been one long, fluid sentence of many clauses, parentheses, and grammatical subjects. Syntax traces a mazy path, and tenses alternate between present, predicted future, and again present.

Thus the verse articulates not just what is happening now but also an understanding of how what is happening now will be superseded—a hindsight projected forward. Not innocence and the "freshness of a dream" but the voice of experience, which knows that what is immediate will be over, so that immediacy itself is tinged with melancholy. Prospective nostalgia.

At this point the disembodied narrator acquires a voice:

O Nightingale!

(line 13)

What does it mean to call upon a nightingale and to do so, moreover, with that most conventionally poetic of forms of address—the apostrophic O? It is, of course, to invoke the most poetic of birds. Since Ovid's *Metamorphoses*, the nightingale has represented human lament made natural (Philomel), and since Coleridge and Keats and Wordsworth's own "Solitary Reaper," it has signified poets' desire to—and difficulty in—encapsulating the sound of nature in their own songs. Invoking it here, Wordsworth aligns himself with these poets. He makes Rydal not, as at first seemed, a real place being evoked by discriminating observation so much as a ground on which the poet ponders the relation of poetry to nature and his own place in the poetic tradition.

Matters become more difficult in the next lines:

Who ever heard thy song
Might here be moved, till Fancy grows so strong
That listening sense is pardonably cheated
Where wood or stream by thee was never greeted.

(lines 13–16)

It turns out that the nightingale has never been heard at Rydal: the Lake District is out of the species' range. In speaking to it in its absence as if it were present, Wordsworth calls into question the poetic conceit of apostrophe that mobilized the nightingale in Milton, Coleridge, and Keats—a foundational conceit of the ode and of the nature lyric. He self-reflexively asks where poetic "fancy" leads. What is the responsibility of a discourse that authorizes itself by calling upon what is not and never has been present? In the text world that the poet writes and the reader reads, the nightingale is simultaneously a fanciful presence-to-voice and an absence to eye and ear. In the real world that the poet supposedly surveys in the imagined scene of his poem, the bird becomes doubly absent, because its absence is now noticed as a lack. The real place is now perceived as incomplete—deprived, even—without the bird that the poet is able to fancy being there. Thus the apostrophe to this of all birds makes an issue of the poetic song's contradictory relationship of dependence on and independence from the real experience that it seems to be narrating. "O Nightingale" is a means of launching an exploration, which the whole poem will turn out to pursue, of verse/song's relationship to originary experience, to imaginative invention, and to textuality (its own status as text and a tradition of prior texts).

> Surely, from fairest spots of favoured lands,
> Were not some gifts withheld by jealous hands,
> This hour of deepening darkness here would be
> As a fresh morning for new harmony;
> And Lays as prompt would hail the dawn of Night
>
> (lines 17–21)

Rydal is not Tempe, and Wordsworth is too committed to the real as it is in the here and now to indulge his desire to be the Ovidian poet who imagines it so. He resents this: as the imputation of blame made by "jealous hands" suggests, the lack of a nightingale to come to the poet's call symbolizes a world deprived of gifts by a god who takes pleasure in withholding (the withholding hands are those of a resentful envier of the world's sensual beauty—and jealousy is a Deadly Sin—a Miltonic God). The fallen world, rather than a nature animated by the metamorphoses of creative desire, is the world that Wordsworth inhabits; he does not commit itself wholly to the fantastical—the made-up world, the airy nothings—which, as the apostrophe shows, the poet can call up ("but will they come?" he says with Hotspur).[11] Acknowledging the withholding, he makes it all the more a loss by imagining, in the diminished form of a possibility that can never come about, a world fulfilled with birdsong: were nightingales present, a twilight chorus would make night "fresh" with "new" song; the dawn would be renewed at dusk; night would enlighten rather than endarken. The nightingale's song, his "Lay," is openly an emblem of the tradition of poetic song that is not quite possible here.

The impossible fancy turns out to be more than merely fanciful because, even though it acknowledges lack, it has the unexpected effect of changing the poet's perception of the actual scene, so that he now emphasizes a form of dawn at dusk, a kind of light in darkness, that *is* present:

> A *dawn* she has both beautiful and bright,
> When the East kindles with the full moon's light;
> Not like the rising sun's impatient glow
> Dazzling the mountains, but an overflow
> Of solemn splendour, in mutation slow.
>
> (lines 22–26)[12]

Moonrise brings about a diminished reflection of dawn that is not a dawn but a *dawn*—the italics indicating its "as it were" not-quite-ness; its analogical status, like but not actually the real, impatient, dazzling thing. Moonlight is itself reflected sunlight, so this dusk-dawn is nature's self-reflection, its re-presentation of itself—an after-image, so that in writing "*dawn*" it is as if the poet were merely recording nature analogizing itself, rather than himself introducing illustrative images from elsewhere. Perhaps no apostrophizing of an exotic and poetic nightingale is needed at Rydal, for the place reflects itself to the observing poet on the spot. It has its own process of representation to enable his writing, offering, not as real but as image or echo, a renewal of what is past—another dawn that occurs just when daylight fades and darkness threatens. And it is writing, rather than speech or song, that is appropriate to articulate this time-overcoming self-doubling, for *dawn* is a textual effect: the italics that indicate the *dawn*'s fanciful status belong to manuscript and print but not to oral communication. Thus they alert us to the poem as textual rather than oral: the poetry of evening is a self-consciously secondary poetry, because writing, for Wordsworth, is secondary to, and a paler, lesser reflection of the oral song (the nightingale song as poetic song) that flows from immediate response to nature the first time round (the real dawn). Late poetry is moonbeams rather than sunlight—the slow mutations of marks on a page rather than the full-throated melody of a bird.

What is accomplished in this moonlit textuality is the discovery of a possibility retrieved from defeat by virtue of acceptance of that defeat—and from past poetry accepted as past and not repeated or rewritten. Because Wordsworth accepts the absence of the nightingale—and the consequential impossibility of dusk being a new dawn full of birdsong/poetsong, a dawn of "prompt" "lays"—he can turn from fantasy to reality and perceive reality changed. It is not so much that he finds strength in what remains behind as that he makes verse a reflection of aspects of the world (and of poetry, his own and others') that are seen to reflect, and so represent, what is gone or never was. Embracing secondariness, he avoids the retreat from the fantasy of full oral presence becoming simply a lament. Instead, he adopts lessness as the best of a bad job, proffering a less-full, less-immediate poetry: writing as a reflection of a reflection. It is a late show on the page instead of a song of plenitude transferred from a nature that is at the full. "Overflow" is a significant word in this process: in admiring the moonlight's "overflow / Of solemn splendour, in mutation slow," Wordsworth alludes to, only to redefine, his famous poetic credo of 1800 (first redefined in 1803).[13] As a model for poetry, the moonlight's illumination of the scene is no "spontaneous overflow of powerful feelings" (LB, p. 744): it is not immediate but indirect and characterized by gradual change; it is not a matter of strong emotion but "solemn splendour." And the phrase is ambiguous. Is the moonlight an overflow possessed of/possessing solemn splendor, or is solemn splendor the thing of which the moonlight is an overflow? If the former, then we are reminded that the illumination of the scene is not a thing-in-itself but an excess of something else (moonlight) that is itself an excess of something else (sunlight). But if the latter, then the moonlit scene is a spilling over of an effect (solemn splendor) whose origins and whereabouts are unknown. In both cases, the status of "overflow" is brought into focus: we see it has no simple, spontaneous, or direct relation to a thing of which it is the spilling over. The sunlight, which is moonlight's origin, has disappeared; splendor is immaterial and unlocatable. The overflow is a supplementary presence, an excess, a not-quite-independent entity, an after-effect, a presence that marks an absence of origin—but at least as a vestige it is more present than the utterly absent nightingale song. Poetry as overflow is now, it follows, an indirect, tardy, metamorphosis of a foregone thing—a trace of a cause recessed in space and time that was and is not to be instantly and wholly met by an answering song that contains it. The rising sun, Wordsworth says, is "impatient" and "dazzling"—too fast and too powerful to be visualized in its pomp; the nightingale is elsewhere. For songs the poet has to substitute writings because, as slow, gradually produced, and distanced reflections, writings are traces of an inspiring full presence that can no longer be, if it ever was, met on the full (i.e., adequately encompassed by verse-songs that it inspires). To be an evening poet, then, is to renounce the Romantic poetic, epitomized by the nightingale, that poetry—as song, as oral response to the world impinging on the mind/body—can meet all motion and become its soul. It is to work out what is implied in the Immortality Ode: the aging poet volunteers a variation on what was first announced in that work. Not only is the hour of splendor gone but also the poem that recorded its loss: the new Voluntary is self-consciously belated with regard both to past experience and to the poetry that lamented the recession of that experience.

If the observing Wordsworth is fixed "by the side of Rydal Mere" as the moon rises, he can at least conjure up the scenario to which he cannot give a local habitation and a name. He imagines the nightingale, following spring's royal progress across the globe, in an allegory of the kind of reception he wanted for his own poetry but knew it would not get:

> Wanderer by spring with gradual progress led,
> For sway profoundly felt as widely spread;
> To king, to peasant, to rough sailor, dear,
> And to the soldier's trumpet-wearied ear;
> How welcome wouldst thou be to this green Vale
> Fairer than Tempe!
>
> (lines 27–32)

Universally welcomed, the songster is an idealized poet, a free spirit, exempted by all from any responsibility other than that to its own singing:

> Yet, sweet Nightingale!
> From the warm breeze that bears thee on alight
> At will, and stay thy migratory flight;
> Build, at thy choice, or sing, by pool or fount,
> Who shall complain, or call thee to account?
>
> (lines 32–36)

At this point, the futility (absurdity?) of complaining to a bird brings the apostrophizing poet down to earth, grounding the poem in an acceptance of the limits of poetic imagination and thus preparing for a concluding, general moral:

The wisest, happiest, of our kind are they
That ever walk content with Nature's way,
God's goodness measuring bounty as it may;
For whom the gravest thought of what they miss,
Chastening the fulness of a present bliss,
Is with that wholesome office satisfied,
While unrepining sadness is allied
In thankful bosoms to a modest pride.

(lines 37–44)

Here the shift from apostrophe to impersonal pronouncement and from the bird to the generic "they" is an effort to attain the authority of factual narrative that is reinforced by triplet rhymes protracting sonic harmony. Wordsworth seeks to promulgate, as uncontroversial fact, a way of living in which less and lack are to be accepted or even welcomed. His effort is to create a balance between contentment with what we have—what nature gives—and the consciousness of diminution—including diminution from past poems that first wrestled with the problem—that limits the wholeness of "present bliss." It is an argument for the virtue of chastening bliss: sadness teaches "the wisest" and "happiest" to be thankful for what is given and thus they discover that the yearning for what they do not have is a source not of dissatisfaction but of gratitude. "Thankful bosoms" learn to value, to have a modest pride (not too much, not sinful) in, what *is* given—whereas unchastened bliss might be too present and too full to allow awareness of what it involves (except in the imaginary pre-lapsarian nightingale-world that poetry can call up from nowhere). It is not, then, on plenitude overflowing but on plenitude restrained that Wordsworth now wants to found his poetry (a "measured bounty" in controlled, neoclassical couplets and regular pentameter measures). Rydal Mere prompts a self-consciously lesser, tamer poetry for a twilight poet: "goodness" and "fulness" are measured and chastened so that neither bounty nor bliss are experienced whole, unmarked by consciousness of lack and lapse. Wholeness is then recuperated in lesser form as the "wholesome," a properly limited and thus virtuous degree of a whole that does not appear. This is a moonlight morality and a textual one too, since moonlight and textuality are both, in the poem's terms, partial and diminished reflections of the original, sensual immediacy of the full-on thing, itself already absent and lamented as such. As an outwork and after-poem to the Immortality Ode, the Voluntary accepts that the subjective intensity of the initial revelation of loss cannot be renewed in full. If then the hour of splendor was lost, now the revelation of its loss is, if not lost, then at least diminished by distance.

"Gravest thought of what they miss" hints at graves, as well as gravity—the weight of death; it proves hard to make such thought mutate into contentment and satisfaction. Indeed, the strength of underlying grief is suggested by the syntactical convolutions and grammatical uncertainties that appear as Wordsworth tries to make loss and lack feel good, as well as justify them as part of God's plan. Syntax tangles, sense muddies, and the clarity of the couplet "The wisest, happiest, of our kind are they / That ever walk content with Nature's way" is dissipated. Is "God's goodness" an alternative description of "Nature's way" or a new concept? Does "wholesome office" refer to walking content with nature's way or to measuring bounty? (In which case who or what is doing the measuring? Does God's goodness measure bounty? If so, it is a tautological self-reflexivity on its part.) How removed from spontaneous giving and gratitude it all is: sadness cannot be repining, bounty must be measured, fullness chastened, pride modest. Wordsworth can balance these opposites only because his terms are so abstract that nobody in particular has to be imagined struggling to live them out. Meanwhile the grammar is so indirect that God, as the origin of all this limitation and restriction, is insulated from responsibility for it. By the end, God is to be neither angrily reviled nor patiently endured, but thanked by those who have disciplined themselves to understand the sorrow he inflicts as a good. But Wordsworth makes them seem like functionaries quietly proud of, and grateful for, their position of self-subordination to a regime that restricts bounty and manipulates lack. It is a portrait of complicity: Wordsworth's resort to generality produces only a spurious authority as he undoes his neat conclusion in a mass of self-contradictions that neither satisfactorily resolve the underlying tensions nor adequately comprehend the earlier exploration of poetry's relationship to absence, lack, and overflow. Coleridge remarked, years after writing "The Rime of the Ancient Mariner," that the concluding moral obtruded too openly on the poem. The same is true of the Evening Voluntaries: Wordsworth fails when he attempts to translate his subtle reflections on the evanescence of passing experience into ringing moral axioms. He was, in effect, a greater poet than he knew—or at least, than he knew how to translate into a generalized sound-bite wisdom (a logophilic transposition of his need for poetic resolution into divine law).

And it was, in part, to escape the burden of trying to do so that he avoided writing *The Recluse*.

Reflection on Reflections: The Fourth Voluntary

The fourth poem in the sequence epitomizes the drama of the sequence as a whole: it offers a new, subtle and sensitive mode of articulating transience and interfusion (a nature of echoes, reflections, and after-effects, too mobile to be encapsulated). It attempts to bear with a diminished, twilight participation in the world (a state of lessness). But it is unable to rest content with diminution, rebelling against calm acceptance of evening as a temporal and mental state. It reveals a poet who, rather than attempt to define the human/world relationship on behalf of the divine word, turns in his unrest to contemptuous dismissal of the plentitude that once he yearned to possess and lamented having lost. The poem represents the evening view as an oscillation between a delicate composure and an angry vehemence: Wordsworth writes both to reconcile himself to being a poet for whom even loss no longer has the freshness of a dream and to complain at a world (a world-self) that keeps reminding him of the fullness he no longer wishes either to have or to regret. This veering between acknowledgement and asperity is made possible by the Voluntary form, which is, on the one hand, loose and open-ended enough to structure subjectivity as shifting and elusive after-images and, on the other, able, through the compression produced by rhyming couplets, to achieve statements of ringing generality.

Again, the poem opens with a Rydal view:

Soft as a cloud is yon blue Ridge—the Mere
Seems firm as solid crystal, breathless, clear,
And motionless; and, to the gazer's eye,
Deeper than Ocean, in the immensity
Of its vague mountains and unreal sky!

(lines 1–5; YR, pp. 167–68)

Here, deixis ("yon") gestures to the view's local reality, placing the reader alongside a narrator who is pointing out the scene, only for the narrator to withdraw, remaining coy about who he is and where he stands (he appears only as a generic "gazer" rather than a first-person guide). The effect of this is to render the scene present and distinct only to make its status uncertain, reinforcing the vagueness and unreality displayed by the reflections in the mere. It is this world—firm, "solid," "clear"—*and* a metamorphosed other world: ridges softened into clouds, water hardened into crystal, lake enlarged into ocean and into mountains and sky. Evening is here no simple decline: it opens new vistas and depths; it mutates solid into liquid and into air; it is a kind of alchemy (as "mutation" in the previous Rydal Voluntary suggests). Perhaps, again, it is an allegory of poetry—of this poetry, though Wordsworth does not here embody the allegorical relationship in a being that partakes of both, as in the nightingale. Instead, while keeping his narratorial position unspecified, he adopts the verbal forms of a tour guide or natural historian who lists a place's features and their significance. Imperatives command readers to "turn" and to "observe"—a characteristic device of eighteenth-century landscape poems:

> But, from the process in that still retreat,
> Turn to minuter changes at our feet;
> Observe how dewy Twilight has withdrawn
> The crowd of daisies from the shaven lawn,
> And has restored to view its tender green,
> That, while the sun rode high, was lost beneath their dazzling sheen.
>
> (lines 6–11)

These lines replace the fluid observation of the poem's opening lines with the pedantic didacticism of a well-meaning schoolmaster giving a botany lesson. But the aim is, as when Pope or Johnson commanded readers to "see," to enable a rapid pointing of a moral on the basis of a scene arranged into examples of a general truth. The withdrawn daisies, folded in twilight, revealing the green grass that they obscure when open at noon, are

> —An emblem this of what the sober Hour
> Can do for minds disposed to feel its power!
> Thus oft, when we in vain have wished away
> The petty pleasures of the garish day,
> Meek Eve shuts up the whole usurping host
> (Unbashful dwarfs each glittering at his post)
> And leaves the disencumbered spirit free
> To reassume a staid simplicity.
>
> (lines 12–19)

"Emblem" is the key word: Wordsworth has in mind, as he writes in this manner, the emblems of George Wither, which draw general moral lessons from set-piece, impersonal descriptions.[14] But as instructive as the moral about "staid simplicity" disencumbering the spirit is the poem's distance from the Wordsworth of old. His 1804 vision of nature as reciprocal pleasuring, recalled in memory after the event, is rejected: the folded daisies are long way from a "host of . . . daffodils" "dancing in the breeze" (lines 4, 6; 1807, II, pp. 49–50). Now, recall does not renew so much as remind of loss: the poet of evening makes seriousness and profundity conditional upon relief from or repression of sensuality, and upon lateness, defined as the relief that decline brings from the heated business of life at its noon. And he is confident enough in his emblematic method to speak for all: the disembodied, removed narrator assumes the reader's consent as he says "we in vain have wished." Flowers and sunlight on the lawn are now distracting, trivial, and tawdry.

After this smoothly drawn moral, the ending is unexpectedly bitter. It turns out that Wordsworth cannot rest content on his gloomy turf; he anticipates the return of day not as new dawn of life and hope but as a renewal of distraction and glare:

'Tis well—but what are helps of time and place,
When wisdom stands in need of nature's grace;
Why do good thoughts, invoked or not, descend,
Like Angels from their bowers, our virtues to befriend;
If yet To-morrow, unbelied, may say,
"I come to open out, for fresh display,
The elastic vanities of yesterday?"

(lines 20–26)

Tomorrow's is the only ventriloquized voice in the poem. Through it, Wordsworth gives voice to Time and speaks, thereby, a prophetic insight into the nature of nature but speaks against his expressed sympathy for staid simplicity. Daylight returns to deliver not grace but glitter, not the wisdom of peace but the vanity of activity. Time's self-definition is grim: the abstraction of the re-opening daisies as "elastic vanities of yesterday" is dismissive—an extraordinary statement for a poet who had invested so much not only in nature but in the renewal of the past in the present. Wordsworth here is as unsentimental in turning away from the romantic motifs of his youth as the late Yeats was to be. He is bleak and unsparing: staid simplicity may be preferred but it does not last. The night/day opposition on which all subsists is a punishing treadmill. There is no resolution—genuine or spurious—no contrived conclusion involving self-contradiction and self-qualification.

The Owlet's Cry: The Fifth Voluntary

Resolution does not come in the next Voluntary either. As the sequence continues it becomes more and more evident that it demonstrates the variety and difference possible within a form that, because it hybridizes improvisation and tradition, liberates Wordsworth from close conformity either to older poets or to his own old innovations (by now themselves a settled style with a forty-year history). The sequence establishes a late style of self-differentiation and self-argument via a new modeled past: adapting old poets is a way of avoiding repeating oneself.

The fifth Voluntary takes the unexpected turn of Coleridgeanizing Wordsworth's own poetic past—a turn probably brought about by the fact that in 1833, like Dorothy's, Coleridge's body was breaking down (he died, after a long period bedridden, in July 1834). The scene mirrors the two previous poems, opening with a lake view (of Grasmere); the scenario—silence and stillness falling as day turns toward night—recalls that of the very first Voluntary:

> THE leaves that rustled on this oak-crowned hill,
> And sky that danced among those leaves, are still;
> Rest smooths the way for sleep; in field and bower
> Soft shades and dews have shed their blended power
> On drooping eyelid and the closing flower[.]
>
> (lines 1–5; YR, pp. 169–70)

Eyelid and flower are not quite synecdoches but they serve a similar purpose: after the opening evocation of sights and sounds at a distance, the poem zooms in to focus on the precise effects of widespread and intangible processes (shades and dews).

The next lines, though continuing one fluid present-tense sentence, reveal the poem's chief concern: how to configure a poetic relationship to being belated not just to the loss of fulness but also to past poetry that had already lamented and defined that loss so powerfully. They do so by calling up the setting and phrasing of "Frost at Midnight." An owlet breaks the silence and prompts the poet to muse about his own utterance:

> Sound is there none at which the faintest heart
> Might leap, the weakest nerve of superstition start;
> Save when the Owlet's unexpected scream
> Pierces the ethereal vault; and 'mid the gleam
> Of unsubstantial imagery—the dream,
> From the hushed vale's realities, transferred
> To the still lake, the imaginative Bird
> Seems, 'mid inverted mountains, not unheard.

(lines 6–13)

It is the relation of silence and sound, and of the voiced and heard, that the owlet's scream surprises the poet into considering—and this only after it opens a parenthesis (interrupting the thought-narration as the "unexpected scream" interrupted the silent vale) in which the visual relation of reality to imagination and to dream is renegotiated. Thus the owl call acts as the absent nightingale's song was previously desired to act in "By the Side of Rydal Mere." It is thus a real sound traversing a real vale (in fact, *realizing* it—piercing its ethereality—by animating its evanescent spiritual processes as one sensed articulation). As such it anchors, in an audible trajectory with an inferred if not exactly located point of origin, the unsubstantial image transference that turns the still lake into upside-down mountains. While this transference is the work of evening light, it is also a figure of imagination's immaterializing tendency (the "gleam" that derives a "dream / From the hushed vale's realities" echoes the 1807 "gleam" that is the "poet's dream" and 1802/1807 "visionary gleam"[15]). It might invert the place utterly, might overturn its order so it becomes a topsy-turvy mirror world where purely fantastical things seem substantial—where an "imaginative [i.e., imagined] bird" can be sensed (as Wordsworth had hoped to make the imagined nightingale heard in his earlier Voluntary). But transference is held within the parenthesis and its effect is limited: the imaginative bird is not positively heard but only "seems" "not unheard"; the inverted mountains license only the inversion of the litotes rather than a straightforward declarative. Wordsworth's fantasy about fantasy remains tentative. In the end, the owlet's cry, piercing the silence, may prompt, but also anchors, a thought process that imagines reality self-transforming into an imaginary second nature whose inversions are sensed as real. In this respect Wordsworth arrives again at "Frost at Midnight," though by a different route, for in Coleridge's poem the owlet's cry spurred reflective musing about the relationship of fantasy and sensed reality that in turn enabled a changed relationship to the experienced moment.

Coleridge turned, altered, to the sounds of his infant son breathing. Wordsworth turns to the owl itself:

> Grave Creature!—whether, while the moon shines bright
> On thy wings opened wide for smoothest flight,
> Thou art discovered in a roofless tower,
> Rising from what may once have been a Lady's bower;
> Or spied where thou sit'st moping in thy mew
> At the dim centre of a churchyard yew;
> Or, from a rifted crag or ivy tod
> Deep in a forest, thy secure abode,
> Thou giv'st, for pastime's sake, by shriek or shout,
> A puzzling notice of thy whereabout
>
> (lines 14–23)

Here Wordsworth calls into renewed voice the syntax and imagery of Coleridge's 1798 apostrophizing of evening. The "whether"/"or" construction and the brightly shining moon call upon "Frost at Midnight"; the roofless tower and lady's bower bring "Christabel" to mind. If the owl's haunts are fanciful locations belonging to poetry (the Gothic romance, the churchyard elegy[16]), Wordsworth is secure in his flight of fancy because he is apostrophizing the night-bird, calling it into imaginary dialogue to respond to its actual "shriek or shout" and to echo the old inspiring call of the friend whose poetic voice had now fallen silent. At this point, he enters in the first person for only the second time in the entire sequence of Voluntaries. "May the night never come, nor day be seen, / When I shall scorn thy voice or mock thy mien!" (lines 24–25) is a heartfelt, moving entreaty because it is unexpectedly confessional: it honors Coleridge as well as the owl, after years of distance in which anger and scorn, if not mockery, had tainted admiration and fellow feeling.

The poem ends on a Coleridgean note when, as in "Frost at Midnight," a second aside breaks the narration to acknowledge another owl call.

In classic ages men perceived a soul
Of sapience in thy aspect, headless Owl!
Thee Athens reverenced in the studious grove;
And, near the golden sceptre grasped by Jove,
His Eagle's favourite perch, while round him sate
The Gods revolving the decrees of Fate,
Thou, too, wert present at Minerva's side—
Hark to that second larum!—far and wide
The elements have heard, and rock and cave replied.

(lines 26–34)

The final exclamation closes with a momentary aside rather a general conclusion. A startling interruption, it nevertheless fulfills the poem's continuing thought-stream, its persistent concern with the necessary conditions required by imagination (a poet's equivalent of the Greeks placing the owl among their gods). It actualizes the calling into being of poetic voice as the poet finds himself called upon by other voices not of his own making (and it also calls upon the reader to witness, as if present in the scene with poet and bird). The Boy of Winander is also invoked here, for it is the fact that the owl is not to be summoned at the poet's will, but interrupts his musings, that calls him out of himself and allows him to respond as the auditory center of the entire experienced spatiotemporal moment, uniting evening's transient transfers and bringing them to voice when at the poem's beginning all was silent. The owl's cry, occurring unexpectedly in the scene, enables Wordsworth's retrieval of voice from gathering silence and affirmation of life in oncoming darkness; it is a twilight call that the poet, without mere fantasy, can invoke in verse and by so doing renew his calling as a poet, a poet whose imagination begins in and returns to a nature animate in the form of sound. The echoes of Coleridge suggest that in doing so Wordsworth also calls up his voice by calling on his now-silent friend's—itself called into sound by the overheard owl in Nether Stowey. In this sense the poem is a valediction as a form of homage, making the dying Coleridge sing as he sang in 1798. Here, then, a revisionary renewal of Wordsworth's voice as nature-poet is made possible by a self-consciously late return to the past under the pressure of oncoming death—Wordsworth achieves a Voluntary revival of Coleridge's poem about breaking silence because he knows that Coleridge's voice will soon fall silent forever.

Sea Voices: The Sixth Voluntary

The sixth poem in the sequence, meditating on the relationship of natural sounds and poet's song, reveals that the sequence, cumulatively, is a set of variations considering the poet's calling in the process of evoking the scenes that call him into verse in the here and now. It unfolds, by this point, not as a developmental narrative but as a variety of exemplifications of what it is to be a poet, each provoked by a present moment but at the same time motivated by past poems.

The sixth Voluntary has behind it the stanzas written about Peele Castle, after John Wordsworth's death by shipwreck. Those stanzas attempted to contain the unreliable violence of nature by the calm formality of art, to allay the sea storm in the harmony of verse. The new poem, prompted by a return to the coast a few miles north of the castle, echoes the attempt at propitiation but from a late perspective in which art's perfection is insufficient. Written in 1833, in the 1835 publication the personal context was signaled by an explanatory title.[17] The title, "On a High Part of the Coast of Cumberland" locates the spot it evokes. A subtitle, "Easter Sunday April 7," identifies the most significant day of the Christian year as its time of writing—a day of thanksgiving for the resurrection of the suffering Christ and the consequent redemption of humankind from sin. A further subtitle, "The Author's Sixty-third Birthday" marks the poem's occasion as a significant day in his own life. Together, the title and subtitles suggest that a coincidence of the two festivals, which marks the day out of the normal run of time, engenders a meditation on the intersection of the human and divine made by a man conscious that he is aging. Place is also highlighted by the coincidence: it is a day when one remembers where one was.

> THE Sun, that seemed so mildly to retire,
> Flung back from distant climes a streaming fire,
> Whose blaze is now subdued to tender gleams,
> Prelude of night's approach with soothing dreams.
> Look round;—of all the clouds not one is moving;
> 'Tis the still hour of thinking, feeling, loving.
>
> (lines 1–6; YR, pp. 171–72)

The imperative—almost an exclamation—"Look round" puts the reader in the scene, suggesting a narrator conversing informally and animatedly. He has something to show—stillness—and is immediately sure of what it means. It means that, motion arrested, the "hour" is a spot of time, a marked-out moment and also a late renewal of a spot as created in his own early poetry, for "the still hour of thinking, feeling, loving" alludes, as had a previous Voluntary, to the 1798 "Lines Written at a Small Distance from My House." Carpe diem, Wordsworth told his sister in 1798; now in 1833/1835 he revives the joyous recognition of a time of openly available love and feeling. Revisiting his old text, however, also inflects the recognition with an awareness of loss: that time was past; Dorothy was now housebound, disabled, demented.

Suffering is not considered biographically, so as not make the text an embarrassing breach of the private, or to invite pity, or to limit the poem's applicability to others. It is, however, invoked by the Easter setting and is implicit in Wordsworth's way of seeing and hearing:

> Silent, and stedfast as the vaulted sky,
> The boundless plain of waters seems to lie:—
> Comes that low sound from breezes rustling o'er
> The grass-crowned headland that conceals the shore!
> No; 'tis the earth-voice of the mighty sea,
> Whispering how meek and gentle he *can* be!

(lines 7–12)

The question-and-answer format is stagey but serves to highlight the noun "earth-voice"—novel and mysterious yet presented as if needing no explanation. As a "low sound" that whispers, it is, perhaps, the resonance of waves breaking on shore, below the high coast. It is, at all events, the sound of the sea transmuted, so that it emanates from the sea's opposite—earth. The sea thus has power to transmit its sonic presence beyond itself, through solid rock.

Hearing the earth-voice, Wordsworth feels called upon to speak. He addresses God:

> Thou Power supreme! who, arming to rebuke
> Offenders, dost put off the gracious look,
> And clothe thyself with terrors like the flood
> Of ocean roused into its fiercest mood

(lines 13–16)

The sea, having been part of the observed scene, now becomes a simile for God's wrath, allowing the poem to make a transition from the particular to the general and from apostrophe to entreaty, as is appropriate on Easter Sunday, the day on which the resurrection redeems humankind from God's anger:

> Whatever discipline thy Will ordain
> For the brief course that must for me remain;
> Teach me with quick-eared spirit to rejoice
> In admonitions of thy softest voice!
> Whate'er the path these mortal feet may trace,
> Breathe through my soul the blessing of thy grace,
> Glad, through a perfect love, a faith sincere
> Drawn from the wisdom that begins with fear;
> Glad to expand; and, for a season, free
> From finite cares, to rest absorbed in Thee!
>
> (lines 17–26)

This appeal to God is couched in conventional Anglican terminology; its vocabulary verges on the hackneyed (life is a "brief course" and a "path"). Yet it is not, in context, clichéd, for the commonplace expressions serve the purpose of subsuming the individual's entreaty in the traditional and communal language of prayer. There is humility in this gesture for a poet with exceptional verbal power at his disposal, and it allows him to make common cause of his fears and hopes. What began as an exceptional occasion for one witness (who points it out to a reader) becomes ritualized: the ending could be said together by the worshippers in church (a Voluntary as the organist's personal, improvised contribution to a congregation's act of entreaty). And it is for this reason more successful than were the attempts in the earlier *Ecclesiastical Sketches* to reconcile individual and community through the historical institution of the church—doctrine and liturgy—as represented by sonnet form. Here Wordsworth does not preach, lecture, or equate poetic form with a temporally realized eternal order; he beseeches in terms in which, for centuries, others have used to give form to their needs. In doing so, he accepts vulnerability as his own and others' lot. For Wordsworth at sixty-three, intimations are sonic in form (his spirit must be quick-eared) and do not suggest immortality; they are "admonitions" that, here in this place on this of all days, may for once hold in abeyance the terrors and fierceness of divine rebukes. God's "softest voice" is a sea-sound, a breeze, a whisper, that aereates (or inspires) the poet's fearful and crushed self ("glad to expand") and leaves his spirit blended in the divine, like the sea's voice in that of earth or like the poem's voice in that of communal prayer. But this absorption brings neither joy nor ecstasy but relief and "rest" (finally won after many appositional phrases delay its arrival and therefore especially prized). Rest is all the more precious for its brevity and fragility, and it may, at best, anticipate a loss of self in God that occurs beyond this world.

Sea Songs: The Seventh Voluntary

The next poem is the final new poem of the 1835 sequence and also its culmination. Latent with the musings prompted by evening in the previous voluntaries, it is self-reflexive, explicitly considering the relation of human song to the sights and sounds of nature even as it attempts to make its own words move to the motion of the sea. It is an effort to bring the voluntaries to a quiet climax by exemplifying what they have discussed and sought to capture—a poised coincidence of human and nonhuman utterance to hold momentarily in the face of loss, lapse, and lessened power while darkness gathers.

> THE sun is couched, the sea-fowl gone to rest,
> And the wild storm hath somewhere found a nest;
> Air slumbers—wave with wave no longer strives,
> Only a heaving of the deep survives[.]
>
> (lines 1–4, YR, pp. 173–74)

The personifications tame nature's violence and domesticate its intangibility: the storm is another seabird seeking shelter; air sleeps. Strife is evoked as a completed activity: the simply present action is slumber. Even the "heaving" that indicates troubled waters is to be a vestige of the past: "A tell-tale motion! soon will it be laid, / And by the tide alone the water swayed" (lines 5–6). This is a self-authorizing gesture: after his successful evocation of nature coming to rest, the poet knows, and tells us he knows, how to tell this tale, how to move to its motion. Buoyed on his ability to echo the sea's tidal swaying in his couplet rhymes (word-sound moving on only after it is first repeated), he licenses himself to sum up the meaning of what he sees and hears:

> Stealthy withdrawings, interminglings mild
> Of light with shade in beauty reconciled—
> Such is the prospect far as sight can range,
> The soothing recompence, the welcome change.
>
> (lines 7–10)

If the word "prospect," here offered to the reader by a disembodied narrator, affiliates the poem to the eighteenth-century landscape verse of Thomson and Dyer (both favorites of Wordsworth's), the understanding of the view is more subtle, complex, and self-reflexive than in *The Seasons* or "Grongar Hill." The prospect is no static, framed picture over and against the stationed viewer; it is an experience of place made by a ranging sight whose own motion lets it register the present as an intersection of traces of greater activity that have now ended. It is possible for the seeing poet to articulate these subtle traces (and to condense them into "welcome change") because the poem as commentary also moves by stealth—mingling present, past, and future in its syntax and before even declaring the observer poet's stance and identity.

Grammar is stealthy too: in the next line the construction "Where, now," leads the reader to expect temporal contrast as in the previous lines (i.e., "where now the ships are so and so, they were such and such"). But in fact "Where, now" does not govern a contrast but begins a question, "are" having been elided—so the poem subtly diverges from the path it has led readers to expect.

> Where, now, the ships that drove before the blast,
> Threatened by angry breakers as they passed;
> And by a train of flying clouds bemocked;
> Or, in the hollow surge, at anchor rocked
> As on a bed of death?
>
> (lines 11–15)

"As on a bed of death." This image—a ship at anchor as a suffering person tossing on a deathbed (John Wordsworth dying as his ship broke on the rocks?)—is extraordinary, not least because the emphasis on calm and peace makes it so unexpected. The storm had been allayed in the poem; here, however, not just danger and violence but death itself is suddenly declared and in such a formally poetic simile that it is notably an introduction from elsewhere. It is markedly the poet-observer's shaping of the scene and thus suggests that a focus on, or even a witnessing of, the agonies of dying is what he cannot help transplanting to the sea, even when peaceful. The storm may be tamed by the poetic figure that "birdifies" it—returning it to its nest—but the sea-surge spawns a kind of figure that is potentially unstoppable—analogy, which likens one thing to another without limit. Slipping into this figure, Wordsworth is off guard; he is lured by the poet's temptation of discovering likeness in difference to reveal, in a graphic image, what the sea is, at bottom, beneath all his careful attempts to lay its menace to rest on this occasion. Death ends all analogies, of course, but it also engenders all figuration in so far as figuration is an effort to assuage and defer it.

Death is also deferred through rhyme. The couplet form ensures past sounds are not lost at once: like the subtly changing sound of waves, the rhyme gradually modulates through repetition, enacting (as the reader learns to anticipate the chime) the foreimagining of hindsight as well as the recurrence of the past. What is produced, in the interplay with sense, is a sound pattern characterized by a kind of temporal swaying rather than a progression from start to end. The sea-sound of evening may spawn images of death but can be taken up sonically as a transitional state—after the main thing, before finality—that is sustained, despite its brevity and consequent fragility, by this lulling rhyming, wave-like, tide-like, back and forth—sustained so the poem can rock there but defer the end (Death itself).

Rhyme reinforces sense: Wordsworth introduces God as a still greater power than death, who cares to redeem vulnerable humanity from its grip. Not all are rocked on the deathbed of the deep;

> Some lodge in peace,
> Saved by His care who bade the tempest cease;
> And some, too heedless of past danger, court
> Fresh gales to waft them to the far-off port[.]

(lines 15–18)

Here the poem takes another surprising turn. We might expect at this point a Christian moral to be drawn about the need to accept God's saving grace rather than carry on heedless of a deathly peril that is not as past as it seemed. But instead, Wordsworth attempts to lift his view out of danger: the ships, he says, are "hanging sea and sky between" (line 19). "Hanging" attempts to subsume "rocking"—to suspend the ships above the deathly sea-swell, safe in mid-air.

Having hung the saved and the heedless—ships in harbor and ships putting out to sea—in an airy nowhere land, Wordsworth is moved to consider their position. Where are they?

> Not one of all those winged powers is seen,
> Seen in her course, nor 'mid this quiet heard[.]
>
> (lines 20–21)

Unreal: not actually seen or heard but only imagined. The real scene has, it turns out, prompted a mind's-eye picture of what is not actually present. A difference thus appears between the poem as a record of a prospect and the poem as means of making mental pictures of what is not there. But this is a more controlled, limited difference than that introduced by analogy; indeed, its function is to supersede the disturbing power of analogy to make something become like something else that one wanted to keep separate. Whereas analogy brought a person's death-throes home to the rocking boat, the imagined ships can be clearly distinguished from the real. The poet reasserts control of his narrative and of his imagination, keeping death rhetorically at bay by insisting that he knows what belongs to the actual scene and what does not. But does he protest too much? "Not one of all . . ." is so vehemently enumerative that we are alerted to an eagerness to deny, and therefore to the power of that which is being denied. Figures of death can only be banished if the poet is seen to have established limits to figuration that arise from experience of the real. Once more, Wordsworth binds himself to actuality—the here and now—because of the both exhilarating and dangerous tendency of his writing to connect the present with other places and other times, a tendency that articulates a life but also raises the dead.

What follows the setting of limits and the return to the actual is the hope that song might arise in the real world—song, therefore, that the poet could witness; song that would legitimize his own sea-song:

> Yet oh! how gladly would the air be stirred
> By some acknowledgment of thanks and praise,

Soft in its temper as those vesper lays
Sung to the Virgin while accordant oars
Urge the slow bark along Calabrian shores;
A sea-born service through the mountains felt
Till into one loved vision all things melt:
Or like those hymns that soothe with graver sound
The gulfy coast of Norway iron-bound;
And, from the wide and open Baltic, rise
With punctual care, Lutherian harmonies.

(lines 22–32)

Here the Calabrian lays achieve a sonic harmony between sea, the rhythm of the oars plying the sea, and the mountains. Sound transcends itself into a union of humankind and nature effected by a communication of feeling ("through the mountains felt") and then into a melding vision ("all things melt"). The Scandinavian hymns are more sober but are also organic stirrings of place into song. Both seem perfect models of Wordsworthian poetry, arising from and accepted by the fells. And yet, while exemplary, they remain foreign—not here or now. Wordsworth's idealizing fantasy of the shore as a site of choral interchange between sea and earth, humans and nature, is not claimed as the poet's, save in the respect that it is he who imagines it happening elsewhere. It is a fantasy, a mind's-ear projection, but not a visionary state in which, being where and when he is, he can himself dwell. British shores do not resound with sailors' songs.

This seems disappointing, and the poet is forced back onto himself—talking to himself in the absence of songs of praise, only to tell himself to cease and listen to the quiet. If sound fails, sight does not, and neither, it turns out, does silence:

Hush, not a voice is here! but why repine,
Now when the star of eve comes forth to shine
On British waters with that look benign?

(lines 33–35)

The star of eve—evoking the star of Bethlehem—is a portent, even if God's own appearance is deferred. Its coming forth ends the suspense of the liminal post-storm, pre-calm state. It is another "tell-tale motion," a sign that the poet is confident he can interpret because it is local and experienced as opposed to fanciful and imaginary (British rather than Calabrian or Norwegian). On its basis, he arrives, if not at song, then at least at the vehement speech of apostrophe. He raises himself to the language of prophecy, no longer musing quietly to himself but exhorting sailors (all sailors—and implicitly readers) in Biblical tones:

> Ye mariners, that plough your onward way,
> Or in the haven rest, or sheltering bay,
> May *silent* thanks at least to God be given
> With a full heart; "our thoughts are heard in heaven."
>
> (lines 36–39)

"British waters" inspire a less formalized and less ecclesiastical hymn (or vesper, or Evening Voluntary)—heartful thanks in the form of a speech that is not speech, a poetic speech read silently and heard in the head (rather than chanted or sung), of which this poem is an example and a model. The voice of a "full heart" (no utter disburdening or cathartic release into song), it stems from and recreates a stealthier and more vestigial reciprocity that can be inferred in silence. "Heard in heaven," it is a spiritual rather than material communication: song as telepathy modeled on the inferred speech of reading. As such it is the apotheosis of the poetic communication of which this very poem is an example—silent reader accessing the mind of the inferred poet across the page.

Telling the tale of disappearing traces, Wordsworth finds his own form of evensong. Apostrophizing the mariners, he offers his "lay," quiet as it is, to them and on their behalf. It is his and, he suggests, their way of thanking the God who makes local waters, for now at least, benign. These thanks are not tightly institutional, for they are an immediate communication with heaven: no church formula or public ritual intervenes. But they are Anglican, for the improvised Voluntary is a form of worship that the individual artist (organist/poet) is licensed to offer to the congregation. As such, they are British—forms of worship less demonstrative than the Calabrians', less punctual than the Norwegians', more heartfelt than either. An undertone of nationalism is audible.

They are British not least because the last phrase is a quotation from a much beloved British poet. Edward's Young's *Night Thoughts* was an extended response to the deaths of the poet's wife, stepdaughter, and stepdaughter's husband. It was an appropriate text, reminded as Wordsworth was on the Cumberland coast of his brother's and children's deaths. And the quoted phrase befitted John Wordsworth's death at sea, drowned in his prime before he had achieved his ambitions, since, in context, it summed up Young's argument that we must make the best of our lives, however petty, given that we cannot alter our past however unworthy we retrospectively think our actions were and given that death may allow us no time to change in the future. It is not by the greatness of our deeds, limited as they are by circumstances, that we give ourselves meaning and virtue. It is, Young suggests, the thought, the intended purpose to do well, that justifies us and opens a communication with God:

> every moment pays.
> If nothing more than purpose in thy power;
> Thy purpose firm, is equal to the deed:
> Who does the best his circumstance allows,
> Does well, acts nobly; angels could no more.
> Our outward act, indeed, admits restraint;
> 'Tis not in things o'er thought to domineer;
> Guard well thy thought; our thoughts are heard in heaven.[18]

As borrowed by Wordsworth, the line, to those who know its origins, suggests that thought reaches beyond this world, to an ideal audience that accepts and cares for the thinker, while actions—the audible and visible singing of the Calabrians and Norwegians—find their audience within the world. Thoughtful thanks—like the silently read thought of poetic writing—are heaven directed and received; they escape the "iron-bound" world of created nature. Sensual praise, however, remains within it, able to displace but not banish the specter of death. Wordsworth thus turns away from the world, even when that world is made by song into a visionary union of humankind and nature—a major change of direction for the poet who had sought such unions above all. This turn subsumes the turnings away from daylit nature made earlier in the Voluntaries: it is not a rejection of nature/human union, as "elastic vanities" was, but a need to set it aside on the basis that it is not enough. Reminded by age and by location of death's looming presence in his past and future, Wordsworth seeks an alternative destination for his verse: God is the imagined haven of the Word— but since He is not a being of flesh and blood, the ideality of thought rather than the sensuality of song is stressed as the means of communication.

Poetry is distanced from its materiality and its communality as it aspires to escape nature and transcend time—all the more so because the aspiration is made by silently borrowing a line from a poem made for individual silent reading rather than oral recitation. Young's verses are night thoughts and so are analogous to Evening Voluntaries. They are not communal vespers.

The ending seems declarative and positive—"our thoughts are heard in heaven." Yet it is also tentative, because it is in quotation marks—Wordsworth's words are not his own. If the quotation bolsters his authority by deriving it from Young's, it nevertheless reveals that he feels it needs bolstering. Wordsworth borrows Young's confidence in, as it were, wording one's way from earth to heaven, and this implies his own relative lack of confidence. But this tentativeness is attractive because it acknowledges vulnerability and fear, rather than sheltering in the comforts of doctrine or certainties of dogma. The declarative positiveness turns out to be a plea—a hope against hope that Britons may silently thank God and so find their way beyond their earthly plight. But the poet knows his urgings may not be taken up: there is no guarantee his words will become Britons' words; he cannot speak univocally or communally with certainty; he cannot be sure of an audience in this world or the next. The spiritual journey that is the poem's final gesture is made in a fragile vessel launched in a brief moment of calm that will not last.

Tail Pieces

In 1835 Wordsworth ended the sequence with two poems from the past, as if to show that the moment was less brief than it seems in the new Voluntaries. However, though these poems assert continuity of concern by virtue of their inclusion, what they say reveals the difference between the late Wordsworth and his own—and others'—earlier verse. The first, "The sun has long been set," from 1804, differs because it, so to speak, lacks lack (YR, p. 175). Also absent are loss, echo, and trace, as is anticipation of darkness and death. Nature is alive and enlivening, fully present and available, to be enjoyed to the full in the moment, with no sense of its being a relic of a prior, livelier state. Printed after the other Evening Voluntaries, the poem thus seems distinctly out of place. But it is, however, contextualized by what precedes it. The seizing of the moment that it enthuses about and the endorsement of innocent bliss it concludes with are qualified by the earlier poems in which bliss is tempered, and the better for being tempered, by awareness of lack. After those complex poems of experience, this one reads as a charming but slight song of innocence.

It is followed by another song of experience—a poem compiled entirely from lines from old poets. Wordsworth concludes the Voluntaries with a cento. By doing so, he highlights the indebtedness of his language to crepuscular verse of the past: "a fine stanza of Akenside, connected with a still finer from Beattie, by a couplet of Thomson" (YR, p. 175) formally indicate that his work updates, rather than breaks with, a decorous tradition. He advertises the continuity of his late style with the diction and form of eighteenth-century verse—and with its mood (YR, p. 177). To be a poet of evening, then, finally, is to acknowledge publicly a reconciliation with the poets admired in youth but rejected in the revolutionary 1790s. If this is a conservative return, the cento nevertheless reveals, capping the sequence, what is at stake in the previous Voluntaries: less obtrusively, they also assemble fragments of eighteenth-century poems.

As a sequence assembled in print, the Evening Voluntaries possess a complex internal relationship—variations on central concerns—like the 1815 Inscriptions I examined in Chapter 2. The hybridization of the open-ended form and conversational voice of Wordsworth's and Coleridge's 1790s verse with the couplets, disembodied narrators, and personifications of eighteenth-century landscape poetry achieves things neither Wordsworth's poetic predecessors nor Wordsworth had quite done before. It enables delicate evocations of the temporal being of a self-consciously belated and aging writer, aware of his declining years and weakening senses, and reminded of his more vigorous past (including his past writing). Occasionally angry about the world of passion and action the earlier Wordsworth had relished, the Voluntaries embrace but also chafe at the diminution brought about by age: Wordsworth places each poem so that it displaces the perspectives offered by the others before those perspectives settle into doctrine. Restless and revisionary, the Voluntaries resist the typical twilight mood of eighteenth-century evening poetry: they do not indulge nostalgic melancholy but instead find unexpected value in the late moment, in a space/time of after-effects and residues that bespeak loss, lapse, and lack; they also articulate a liminal state, poised between before and after, and articulate a way of bearing toward an ending not yet reached. For all these reasons they are original, innovative, thought-provoking, moving—perhaps the most profound meditations on life and on poetry-making from the viewpoint of age not just within Wordsworth's own oeuvre but in English poetry up to that time.

Elegiac Musing and Generic Mixing

Your hands, my dear friend, have failed, as well as my eyes. . . . Last
year has robbed me of Coleridge, of Charles Lamb—James Losh—Rudd
of Trinity—and Fleming just gone—and other Schoolfellows and
Contemporaries. I cannot forget that Shakespear, who scarcely survived
50—(I am near the close of my 65th year) wrote:
> *In me that time of life thou dost behold*
> *When yellow leaves, or few or none, do hang upon the bough*
How much more reason have we to break out into such a strain?
>> —Wordsworth to Lonsdale, 2 February 1835; LY, III, p. 19

Elegy is a form of poetry natural to the reflective mind. It may treat of
any subject, but it must treat of no subject for itself; but always and
exclusively with reference to the poet. As he will feel regret for the Past
or Desire for the Future, so Sorrow and Love became the principal themes
of Elegy. Elegy presents every thing as lost and gone or absent and future.
>> —Coleridge, 23 October 1833, TT, I, pp. 444–45

From the mid-1830s, it was Wordsworth's fate, as he aged, to find his family,
friends, and fellow poets dying before him; in his later letters sorrow at
their loss, regret at the departure of old times, and anticipation of his own
coming death are some of his most frequently expressed emotions. These
feelings led him to write poems memorializing and mourning the dead—
poems, however, that did not quite fit any of the recognized genres for such
occasions, though they did echo, with a more personal note, the nature
memorials he had been writing since "Yew Trees" and since his Scottish

tours. Elegies and epitaphs, however, in the traditional sense, eluded him: he tried writing an epitaph for Lamb but when it reached 131 lines, he had to accept that it had exceeded the bounds of a genre he valued for its terse, detached formality.[1] A piece commemorating Beaumont was a putative inscription for a garden monument, but it was too long to imagine it being chiseled on stone. A commemorative poem for Edith Southey was a sonnet; rarely did he attempt the formal elegy, whether pastoral, with its traditional cast of swains, or funerary, with its expected form of graveside oration. Wordsworth needed a less predetermined form that would allow him to combine private feeling with public commemoration in ways that developed the kind of poetry that the dead person had, when living, admired him for writing.[2] His memorializations of the dead were often generic and stylistic tributes to others' appreciation of his poetry: he renewed the verse, and the verse genres, particularly associated with each dead friend. These genres were mostly of his own manufacture: a memorial to Sarah Hutchinson was a hybrid of conversation poem and inscription with a poem on the naming of places; the tribute to his fellow poets—two of them ballad singers—was an "Extempore Effusion"; the commemorations of Beaumont and of Scott were "Elegiac Musings" and "Musings."[3] Although the forms employed were varied—couplets, blank verse, tetrameter quatrains—the titles all stressed immediacy, suggesting that these elegies took their form from a spontaneous overflow of powerful feeling into thought or speech. They were elegiac in Coleridge's sense of "a form of poetry natural to the reflective mind" and were modeled on the "natural" poetry that Coleridge had taught Wordsworth to manufacture ("effusion" being a title invented by Coleridge to designate his conversation poems; "musings" referring to Coleridge's rambling meditation "Religious Musings"). In effect, after 1834, Wordsworth's commemorative poetry constituted acts of homage[4]—poetic evidence that formative relationships had, despite an increasing distance that death had only confirmed, remained informing influences.

Late-life elegiac poems are different from those the poet found himself called to write earlier in his career.[5] When shipwreck robbed Wordsworth of a brother in 1805, he felt betrayed by the nature that could so cruelly cut down a young man of whom so much was hoped. Trying to bear with his loss and the anger it caused him, Wordsworth found himself braced by art's static, achieved polish. In the "Elegiac Stanzas Suggested by a Picture of Peele Castle in a Storm," the disruptive power of grief, arising from a disturbingly violent nature, is stilled by the formal perfection of art.[6]

The later memorials have less anger to displace. The death, in age, of old friends produced regret rather than suffering, a rueful willingness rather than outraged refusal to accept loss.[7] Anxiety, rather than anguish, was now the mood: Wordsworth was reminded that his own death must be near and was unsure whether to welcome or fear this. Knowing he was a public figure and that many of those he mourned also had been—or would gain a degree of publicity by being made the subjects of his poems—he knew that his comments on their lives would be noticed. What was a private need to recollect was also a public task to do justice: epitaphic or obituary.[8]

Commemorating Fellow Poets

At the end of 1835, hearing of James Hogg's death, Wordsworth was moved to elegize the balladeer who had introduced him to Yarrow and its folk-song culture. The "Extempore Effusion upon the Death of James Hogg," the finest of the late elegiac pieces, mourned not just Hogg but many fellow poets, among them Coleridge and Scott. The title signaled that the poem was not a traditional elegy and associated it with Coleridge, who had applied the name "effusion" to his poems in 1796, referring to pieces that took their form from a stream of spontaneous meditation or conversation. "Extempore," meanwhile, linked the poem to the song performances for which Hogg and his family was known, renditions of ballads learned orally. Wordsworth, as we saw in Chapter 3, had drawn on them for his own textual Yarrow ballads. Thus the title of his poem was a homage to the ballad tradition and to his poetic peers' textual versions of spontaneous oral poetry. What Wordsworth produced, however, did not sit firmly in either of the genres the title invoked. It was not, like Coleridge's effusions, a blank-verse meditation or extended sonnet; nor was it in ballad meter. Its stanza form is unusual—four lines: lines 1 and 3 having nine syllables and being unrhymed, and lines 2 and 4 having eight syllables and rhyming with each other; the meter, iambic. It bears a slight resemblance to William Hamilton's song "The Braes of Yarrow," to which Wordsworth made a verbal allusion,[9] but that stanza has longer and more various lines. It also has some likeness to the most famous elegiac stanza of all—the iambic pentameter quatrains of Gray's "Elegy Written in a Country Churchyard." And yet its differences from the formal models to which it alludes are more significant than the similarities: Wordsworth may place himself in the lineage of Gray and of the Scottish songs, but he keeps his lyrical measure on a shorter rein with less frequent rhyme. The result is song-like—rather than conventional song form—a stanza in which the recurring contrast of longer and shorter lines isolates statements and images to the reader's eye and ear. Wordsworth aims for pithiness by a form demanding self-restraint.

If the short, separately presented lines are terse, the images they present are also pregnant. Much of the poem's pathos stems from the use of images that, Wordsworth knows, readers will associate with his and his fellow poets' lives and writings. The golden groves of Yarrow and the moldering ruins wherein Scott is buried are redolent of Scott's border lays; the "clouds that rake the mountain-summits" (line 21)[10] bespeak Wordsworth's own Lakeland verse; the "sunless land" (line 24) evokes the "sunless sea" of Coleridge (the subject of the previous stanza).[11] Memorializing private friendship with friends who were also poets, and also public figures, allows Wordsworth to rely on prior knowledge and existing sympathy. His allusions, formal and verbal, hold sway as a poetic mode because readerly recognition is strong enough for commemoration of the lives of the deceased and justification of the feelings of the bereaved not to be needed. But the retrieval that the allusions make is partial, fragmentary: it suffices to offer tribute to the dead but not to revive their work as a continuing tradition. Wordsworth looks to commemoration, not to renewal—either on earth or in heaven. He ends with a finality born of perfect control of form and image, a finality that is also a fantasy about Romantic poetry finding, along with its poets, a rightful resting place:

> No more of old romantic sorrows,
> For slaughtered Youth or love-lorn Maid!
> With sharper grief is Yarrow smitten,
> And Ettrick mourns with her their Poet dead.
>
> (lines 41–44)

The poet is reunited with the named locality that gave rise to him—a death into nature, which becomes his true mourner: this is a fantasy of total acceptance that, for the poet of Lorton yew, Coleorton, Ellan I Vow, Rydal Park, Donnerdale, and Moresby is a consummation devoutly to be wished. It is, as it were, Wordsworth's dying wish, his last word.

Only it is not. Wordsworth did not end with the poised pathos of the "Effusion"; the majestic impersonality of its conclusion was not his last elegy for poetry and the poet. In 1841 he wrote another not-quite elegy about his feelings as the survivor of Scott. On tour in Italy in 1837, where Scott had gone to recover his health in 1832, Wordsworth found himself brooding on the dead, and their remains, rather than impressed by paintings and architecture. On the Campo Santo, Pisa, he was taken with the burials, in ground supposedly composed of soil brought from the hill of Calvary. He described it in a tour memorial, "Musings Near Aquapendente" as

> a capacious field
> That to descendants of the dead it holds
> And to all living mute memento breathes,
> More touching far than aught which on the walls
> Is pictured, or their epitaphs can speak,
> Of the changed City's long-departed power,
> Glory, and wealth, which, perilous as they are,
> Here did not kill, but nourished, Piety.
>
> (lines 162–69)[12]

For the author of the "Essays upon Epitaphs," the preference for the grave's "mute memento" over the written epitaph is surprising. It suggests disenchantment with the poet's memorializing art but is also a return to the Wordsworth of "The Brothers" and "We Are Seven"—a fantasy of an unbroken oral community, still so closely linked to a place that the lives of the local dead can be preserved in memory and speech without the need for writing.

Wordsworth contrasts the community of Pisa with the isolation of Scott, dying in Italy far from his family, friends, and beloved Borders landscape, and with himself, a tourist far from his home, his domestic circle (depleted by death), and the Lakes. Restless and out on a limb, Wordsworth elegizes the lonely Scott by imagining him thinking elegiacally of the days they had spent together during their vigorous youth:

> "The Wizard of the North," with anxious hope
> Brought to this genial climate, when disease
> Preyed upon body and mind—yet not the less
> Had his sunk eye kindled at those dear words
> That spake of bards and minstrels; and his spirit
> Had flown with mine to old Helvellyn's brow,

Where once together, in his day of strength,
We stood rejoicing, as if earth were free
From sorrow, like the sky above our heads.
Years followed years, and when, upon the eve
Of his last going from Tweed-side, thought turned,
Or by another's sympathy was led,
To this bright land, Hope was for him no friend,
Knowledge no help; Imagination shaped
No promise. Still, in more than ear-deep seats,
Survives for me, and cannot but survive
The tone of voice which wedded borrowed words
To sadness not their own, when, with faint smile
Forced by intent to take from speech its edge,
He said, "When I am there, although 'tis fair
'Twill be another Yarrow." Prophecy
More than fulfilled, as gay Campania's shores
Soon witnessed, and the city of seven hills,
Her sparkling fountains and her mouldering tombs;
And more than all, that Eminence which showed
Her splendors, seen, not felt, the while he stood
A few short steps (painful they were) apart
From Tasso's Convent-haven, and retired grave.

(lines 57–84)

As Stephen Gill and Peter Manning have noted, in mentioning Scott's remark about Yarrow, Wordsworth is quoting Scott quoting Wordsworth's poem alluding to Scott's poetry.[13] The allusive trail reunites the poets even as the anecdote speaks of parting, absence, and homesickness—all of which, Wordsworth goes on to show, making Scott stand in for himself, were the poet's feelings in Italy. Sublime elegism, as Keats might have said; Wordsworth writes Scott in his own image, lamenting his own loss of home, friends, and past times by imagining the experience of a "Wizard of the North" now too sick still to subject the land to his literary spells, even when visiting the home of that master of romance, Tasso. The land of poetic imagination is absent, lost.

Wordsworth stops there, before pathos becomes sentimentality and identification becomes self-indulgence. The elegist is tired of elegizing; he turns aside, as if to admit that the home he has left behind is too reduced by deaths such as Scott's, too full of memories of a fuller, departed past, to dwell upon. He presents this turn as the outcome of a self-reflexive questioning forced upon him by the process of "musing" on his and Scott's careers. In a late equivalent of the famous moment of crisis in the Simplon Pass, he is brought to question his vocation:

> why should Poesy
> Yield to the lure of vain regret, and hover
> In gloom on wings with confidence outspread
> To move in sunshine?
>
> (lines 85–88)

It is a fundamental question, no less challenging than that posed by the Simplon discovery (which Wordsworth had been revising after his Italian tour, eighteen months before writing "Aquapendente") that imagination may not be sustained by nature (a discovery that is itself a displacement of the boy's dawning experience that nature has death at its heart). How not to hover in gloom when the regions that sustained one's poesy have been darkened by death? Wordsworth is put on his mettle—or rather, stages the Italian landscape as the scene of a drama of self-loss and self-recollection. It lures him to pathos and lament, but he rebounds, recognizing that poetic slackness—and silence—lies along the path of retrospective vicarious identification with the sick and the dead. There is a modest acceptance of emotional limit in this recognition: he accepts that, after all, he is not Scott; though homesick, he is not dying, nor are his energies as a tourist and a writer spent. It would be self-indulgent to keep imagining the world through Scott's eyes. As in *The Prelude*, then, the traveling poet turns from alluring but vicarious involvement in a nature that is not his home and apostrophizes himself:

> Utter thanks, my Soul!
> Tempered with awe, and sweetened by compassion
> For them who in the shades of sorrow dwell,
> That I—so near the term to human life
> Appointed by man's common heritage,
> Frail as the frailest, one withal (if that
> Deserve a thought) but little known to fame—
> Am free to rove where Nature's loveliest looks,

Art's noblest relics, history's rich bequests,
Failed to reanimate and but feebly cheered
The whole world's Darling—free to rove at will
O'er high and low, and if requiring rest,
Rest from enjoyment only.

(lines 88–100)

This is certainly as egotistical as *The Prelude*, for Wordsworth not only thanks, but also implicitly praises, his own soul for allowing him freedom to live, at liberty, though unfavored by fame, when the famous Scott, now dead, was too weak to do so. Payback time: Wordsworth had long envied Scott's popularity; now, he finds, talking to himself, that it was better to have had himself for an admiring audience, better to have had to rely upon the inner resource of his self-love.

Such egotism can only be justified if, for all its defensive self-regard, it authorizes the old poet to begin again, articulating new experience anew, rather than pitying himself for days gone by and friendships lost. Wordsworth's self-congratulation must also be a self-spurring. And to some extent it is—although after 1842 there would not be much new verse to come. But the determination to work out in verse the experiences of seeing places he had never before seen is present: the thanksgiving for survival is also an energetic embrace of the future. It is energetic at the levels of syntax and measure—rhythmical verse sentences move dynamically; energetic too in its eschewal of frippery and preparedness to embrace the awkward in order to articulate the processes of consciousness. The phrase "ear-deep seats" (line 71) is an example of this awkwardness: the diction is plain but the compound adjective is novel, and its effect, in combination with the noun, is an oddly materializing way of describing a sound lodged "along the heart" (to use an earlier physicalizing metaphor for emotional endearment ["Tintern Abbey," line 29]). It's both ordinary and extraordinary, and incongruous without being mellifluous, almost a token of a refusal to make pleasing images and sounds. It is coupled with a Miltonic syntax in which the parts of speech that resolve clauses may be deferred through subordinate clauses and parentheses for many lines. This delaying of resolution demands that the reader stay in the game for a long time, tracing emerging syntactical relations until the deferred gratification finally arrives (as in "free to rove" [line 95], a phrase repeated so it motivates further instances of liberty). Thus Wordsworth's address to his own soul affirms faith, through syntactical energy and verbal originality, in moving forward through time to a receding future. It is not formally backward-looking, not elegiac, because it is the representation of a muscular thought process that restlessly works toward a state of understanding that has the air of finality about it (when the resolving concept is finally articulated, it has accrued a weight accumulated over a long period of expectation). Wordsworth's late recourse—almost, poetically, his last resort—when faced by the depredations of death on his imagination is to return to his own company, his self-authorizing mind, which is capable of overcoming setbacks from outside. A great elegist, in the end he turned from the seductions, demands, and sadnesses of elegy to the old "pastures new" attainable by a reassertion of the Miltonic style that powered the poem "on the growth of my own mind."

Notes

Introduction

1. On dismissals of Wordsworth in these terms, see Trott, "Wordsworth and the Parodic School"; Schoenfield, *Law, Labor*, pp. 189–223.

2. See Gill, *Wordsworth and the Victorians*.

3. Seminal readings of this kind include Abrams, "Structure and Style" and *Natural Supernaturalism*; Bloom, "Internalization of the Quest Romance"; Hartman, "Wordsworth, Inscriptions."

4. See, e.g., Hartman, *Wordsworth's Poetry*; Beer, *Wordsworth in Time*; Jonathan Wordsworth, *Wordsworth: The Borders of Vision*.

5. Hartman, *Unremarkable Wordsworth*, p. 14.

6. Arnold, *Poems of Wordsworth*, p. xii. J. S. Mill had also suggested that "little of value was added in the latter part of the author's life" (*Autobiography and Other Writings*, p. 88).

7. Garrod, *Wordsworth*, p. 138.

8. Sperry, *Wordsworth's Anti-Climax*.

9. McFarland, *Wordsworth: Intensity and Achievement*, p. 89. The best summary of the development of this view in the twentieth century is John Williams, *Wordsworth: Critical Issues*, pp. 197–208.

10. Hartman, *Unremarkable Wordsworth*, p. 14.

11. Bloom, *Western Canon*, pp. 249–50.

12. See Levinson, *Wordsworth's Great Period Poems*; Liu, *Wordsworth: The Sense of History*; Simpson, *Wordsworth's Historical Imagination*.

13. McGann, *Romantic Ideology*.

14. E.g. Roe, *Politics of Nature*, pp. 159–80; Bate, *Romantic Ecology*; Rzepka, "Pictures of the Mind"; Walford Davies, "Romantic Hydrography."

15. Curran, *Poetic Form*; Ross, *Contours of Masculine Desire*; Bewell, *Wordsworth and the Enlightenment*; Lee, *Slavery and the Romantic Imagination*, pp. 194–222; Wyatt, *Wordsworth and the Geologists*; Heringman, *Romantic Rocks*; Wiley, *Romantic Geography*; Hess, *Wordsworth and the Ecology of Authorship*; Carlson, *Romantic Marks and Measures*.

16. Bushell, *Re-reading* The Excursion; Hickey, *Impure Conceits*; Ryan, *Romantic Reformation*, pp. 80–118; "'The Excursion': A Bicentenary Celebration"; Boyson, *Wordsworth and the Enlightenment*, pp. 153–83. On the *White Doe*, see Manning, *Reading Romantics*; Page, *Wordsworth and the Cultivation of Women*, pp. 112–46.

17. McGann, *Beauty of Inflections*, p. 313.

18. The essays were collected in Hartman, *Unremarkable Wordsworth*, pp. 75–119.

19. Galperin, *Revision and Authority*, p. 2.

20. Gill, *Wordsworth and the Victorians*, 40–80.

21. Manning, *Reading Romantics*, p. 291.

22. Also, Manning, "Wordsworth's 'Illustrated Books and Newspapers'"; Gill, *Wordsworth and the Victorians*, pp. 81–113; and Erickson, *Economy of Literary Form*, pp. 49–70. The impetus of Manning's and Erickson's book-history work is continued in my *The Late Poetry of the Lake Poets: Romanticism Revised*.

23. Manning, "Wordsworth and William Cobbett," and "Other Scene of Travel." On Wordsworth's later poems of place, see also Gravil, *Wordsworth's Bardic Vocation*, pp. 245–66.

24. Manning, "Wordsworth at St. Bees."

25. Chandler, *Wordsworth's Second Nature.*

26. Larkin, "Wordsworth's 'After-Sojourn.'"

27. Connell, *Romanticism, Economics*, p. 176.

28. Shaw, *Waterloo*, pp. 140–64.

29. Gravil, *Wordsworth's Thanksgiving Ode.*

30. Cox, "From Pantomime to Poetry"; see also his *Poetry and Politics*, p. 220.

31. Cox, "Cockney Excursions" and "Thinking Rivers."

32. On this argument, see Mahoney, *Romantics and Renegades.*

33. Gill, *Wordsworth and the Victorians* and *Wordsworth's Revisitings.*

34. See Donaldson, "Down the Duddon"; Yoshikawa, *Invention of Tourism.*

35. Simonsen, *Wordsworth and Word-Preserving Arts.* See also the sales data in St Clair, *Reading Nation*, pp. 660–64.

36. On which, see Newlyn, *Reading, Writing, and Romanticism*, pp. 91–99, 104–9; Zimmerman, *Romanticism, Lyricism and History*, pp. 75–76.

37. Kelley, *Wordsworth's Revisionary Aesthetics*, pp. 156–69, 170–92.

38. Robin Jarvis, "Shades of Milton"; Shaw, "Wordsworth's 'Dread Voice.'"

39. Gravil, *Wordsworth's Bardic Vocation*; Garrett, *Wordsworth and the Writing of the Nation.*

40. Simon Jarvis, *Wordsworth's Philosophic Song*; Walker, *Marriage, Writing and Romanticism.*

41. Page, *Wordsworth and the Cultivation of Women*, pp. 112–46.

42. Heringman, *Romantic Rocks*, p. 57.

43. Miller, *Invention of Evening*, pp. 81–111.

44. Developing discussions of the earlier poetry by, among many, Liu, *Wordsworth: The Sense of History*; Baron, *Language and Relationship in Wordsworth's Writing*; Goodman, *Georgic Modernity*, pp. 106–43; and of historicity in Siskin, *The Historicity of Romantic Discourse*, pp. 114–24.

45. Precedents for the earlier Wordsworth, include Liu, "Power of Formalism"; Wolfson, *Formal Charges.*

46. On versions, see Stillinger, *Coleridge and Textual Instability*; Leader, *Revision and Romantic Authorship*, pp. 21–77. On the poet's presentation in collected editions, see Piper, *Dreaming in Books*, pp. 55–58. On the poet as professional author and man of letters, see Klancher, *Making of English Reading Audiences*, pp. 138–39, 148–50; Eagleton, *Ideology of the Aesthetic*, p. 65; Woodmansee, *Author, Art*, p. 73; Rose, *Authors and Owners.* On Wordsworth

as a professional, see Hess, *Authoring the Self*; Goldberg, *Lake Poets*, pp. 190–221; Schoenfield, *Law, Labor*; Pfau, *Wordsworth's Profession*.

47. See Raymond Williams, *Country and the City*; Barrell, *Idea of Landscape*; Daniels, *Fields of Vision*; Simpson, *Wordsworth, Commodification*.

48. See Stafford, "'Inhabited Solitudes'"; Janowitz, *England's Ruins*, pp. 117–26.

49. Here, I am in dialogue with Baron, *Language and Relationship*; Langan, "Understanding Media in 1805"; McLane, "On the Use and Abuse of 'Orality'"; Duncan, *Scott's Shadow*. On colonization within Britain, see Crawford, *Devolving English Literature*; Kerrigan, *Archipelagic English*.

50. See Leader, *Revision and Romantic Authorship*, pp. 21–77; Bushell, *Text as Process*; Bennett, in *Wordsworth Writing*, examines Wordsworth's dematerialization of his own practice.

51. Here, I develop arguments made by Cox, "Thinking Rivers."

52. See, e.g., Cox, *Poetry and Politics*; Franklin, *Byron's Heroines*; Stabler, *Byron, Poetics and History*; Chandler, *England in 1819*.

53. Goodridge, *Nineteenth Century Labouring-Class Poets*; Haywood, *Revolution in Popular Literature*; Janowitz, *Lyric and Labour*. Also, Keegan, *British Labouring-Class Nature Poetry*.

54. See, on revising genre in the act of reading past examples, Prins, "What Is Historical Poetics?" For particular forms read historically, see Tucker, *Epic*; Phelan, *Nineteenth-Century Sonnet*.

55. Larkin, *Wordsworth and Coleridge*; Said, *On Late Style*; Prynne, *Field Notes*.

56. See Curran, *Poetic Form*, pp. 180–203.

57. A debate begun by Manning's fine essay "Wordsworth in Youth and Age."

58. Cf. Simpson, *Wordsworth, Commodification*, p. 53: his poems are "demanding paradigms for understanding a history in which we are still entangled."

Part I

1. Hartman, *Unremarkable Wordsworth*, p. 133.

2. See Kelley, *Wordsworth's Revisionary Aesthetics*, pp. 156–69; Zimmerman, *Romanticism, Lyricism and History*, pp. 75–76.

3. For the comparison see Raymond Williams, *Country and the City*, pp. 128–32. On class tensions in Austen, see, among many discussions, Duckworth, *Improvement of the Estate*; and Roberts, *Jane Austen*.

Chapter 1

1. See Bates, *Wordsworth's Poetic Collections*, pp. 77–100.

2. In Jeffrey's review of the *White Doe*, 355–63. On Wordsworth's modeling of a select audience for a work he feared would be unpopular, see Clarke, "'Fit though Few.'"

3. On collecting works to establish reputation and legacy, see Gamer, *Romanticism*, pp. 16–53; Erickson, *Economy of Literary Form*, pp. 49–70.

4. On the Gothic metaphor and Wordsworth's self-portrayal, see Duggett, *Gothic Romanticism*, pp. 143–68.

5. On Wordsworth's somewhat porous and provisional categorizations, see Duff, "Wordsworth and the Language of Forms."

6. Jeffrey, review of *Poems, in Two Volumes*. On Jeffrey's attacks and Wordsworth's responses, see Owen, "Wordsworth and Jeffrey."

7. Coleridge, *Friend*, II, pp. 286–87.

8. On this self-imaging, see Mole, *Byron's Romantic Celebrity*.

9. The Preface promised the poems would throw over their subjects "a certain colouring of imagination" (LB, p. 743).

10. See Klancher, *Making of English Reading Audiences*, pp. 138–39, 148–50; Newlyn, *Reading, Writing, and Romanticism*, pp. 91–99. See Hess, *Authoring the Self*, pp. 220–33 on Wordsworth's ambivalent relationship to reviews.

11. Salient examples include Weiskel, *Romantic Sublime*, pp. 195–204; Caruth, *Empirical Truths*, pp. 44–57, 147–51; Potkay, *Wordsworth's Ethics*.

12. One among many is Jacobus, *Romanticism, Writing and Sexual Difference*.

13. The most germinal text is de Man, *Rhetoric of Romanticism*.

14. Hartman, *Unremarkable Wordsworth*, remains the seminal study.

15. E.g., Bloom, *Anxiety of Influence*.

16. See, e.g., Chase, *Decomposing Figures*.

17. McGann, *Romantic Ideology*, pp. 67–68, 88.

18. Hartman, *Unremarkable Wordsworth*, p. 133.

19. On Coleridge's frustration at Wordsworth on the Scottish tour, see my *Romantic Poetry and Literary Coteries*, chapter 3.

20. Dorothy Wordsworth, *Recollections of a Tour*, p. 83; CN, I, 1469.

21. Dorothy Wordsworth, *Recollections of a Tour*, p. 92.

22. On this see Matlak, "Wordsworth and the 'Great Terror.'"

23. On the invasion fears, see Banks, "Rhetorical Missiles."

24. See Liu, *Wordsworth: The Sense of History*, pp. 480–95.

25. For the dating of the poem, see Ringler, "Genesis of Cowper's 'Yardley Oak.'"

26. Cowper, *Life and Posthumous Writings*, III, pp. 405–16.

27. Culler, "Apostrophe," 63; de Man, "Autobiography as Defacement," in *Rhetoric of Romanticism*, pp. 67–81; Chase, *Decomposing Figures*.

28. Culler, "Apostrophe," 63.

29. But see Clymer's critique of de Man's equation of apostrophe and prosopopeia and demonstration that Cowper is not comprehended by his argument: Clymer, "Graved in Tropes." For further critique, see Kneale, *Romantic Aversions*, pp. 11–27.

30. De Man, *Rhetoric of Romanticism*, p. 78.

31. Culler, "Apostrophe," 67.

32. Burke, *Reflections on the Revolution*, p. 120.

33. Burke, *Reflections on the Revolution*, p. 173.

34. *The Task, 1785*, III, 746–56. Details of the events which lay behind Cowper's angry lines can be found in Hyams, *Capability Brown*, p. 44.

35. On Cowper's bleak articulation of political decline via images of landscape, see Feingold, *Nature and Society*, pp. 144–55, 162–63, 182–83; Newey, *Cowper's Poetry*, pp. 165–207; Goodman, *Georgic Modernity*, pp. 72–94.

36. Madden Ballad Collection, vol. XV.

37. The historian of ballads Mark Philp writes that by 1798 reformist songs had "dwindled to a handful" while "loyalist broadsides and tracts [funded by] government subsidies . . . sold throughout the country at very low prices." Philp et al., "Music and Politics."

38. As Jonathan Wordsworth points out, it was Wordsworth's receipt of "Yardley Oak" in Hayley's *Life*, coupled with the sight of Lorton yew in September 1804, that prompted him to write "Yew Trees." *Wordsworth: The Borders of Vision*, pp. 279, 442.

39. Corrected MS draft taken from Wordsworth, *Poems, in Two Volumes*, pp. 669–71.

40. Hartman notes the "adjacence" of the depersonalized voice of "Yew Trees" to the "poetic tradition in which a tree . . . is made to speak," deciding that "the poet has subsumed or refined an archaic genre" without seeing that the subsumption involved the direct excision of textual borrowings. In *Unremarkable Wordsworth*, p. 132.

41. Cf. Hartman, *Unremarkable Wordsworth*, p. 146, where Cowper's presence is briefly considered.

42. MS draft in *Poems, in Two Volumes*, p. 667.

43. "Eugh" and "Ew" in the manuscripts became "Yew" on publication.

44. Hartman, *Unremarkable Wordsworth*, p. 133.

45. Hartman, *Unremarkable Wordsworth*, pp. 140–46.

46. On Wordsworth's attainment of uncanny objectivity, see Ferguson, *Wordsworth: Language as Counter-Spirit*. Also see Rifaterre, "Interpretation and Descriptive Poetry," in which the poem's referentiality to historical particulars is said to be merely gestural.

47. De Man, *Rhetoric of Romanticism*, pp. 77–78.

48. See Hartman, *Unremarkable Wordsworth*, p. 136. While viewing Wordsworth as an epitaphic poet, Bewell, in *Wordsworth and the Enlightenment*, pp. 187–217, historicizes this "mythic" quality by placing him in an eighteenth-century tradition of writing impersonally about death.

49. Hartman, *Unremarkable Wordsworth*, pp. 140–46.

Chapter 2

1. For Barrell, "overlooking" describes an idealization of the landscape born of distance: the prospect poet's lack of involvement in the landscape as a place of production allowed him to separate "objects "from the[ir] intellectual, emotional, historical associations." *Idea of Landscape*, pp. 58–59.

2. See Simonsen, *Wordsworth and Word-Preserving Arts*, pp. 69–101 (Wordsworth's collaboration with Beaumont) and pp. 38–69 (typographic inscription).

3. On Wordsworth's changed poetics in this context, see Kelley, *Wordsworth's Revisionary Aesthetics*, pp. 156–69; Pearson, "Coleorton's 'Classic Ground.'"

4. On this, see Zimmerman, *Romanticism, Lyricism and History*, pp. 75–76.

5. On the dedication and its implications, see Mahoney, *Romantics and Renegades*, p. 120.

6. Addison, *Letter from Italy*.

7. Nichols, *History and Antiquities*, III, part II, pp. 651–60.

8. In vol. IX.

9. Hazlitt, *Spirit of the Age*, p. 196.

10. On this history, see Hartman, "Wordsworth, Inscriptions."

11. On the idealizing function of Georgic, see Raymond Williams, *Country and the City*; Barrell, *English Literature in History*; Bermingham, *Landscape and Ideology*.

12. Line 13 of "Written at the Request of Sir George Beaumont, Bart., and in his Name, for an Urn, placed by him at the Termination of a newly-planted Avenue, in the same Grounds," in 1815, II, p. 290.

13. Repton, *Fragments on the Theory*, p. viii; Daniels, *Fields of Vision*, p. 83.

14. About £140,000 in 2018 values.

15. Nichols, *History and Antiquities*, III, part II, p. 739.

16. Hon. John Byng, 1789, quoted in Stewart, *History of Coal Mining*, p. 101.

17. Brydges, ed., *Topographer for the Year 1790*, p. 94: "The park is gone, the trees are cut down; only a fragment of the house remains. . . . Dirty Coal-Mines surround it."

18. In 1760 Joseph Boultbee took out a twenty-one-year lease on Beaumont's Paddock Colliery, farm, and woods, agreeing to pay a rent of £140 per annum and to produce no more than 10,000 loads of coal a year. He also leased Newbold Field Colliery at £50 a year.

19. *English Reports*, vol. XXXI: *Chancery*, vol. XI, Beaumont v. Boultbee, pp. 695–700.

20. Curtis, *Topographical History*, p. 44.

21. A description of the Snibston pit, a mile from Coleorton, taken in 1842. From the official report of the Children's Employment Commission, 1842.

22. Owen and Brown, *Collector of Genius*, p. 93.

23. *English Reports*, vol. XXXII: *Chancery*, vol. XII, Beaumont v. Boultbee (1805), p. 1126.

24. With an additional legacy of landed estate, Beaumont's income rose to circa £8,000 a year—about £2 million in 2018 terms.

25. That is, to rent the land out as Beaumont's agent and spend the incoming money on landscaping it.

26. For these financial transactions, see Worthen, *Life of William Wordsworth*, chapter 2.

27. On Wordsworth's anxieties about being a professional poet for the market, see Pfau, *Wordsworth's Profession*, pp. 92–113; Schoenfield, *Law, Labor*.

28. See Goldberg, *Lake Poets*, pp. 3–4, on Wordsworth's complicated relationship with writing—or publishing—for money.

29. "Home at Grasmere," I, 179.

30. See Anderson, "Wordsworth and the Gardens"; Buchanan, *Wordsworth's Gardens*, pp. 89–114; Fay, "Prospects of Contemplation."

31. On Wordsworth's careful negotiation of the patronage relationship, see Gill, *William Wordsworth: A Life*, p. 219; James, "Wordsworth and Literary Friendship."

32. See St Clair, *Reading Nation*, pp. 660–64.

33. On these judgments as the preferred medium of the relationship, see Matlak, *Deep Distresses*, p. 148.

34. See EY, p. 490, and MY, I, p. 63 for Wordsworth's engagement with Reynolds and neoclassical art.

35. On this changed style in the poem, see Levinson, *Wordsworth's Great Period Poems*, pp. 101–34.

36. It is probable that Wordsworth already knew Taylor before his arrival at Coleorton, since, in his letters to the poet, Beaumont clearly felt the need to justify Taylor's dismissal by a detailed explanation of his conduct. See Beaumont's letters to Wordsworth, held by the Wordsworth Trust (WLL / Beaumont, George /33/34/35).

37. On Wordsworth and monasticism, see Fay, "Wordsworth's Northumbria."

38. On this unease and the relation between labor value and money value in the poem, see, e.g., Levinson, *Wordsworth's Great Period Poems*, pp. 58–79; Heinzelman, *Economics of the Imagination*, pp. 196–233; Schoenfield, *Law, Labor*, pp. 31–60.

39. See Campbell, *The Hermit in the Garden*.

40. On anxieties about labor and value, see Simpson, *Wordsworth, Commodification*.

41. On labor, the Georgic, and *The Excursion*, see Goodman, *Georgic Modernity*, pp. 106–43; Schoenfield, *Law, Labor*, pp. 224–52.

42. Milton, "Sonnet 12," line 7.

43. An alternate version of line 625 from the 1827 text of the poem; see Wordsworth, *Excursion*, p. 246.

44. Hartman, *Beyond Formalism*, p. 208.

45. Cf. Chase, "Monument and Inscription."

46. Wordsworthian scholars who explore the coming into focus of his lyrics in the context of printed books—his own books and others' (including guidebooks), include Carlson, *Romantic Marks and Measures*; and Yoshikawa, *Invention of Tourism*. For a survey of the Romantics' inscription poems, see Bernhardt-Kabisch, "Epitaph and the Romantic Poets."

47. Cf. Bennett, *Wordsworth Writing*, pp. 78–100, in which the inscriptions present a form of impossible writing, undoing their stony materiality by their immaterial existence on the reproduced page and in the readers' minds, and vice versa.

48. Cf. Zimmerman, *Romanticism, Lyricism and History*, pp. 75–76.

49. On this poem, see Wiley, *Romantic Geography*, pp. 149–50, 160–69; Garrett, *Wordsworth and the Writing of the Nation*, pp. 70–80; Carlson, *Romantic Marks and Measures*, pp. 103–12.

Part II

1. Terms from de Certeau, *Practice of Everyday Life*. On bringing a space into cultural memory by representing it, see Schama, *Landscape and Memory*, especially pp. 53–74, on the iconography of trees. On renewing visited relics in verse, see Rzepka, "From Relics to Remains." Chandler stresses the importance for Wordsworth of a poetic history that takes into account the myths, tales, and legends by which people endow places they love with meaning. In *Wordsworth's Second Nature*, p. 174.

2. On the national appeal of local memorials, see Stafford, *Local Attachments*; and Garrett, *Wordsworth and the Writing of the Nation*, pp. 69–94 and 149–76. On uniting a national community of readers, see Benedict Anderson, *Imagined Communities*.

3. On the memorial as a tourist poem, see Robin Jarvis, "Wages of Travel"; and Wyatt, *Wordsworth's Poems of Travel*.

4. On this, see Gill, "Wordsworth and Burns"; Stafford, *Local Attachments*, pp. 123–24.

5. McGann, *Romantic Ideology*, pp. 68, 137.

6. See Stafford, *Last of the Race*, pp. 101–8.

7. On the textualization of memory, see Wolfson, *Formal Charges*, p. 104.

8. Here, I offer a textualized development of the emphasis on partnership in Newlyn, *William and Dorothy Wordsworth*.

Chapter 3

1. See chapter 6 of my *The Late Poetry of the Lake Poets*.

2. Jeffrey, review of *Poems, in Two Volumes*, 224, 231.

3. Jeffrey, review of *Marmion*, 3.

4. Jeffrey, review of *The Lady of the Lake*, 270.

5. Crabb Robinson's comment, quoted in Gill, *William Wordsworth: A Life*, p. 459.

6. Stewart, *Crimes of Writing*, p. 115.

7. Duncan, *Modern Romance*, pp. 10–11.

8. See Stewart, *Crimes of Writing*, pp. 122–23, on Scott's means of production of authenticity effects.

9. On Wordsworth's reflections on the poet's position in these poems see Prynne, *Field Notes*; Bewell, *Wordsworth and the Enlightenment*, pp. 81–93.

10. McLane, *Balladeering*, p. 164.

11. On the poem's vexed history, see Manning, *Reading Romantics*, pp. 165–94.

12. "Lord B." is Byron, the popularity of whose semi-Wordsworthian *Childe Harold's Pilgrimage* Wordsworth envied.

13. On the 1803 tour poems, see Prynne, *Field Notes*; Stafford, "'Inhabited Solitudes.'"

14. See McLane, *Balladeering*, p. 168, on Wordsworth's rejection of the pageantry and minstrelsy that placed ballads in a pseudo-medieval past. On minstrelsy as discovered by Thomas Percy, see Groom, *Making of Percy's Reliques*.

15. In Scott's *Minstrelsy of the Scottish Border*, III, pp. 72–79.

16. Percy, *Reliques of Ancient English Poetry*, II, pp. 361–66.

17. "Rare Willie Drowned in Yarrow" appeared in vol. 4, Ramsay, *Tea Table Miscellany*.

18. On the print mechanisms that gave the illusion of sound-production, see Langan, "Understanding Media in 1805"; Manning, "'Birthday of Typography.'" On the actual performance of poetry, see Perkins, "How the Romantics Recited Poetry."

19. On the mediation of Logan's song, see Currie, "Re-visioning James Hogg."

20. See the discussion of these poems and issues in Baron, *Language and Relationship*, pp. 236–41.

21. Jeffrey, in review of *The Excursion*, 1–4.

22. See St. Clair, *Reading Nation*, pp. 660–64.

23. Hogg, *Collected Letters of James Hogg*, I, p. 249.

24. Jeffrey, review of *Reliques of Robert Burns*, 253.

25. Cf. Davis, *Acts of Union*, pp. 129–43.

26. For recent debates concerning Burns's representation of tradition, see Leask, *Robert Burns*.

27. Burns, *Poems and Songs of Robert Burns*, I, p. 170.

28. Burns, *Works of Robert Burns*, I, p. 38. Cf. Noble, "Wordsworth and Burns."

29. Burns, *Works of Robert Burns*, II, p. 399.

30. Wordsworth, *Recollections of a Tour*, p. 76.

31. On Macpherson's production of the past, see Stafford, *Sublime Savage* and *Last of the Race*; Gaskill, *Ossian Revisited* and *Reception of Ossian in Europe*.

32. Contrast Scott's "Glenfinlas" (1800), in which the seer is ignored, to their cost, by the romanticized nobility. The pseudo-medieval ballad is a text full of antique devices but makes no attempt to explore the nature or cause of the superstition of second sight.

33. Hogg, *Brownie of Bodsbeck*, I, pp. i–xii.

34. See Alker and Nelson, "'Ghastly in the Moonlight.'"

35. Jeffrey Robinson identifies it as such, analyses earlier examples, and pleads for its importance as an alternative to visionary lyricism, then and now, in his *Unfettering Poetry*. See especially pp. 256–57.

36. Wordsworth, *Fenwick Notes*, p. 89.

37. Wordsworth, *Recollections of a Tour*, p. 210.

38. As is revealed in fine essays by McLane, "On the Use and Abuse of 'Orality'"; Stafford, "'Dangerous Success.'"

39. T. S. Eliot, "Burnt Norton," lines 151–53.

40. I take the term from Gill's study of the later work, in *Wordsworth's Revisitings*.

Chapter 4

1. The Lycoris figure, and the genesis of the poem, is discussed in Walker, *Marriage, Writing and Romanticism*, p. 122. Also, Thomson, "'Sport of Transmutations.'"

2. Cf. Wolfson: "Manuscripts as well as memories constitute his past, and textual revision reduplicates, perpetuates, and enters into recollection." *Formal Charges*, p. 104.

3. On the dependence of poetic production on the Wordsworth women, see Leader, *Revision and Romantic Authorship*, pp. 21–77; and Page, *Wordsworth and the Cultivation of Women*, pp. 112–46. On its physicality, elided in Wordsworth's representation of it, see Bennett, *Wordsworth Writing*.

4. See Bushell, *Text as Process*, pp. 12–21, 97, and "Composition and Revision."

5. Compare with the argument of Gidal, "Wordsworth's Art of Memory," 445–46, that *The Prelude* "exhibit[s] his very memory itself as a formal structure" analogous to those of museum and guidebook.

6. For instance, in the accounts of Wordsworth's self-recycling in Sykes Davies, *Wordsworth and the Worth of Words*, pp. 261–307. Gill's *Wordsworth's Revisitings* (pp. 123–54) factors in the pressures of the public world.

7. For a discussion of fossils in Charlotte Smith—a poetics of assemblage and conjecture rather than of organic form—see Goodman, "Conjectures on Beachy Head." For assemblage as an aesthetic involving nonhuman entities as actants alongside humans, see Bennett, "Agency of Assemblages."

8. See Khan, "'To the Same,'" for a discussion of the poem as a late work.

9. Cf. Thomson, "Importance of Other People."

10. Mellor, *Romanticism and Gender*, pp. 145–68; Ross, *Contours of Masculine Desire*, p. 106. See Fay, *Becoming Wordsworthian*, on Dorothy's encouragement to perform a version of sorority and femininity for her brother.

11. Cf. Wordsworth, *Shorter Poems*, pp. 252–53.

12. Heringman, *Romantic Rocks*, p. 57, shows a similar recoil at work in the "Kirkstone" ode of 1817.

13. DC MS 84 7r, in Mary's and William's hands. The lines were drafted to follow the words "circumscribing shades" (in line 13 of the 1820 published text). See Wordsworth, *Shorter Poems*, pp. 480–81.

14. The penultimate line of "Ode: Intimations of Immortality."

15. For the text, see Fairer and Gerrard, *Eighteenth-Century Poetry*.

16. Ricks, *Allusion to the Poets*, p. 86.

17. A deleted passage in DC MS 15. See LB, p. 547.

18. On Wordsworth's discovery that "inanimate things came before animate ones" and his consequent questioning of "the priority of language to the being of death disclosed in the sensory object," see Fry, "Green to the Very Door?," 104. On nature as a figure of an absence and writing as a tracing of that absence imbued with death, see Chase, *Decomposing Figures*; and de Man, "Time and History in Wordsworth."

19. Ferguson, *Wordsworth: Language as Counter-Spirit*, pp. 193–94.

20. My interpretation of Hartman's meditation on Wordsworth and the divine fiat in *Unremarkable Wordsworth*, pp. 100–110.

21. Cf. Ferguson, *Wordsworth: Language as Counter-Spirit*, p. 233: "an insistently supplemental pattern, in which the retreat from language is not silence but a translation from one form of language to another."

22. Buckland, *Reliquiae Diluvinae*, p. 193.

23. Larkin, "Wordsworth's 'After-Sojourn,'" 431.

24. On Dorothy's role in "Tintern Abbey" as a component of "a performance of memory, the paradoxical achievement in the present of a future remembrance," see Bennett, *Romantic Poets*, p. 106. See Wolfson, *Romantic Interactions*, pp. 152–78, on William's dependence on Dorothy's subjectivity.

25. Larkin, "Wordsworth's 'After-Sojourn,'" 412.

26. Cf. Walker, *Marriage, Writing and Romanticism*, p. 125.

Part III

1. For these, and counter-arguments more recently, see the Introduction; and Trickett, "Language of Wordsworth's Later Poems."

2. Robert Browning's description from the poem of that name.

3. Recent discussions of Wordsworth and younger poets include Low, *Literary Protégées of the Lake Poets*; Wolfson, *Romantic Interactions*, pp. 152–78; Melnyk, "William Wordsworth and Felicia Hemans"; Kim, *Wordsworth, Hemans*.

Chapter 5

1. See Khan, "Wordsworth's 'The Haunted Tree'."

2. *The Task*, I, 28–37.

3. Letter of 21 June 1820 from Princess Lieven to Prince Metternich, quoted in Smith, *Queen on Trial*, p. 40.

4. Quoted in Smith, *Queen on Trial*, p. 106.

5. "The bill thrown out, but the pains and penalties inflicted" (15 November 1820), reproduced in Smith, *Queen on Trial*, p. 142.

6. Keats gave Wordsworth an inscribed copy of his first collection, *Poems, by John Keats* (1817), and Wordsworth possessed a copy of *Endymion* (1818).

7. Haydon's account is given in *Keats Circle*, II, p. 144. On paganism and Keats, see Barnett, *Romantic Paganism*.

8. The matter is discussed in Walker, *Marriage, Writing and Romanticism*, p. 208; and Roe, *John Keats*, pp. 76–77.

9. See Walker, *Marriage, Writing and Romanticism*, 200–209, on the poem in relation to Keats.

10. *John Keats: Complete Poems*, p. 97.

11. Wordsworth disliked Leigh Hunt's pretty sensuality: see LY, I, p. 124. Leigh Hunt's hamadryads appear in "The Nymphs" (1818), Part I, 87–92 and "The Palace of Pleasure" (1801) canto I, 166. See Roe, *Fiery Heart*. Walker (*Marriage, Writing and Romanticism*, p. 197) shows Wordsworth had in February 1819 been reading Virgil's 10th Eclogue in his friend's Francis Wrangham's translation, comparing it with the Latin original—"Hamadryad" appears there, as does "Lycoris". The Eclogue is also a contributory source for the classicism of Wordsworth's 1819–20 poetry.

12. Cited in *Keats Circle*, II, p. 144.

13. Leigh Hunt, *Examiner*, 1 June, 6 July, 13 July 1817, 345. See Cox, *Poetry and Politics*.

14. Dryden, *Ovid's Metamorphoses*, VIII.

15. Burke, *Reflections on the Revolution*, p. 181.

16. On tree-symbolism, see Daniels, "Political Iconography of Woodland."

17. Burke, *Philosophical Enquiry*, pp. 111, 157.

18. On these classical allusions and their significance for Wordsworth's preference for historical poetry—which takes myth and folktale and retells them—over documentary history, see Chandler, *Wordsworth's Second Nature*, p. 174.

Chapter 6

1. Southey declared in 1833 he had known nothing of the *Corn Law Rhymes* until Wordsworth had put them in his hand (*Life and Correspondence*, VI, p. 218). This must have occurred before March 1832, because on the twenty-ninth of that month, Southey wrote to a friend discussing them familiarly (*New Letters*, II, p. 375). In a letter of 4 December 1833 (LY, II, p. 667), Wordsworth asked William Pearson to bring a copy of the "Corn Law poet's book" to Rydal.

2. Crabb Robinson, *Diary, Reminiscences, and Correspondence*, II, p. 171.

3. *Corn Law Rhymes*, 3rd ed. (London, 1831), p. iv. All subsequent citations are from this edition.

4. This threat appeared in a note added to the declaration in editions from 1833. I cite it here from Elliott, *The Splendid Village: Corn Law Rhymes*.

5. Likewise, retaining radical sympathies, he welcomed the Chartist poet Thomas Cooper, recently released from prison, to Rydal Mount, telling him that the claims of the charter were entirely justified. See Gravil, *Wordsworth's Bardic Vocation*, pp. 347–52.

6. Elliott "spoke of the 'Excursion' as one of the poems destined for immortality. He could quote all its finest descriptive passages." Phillips, *Life, Character and Genius of Ebenezer Elliott*, p. 22.

7. Published in Wordsworth's *Poetical Works* (1836–37). Text from *Last Poems*, pp. 299–304, line 38.

8. Both poets were responding to the evangelical campaign to abolish slavery. They were modifying the blank-verse argument of Cowper's *Task, 1785*, II, 40–46. On Elliott's satiric style and its antecedents among radical poets, see Jones, "Wheat from the Chaff."

9. In a review for the *Quarterly* in late 1833, which was rejected by its editor, Southey praises Elliott's poetry and laments the political agitation yet highlights the plight of the poor as a matter of exploitation, exactly as Wordsworth does. Elliott, *More Verse and Prose*, II, pp. 81–116. See Brown, "Ebenezer Elliott and Robert Southey."

Part IV

1. Prins, "What Is Historical Poetics?," p. 15.

2. Simon Jarvis, "What Is Historical Poetics?," pp. 100–101.

3. Levinson, "What Is New Formalism?."

4. On this, see Galperin, *Revision and Authority*, p. 232.

5. Said, "Thoughts on Late Style."

Chapter 7

1. Levinson, *Wordsworth's Great Period Poems*, p. 116.

2. Gates, "Wordsworth's Mirror of Morality"; Rylestone, *Prophetic Memory*; Hewitt, "Church Building as Political Strategy"; Branch, *Rituals of Spontaneity*; Johnson, *Wordsworth and the Sonnet*; Tomko, "Superstition."

3. More general commentaries on the ideological function of Wordsworth's later Anglicanism include Connell, *Romanticism, Economics*, pp. 121–80; Duggett, *Gothic Romanticism*, pp. 143–68; Ryan, *Romantic Reformation*, pp. 80–118; Gill, *Wordsworth and the Victorians*, pp. 40–80. On the church and sonnet form, see Frey, who in *British State Romanticism* (pp. 86–87) suggests that Wordsworth chooses the church and the sonnet as modes of disciplining the poetic imagination so that its liberty is invested in the historical order of tradition.

4. Cf. Easterlin, who delineates the tension between conformity to the liturgy of the church and to personal experience (the latter represented in images of maternal love). *Wordsworth and the Question*, pp. 146, 150.

5. Manning observes that in 1820 Wordsworth implied, in "Processions," that religion is invented rather than revealed. He valued it, institutionalized in the church and its clergy, as a historical force, both local and national, making for moral, social, and national cohesion. "Cleansing the Images," 315.

6. Charges made in Francis Jeffrey's review of *Thalaba the Destroyer*, 63–83.

7. Phelan, *Nineteenth-Century Sonnet*, p. 14. See also Curran, "Wordsworth's Sonnets."

8. Cf. Robinson, " 'Still Glides the Stream.' "

9. See Donaldson, "Down the Duddon"; Gill, "Wordsworth and *The River Duddon*."

10. See Fay, "Question of Loyalty."

11. In the Preface to *Lyrical Ballads*, Wordsworth argued that meter's "power" to "give pleasure" over time, "from generation to generation," derived from its association, according to the "concurring testimony of ages" with "particular poems" (LB, pp. 754, 755, 757).

12. The English tradition of "change ringing"—ringing church bells in sets of permutations—was developed in the seventeenth century and spread by practice and also by the publication of handbooks.

13. Gates, "Wordsworth's Mirror of Morality," 130–31.

14. Wordsworth, *Fenwick Notes*, p. 133.

15. On Wordsworth's representations of Druidism, see Gravil, *Wordsworth's Bardic Vocation*, pp. 25–33.

16. The Roman historian Dio Cassius was the source.

17. In the 1805 *Prelude*, Wordsworth treated Stonehenge as a Druid "sacrificial altar, / Fed with living men," as if following the theories of Edward Davies, and imagined himself as a Druid priest, tracing figures of the heavens in the patterns of stones they arranged on earth, "gently charm'd, / Albeit with an antiquarian's dream" (XII, 338–53). He rewrote his *Prelude* vision in *The Excursion*, replacing his visionary response to Stonehenge with a description of Swinside, secluded beneath the sheltering arms of the fell Black Comb, near the coast (IX, 685–706).

18. On Wordsworth's rendition of this history, see Wright, "Vile Saxons and Ancient Britons."

19. Setzer, "Precedent and Perversity," 434. Cf. Galperin, *Revision and Authority*, p. 238: Wordsworth places "politics . . . in the service of his art, which more than ever—at the terminus of his career—had become a private sphere."

20. *Prelude*, XI, 335.

21. On this tendency to undermine the support of the death penalty that the sonnets had embodied, see Canuel, *Shadow of Death*, pp. 75, 79; and Galperin, *Revision and Authority*, pp. 25, 238, 242.

Chapter 8

1. See Miller, *Invention of Evening*, pp. 81–111.

2. Cf. Castell, "Wordsworth, Silence."

3. Lines 9–14.

4. Wordsworth had included Mickle's and Finch's poems among those he selected for an anthology he prepared. See Wordsworth, *Poems and Extracts*, pp. 9–11, 52.

5. On sound's materiality in Wordsworth, see Mathes, "Listening Not Listening."

6. This couplet (lines 24–25), present in the manuscript draft, was omitted on first publication but included in later editions. See Wordsworth, *Last Poems*, p. 237.

7. Cf. Simon Jarvis, "Wordsworth's Late Melodics."

8. On this, see Speitz, "Wordsworthian Acoustic Imagination."

9. On the source of the phrase "lucid intervals," see Martin, "Lucid Intervals." The poem is briefly discussed by Simon Jarvis in *Wordsworth's Philosophic Song*, p. 196.

10. Cf. Galperin, *Revision and Authority*, p. 2 (see the Introduction above for a discussion).

11. Shakespeare, *Henry IV*, pt. I, act 3, scene 1, 57.

12. Lines 24–26 were present in the manuscript draft but not in the first publication. They were included in editions from 1836. See Wordsworth, *Last Poems*, p. 239.

13. In "The Solitary Reaper" Wordsworth ponders how to represent a vale "overflowing" with the song of the Highland girl that is and is not like a nightingale; here, the translation of oral plenitude in print is not the issue, but rather the registration of what appears by virtue of its absence. See Prynne, *Field Notes*.

14. He included Wither's verse in the Lowther album. See Wordsworth, *Poems and Extracts*, pp. 33–41.

15. "Elegiac Stanzas Suggested by a Picture of Peele Castle in a Storm," lines 14, 16; Immortality Ode, line 57.

16. Wordsworth calls to the owls in Gray's "Elegy" and Milton's "Il Penseroso."

17. See Wordsworth, *Last Poems*, p. 243.

18. Young, *Night Thoughts*, Night II, lines 88–95.

Coda

1. See Scodel, *English Poetic Epitaph*, pp. 384–407; Matthews, "Epitaphs"; Depew, "Wordsworth on Epitaph."

2. In the first of his "Essays upon Epitaphs," Wordsworth argued that mental "transports" and "turns of conflicting passion" "might constitute the life and beauty of a funeral Oration or elegiac Poem" but were not suitable for epitaphs (Wordsworth, *Prose Works*, II, p. 60).

3. In this respect employing a generic mixing that David Duff has seen as characteristic of Romanticism. Duff, *Romanticism*, pp. 1–16. See also Curran, *Poetic Form*, pp. 180–203.

4. Esther Schor has traced the concept of mourning as a "debt" in *Bearing the Dead*.

5. On the early elegies, see Woof, "Wordsworth Learns."

6. See Holt, "Aspects of Wordsworth's Poetry": "It is simultaneously an elegy to Wordsworth's old writings and his first attempts at creating a new kind of poetry, but one that is still in the process of constructing itself from the remains of his old work." See also Swaab,

"Wordsworth's Elegies"; Clucas, "Consecration, and the Poet's Dream," arguing that Words-worth forces himself to relinquish each consoling fiction, rather than create what Sacks called "elegiac images of consolation" (*English Elegy*, p. 33).

7. In *Buried Communities*, Fosso suggests that after John's and the children's deaths, Wordsworth's mode of mourning changed from a focus on the community of the living and dead to a more orthodox form: "Wordsworth . . . began to move from the churchyard to the church" (p. 194).

8. Bewell, *Wordsworth and the Enlightenment*, pp. 187–217, reads *Lyrical Ballads* in the light of "Essays upon Epitaphs."

9. Gill, *William Wordsworth: A Life*, pp. 376–77.

10. First published in the *Newcastle Journal*, 5 December 1835. See Wordsworth, *Last Poems*, pp. 305–7.

11. See Newlyn, *William and Dorothy Wordsworth*, pp. 287–88.

12. Published in Wordsworth, *Poems, Chiefly of Early and Late Years*, pp. 97–112.

13. Gill, *Wordsworth's Revisitings*, pp. 155–70; Manning, "The Other Scene of Travel": Wordsworth "is at once his own elegiac subject and the chronicler of his times, re-presenting his earlier works and ensuring his place for posterity" (p. 108).

Bibliography

Abbott, Ruth. "Wordsworth's Notebooks" (forthcoming).

Abrams, M. H. "Structure and Style in the Greater Romantic Lyric," in *From Sensibility to Romanticism: Essays Presented to Frederick A. Pottle*, ed. Frederick W. Hilles and Harold Bloom (New York: Oxford UP, 1965), pp. 527–60.

———. *Natural Supernaturalism: Tradition and Revolution in Romantic Literature* (New York: W. W. Norton, 1971).

Addison, Joseph. *A Letter from Italy, to the Right Honourable Charles Lord Halifax* (London, 1709).

Alker, Sharon, and Holly Faith Nelson. "'Ghastly in the Moonlight': Wordsworth, Hogg and the Anguish of War," *Studies in Hogg and His World*, 15 (2004), 76–89.

Anderson, Anne. "Wordsworth and the Gardens of Coleorton Hall," *Garden History*, 22 (1994), 206–17.

Anderson, Benedict. *Imagined Communities: Reflections on the Origin and Spread of Nationalism* (London: Verso, 1983).

Arnold, Matthew. *Poems of Wordsworth* (London: Macmillan, 1888).

Banks, Brenda. "Rhetorical Missiles and Double-Talk: Napoleon, Wordsworth, and the Invasion Scare of 1804," in *Romanticism, Radicalism, and the Press*, ed. Stephen Behrendt (Detroit, MI: Wayne State UP, 1997), pp. 103–19.

Barnett, Suzanne L. *Romantic Paganism. The Politics of Ecstasy in the Shelley Circle* (New York: Palgrave, 2017).

Baron, Michael. *Language and Relationship in Wordsworth's Writing* (London: Longman, 1995).

Barrell, John. *The Idea of Landscape and the Sense of Place, 1730–1840: An Approach to the Poetry of John Clare* (Cambridge: Cambridge UP, 1972).

———. *English Literature in History, 1730–1780: An Equal, Wide Survey* (London: Hutchinson, 1983).

Bate, Jonathan. *Romantic Ecology: Wordsworth and the Environmental Tradition* (London: Routledge, 1991).

Bates, Brian R. *Wordsworth's Poetic Collections, Supplementary Writing and Parodic Reception* (London: Pickering & Chatto, 2012).

Beaumont, Sir George. MS letters to Wordsworth. Jerwood Centre, Wordsworth Trust (WLL / Beaumont, George / 33/ 34/ 35).

Beer, John. *Wordsworth in Time* (London: Faber and Faber, 1979).

Bennett, Andrew. *Romantic Poets and the Culture of Posterity* (Cambridge: Cambridge UP, 1999).

———. *Wordsworth Writing* (Cambridge: Cambridge UP, 2007).

Bennett, Jane. "The Agency of Assemblages," in *Vibrant Matter: A Political Ecology of Things* (Durham, NC: Duke UP, 2010), 28–30.

Bermingham, Ann. *Landscape and Ideology: The English Rustic Tradition, 1740–1860* (Berkeley: U of California P, 1986).

Bernhardt-Kabisch, Ernest. "The Epitaph and the Romantic Poets: A Survey," *Huntington Library Quarterly*, 30 (1967), 113–46.

Bewell, Alan. *Wordsworth and the Enlightenment: Nature, Man and Society in the Experimental Poetry* (New Haven, CT: Yale UP, 1989).

Bloom, Harold. "The Internalisation of the Quest Romance," in *Romanticism and Consciousness: Essays in Criticism*, ed. Harold Bloom (New York: W. W. Norton, 1970), pp. 3–23.

———. *The Anxiety of Influence: A Theory of Poetry* (New York: Oxford UP, 1973).

———. *The Western Canon: The Books and School of the Ages* (New York: Harcourt Brace, 1994).

Boyson, Rowan. *Wordsworth and the Enlightenment Idea of Pleasure* (Cambridge: Cambridge UP, 2012).

Branch, Lori. *Rituals of Spontaneity: Sentiment and Secularism from Free Prayer to Wordsworth* (Waco, TX: Baylor UP, 2006).

Brown, Simon. "Ebenezer Elliott and Robert Southey: Southey's Break with *The Quarterly Review*," *Review of English Studies*, 22 (1971), 307–11.

Brydges, Sir Egerton, ed. *The Topographer for the Year 1790*, vol. 2 (London, 1790).

Buchanan, Carol. *Wordsworth's Gardens* (Lubbock: Texas Tech UP, 2001).

Buckland, William. "An Assemblage of Fossil Teeth and Bones," *Philosophical Transactions of the Royal Society*, 112 (1822), 171–236.

———. *Reliquiae Diluvinae: or, Observations on the Organic Remains Contained in Caves, Fissures, and Diluvial Gravel, and on Other Geological Phenomena, Attesting the Action of an Universal Deluge* (London: John Murray, 1823).

Burke, Edmund. *Reflections on the Revolution in France*, ed. Conor Cruise O'Brien (Harmondsworth: Penguin, 1982).

———. *A Philosophical Enquiry into the Origin of Our Ideas of the Sublime and the Beautiful*, ed. James T. Boulton (Oxford: Oxford UP, 1987).

Burns, Robert. *The Works of Robert Burns: With an Account of His Life*, ed. James Currie, 2nd ed., 4 vols. (London: Cadell and Davies, 1801).

———. *The Poems and Songs of Robert Burns*, ed. James Kinsley, 3 vols. (Oxford: Oxford UP, 1968).

Bushell, Sally. *Re-Reading "The Excursion": Narrative, Response and the Wordsworthian Dramatic Voice* (Aldershot: Ashgate, 1999).

———. *Text as Process: Creative Composition in Wordsworth, Tennyson, and Dickinson* (Charlottesville: U of Virginia P, 2009).

———. "Composition and Revision," in *William Wordsworth in Context*, ed. Andrew Bennett (Cambridge: Cambridge UP, 2015), 27–37.

Byron, George Gordon, Lord. *Byron's Letters and Journals*, ed. Leslie A. Marchand, 12 vols. (London: John Murray, 1977–82).

————. *The Complete Poetical Works*, ed. Jerome J. McGann and Barry Weller, 7 vols. (Oxford: Oxford UP, 1980–91).

Campbell, Gordon. *The Hermit in the Garden: From Imperial Rome to Ornamental Gnome* (Oxford: Oxford UP, 2013).

Canuel, Mark. *The Shadow of Death: Literature, Romanticism, and the Subject of Punishment* (Princeton, NJ: Princeton UP, 2007).

Carlson, Julia S. *Romantic Marks and Measures: Wordsworth's Poetry in Fields of Print* (Philadelphia: Pennsylvania UP, 2016).

Caruth, Cathy. *Empirical Truths and Critical Fictions: Locke, Wordsworth, Kant, Freud* (Baltimore: Johns Hopkins UP, 1990).

Castell, James. "Wordsworth, Silence, and the Nonhuman," *Wordsworth Circle*, 45 (2014), 58–61.

Chandler, James. *Wordsworth's Second Nature: A Study of the Poetry and Politics* (Chicago: U of Chicago P, 1984).

————. *England in 1819: The Politics of Literary Culture and the Case of Romantic Historicism* (Chicago: U of Chicago P, 1998).

Chase, Cynthia. *Decomposing Figures: Rhetorical Readings in the Romantic Tradition* (Baltimore: Johns Hopkins UP, 1986).

————. "Monument and Inscription: Wordsworth's Lines," *Diacritics*, 17 (1987), 65–77.

Children's Employment Commission. *On the Employment of Children and Young Persons in the Mines of the Warwickshire and Leicestershire Coal-Fields, and on the State, Condition, and Treatment of Such Children and Young Persons* (London: HMSO, 1842).

Clancey, Richard W. *Wordsworth's Classical Undersong: Education, Rhetoric and Poetic Truth* (Houndmills: Macmillan, 2000).

Clarke, Matthew. "'Fit though Few': Anxiety and Ideology in Wordsworth's *Excursion* Quarto," *SiR*, 55 (2016), 257–81.

Clucas, Thomas. "'The Consecration, and the Poet's Dream': Evasion and Revision in the Elegies for John Wordsworth," *European Romantic Review*, 27 (2016), 601–21.

Clymer, Lorna. "Graved in Tropes: The Figural Logic of Epitaphs and Elegies in Blair, Gray, Cowper, and Wordsworth," *ELH*, 62 (1995), 347–86.

Coleridge, Samuel Taylor. *Collected Notebooks of Samuel Taylor Coleridge*, ed. Kathleen Coburn, 5 vols. (Princeton. NJ: Princeton UP, 1957–2002).

————. *The Friend*, ed. Barbara E. Rooke, 2 vols. (Princeton, NJ: Princeton UP, 1969).

————. *Biographia Literaria*, ed. James Engell and W. Jackson Bate, 2 vols. (Princeton, NJ: Princeton UP, 1983).

————. *Table Talk*, ed. Carl Woodring, 2 vols. (Princeton, NJ: Princeton UP, 1990).

————. *Poetical Works*, ed. J. C. C. Mays, 6 vols. (Princeton, NJ: Princeton UP, 2001).

Connell, Philip. *Romanticism, Economics and the Question of "Culture"* (Oxford: Oxford UP, 2001).

Cowper, William. *The Life and Posthumous Writings of William Cowper*, ed. William Hayley, 3 vols. (London: Joseph Johnson, 1803–4).

————. *The Task, 1785* (London: Joseph Johnson, facsimile ed., 1973).

Cox, Jeffrey N. *Poetry and Politics in the Cockney School: Keats, Shelley, Hunt and Their Circle* (Cambridge: Cambridge UP, 1998).

————. "Cockney Excursions," *Wordsworth Circle*, 42 (2011), 106–15.

———. "Thinking Rivers: The Flow of Influence, Wordsworth-Coleridge-Shelley," keynote presentation, Coleridge Summer Conference, Bristol, 2016.

———. "From Pantomime to Poetry: Wordsworth, Byron, and Harlequin Read Waterloo," *SiR*, 56 (2017), 321–40.

Crabb Robinson, Henry. *Diary, Reminiscences, and Correspondence* (London: Macmillan, 1870; 1872).

Crawford, Robert. *Devolving English Literature*, 2nd ed. (Edinburgh: Edinburgh UP, 2000).

Crockett, Bryan. "Negotiating the Shade: Wordsworth's Debt to Ovid," *Classical and Modern Literature*, 11 (1991), 109–18.

Culler, Jonathan. "Apostrophe," *Diacritics*, 7 (1977), 59–69.

Curran, Stuart. *Poetic Form and British Romanticism* (Oxford: Oxford UP, 1986).

———. "Wordsworth's Sonnets," in *Wordsworth's Poetry and Prose*, ed. Nicholas Halmi (New York: Norton, 2014), pp. 672–78.

Currie, Janette. "Re-visioning James Hogg: The Return of the Subject to Wordsworth's 'Extempore Effusion,'" *Romantic Textualities: Literature and Print Culture, 1780–1840*, 15 (2005), 8–28.

Curtis, John. *A Topographical History of the County of Leicester* (Ashby de la Zouch: W. Hextall, 1831).

Daniels, Stephen. "The Political Iconography of Woodland in Later Georgian England," in *The Iconography of Landscape*, ed. Denis Cosgrove and Stephen Daniels (Cambridge: Cambridge UP, 1980), pp. 43–82.

———. *Fields of Vision: Landscape Imagery and National Identity in England and the United States* (Cambridge: Polity Press, 1993).

———. *Humphry Repton: Landscape Gardening and the Geography of Georgian England* (New Haven, CT: Yale UP, 1999).

Davis, Leith. *Acts of Union: Scotland and the Literary Negotiation of the British Nation, 1707–1830* (Stanford, CA: Stanford UP, 1998).

de Certeau, Michel. *The Practice of Everyday Life* (Berkeley: U of California P, 1984).

de Man, Paul. *The Rhetoric of Romanticism* (New York: Columbia UP, 1984).

———. "Time and History in Wordsworth," in *Romanticism*, ed. Cynthia Chase (London: Longman, 1993), pp. 55–77.

Depew, Bradley. "Wordsworth on Epitaph: Language, Genre, Mortality," *ELH*, 79 (2012), 963–88.

Donaldson, Christopher. "Down the Duddon: Wordsworth and His Literary Pilgrims," *Literary Imagination*, 15 (2013), 186–209.

Dryden, John. *Ovid's Metamorphoses in Fifteen Books* (London, 1717).

Duckworth, Alistair M. *The Improvement of the Estate: A Study of Jane Austen's Novels* (Baltimore: Johns Hopkins UP, 1971).

Duff, David. "Wordsworth and the Language of Forms: The Collected Poems of 1815," *Wordsworth Circle* 34 (2003), pp. 86–90.

———. *Romanticism and the Uses of Genre* (Oxford: Oxford UP, 2009).

Duggett, Tom. *Gothic Romanticism: Architecture, Politics, and Literary Form* (Houndmills: Palgrave, 2010).

Duncan, Ian. *Modern Romance and Transformations of the Novel: The Gothic, Scott, Dickens* (Cambridge: Cambridge UP, 1992).

———. *Scott's Shadow: The Novel in Romantic Edinburgh* (Princeton, NJ: Princeton UP, 2007).

Eagleton, Terry. *The Ideology of the Aesthetic* (Oxford: Oxford UP, 1990).

Easterlin, Nancy. *Wordsworth and the Question of Romantic Religion* (Lewisburg, PA: Bucknell UP, 1996).

Elliott, Ebenezer. *Corn Law Rhymes,* 3rd ed. (London: B. Steill, 1831).

———. *The Splendid Village, Corn Law Rhymes and Other Poems* (London: B. Steill, 1833).

———. *More Verse and Prose by the Corn Law Rhymer,* 2 vols. (London: C. Fox, 1850).

English [Law] Reports, vol. XXXI: *Chancery,* vol. XI, Beaumont v. Boultbee (London: W. Green, 1903), 695–700.

Erickson, Lee. *The Economy of Literary Form: English Literature and the Industrialization of Publishing, 1800–1850* (Baltimore: Johns Hopkins UP, 1996).

Everett, Nigel. *The Tory View of Landscape* (New Haven, CT: Yale UP, 1994).

"'The Excursion': A Bicentenary Celebration." Special issue, *Wordsworth Circle,* 45 (2014).

Fairer, David, and Christine Gerrard. *Eighteenth-Century Poetry: An Annotated Anthology* (Oxford: Blackwell, 2004).

Fay, Elizabeth A. *Becoming Wordsworthian: A Performative Aesthetic* (Amherst, MA: U of Massachusetts P, 1995).

Fay, Jessica. "Prospects of Contemplation: Wordsworth's Winter Garden at Coleorton, 1806–1811," *European Romantic Review,* 24 (2013), 307–15.

———. "A Question of Loyalty: Wordsworth and the Beaumonts, Catholic Emancipation and Ecclesiastical Sketches," *Romanticism,* 22 (2016), 1–14.

———. "Wordsworth's Northumbria: Bede, Cuthbert, and Northern Medievalism," *Modern Language Review,* 111 (2016), 917–35.

Feingold, Richard. *Nature and Society: Later Eighteenth-Century Uses of the Pastoral and Georgic* (New Brunswick, NJ: Rutgers UP, 1978).

Ferguson, Frances. *Wordsworth: Language as Counter-Spirit* (New Haven, CT: Yale UP, 1977).

Fosso, Kurt. *Buried Communities: Wordsworth and the Bonds of Mourning* (Albany: SUNY P, 2004).

Franklin, Caroline. *Byron's Heroines* (Oxford: Oxford UP, 1992).

Frey, Anne. *British State Romanticism: Authorship, Agency, and Bureaucratic Nationalism* (Stanford, CA: Stanford UP, 2010).

Fry, Paul H. "Green to the Very Door? The Natural Wordsworth," in *The Wordsworthian Enlightenment: Romantic Poetry and the Ecology of Reading,* ed. Helen Regueiro Elam and Frances Ferguson (Baltimore: Johns Hopkins UP, 2005), pp. 97–111.

———. *Wordsworth and the Poetry of What We Are* (New Haven, CT: Yale UP, 2008).

Fulford, Tim. *The Late Poetry of the Lake Poets: Romanticism Revised* (Cambridge: Cambridge UP, 2013).

———. *Romantic Poetry and Literary Coteries: The Dialect of the Tribe* (New York: Palgrave, 2015).

Galperin, William H. *Revision and Authority in Wordsworth: The Interpretation of a Career* (Philadelphia: U Pennsylvania P, 1989).

Gamer, Michael. *Romanticism, Self-Canonization, and the Business of Poetry* (Cambridge: Cambridge UP, 2017).

Garrett, James M. *Wordsworth and the Writing of the Nation* (Aldershot: Ashgate, 2008).

Garrod, H. W. *Wordsworth* (Oxford: Oxford UP, 1923).

Gaskill, Howard. *Ossian Revisited* (Edinburgh: Edinburgh UP, 1991).

———. *The Reception of Ossian in Europe* (London: Bloomsbury, 2008).

Gates, Barbara T. "Wordsworth's Mirror of Morality: Distortions of Church History," *Wordsworth Circle*, 12 (1981), 129–32.

Gidal, Eric. "Wordsworth's Art of Memory," *SiR*, 37 (1998), 445–75.

Gill, Stephen. *William Wordsworth: A Life* (Oxford: Oxford UP, 1989).

———. *Wordsworth and the Victorians* (Oxford: Oxford UP, 1998).

———. "Wordsworth and *The River Duddon*," *Essays in Criticism*, 57 (2007), 22–41.

———. *Wordsworth's Revisitings* (Oxford: Oxford UP, 2011).

———. "Wordsworth and Burns," in *Burns and Other Poets*, ed. David Sergeant and Fiona Stafford (Edinburgh: Edinburgh UP, 2012), pp. 156–67.

Goldberg, Brian. *The Lake Poets and Professional Identity* (Cambridge: Cambridge UP, 2007).

Goodman, Kevis. *Georgic Modernity and British Romanticism: Poetry and the Mediation of History* (Cambridge: Cambridge UP, 2004).

———. "Conjectures on Beachy Head: Charlotte Smith's Geological Poetics and the Ground of the Present," *ELH*, 81 (2014), 983–1006.

Goodridge, John, ed. *Nineteenth Century Labouring-Class Poets, 1800–1900*, 3 vols. (London: Pickering and Chatto, 2003).

Gravil, Richard. *Wordsworth's Bardic Vocation, 1787–1842* (Houndmills: Macmillan, 2003).

———. *Wordsworth's Thanksgiving Ode in Context* (Tirril, Cumbria: Humanities-Ebooks, 2015).

Groom, Nick. *The Making of Percy's Reliques* (Oxford: Oxford UP, 1999).

Hardy, Thomas. *The Life and Work of Thomas Hardy*, ed. Michael Milgate (Houndmills: Macmillan, 1984).

Hartman, Geoffrey H. *Wordsworth's Poetry, 1787–1814* (New Haven, CT: Yale UP, 1964).

———. *Beyond Formalism: Literary Essays 1958–1970* (New Haven, CT: Yale UP, 1971).

———. "Wordsworth, Inscriptions, and Romantic Nature Poetry," in Hartman, *Beyond Formalism*, pp. 206–30.

———. *The Unremarkable Wordsworth* (Minneapolis: U Minnesota P, 1987).

Haywood, Ian. *The Revolution in Popular Literature: Print, Politics and the People, 1790–1860* (Cambridge: Cambridge UP, 2004).

Hazlitt, William. *The Spirit of the Age*, 2nd ed. (London: H. Colburn, 1825).

Heinzelman, Kurt. *The Economics of the Imagination* (Amherst: U Massachusetts P, 1980).

———. "Poetry and Real Estate: Wordsworth as Developer," *Southwest Review*, 84 (1999), 573–88.

Heringman, Noah. *Romantic Rocks, Aesthetic Geology* (Ithaca, NY: Cornell UP, 2004).

Hess, Scott. *Authoring the Self: Self-Representation, Authorship, and the Print Market in British Poetry from Pope through Wordsworth* (London: Routledge, 2005).

———. *William Wordsworth and the Ecology of Authorship: The Roots of Environmentalism in Nineteenth-Century Culture* (Charlottesville: University of Virginia Press, 2012).

Hewitt, Regina. "Church Building as Political Strategy in Wordsworth's 'Ecclesiastical Sonnets,'" *Mosaic*, 25 (1992), 31–46.

Hickey, Alison. *Impure Conceits: Rhetoric and Ideology in Wordsworth's "Excursion"* (Stanford, CA: Stanford UP, 1997).

Hill, Alan G. "Wordsworth, Boccacio, and the Pagan Gods of Antiquity," *Review of English Studies*, 45 (1994), 26–41.

Hogg, James. *The Brownie of Bodsbeck and Other Tales*, 2 vols. (Edinburgh: Blackwood and Murray, 1818).

———. *Collected Letters of James Hogg*, ed. Gillian Hughes, 3 vols. (Edinburgh: Edinburgh UP, 2004).

Holt, James, "Aspects of Wordsworth's Poetry in the 'Elegiac Stanzas,'" http://jameshholt .blogspot.com/2011/05/aspects-of-wordsworths-poetry-in.html.

Hyams, Edward. *Capability Brown and Humphry Repton* (London: Scribner, 1971).

Jacobus, Mary. *Romanticism, Writing and Sexual Difference* (Oxford: Oxford UP, 1989).

James, Felicity. "Wordsworth and Literary Friendship," in *The Oxford Handbook of William Wordsworth*, ed. Richard Gravil and Daniel Robinson (Oxford: Oxford UP, 2015).

Janowitz, Anne K. *England's Ruins: Poetry and the National Landscape, 1760–1820* (Oxford: Blackwell, 1990).

———. *Lyric and Labour in the Romantic Tradition* (Cambridge: Cambridge UP, 1998).

Jarvis, Robin. "Shades of Milton: Wordsworth at Vallombrosa," *SiR*, 25 (1986), 483–504.

———. "The Wages of Travel: Wordsworth and the Memorial Tour of 1820," *SiR*, 40 (2001), 321–43.

Jarvis, Simon. *Wordsworth's Philosophic Song* (Cambridge: Cambridge UP, 2006).

———. "Wordsworth's Late Melodics," in *Wordsworth's Poetic Theory: Knowledge, Language, Experience*, ed. Alexander Regier and Stefan H. Uhlig (New York: Palgrave, 2010), pp. 158–75.

———. "What Is Historical Poetics?" in *Theory Aside*, ed. Jason Potts and Daniel Stout (Durham, NC: Duke University Press, 2014), pp. 97–116.

Jeffrey, Francis. Review of *Thalaba the Destroyer*, by Robert Southey, *Edinburgh Review*, 1 (October 1802), 63–83.

———. Review of *Poems, in Two Volumes*, by William Wordsworth, *Edinburgh Review*, 11 (October 1807), 214–31.

———. Review of *Marmion*, by Walter Scott, *Edinburgh Review*, 12 (April 1808) 1–13.

———. Review of *Reliques of Robert Burns*, R. H. Cromek, publ., *Edinburgh Review*, 13 (January 1809), 249–76.

———. Review of *Lady of the Lake*, by Walter Scott, *Edinburgh Review*, 16 (August 1810), 263–93.

———. Review of *The Excursion*, by William Wordsworth, *Edinburgh Review*, 24 (November 1814), 1–4.

———. Review of *The White Doe of Rylstone*, by William Wordsworth, *Edinburgh Review*, 25 (October 1815), 355–63.

Johnson, Lee M. *Wordsworth and the Sonnet* (Copenhagen: Rosenkilde and Bagger, 1973).

Johnston, Kenneth R. *Wordsworth and "The Recluse"* (New Haven, CT: Yale UP, 1984).

Jones, Steven E. "The Wheat from the Chaff: Ebenezer Elliott and the Canon," in Jones, *Satire and Romanticism* (New York: St Martin's Press, 2000), pp. 199–220.

Keats, John. *Poems, by John Keats* (London: C. and J. Ollier, 1817).

———. *Endymion* (London: Taylor and Hessey, 1818).

———. *John Keats: Complete Poems*, ed. Jack Stillinger (Cambridge, MA: Harvard UP, 1982).

The Keats Circle: Letters and Papers, 1816–1879, ed. Hyder E. Rollins (Cambridge, MA: Harvard UP, 1958).

Keegan, Bridget. *British Labouring-Class Nature Poetry, 1730–1837* (New York: Palgrave, 2008).

Kelley, Theresa M. *Wordsworth's Revisionary Aesthetics* (Cambridge: Cambridge UP, 1998).

Kerrigan, John. *Archipelagic English: Literature, History, and Politics, 1603–1707* (Oxford: Oxford UP, 2008).

Khan, Jalal Uddin. "The Theme of Duty in Wordsworth's 'Addressed to —— On the Longest Day,'" *English Language Notes*, 34 (1996), 40–47.

———. "'To the Same [Lycoris]': Wordsworth's Uses of Dorothy and Coleridge in a Post-Napoleonic Dialogical Context," *Forum for Modern Language Studies*, 33 (1997), 315–27.

———. "Wordsworth's 'The Haunted Tree': A Political and Dialogical Reading," *Forum for Modern Language Studies*, 38 (2002), 241–51.

Kim, Benjamin. *Wordsworth, Hemans, and Politics, 1800–1830: Romantic Crises* (Lewisburg, PA: Bucknell UP, 2013).

Klancher, Jon. *The Making of English Reading Audiences, 1790–1832* (Madison, WI: U of Wisconsin P, 1987).

Kneale, J. Douglas. *Romantic Aversions: Aftermaths of Classicism in Wordsworth and Coleridge* (Montreal: McGill UP, 1999).

Langan, Celeste. "Understanding Media in 1805: Audiovisual Hallucination in *The Lay of the Last Minstrel*," *SiR*, 40 (2001), 49–70.

Larkin, Peter. "Wordsworth's 'After-Sojourn': Revision and Unself-Rivalry in the Later Poetry," *SiR*, 20 (1981), 409–36.

———. *Wordsworth and Coleridge: Promising Losses* (New York: Palgrave, 2012).

Leader, Zachary. *Revision and Romantic Authorship* (Oxford: Oxford UP, 1996).

Leask, Nigel. *Robert Burns and Pastoral: Poetry and Improvement in Late Eighteenth-Century Scotland* (Oxford: Oxford UP, 2010).

Lee, Debbie. *Slavery and the Romantic Imagination* (Philadelphia: Pennsylvania UP, 2002).

Leigh Hunt, James. "The Palace of Pleasure," in *Juvenilia; or a Collection of Poems: Written between the Ages of Twelve and Sixteen* (London, Rivington, 1801).

———. "The Nymphs," in *Foliage: or, Poems Original and Translated* (London: C. and J. Ollier, 1818).

Levinson, Marjorie. *Wordsworth's Great Period Poems: Four Essays* (Cambridge: Cambridge UP, 1986).

———. "What Is New Formalism?" *PMLA*, 122 (2007), 558–69.

Liu, Alan. *Wordsworth: The Sense of History* (Stanford, CA: Stanford UP, 1989).

———. "The Power of Formalism: The New Historicism," *ELH*, 56 (1989), 721–72.

Low, Dennis. *The Literary Protégées of the Lake Poets* (Aldershot: Ashgate, 2006).

Madden Ballad Collection, vol. XV, Special Collections, Cambridge University Library.

Mahoney, Charles. *Romantics and Renegades: The Poetics of Political Reaction* (New York: St Martin's Press, 2003).

Mahoney, John L. "Reynolds and Wordsworth: The Emergence of a Post-Enlightenment Aesthetic," *Studies on Voltaire and the Eighteenth Century*, 305 (1992), 1502–5.

Manning, Peter J. *Reading Romantics: Text and Context* (Oxford: Oxford UP, 1990).

———. "Wordsworth at St. Bees: Scandals, Sisterhoods, and Wordsworth's Later Poetry," in Manning, *Reading Romantics*, pp. 273–99.

———. "Cleansing the Images: Wordsworth, Rome, and the Rise of Historicism," *Texas Studies in Language and Literature*, 33 (1991), 271–326.

———. "Wordsworth in the *Keepsake*, 1829," in *Literature in the Marketplace: Nineteenth-Century British Publishing and Reading Practices*, ed. John O. Jordan and Robert L. Patten (Cambridge: Cambridge UP, 1995), pp. 44–72.

———. "'The Birthday of Typography': A Response to Celeste Langan," *SiR*, 40 (2001), 71–84.

———. "The Persian Wordsworth," *European Romantic Review*, 17 (2006), 189–96.

———. "William Wordsworth and William Cobbett: Scotch Travel and British Reform," in *Scotland and the Borders of Romanticism*, ed. Leith Davis, Ian Duncan, and Janet Sorensen (Cambridge: Cambridge UP, 2004), pp. 153–69.

———. "The Other Scene of Travel: Wordsworth's 'Musings Near Aquapendente,'" *The Wordsworthian Enlightenment: Romantic Poetry and the Ecology of Reading*, ed. Helen Rugueiro Elam and Frances Ferguson (Baltimore: Johns Hopkins UP, 2005), pp. 191–211.

———. "Wordsworth's 'Illustrated Books and Newspapers' and City Media," in *Romanticism and the City*, ed. Larry H. Peer (New York: Palgrave, 2011), pp. 223–40.

———. "Wordsworth in Youth and Age," *European Romantic Review*, 25 (2014), 385–96.

Martin, Philip W. "Lucid Intervals: Dryden, Carkesse, and Wordsworth," *Notes and Queries*, 33 (1986), 42–44.

Mathes, Carmen Faye. "Listening Not Listening: William Wordsworth and the Radical Materiality of Sound," *European Romantic Review*, 28 (2017), 315–24.

Matlak, Richard. *Deep Distresses: William Wordsworth, John Wordsworth, Sir George Beaumont, 1800–1808* (Newark, NJ: U of Delaware P, 2003).

———. "Wordsworth and the 'Great Terror' of 1803–05," *Wordsworth Circle*, 46 (2015), 21–25.

Matthews, Samantha. "Epitaphs, Effusions and Final Memorials: Wordsworth and the Grave of Charles Lamb," *Charles Lamb Bulletin*, 118 (2002), 49–63.

McFarland, Thomas. *William Wordsworth: Intensity and Achievement* (Oxford: Oxford UP, 1992).

McGann, Jerome J. *The Romantic Ideology: A Critical Investigation* (Chicago: U of Chicago P, 1983).

———. *The Beauty of Inflections: Literary Investigations in Historical Method and Theory* (Oxford: Oxford UP, 1985).

McLane, Maureen N. "On the Use and Abuse of 'Orality' for Art: Reflections on Romantic and Late Twentieth-Century Poiesis," *Oral Tradition*, 17 (2002), 135–64.

———. *Balladeering, Minstrelsy, and the Making of British Romantic Poetry* (Cambridge: Cambridge UP, 2008).

Mellor, Anne K. *Romanticism and Gender* (London: Routledge, 1993).

Melnyk, Julie. "William Wordsworth and Felicia Hemans," in *Fellow Romantics: Male and Female British Writers, 1790–1835*, ed. Beth Lau (Burlington, VT: Ashgate, 2009), pp. 139–58.

Mill, J. S. *Autobiography and Other Writings*, ed. Jack Stillinger (Boston: Houghton Mifflin, 1969).

Miller, Christopher R. *The Invention of Evening: Perception and Time in Romantic Poetry* (Cambridge: Cambridge UP, 2006).

Mole, Tom. *Byron's Romantic Celebrity: Industrial Culture and the Hermeneutic of Intimacy* (New York: Palgrave, 2007).

Moorman, Mary. *William Wordsworth—A Biography: The Later Years, 1803–1850* (Oxford: Oxford UP, 1965).

Newey, Vincent. *Cowper's Poetry: A Critical Study and Reassessment* (Liverpool: Liverpool UP, 1982).

Newlyn, Lucy. *Reading, Writing, and Romanticism: The Anxiety of Reception* (Oxford: Oxford UP, 2000).

———. *William and Dorothy Wordsworth: "All in Each Other"* (Oxford: Oxford UP, 2013).

Nichols, John. *History and Antiquities of the County of Leicester*, 4 vols. (London: J. Nichols, 1795–1811).

Noble, Andrew. "Wordsworth and Burns: The Anxiety of Being Under the Influence," in *Critical Essays on Robert Burns*, ed. Carol McGuirk (New York: G. K. Hall, 1998), pp. 49–62.

Owen, Felicity, and David Blayney Brown. *Collector of Genius: a Life of Sir George Beaumont* (New Haven, CT: Yale UP, 1988).

Owen, W. J. B. "Wordsworth and Jeffrey in Collaboration," *Review of English Studies*, 15 (1964), 161–67.

Page, Judith W. *Wordsworth and the Cultivation of Women* (Berkeley: U of California P, 1994).

Parrinder, Patrick. *Authors and Authority: English and American Criticism, 1750–1990* (London: Macmillan, 1977).

Pearson, Thomas. "Coleorton's 'Classic Ground': Wordsworth, the Beaumonts, and the Politics of Place," *Charles Lamb Bulletin*, 89 (1995), 9–14.

Percy, Thomas. *Reliques of Ancient English Poetry*, 3 vols. (London, 1765).

Perkins, David. "How the Romantics Recited Poetry," *SEL*, 31 (1991), 655–71.

Pfau, Thomas. *Wordsworth's Profession: Form, Class and the Logic of Early Romantic Cultural Production* (Stanford, CA: Stanford UP, 1997).

Phelan, Joseph. *The Nineteenth-Century Sonnet* (New York: Palgrave, 2005).

Phillips, George "January" Searle. *The Life, Character and Genius of Ebenezer Elliott* (London: C. Gilpin, 1850).

Philp, Mark, Roz Southey, Caroline Jackson-Houlston, and Susan Wollenberg, "Music and Politics, 1793–1815," in *Resisting Napoleon: The British Response to the Threat of Invasion, 1797–1815*, ed. Mark Philp (Aldershot: Ashgate, 2006), pp. 173–204.

Piper, Andrew. *Dreaming in Books: The Making of the Bibliographic Imagination in the Romantic Age* (Chicago: U of Chicago P, 2000).

Potkay, Adam. *Wordsworth's Ethics* (Baltimore: Johns Hopkins UP, 2012).

Prins, Yopie. "What Is Historical Poetics?," *MLQ*, 77 (2016), 13–40.

Prynne, J. H. *Field Notes: "The Solitary Reaper" and Others* (Cambridge: Barque Press, 2007).

Ramsay, Allan. *Tea Table Miscellany: or, a Collection of Choice Songs, Scots and English*, 4 vols. (London, 1763).

Repton, Humphry. *Fragments on the Theory and Practice of Landscape Gardening* (London: J. Taylor, 1816).

Ricks, Christopher. *Allusion to the Poets* (Oxford: Oxford UP, 2002).

Rifaterre, Michael. "Interpretation and Descriptive Poetry," *New Literary History*, 4 (1973), 229–57.

Ringler, R. N. "The Genesis of Cowper's 'Yardley Oak,'" *English Language Notes*, 5 (1967–68), 27–32.

Roberts, Warren. *Jane Austen and the French Revolution* (London: Macmillan, 1979).

Robinson, Daniel. "'Still Glides the Stream': Form and Function in Wordsworth's River Duddon Sonnets," *European Romantic Review*, 13 (2002), 449–64.

Robinson, Jeffrey C. *Unfettering Poetry: Fancy in British Romanticism* (New York: Palgrave, 2006).

Roe, Nicholas. *The Politics of Nature: Wordsworth and Some Contemporaries* (New York: Macmillan, 1992).

———. *John Keats and the Culture of Dissent* (Oxford: Oxford UP, 1997).

———. *Fiery Heart: The First Life of Leigh Hunt* (London: Pimlico, 2005).

Rose, Mark. *Authors and Owners: The Invention of Copyright* (Cambridge, MA: Harvard UP, 1993).

Ross, Marlon B. *The Contours of Masculine Desire: Romanticism and the Rise of Women's Poetry* (Oxford: Oxford UP, 1990).

Ruddick, William. "Subdued Passion and Controlled Emotion: Wordsworth's 'Extempore Effusion upon the Death of James Hogg,'" *Charles Lamb Bulletin*, 87 (1994), 98–110.

Ruoff, Gene. "Wordsworth's 'Yew-Trees' and Romantic Perception," *Modern Language Quarterly*, 34 (1973), 146–60.

Ryan, Robert. *The Romantic Reformation: Religious Politics in English Literature, 1789–1824* (Cambridge: Cambridge UP, 1997).

Rylestone, Anne L. *Prophetic Memory in Wordsworth's Ecclesiastical Sonnets* (Carbondale, IL: Southern Illinois UP, 1991).

Rzepka, Charles. "Pictures of the Mind: Iron and Charcoal, 'Ouzy' Tides and 'Vagrant Dwellers' at Tintern, 1798," *SiR*, 42 (2003), 155–85.

———. "From Relics to Remains: Wordsworth's 'The Thorn' and the Emergence of Secular History," *Romanticism on the Net*, 31 (2003), http://www.erudit.org/revue/ron/2003/v/n31/008696ar.html.

Sacks, Peter. *The English Elegy: Studies in the Genre from Spenser to Yeats* (Baltimore: Johns Hopkins UP, 1985).

Said, Edward. "Thoughts on Late Style," *London Review of Books*, 26, no. 15 (2004), 3–7.

———. *On Late Style: Music and Literature Against the Grain* (New York: Pantheon, 2006).

Schama, Simon. *Landscape and Memory* (New York: Knopf, 1995).

Schoenfield, Mark. *Law, Labor and the Poet's Contract: The Professional Wordsworth* (Athens GA: U of Georgia P, 1996).

Schor, Esther. *Bearing the Dead: The British Culture of Mourning from the Enlightenment to Victoria* (Princeton, NJ: Princeton UP, 1994).

Scodel, Joshua. *The English Poetic Epitaph: Commemoration and Conflict from Jonson to Wordsworth* (Ithaca, NY: Cornell UP, 1991).

Scott, Sir Walter. "Glenfinlas," in *Minstrelsy of the Scottish Border*, 2nd ed., 3 vols. (Edinburgh: Longman and Rees, 1803).

———. *The Lay of the Last Minstrel* (Edinburgh: Constable, 1805).

———. *Marmion: A Tale of Flodden Field* (Edinburgh: Constable, 1808).

———. *The Lady of the Lake: A Poem* (Edinburgh: Ballantyne, 1810).

———. *The Lord of the Isles: A Poem* (Edinburgh: Constable, 1815).

Setzer, Sharon. "Precedent and Perversity in Wordsworth's *Sonnets Upon the Punishment of Death*," *Nineteenth-Century Literature*, 50 (1996), 427–47.

Shakespeare, William. *Henry IV, Part One*, ed. Barbara A. Mowatt and Paul Werstine (New York: Washington Square Press, 1994).

Shaw, Philip. *Waterloo and the Romantic Imagination* (New York: Palgrave, 2002).

———. "Wordsworth's 'Dread Voice': Dora, Ovid and the Later Poetry," *Romanticism*, 8 (2002), 34–48.

Simonsen, Peter. *Wordsworth and Word-Preserving Arts: Typographic Inscription, Ekphrasis and Posterity in the Later Work* (Houndmills: Palgrave, 2007).

Simpson, David. *Wordsworth's Historical Imagination: The Poetry of Displacement* (New York: Methuen, 1987).

———. *Wordsworth, Commodification and Social Concern: The Poetics of Modernity* (Cambridge: Cambridge UP, 2009).

Siskin, Clifford. *The Historicity of Romantic Discourse* (Oxford: Oxford UP, 1988).

Smith, E. A. *A Queen on Trial: The Affair of Queen Caroline* (Stroud: Alan Sutton, 1993).

Southey, Robert. *The Life and Correspondence of Robert Southey*, ed. C. C. Southey, 6 vols. (London: Longman, Brown, Green, and Longmans, 1849).

———. *New Letters of Robert Southey*, ed. Kenneth Curry, 2 vols. (New York: Columbia UP, 1965).

Speitz, Michele, "The Wordsworthian Acoustic Imagination, Sonic Recursions, and 'that dying murmur,'" *Studies in English Literature, 1500–1900*, 55 (2015), 621–46.

Sperry, Willard. *Wordsworth's Anti-Climax* (Cambridge, MA: Harvard UP, 1935).

St Clair, William. *The Reading Nation in the Romantic Period* (Cambridge: Cambridge UP, 2004).

Stabler, Jane. *Byron, Poetics and History* (Cambridge: Cambridge UP, 2002).

Stafford, Fiona J. *Sublime Savage: James Macpherson and the Poems of Ossian* (Edinburgh: Edinburgh UP, 1988).

———. "'Dangerous Success': Ossian, Wordsworth, and English Romantic Literature," in *Ossian Revisited*, ed. H. Gaskill (Edinburgh: Edinburgh UP, 1991), pp. 49–72.

———. *The Last of the Race: The Growth of a Myth from Milton to Darwin* (Oxford: Oxford UP, 1994).

———. "'Inhabited Solitudes': Wordsworth in Scotland, 1803," in *Scotland, Ireland, and the Romantic Aesthetic*, ed. David Duff and Catherine Jones (Lewisburg, PA: Bucknell UP, 2007), pp. 93–113.

———. *Local Attachments: The Province of Poetry* (Oxford: Oxford UP, 2010).

Stelzig, Eugene L. "Mutability, Ageing and Permanence in Wordsworth's Later Poetry," *Studies in English Literature*, 19 (1979), 623–44.

Stewart, Samuel T. *A History of Coal Mining in Coleorton and the Local Area* (Ashby de la Zouch: S. Stewart, 2014).

Stewart, Susan. *Crimes of Writing: Problems in the Containment of Representation* (Oxford: Oxford UP, 1991).

Stillinger, Jack. *Coleridge and Textual Instability: The Multiple Versions of the Major Poems* (Oxford: Oxford UP, 1994).

Stryer, Steven. "'A Loftier Tone': 'Laodamia,' the Aeneid, and Wordsworth's Virgilian Imagination," *Studies in Philology*, 112 (2015), 575–97.

Swaab, Peter. "Wordsworth's Elegies for John Wordsworth," *Wordsworth Circle*, 45 (2014), 30–39.

Sykes Davies, Hugh. *Wordsworth and the Worth of Words* (Cambridge: Cambridge UP, 1986).

Thomson, Douglas H. "'Sport of Transmutations': The Evolution of Wordsworth's 'To Lycoris,'" *SEL*, 27 (1987), 581–93.

Thomson, Heidi, "The Importance of Other People and the Transmission of Affect in Wordsworth's Lyric Poetry," *Modern Language Review*, 110 (2015), 969–91.

Tomko, Michael. "Superstition, the National Imaginary, and Religious Politics in Wordsworth's *Ecclesiastical Sketches*," *Wordsworth Circle*, 39 (2008), 16–19.

Trickett, Rachel. "The Language of Wordsworth's Later Poems," *Wordsworth Circle*, 21 (1990), 46–51.

Trott, Nicola. "Wordsworth and the Parodic School of Criticism," in *The Satiric Eye: Forms of Satire in the Romantic Period*, ed. Steven E. Jones (New York: Palgrave, 2003), pp. 71–97.

Tucker, Herbert. *Epic: Britain's Heroic Muse, 1790–1910* (Oxford: Oxford UP, 2008).

Walford Davies, Damian. "Romantic Hydrography: Tide and Transit in 'Tintern Abbey,'" in *English Romantic Writers and the West Country*, ed. Nicholas Roe (Houndmills: Palgrave, 2010), pp. 218–36.

Walker, Eric C. *Marriage, Writing and Romanticism: Wordsworth and Austen after War* (Stanford, CA: Stanford UP, 2009).

Weiskel, Thomas. *The Romantic Sublime: Studies in the Structure and Psychology of Transcendence* (Baltimore: Johns Hopkins UP, 1986).

Wiley, Michael. *Romantic Geography: Wordsworth and Anglo-European Spaces* (New York: Palgrave, 1998).

Williams, John. *William Wordsworth: Critical Issues* (New York: Palgrave, 2002).

Williams, Raymond. *The Country and the City* (London: Chatto and Windus, 1973).

Woodmansee, Martha. *The Author, Art, and the Market: Rereading the History of Aesthetics* (New York: Columbia UP, 1994).

Woof, Pamela. "Wordsworth Learns to Write Elegy," *Wordsworth Circle*, 46 (2015), 70–79.

Wolfson, Susan J. *Formal Charges: The Shaping of Poetry in British Romanticism* (Stanford, CA: Stanford UP, 1997).

———. *Romantic Interactions: Social Being and the Turns of Literary Action* (Baltimore: Johns Hopkins UP, 2010).

Wordsworth, Dorothy. *Recollections of a Tour Made in Scotland A.D. 1803*, ed. J. C. Shairp, 3rd ed. (Edinburgh: D. Douglas, 1875).

Wordsworth, Jonathan. *William Wordsworth: The Borders of Vision* (Oxford: Oxford UP, 1982).

Wordsworth, William. *Poems, in Two Volumes* (London: Longman, 1807).

———. *Concerning the Convention of Cintra* (London: Longman, 1809).

———. *Poems by William Wordsworth: Including Lyrical Ballads, and the Miscellaneous Pieces of the Author. With Additional Poems, a New Preface, and a Supplementary Essay* (London: Longman, 1815).

———. *A Letter to a Friend of Robert Burns* (London: Longman, 1816).

———. *The River Duddon, a Series of Sonnets: Vaudracour and Julia: and Other Poems. To which is annexed, a topographical description of the country of the Lakes, in the North of England* (London: Longman, 1820).

———. *The Poetical Works of William Wordsworth*, 5 vols. (London: Longman, 1827).

———. *Yarrow Revisited, and Other Poems* (London: Longman, 1835).

———. *Poetical Works* (London: E. Moxon, 1836–37).

———. *Yarrow Revisited*. 2nd ed. (London: Longman, 1836).

———. *Poems, Chiefly of Early and Late Years* (London: E. Moxon, 1842).

————. *Kendal and Windermere Railway: Two Letters Reprinted from the Morning Post. Revised, with Additions* (London: Whitaker and E. Moxon, 1845).

————. *The Poems of William Wordsworth, D.C.L* (London: E. Moxon, 1845).

————. *Poems and Extracts Chosen by William Wordsworth for an Album Presented to Lady Mary Lowther, Christmas 1819* (London: H. Frowde, 1905).

————. *The Letters of William and Dorothy Wordsworth: The Early Years, 1787–1805*, ed. Ernest De Selincourt, rev. Chester L. Shaver (Oxford: Oxford UP, 1967).

————. *The Letters of William and Dorothy Wordsworth: The Middle Years, 1806–20*, ed. E. de Selincourt, rev. Mary Moorman and Alan G. Hill, 2 vols. (Oxford: Oxford UP, 1969–70).

————. *The Prose Works of William Wordsworth*, ed. W. J. B. Owen and Jane Worthington Smyser, 3 vols. (Oxford: Oxford UP, 1974).

————. *The Letters of William and Dorothy Wordsworth: The Later Years*, ed. E. de Selincourt, rev. Alan G. Hill, 4 vols. (Oxford: Oxford UP, 1978–88).

————. *Poems, in Two Volumes, and Other Poems, 1800–1807*, ed. Jared Curtis (Ithaca, NY: Cornell UP, 1983).

————. *Shorter Poems, 1807–1820*, ed. Carl H. Ketcham (Ithaca, NY: Cornell UP, 1989).

————. *Lyrical Ballads, and Other Poems, 1797–1800*, ed. James Butler and Karen Green (Ithaca, NY: Cornell UP, 1992).

————. *Last Poems, 1821–1850*, ed. Jared Curtis (Ithaca, NY: Cornell UP, 1999).

————. *William Wordsworth: The Critical Heritage: Volume I, 1793–1820*, ed. Robert Woof (London: Routledge, 2001).

————. *Sonnet Series and Itinerary Poems, 1820–1845*, ed. Geoffrey Jackson (Ithaca, NY: Cornell UP, 2004).

————. *The Excursion*, ed. Sally Bushell, James A. Butler, and Michael C. Jaye (Ithaca, NY: Cornell UP, 2007).

————. *The Fenwick Notes of William Wordsworth*, ed. Jared Curtis (Tirril, Cumbria: Humanities-Ebooks, 2007).

Worthen, John. *The Life of William Wordsworth: A Critical Biography* (Chichester: Wiley, 2014).

Wright, Paul. "Vile Saxons and Ancient Britons: Wordsworth, the Ambivalent Welsh Tourist," in *Dangerous Diversity: The Changing Faces of Wales: Essays in Honour of Tudor Bevan*, ed. Katie Gramich and Andrew Hiscock (Cardiff: U Wales P, 1998), pp. 64–81.

Wu, Duncan, and Nicola Trott, "Three Sources for Wordsworth's *Prelude* Cave," *Notes and Queries*, 38 (1991), 298–99.

Wyatt, John. *Wordsworth and the Geologists* (Cambridge: Cambridge UP, 1995).

————. *Wordsworth's Poems of Travel, 1819–1842: Such Sweet Wayfaring* (Houndmills: Palgrave Macmillan, 1999).

Yoshikawa, Saeko. *William Wordsworth and the Invention of Tourism, 1820–1900* (Farnham: Ashgate, 2014).

Young, Edward. *Night Thoughts* (London, 1742–45).

Zimmerman, Sarah M. *Romanticism, Lyricism and History* (Albany: SUNY P, 1999).

Index

Acknowledgments

Part of Chapter 1 appeared in "Cowper, Wordsworth, Clare: the Politics of Trees," *John Clare Society Journal,* 14 (1995), 47–59; part of Chapter 5 was published in "Wordsworth's 'The Haunted Tree' and the Sexual Politics of Landscape," in *Placing and Displacing Romanticism*, ed. Peter J. Kitson (Aldershot: Ashgate, 2003); part of Chapter 7 was published in "Wordsworth and Southey: Stone Circles and the Uses of the Prehistoric," in *The Harp and the Constitution*, ed. Joanne Parker (Leiden: Brill, 2015). Alan Vardy, Julia Carlson, David Fairer, Michael Gamer, Stephen Gill, Ian Haywood, Peter Larkin, Peter J. Manning, Dahlia Porter, and Peter Simonsen read drafts: I am most grateful to them. Jessica Fay provided useful information on Beaumont's letters. At the Press, Jerry Singerman was everything you'd always hoped an editor might be. Andrew Lacey caught many an error and compiled the index.